KING LEAR
IN CONTEXT

ANTHEM PERSPECTIVES IN LITERATURE

Titles in the **Anthem Perspectives in Literature** series
are designed to contextualize classic works of literature for readers
today within their original social and cultural environments. The books
present historical, biographical, political, artistic, moral, religious and
philosophical material from the period that enable readers to understand
a text's meaning as it would have struck the original audience. These
approachable but informative books aims to uncover the period and the
people for whom texts were written; their values and views, their anxieties
and demons, what made them laugh and cry, their loves and hates.
The series is targeted at high-achieving A-level, International
Baccalaureate and Advanced Placement pupils, first-year
undergraduates and an intellectually curious audience.

KING LEAR IN CONTEXT

THE CULTURAL BACKGROUND

Keith Linley

ANTHEM PRESS

Anthem Press
An imprint of Wimbledon Publishing Company
www.anthempress.com

This edition first published in UK and USA 2015
by ANTHEM PRESS
75–76 Blackfriars Road, London SE1 8HA, UK
or PO Box 9779, London SW19 7ZG, UK
and
244 Madison Ave #116, New York, NY 10016, USA

British Library Cataloguing-in-Publication Data
A catalogue record for this book is available from the British Library.

Library of Congress Cataloging-in-Publication Data
Linley, Keith.
King Lear in context : the cultural background / Keith Linley.
pages cm. – (Anthem perspectives in literature)
Includes bibliographical references and index.
ISBN 978-1-78308-373-2 (papercover : alk. paper)
1. Shakespeare, William, 1564–1616. King Lear. 2. Literature and society–England–
History–16th century. 3. Literature and society–England–History–17th century.
4. Kings and rulers in literature. 5. Lear, King of England (Legendary character)–
In literature. I. Title.
PR2819.L55 2015
822.3'3–dc23
2014049086

ISBN-13: 978 1 78308 373 2 (Pbk)
ISBN-10: 1 78308 373 5 (Pbk)

Cover image © Andrew_Howe/iStockphoto.com

This title is also available as an ebook.

CONTENTS

INTRODUCTION

About This Book

This book concentrates on the contexts from which *King Lear* emerges, those characteristics of life in early Jacobean England which are reflected in the values and views Shakespeare brings to the text and affect how a contemporary might have responded to it. These are the primary, central contexts, comprising the writer, the text, the audience and all the views, values and beliefs held by these three. The actions taken and words spoken by the characters do not all represent Shakespeare's own views, but they will have evoked ethical judgements from the audience in line with the general religious and political values of the time. There would have been a range of differing responses, though the fundamentals of right and wrong would have been broadly agreed. These primary contexts, this complicity of writer, audience and text and their shared mediation of the play, are the prime concern of this book.

Where relevant, the book also focuses on a range of secondary contexts. A play does not come into being without having a background and does not exist *in vacuo*. It will have its own unique features, but it will have characteristics inherited from its author, as well as sources derived from and traits resembling the writing of its time. Other secondary contexts – the actors, their companies, the acting space, the social mix of general audiences – do not figure in this study except as occasional incidentals. However, the first recorded performance of *King Lear* was at court, and the book discusses that unique audience.

There are tertiary contexts too. There is the afterlife of a text (its printed form, how subsequent ages interpreted it on stage and changed it) – what is called its performance history. And there is the critical backstory, showing how critics of subsequent times bring their own agendas and the values and prejudices of their period to analysis of a text. These are referenced incidentally where they seem useful and relevant, but are not a major concern. The 'Further Reading' list provides broad guidance on the critical and performance history, and any scholarly edition of *King Lear* will cover these areas in greater detail.

This book is for students preparing assignments and exams for Shakespeare modules. The marking criteria at any level explicitly or implicitly require students to show a consistently well-developed and consistently detailed understanding of the significance and influence of contexts in which literary texts are written and understood. This means responding to the play in the ways Shakespeare's audience would have done. You will not be writing a history essay, but along with considering the play as a literary vehicle communicating in dramatic form, you will need to know something of how Shakespeare's audience might have reacted. A text is always situated in some way within its historical setting. The automatic correlatives in this case would have been the classics (for the educated), the Bible, Christian ethics and the society of the day; the latter means they would view the play in the light of what had happened in recent history and what was currently happening in the court, in the city, in the streets, on the roads and in the villages. No one could watch *King Lear* and not think of King James, nor hear the comments on flattery by Kent and the Fool and not think of the court. References to social problems, the corruption of public life, the actuality of family breakdown before their eyes, would all evoke a disturbing sense of recognition.[1]

The following material will enable you to acquire a surer grasp of this cultural context – the socio-political conditions out of which the play emerged, the literary profile prevailing when it was written, and the religious-moral dimensions embedded in it. The setting is pagan, but since *Lear* was written in an age of faith, when the Bible's teachings and sermons heard in church formed part of everyone's mindset, it is vital to recreate those factors, for the actions of the characters would have been assessed by Christian criteria. You may not agree with the values of the time or the views propounded in the play, but you do need to understand how belief mediated the possible responses of the court that watched the tragedy on 26 December 1606. A concept key to this book's approach is that *Lear* is full of sins, transgressions, boundary crossing and rule breaking – in the personal world and in the public and political arenas. Alerted to the subversive behaviour of the characters, the audience would expect that the unrepentant would be punished and damned and those repenting be brought to new understanding, forgiving and being forgiven. What partly makes it a tragedy, not just a story of the good being saved and the bad punished, is that some of the good and repentant will also be sacrificial victims. Though biblical values would be applied to the action, there is much more going on scene by scene than a series of echoes of or allusions to what the

Bible says about virtue and vice. Interwoven are political concerns about rule (of the self, of a state), public service and the dangers of appetite unrestrained. This study of these contexts will complete your preparation.

What Is the Primary Context?

Any document – literary or non-literary – comes from an environment and has that environment embedded in it, overtly and covertly. Its context is the conditions which produced it, the biographical, social, political, historical and cultural circumstances which form it, and the values operating within it and affecting the experience of it, including what the author may have been trying to say and how the audience may have interpreted it. A text in isolation is simply a collection of words carrying growing, developing meanings as the writing/performance progresses. It is two-dimensional – a lexical, grammatical construct and the sum of its literal contents. It has meaning, we can understand what it is about, how the characters interact, but context provides a third dimension, making meaning comprehensible within the cultural values of the time. Primary context is the sum of all the influences the writer brings to the text and all the influences the viewer/reader deploys in experiencing it. Knowing the cultural context enriches that experience. This book concentrates on the archaeology of the play, recovering how it would be understood in 1606, unearthing the prevailing attitudes of the time, and displaying the factors that shaped its meaning for that audience in 1606. These are the significations of society embedded in the text that, added together, make it what Shakespeare intended it to be – or as close as we can be reasonably sure for, of course, it is impossible to definitively say what the author may have meant at any one point. Our views about the text stem from our attitudes, our prejudices, our priorities, but we always have to understand the context in which something from the past was said or done if we are to understand what the text was meant to mean. Recovering the mindset, nuances and values Shakespeare works into *Lear* and how his audience would have interpreted them means recovering the Elizabethan-Jacobean period. To achieve that a range of aspects is considered, but two key contextual areas dominate the approach of this book: the religious-moral and the socio-political. Supposedly set in pagan pre-Roman Britain, the play has few explicit verbal echoes of the Bible, but the multiple transgressions it presents would have been interpreted by the audience in terms of the scriptural upbringing most of them would have had. Its setting among courtiers and its focus on the breakdown of the royal family automatically brings into play considerations related to kingship, rule and family, subjects constantly debated in pre–Civil War England. Sin, subversion, transgression and reversals abound in the play.

Cultural historians aim to recover 'the commonplaces, the unargued presuppositions', and 'the imperative need, in any comparative discussions of epochs, [is] first to decide what the norm of the epoch is'.[2] Once the typical and orthodox values are established, it is then essential to register significant divergences from them. Part I looks broadly at the 'world view' of the time, the normative inherited past which shaped how the Jacobeans thought about God, the world, sin, death, the Devil, the social structure, family and gender relationships, and also the Jacobean present with its social change, political matters, connections between the play and the wider literary world, and the features expected in a tragedy. Most importantly, it considers the religious beliefs that informed the likely judgements made of the actions in the play and suggests a number of socio-political allusions that gave the drama a topical dimension – two areas not previously given much attention. Part II gives a scene-by-scene identification and discussion of the recurrent sins, transgressions and subversions. Crucial to the religious context are three moral matrices against which conduct in the play would have been measured: the Ten Commandments, the Seven Deadly Sins and the Seven Cardinal Virtues. You need to absorb them thoroughly as they recur constantly (Chapters 3 and 4). These ethical contexts decode the hidden nuances and inflexions of meaning which would have coloured a contemporary audience's responses to the story of Lear and his daughters. There will have been many different responses, but in the area of religious and moral values there will have been many shared reactions.

There is always a gulf between what people are supposed to do or believe and what they actually do or believe. *Lear* demonstrates this. Edgar's closing precept demands that there should be a match between what we feel and what we say. The play demonstrates what happens when idealized fantasies of expected conduct and rule are countered by the harsh realities of how people actually behave. Machiavelli's version of 'the mirror for princes' claimed:

> I have thought it proper to represent things as they are in real truth, rather than as they are imagined. [...] The gulf between how one should live and how one does live is so wide that a man who neglects what is actually done for what should be done learns the way to self-destruction rather than self-preservation.[3]

Ignorance, indifference, rebelliousness, purposeful wickedness and laziness account for these discrepancies. Goneril, Regan and Edmund's deviations from normative behaviour are motivated by deliberate ambition. They know they are doing evil, but do not care. Their goal is power and any means that gives them dominance is acceptable: 'All with me's meet, that I can fashion fit' (I. ii.).

Further Reading

Editions of the play with useful introductions and reading lists

All give textual history, discuss sources, raise key issues and review recent criticism.

The Arden Shakespeare (ed. Kenneth Muir, 1963)
The Arden Shakespeare (ed. R. A. Foakes, 1997)
The New Cambridge Shakespeare (ed. Jay L. Halio)
The Oxford Shakespeare (ed. Stanley Wells)
Norton Critical Edition (ed. Grace Ioppolo)

Broader guides

'*King Lear*': *A Critical Guide* (ed. Andrew Hiscock, Lisa Hopkins)
Includes critical history, a guide to online resources and a range of chapters on individual issues
'*King Lear*': *New Critical Essays* (ed. Jeffrey Kahan)
A variety of approaches, from post-colonialism and new historicism to psychoanalysis and gender studies, with performance and textual history
'*King Lear*': *New Casebooks* (ed. Kiernan Ryan)
A valuable range of essays on key issues

Other critics

Janet Adelman, *Suffocating Mothers*
A. C. Bradley, *Shakespearean Tragedy*
John F. Danby, *Shakespeare's Doctrine of Nature*
Jonathan Dollimore, *Radical Tragedy*
G. B. Harrison, *Shakespeare's Tragedies*
Frank Kermode (ed.), *King Lear: A Casebook of Critical Essays*
G. Wilson Knight, *The Wheel of Fire*
Jan Kott, *Shakespeare: Our Contemporary*
Gary Taylor and Michael Warren (eds.), *The Division of the Kingdoms*
Enid Welsford, *The Fool*

Journal articles

Judith R. Anderson, 'The Conspiracy of Realism: Impasse and Vision in *King Lear*', *Studies in Philology* 84 (1987): 1–23.
Richard Dutton, '*King Lear*, the Triumph of Reunited Britannia, and "The Matter of Britain"', *Literature and History* 12 (1986): 139–51.

Margot Heinemann, 'Demystifying the Mystery of State: *King Lear* and the World Upside Down', *Shakespeare Survey* 44 (1992): 75–84.
Derek Peat, '"And that's true too": *King Lear* and the Tension of Uncertainty', *Shakespeare Survey* 33 (1980): 43–53.

Note: Act and scene references are given with quotations from *King Lear*, but line references are omitted because the different editions (using either Folio or Quarto variants) have different lineation.

Prologue

GRIM EXPECTATIONS

There is the usual shuffling, chatting, giggling, calling out to friends. An audience is settling. It is 26 December 1606. The court is gathering for its customary St Stephen's Day entertainment. The atmosphere is lively. This is a festive occasion; it is Christmas and everyone has dined and wined well. The Palace of Whitehall's banqueting hall is ablaze with candles. Silk dresses rustle and shine. There is excitement and expectation. The King's Men are to perform a new play by Master Shakespeare. The king is eager for entertainment after his less-than-successful hunting trip to Ware in Hertfordshire a few days earlier. Bad weather and poor sport have not put him in a good mood. At least parliamentary problems are adjourned until February, but then there will be the difficult matter of the still-unresolved union between England and Scotland. Committees discussing unification are making little progress. The king dearly wishes union be established, but there is little support in the Commons (or among the commoners – but they do not count). After good food and plenty to drink the audience is somewhat noisy, but not too rowdy, for the king has commanded this performance (or at least agreed to it) and he and the Queen are present. Are the Dukes of Cornwall and Albany there too, to watch their namesakes? Prince Henry is 12, Prince Charles only 6.[1] Perhaps they are allowed to stay up as a treat. Their father might see this play about a foolish king as a useful lesson for them.

The evening's fare is hardly promising; a tragedy called *The True Chronicle History of the Life and Death of King Lear and His Three Daughters*, together with the unfortunate life of Edgar, son and heir to the Earl of Gloucester, and his sullen and assumed humour of Tom of Bedlam'.[2] The opening scene is a king's court. A court within the court? Curious. It is an old story from the chronicles, but with crucial differences, for 'whereas Holinshed and all other writers do declare that Lear was restored to his kingdom by Cordelia his true and loyal daughter, yet in this play Cordelia is hanged by order of the bastard son of the Earl of Gloucester, and Lear dies of grief and old age'.[3] The audience does not know this. The Queen's waiting-women are mostly young and rather light-hearted. This is not their sort of theatre. Though some may be 'over-eares in love' with some of the actors, they will not probably be overly pleased with the play.[4] Last Christmas was much more fun. The Boys of the Chapel performed *All Fools*, and the Queen's Players presented *How to Learn of a Woman to Woo*. Amusing too, but with more serious undertones, were the King's Men's offerings: *Measure for Measure*, *The Comedy of Errors*, *Love's Labours Lost* and *Everyman Out of His Humour*. All spicy, amusing, naughty. You could ignore the darker bits. This play has little to amuse. It is about folly, bad royal judgement, about style and manner of rule, about human cruelty and an irascible old man. It also has some acid comments about society and the court. It will be awkward viewing; James's wilfulness and capriciousness were already all too evident. Apart from the royal family this court audience will be a mix of genuine courtiers, top officials, foreign ambassadors and hangers-on invited to make up the numbers. This latter group, many of them young gallants, generally demanded 'some passages [...] which may relish, and tickle the humour [...] or else good night to the players'.[5] They might be amused by the Fool, but when he disappears at the close of Act III, Scene vi will they have been sufficiently drawn in by the pathos to concentrate until the end?

Shakespeare's age believed in imminent cataclysm, expected the Apocalypse. Sunday sermons spoke of the end of the world and the Last Judgement, visionaries predicted it in pamphlets, theologians and painters described it in words and images. Many parish churches still had frescoes showing the damned falling into everlasting flames attended by grinning devils while the blessed mingle with angels above. Often appearing on the arch between the chancel and nave they were visible to the congregation throughout Sunday service. It was a churchgoing society; even the reluctant attended on Sundays – the law required it. Apocalyptic thinking, expectation of the world's end, had penetrated the English psyche. All sects believed it. But there were other forces feeding this mental state. Jacobeans lived in fear of plague, starvation, social collapse and bloody Catholic outrages or invasion. These hysterias are reflected in *Lear*. Lear calls the gods to visit their wrath on those opposing his will. In emotional desperation he calls them to 'strike flat the thick rotundity o' th' world!' (III. ii.). Ironically it is upon him destruction falls. From the storm on the heath to the deaths at the end and the king's world shattered, the play resembles the coming of judgement at the end of days. Before that the audience witnesses the turning upside-down of fundamental familial norms, heralding the wreck of humanity or 'th'image of that horror'. The play is a microcosm of a society disintegrating. It reflects what the early

1600s seemed to show in real life – a procession of betrayals, unnatural acts of horror, social tensions, plots, lies, poisoning, madness, blinding, pretences, disguises and deaths. The Armageddon wreckage portrayed in the last scene mirrors what some Jacobeans saw as they looked around them. Yet, there is hope. The small band of battered survivors talks of renewal. Albany calls on Kent and Edgar to 'sustain' the 'gored state'. Good redeems life, but it is a close call.

Lear is not James I, but *Lear* is a highly political play concerned with the uses and abuses of power, reflecting contemporary discourses on kingship, education, the role of women and social relationships. It does all this against an unspoken but assumed background of Christian ethics. Though the setting is ostensibly pagan, the moral bases by which the audience judged what it saw are biblical. The issues raised by characters' comments or actions are relevant to the new but already corrupt and creaky Stuart dynasty.[6] To understand how this world is overturned we need to know what were the fundamental beliefs of that world before Lear, Gloucester and their families wreck it. Not all these ways of thinking appear immediately relevant to *Lear*, but they are the normative values, the common assumptions, by which the brutish, unnatural acts, the disturbing subversions of acceptable behaviour on stage, would have been measured.

Part I

THE INHERITED PAST AND THE JACOBEAN PRESENT

Chapter 1

THE HISTORICAL CONTEXT: AN OVERVIEW

Elizabeth I died in 1603 and James VI of Scotland became James I of England. *King Lear* was written between 1603 and 1606, so falls into the Jacobean period (after *Jacobus*, Latin for James). In the wider European literary and political contexts, the period is the waning of the High Renaissance. Historians today call it Early Modern because many features of it are recognizably modern while being early in the evolutions that shaped our world.

The new king, ruling until 1625, was of the Scottish family the Stuarts. They were a dynastic disaster. None was an effective king and kingship is a key theme in *Lear*. James, a learned man but flawed king, shirked the routines of work government involved, disliked contact with his people, drank heavily, was extravagant, impulsive and tactless, constantly in debt, and in perpetual conflict with Parliament. He was a hard-line right-winger in religion and backed the repression of Catholics and Puritans. Sir Anthony Weldon, courtier and politician, banished from court for a book criticizing the Scots, dubbed him 'the wisest fool in Christendom'.[1] The epithet captures something of the discrepancy between his writings on political theory and his practice as a lazy man only intermittently engaged with his role. London celebrated with bonfires when he succeeded peacefully. His apparent engagement with regal duty generated hope, reflected in the mass of appalling, sycophantic eulogistic verse published.[2] During the 15 March 1603 royal procession through the city two St Paul's choristers sang of London as Troynovant (New Troy),[3] no longer a city but a bridal chamber, suggesting a mystical union and new hope.[4]

This sense of promise soon evaporated as his failings and inconsistencies emerged. *King Lear* is underpinned by concerns about kingship and rule (or misrule) of self and others. Misrule of self is a theme running through all Shakespeare's plays, and in *Lear* the major characters, even Cordelia, are guilty of misrule of themselves; each transgress in some way.

The previous monarch, Elizabeth I, a Tudor, was much loved and respected and had been a strong ruler, indeed strong enough to suppress the addressing of many problems which by James's time had become irresolvable. The Tudors (Henry VII, Henry VIII, Edward VI, Mary I and Elizabeth I), ruling 1485–1603, brought relative stability after the turmoil of the Wars of the Roses (though there were various short-lived rebellions against them). Questions of succession, the nature of rulers, the use and limits of monarchical power, the influence of court and the qualities of courtiers, were matters that concerned people throughout the period, and are part of the contexts of *Lear*. Religion was a major area of conflict.[5] Catholic opposition to the new Church of England and Puritan desires for freedom from tight central control created a constant battleground. The effects on society and individual morality of the wealth that the new capitalism and the expansion of trade were creating also worried Jacobean writers. The new individualism, another context, emerges in the self-centred ruthlessness of Goneril, Regan, Edmund and Oswald.

Henry VIII's great achievement (and cause of trouble) was breaking with the Catholic Church of Rome and establishing an independent English church. This inaugurated a period of seismic change called the English Reformation. In 1536 the first Act of Supremacy made Henry Supreme Head of the Church of England. Its rituals and doctrines remained essentially Catholic until the reforms of his son Edward aligned it with the Protestant movements on the Continent. There was some limited alliance with the Protestant Reformation led by Martin Luther, but in many ways the English went their own way. Monasteries and convents were dissolved, the infrastructural features of Catholicism banished, altars stripped of ornament (leaving only the cross and flanking candles), churches emptied of statues and relics, and some murals whitewashed over. New services and prayers were in English rather than Latin, new English translations of the Bible began to appear and there was a Book of Common Prayer to be used in all parish churches. Holy shrines, and saints' days were done away with as idolatrous superstitions. The vicar was to be the only intermediary between a person and God. After a brief, fiery, bloody return to Catholicism under Mary I (1553–58), Elizabeth I succeeded and the bedding-in of the new church continued. The freedom of a reformed English religion, supposedly stripped back to its simple original faith, encouraged the rise of more extreme reformist Protestant sects (not always to the liking of the infant Established Church). These groups, called Non-conformists, Independents or Dissenters, included Puritans, Calvinists[6] and Presbyterians – all Protestant, but with doctrinal differences. Some eccentric sects emerged too, such as the Anabaptists, Brownists and the Family of Love. Religious differences, tensions between different faiths and disagreements within the same faith are persistently present at this time, but despite all the official changes to religion, the essential beliefs in sin, virtue, salvation, the centrality of Christ and the ubiquity of the Devil (the idea that he was everywhere, looking to tempt man) were the same as they always had been, as were the beliefs that sin was followed by punishment and possible damnation and that the world, in decline, would shortly come to an end.

Also persistent is the political discourse on kingship. Elizabeth I (adoringly nicknamed 'Gloriana' after her identification with a character in Spenser's *The Faerie Queene*) ruled 1558–1603, a time long enough to establish her as an icon, particularly as she headed up strong opposition (and victory) against the Spanish. External threats repulsed, the regime was consolidated (though relentlessly under covert attack by Catholicism), but the Elizabethan-Jacobean period was one of unstoppable internal changes, gradually altering the profile and mood of society.[7] Religion, commerce, growing industrialization, increase of manufacture, social relationships, kingship and rule were all in flux. One feature of the period was the unceasing rise in prices, particularly of food, bringing about a decline in the living standards of the poor, for wages did not rise. The rich and the rising middle class could cope with inflation, but the state of the poor deteriorated. Enclosure of arable land (very labour intensive) and its conversion to sheep farming (requiring less labour), raised unemployment among the 'lower orders' or 'baser sort', who constituted the largest proportion (between 80–85 per cent) of the four to five million population. Rising numbers of poor put greater burdens on Poor Relief in small, struggling rural communities and added to the elite's fear of some monumental uprising of the disenchanted. Most of the population worked on the land, though increasing numbers were moving to the few existing cities. Later ages, regarding the Elizabethan era as a 'golden age', talked of 'Merry England' – it was not, except for a small section of rich, privileged aristocrats. Also enjoying greater luxury and comfort were canny merchants (making fortunes from trading in exotic goods from the 'New Worlds' of Asia and the Americas) and the increasingly wealthy, acquisitive 'middling sort' manufacturing luxury goods for the aristocracy. Awareness of the state of the poor and the governing class's emotional detachment from that deteriorating condition is a feature of *Lear* and reflects contemporary hardships. On Sunday 13 March 1603, the Puritan divine Richard Stock delivered a Lent sermon at the Pulpit Cross in St Paul's churchyard, commenting:

> I have lived here some few years, and every year I have heard an exceeding outcry of the poor that they are much oppressed of the rich of this city. […] All or most charges are raised […] wherein the burden is more heavy upon a mechanical or handicraft poor man than upon an alderman.[8]

The Jacobean period was quickly perceived as declining from the high points of Elizabeth's time, with worsening of problems she had been unable or unwilling to rectify during her reign. Economic difficulties, poverty, social conflict, religious dissent and political tensions relating to the role and nature of monarchy and the role and authority of Parliament all remained unresolved. Charismatic, strong rulers (like Elizabeth – and Lear) inspire loyalty though often through fear. Emerging problems are ignored or masked because the ruler disallows discussion of them and councillors fear to raise them. Elizabeth, for example, passed several laws making it treason to even discuss who might succeed her. Such a ruler's death exposes the true state of things. Many of these features are reflected in the contexts of *Lear*. The plan to 'divest' himself of rule, 'interest of territory, cares of state', and the love test, expose flawed thinking and suggest his decision making in general may be faulty. It exposes and activates the fault lines in his family. His strength as ruler and father is a weakness. Too controlling, too dogmatic, too unyielding, obstinately reluctant to go back on his words, especially those rashly spoken, Lear's behaviour raises the question, often asked in James's time, of the place that councillors, personal advisers and Parliament should have in making state decisions.[9]

Strong, purposeful central rule dwindled under James into rule by whim and capricious diktat. His court became more decadent and detached from the rest of the population than his predecessor's. Commerce and manufacture expanded rapidly, triggering a rise in the middle class that provided and serviced the new trades and crafts. Attitudes to religion and freedom from church authority began to develop into resistance, and science began to displace old superstitions and belief in magic. Like all times of transition, the Jacobean period and the seventeenth century in general were exciting for some but unsettling for most, profitable for a few but a struggle for the majority. As always the rich found ways to become richer, and the poor became poorer. Gradually the disadvantaged found men to speak up for them in the corridors of power, in the villages of England and the overcrowded streets of the cities. *King Lear*, a Renaissance *de casibus* tragedy concerned with the fall of a powerful man,[10] is also a typical Jacobean play – dark, cynical, satirical, violent, psychological, exploring character and motive. It is also much concerned with sin, punishment, repentance, redemption and reconciliation.

The first known audience was the court. The new reign and new century were still much overshadowed by the past. Just as Lear's past relationship with his daughters and Gloucester's with his bastard son influence their present, so past events resonated in Whitehall Palace on 26 December 1606.

Chapter 2

THE ELIZABETHAN WORLD ORDER: FROM DIVINITY TO DUST

Strict hierarchy (everything having its place according to its importance in God's order) and organic harmony (everything being part of a whole and having a function to perform) were the overriding principles of the broad orthodox background to how the audience thought their universe was structured (cosmology), how they saw God and religion (theology), and how their place in the order of things was organized (sociology). The disorders and disharmonies upsetting roles and expectations in *King Lear* make it a deeply unsettling threat to established order. It is a play in which the world seems to be falling apart.

Everyone was fairly clear where they were in the universal order, the Great Chain of Being. There were three domains: Heaven, Earth and Hell.[1] God ruled all, was omnipotent (all-powerful) and omniscient (all-knowing). Man was inferior to God, Christ, the Holy Ghost, all the angels, apostles and saints, the Virgin Mary and all the blessed, but superior to all animals, birds, fish, plants and minerals. God ruled Heaven, kings ruled on Earth (and princes, dukes, counts, etc.) and fathers ruled families, like God at home. The chain stretched in descending order of importance from God, through all the hierarchies of existence, to the very bottom – from divinity to dust – all interconnected as contributory parts of God's creation. Each link was a separate group of beings, creatures or objects, connected to the one before and the one after, semi-separate, dependent but partly independent, separate yet part of something greater. Each link had a hierarchy. The human link contained three different ranks: the 'better sort' (monarchs, nobles, gentry), the 'middling sort' (merchants, farmers) and the 'baser sort' or 'lower orders' (artisans, peasants, beggars). The word 'class' was not used then, but these ranks are equivalent to our upper, middle and lower classes.

Cosmology

Astronomically, medieval and Renaissance man thought of Creation, the cosmos, as an all-enveloping Godliness that incorporated Heaven, the human universe and Hell. The universe was thought of as a series of transparent crystal spheres, one inside the other, and each containing a planet. It was a geocentric model – the Earth in the middle, encased in its sphere, enveloped by the Moon's sphere, then Mercury, Venus, the Sun, Mars, Jupiter and Saturn, like the rings of an onion.[2]

The Ptolemaic system

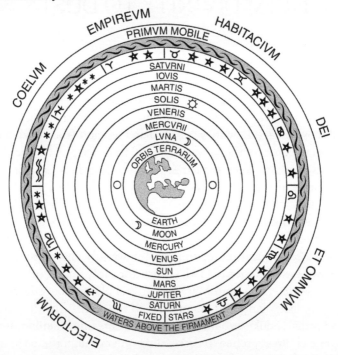

Adapted from engraving for Peter Apian's *Cosmographicus Liber* (*Book of the Universe*, Antwerp 1524). Enclosing the spheres is the 'COELUM EMPIREUM HABITACIUM DEI ET OMNIUM ELECTORUM' (The Empyrean sky, home of God and all the elect – i.e., those judged worthy of Heaven).

Each planet and sphere circled the Earth at different orbital angles and different speeds. After Saturn came the firmament – the fixed stars (divided into 12 seasonal zodiac sectors). Outside this were 'the waters above the firmament' (Genesis 1:7). The tenth sphere, the *Primum Mobile* (First Mover), drove the spheres and then came the all-surrounding Empyrean the domain that was all

God's and all God (i.e., Heaven). Here He was accompanied by the angels and the blessed. The set of concentric crystal balls was imagined by some to hang from the lip of Heaven by a gold chain. This cosmological organization was the Ptolemaic system formulated by the second century AD Graeco-Egyptian astronomer/geographer Ptolemy (Claudius Ptolemaeus). In Tudor times his *Cosmographia* was still being recommended by Sir Thomas Elyot for boys to learn about the spheres.[3]

A man could see the stars, sometimes some of the planets, but not beyond, his vision being blocked by the 'waters'. As the Empyrean, the destination for the virtuous saved, was thus invisible, people needed a visualizable image. It was easier to imagine the blessed 'living' in a celestial city rather than existing spiritually in the heavenly ether, so the idea grew of a heavenly city with towers and gates made of different substances. At the Gate of Pearl, St Peter was supposed to receive each approaching soul and consult his 'Book of Life', recording the person's good and evil, to see if the soul was worthy of entry. Medieval paintings show the *Civitatis Dei* (the City of God) as resembling the walled cities of Italy, France or Germany. Painters often simply depicted the city they knew.[4]

By Shakespeare's time the Ptolemaic system was beginning to be undermined. The great Copernican revolution, supported by Galileo, Kepler and a few others, put the sun at the heart of the universe. It took a long time to become accepted and then filter down to the mass of ordinary people. This idea entered the public domain with Copernicus' study *De Revolutionibus Orbium Coelestium* (*On the Revolutions of the Celestial Spheres*, 1542), but dissemination was impeded by church authorities and the slowness of information spread in those times. In 1603 Sir Christopher Heydon, displaying his knowledge of the new advances, declared, 'Whether (as Copernicus saith) the sun be the centre of the world, the astrologer careth not.'[5] This references the triple belief system in which most people lived: 1. Christian doctrine existing uneasily alongside, 2. the new astronomy and sciences, and 3. old semi-magical beliefs in the authenticity of astrology. Heliocentrism, opposed by other sceptic astronomers (like John Dee), was also frighteningly repressed by dogmatic, authoritarian churches. The Catholic Church's Inquisition enforced conformity persuasively with thumbscrews, the rack and a host of other tortures. The English church had its own courts to question and punish deviations from customary practice and belief; visitations within their diocese enabled bishops to keep vicars and congregations in line and serious infractions could be brought before the Star Chamber.[6] Torture was endemic in England too.

Other beliefs concerning the structure of our world were being transformed. Magellan's circumnavigation of the world without falling off the edge

(1522) showed the Flat Earth theory was inaccurate. Drake's 1580 voyage brought this home more directly to British people when the queen permitted an exhibition to publicize his discoveries. A map displayed at Whitehall Palace made the spherical world visually clear. But how many people saw it? Shakespeare knew of the new development in thinking about the world's shape, as evidenced by Puck's referring to putting 'a girdle round about the earth' (*A Midsummer Night's Dream*, 1595–96) and Lear's demand the gods 'strike flat the thick rotundity of the earth'. To most people, unenlightened by the new discoveries, Earth's roundness and the sun's centrality were unimportant and perhaps still unknown. In an age when the nearest town was often as alien as the moon, 'New Worlds' were places of fantasy and nightmare, inhabited by unnatural beings like the cannibal *anthropophagi*, 'men whose heads/Do grow beneath their shoulders' (*Othello* I. iii. 144–5) and a whole bestiary of strange animals.[7] As long as the sun rose to grow corn, ripen fruit and assist in telling the time and the season, they were indifferent. The centre of their universe was their village. The ordinary farmer would know the stars and some planets but thought of them as belonging to the world of superstition, astrology, weather lore and magic rather than to science and astronomy.

The Great Chain of Being

Earthly creation was thought to be arranged in a set of hierarchical links that made the world order. Man was at the top, followed by animals, birds, fish, plants, minerals. Each stratum of existence had its internal hierarchy organized in order of importance, but man was the pinnacle of God's animal creation. Flawed by Original Sin, with animal weaknesses and negative passions, he was nevertheless part angel, endowed with soul, reason, language, intelligence and sensitivity. Human beings acting morally were an imitation of Christ. Choosing the left-hand way, the path of sin, they resembled the Devil. The conflict between these two aspects made man an angel with horns, but the tensions between virtue and the passions, the perpetual *psychomachia*[8] of life, sparked the interest of literature.

The Great Chain of Being was a construct of human imagining, helping people from the early medieval period to the Renaissance picture how the universe was put together socially and how it worked physically. It was still generally believed in by the majority of Jacobeans, though its physical structure was increasingly challenged by new astronomical research and by socio-economic changes. Most people still thought the cosmos geocentric (centred around Earth). The Renaissance is regarded as a time of change, of new learning and new knowledge. Men were discovering new lands and new ways of thinking about God and society. But this only slowly affected everyday life. The iconoclastic, rationalist, free-thinking, humanist Renaissance Man, daringly breaking through barriers, was an oddity often in conflict with the authorities, confined to small minority groups of progressive artist/scientists/ intellectuals.[9] Seventeenth-century Everyman was conservative and backward-looking in beliefs and lifestyle. If literate, he had few books apart from a Bible, though religious pamphlets and many sorts of non-fiction and fiction books were becoming available.[10] He still went to the wise woman for semi-magical medical help, believed in divination, went to an astrologer to predict a suitable day for travelling or a suitable mate, and still believed the Chain of Being was constructed by God.

Hierarchically arranged, reflecting descending importance, usefulness and perfection, the chain was sometimes imagined instead as a ladder of nature (*scala naturae*). This image suited Christian thinkers because it suggested the idea of rising towards the divine, as each person was supposed to do by virtuous living, cleansing away their earthly faults, purifying them as they metaphorically rose rung by rung to a holiness that prepared their soul for Heaven. Walter Hilton's *The Ladder of Perfection* (written between 1386 and 1396), reflects in its title the image of the step-by-step rise from sin to virtue, presented as a spiritual journey towards Christ-given peace and the peace which was Christ. He is the perfection achieved in climbing the ladder, reached by denying the primacy of the 'anti-Trinity' of mind, reason and will, and trusting faith alone.[11] In the busy, corrupt world of 1606 London, the same belief persisted among the godly sort. These were not just fervent Puritan zealots, but those ordinary folk believing their Christian duty was to live the good life. The good life meant not the carnal life of fleshly pleasures, but the hard-working, devoted life of the family man or woman, whose days were struggled through with Christ's example as their perpetual model. It is important not to underplay the general piety of most people at this time, listening regularly to open-air preachers of different sorts, attending church regularly, and buying, borrowing or having read to them the religious pamphlets pouring off the presses. Printed pamphlet production accelerated from a trickle in 1600 to a flood by the Civil War.[12] Though they lived physically 'by the rule of the flesh', as St Augustine put it, they were dominated by 'the rule of the spirit'.[13] While many lived dedicated Christian lives, others lived at various intermediate stages ranging from occasionally lapsing piety to a more sinful existence, less concerned with virtue than bodily pleasures, and shading down towards outright irreligion and criminality. This vast spectrum was much represented in the City Comedies of the 1600s and in the Revenge Tragedies of the 1580s to 1630s. Shakespeare's Problem Plays (*Troilus and Cressida*, 1601–02; *All's Well That Ends Well*, 1602–04; *Measure for Measure*, 1604), written in the same period as *Lear*, and his late Romances (*Pericles*,

1608–09; *Cymbeline*, 1609–10; *The Winter's Tale*, 1610–11; *The Tempest*, 1611) are concerned with the ethical complexities and ambiguities focused in the tensions between flesh and spirit. *Lear* persistently raises questions of conduct in areas that were of contemporary interest. The audience's responses will have largely been within a Christian, Bible-based context.

Chain or ladder equally suggest unbroken interconnection between all the many phases of created existence between the Creator and dust. Originating in the pre-Christian philosophy of Plato and Aristotle, this idea of hierarchies reflects a Western obsession with taxonomy (classification). Medieval Christian theology assimilated the heavenly hierarchy to fit above the feudal system of human society and the descending levels of the rest of creation. Below earthly life (physically and morally) came the hierarchy of Hell, traditionally thought to be in the bowels of the Earth. Dante (1321) placed it below Gehenna, the rubbish dump outside Jerusalem.[14] The orderliness of God's creation was so embedded in people's minds that disassembling it was like an attack on the foundations of life and faith. Order was part of everything and maintaining order was a form of worship, an acceptance of God as author of that order. Within each dominion – Heaven, Earth and Hell – was a series of graduated structures. In Christian thought the domains of Heaven and Hell, equivalents of the classical world's Olympus (home of the ancient gods) and Hades (the underworld, the place of the dead), had their inhabitants ranked according to priority and power like earthly creation. All three realms had rulers and below them were ranks of diminishing power and diminishing virtue. This was 'a society obsessed with hierarchy'.[15]

Hierarchy of Heaven: God > Christ > the Holy Ghost > Seraphim > Cherubim > Thrones > Dominations > Principalities > Powers > Virtues > Archangels > Angels > the Virgin Mary > the disciples > the saints > the blessed (saved, elect, good souls admitted to Heaven after a virtuous life)[16]

Saints were still intermittently prayed to as intercessors for specific concerns in Protestant England, despite the church having banished such idolatry. It takes generations to change a mindset that has for centuries been integral to thought and elief

Hierarchy of Earth: Man > animals > birds > fish > plants > rocks/minerals

Hierarchy of Hell: Devil/Lucifer/Satan > first hierarchy (Hell's 'nobility'): named devils like Beelzebub, Mephistophelis, Mammon, Belial, etc. > second hierarchy: demons > goblins > imps > incubi/succubi[17] > familiars

Familiars are spirits controlled by a witch/wizard and acting as an assistant. Often they are in animal form. A black cat is commonly thought to be the standard witch's demon familiar, but records include black frogs, dogs and toads. They could take human shape too. Seventeenth-century witch confessions regularly describe a good-looking, blond-haired young man, but with giveaway cloven hoofs. A familiar attached to a necromancer/witch was thought to be a malevolent servant/assistant imp/demon, a limb of Satan, sometimes even Satan himself. If it was benevolent and assisted a white wizard/cunning woman it was sometimes called a fairy. The latter could have mischievous tendencies, like Puck in A Midsummer Night's Dream. They could appear as three-dimensional forms or remain invisible.

Human society's three ranks, degrees or orders were the 'better sort', the 'middling sort' and the 'lower orders' ('commoners' or 'baser sort'). It was thought those of highest rank were there by the grace of God and therefore automatically assumed to be virtuous. They certainly thought themselves superior. Among the classical texts they studied at university was Aristotle's *Nichomachean Ethics*. In his conclusions, they would have found a view to endorse their sense of superiority:

> While [arguments] seem to have power to encourage and stimulate the generous-minded among our youth, and to make a character who is gently born, and a true lover of what is noble, ready to be possessed by virtue, they are not able to encourage the *many* to nobility and goodness. For these do not by nature obey the sense of shame, but only fear, and do not abstain from bad acts because of their baseness but through fear of punishment.[18]

This ignores the fact that many elite men did wrong because they knew they could escape penalty by buying off the law, by family influence or by the psychological power they had over the subordinate majority. The lower orders were thought to be naturally sinful, the middle rank dour money-grubbers. The three-tier feudal system (those who fight, those who pray, those who work) was refined in the Renaissance. 'Those who pray', diminished by the Dissolution of the Monasteries, were assimilated into the upper ranks. 'Those who work' were split into the 'middling sort' and the 'commoners'. The former included the important expanding new masses of bourgeois entrepreneurs (bankers, projectors [speculators], merchants, wealthy clothiers, industrial manufacturers, etc.) that had hardly existed before, but which were driving the astonishing Renaissance explosion of culture and commerce. As money and investment spread through the arteries of European trading, so the bourgeoisie expanded. This rising class was to be a vital feature in Elizabethan-Jacobean social change, hugely increasing the numbers of the 'middling sort', creating confusion about whether powerful 'merchant princes' and 'captains of industry' belonged within the middling rank or among the better sort.[19] The old, simple medieval world, unified in religion by Catholicism, unified socially by the feudal system, was morphing slowly into dynamic new forms. Rising wealth created new types of job. Developing industries created new roles and services. The broad social stratifications were still the same, but the three levels were diversifying into complex new classifications while social/political/commercial interactions were changing in destabilizing, disturbing ways with which many could not easily cope. *Lear* reflects some of these collisions between old and new ways in the references to cozeners, monopolies, courtiers, usurers, and in the behaviour of Goneril, Regan, Edmund and Oswald. Playwright after playwright vilifies usurers and lawyers along with various cheats, hypocrites and ruthless power seekers. These allusions, sprinkled throughout *Lear*, give a satirical edge to the play, reinforcing the darker aspects of the central action.[20] The state of official corruption was highlighted in the oration delivered to James on his arrival in the city. It demanded, 'No more shall bribes blind the eyes of the wise, nor gold be reputed the common measure of a man's worth.' The burden of monopolies, generating taxes that went into the pockets of the monopoly owner, was described as 'most odious and unjust', sucking the marrow out of the life of the people. The legal profession too was indicted: 'Unconscionable lawyers and greedy officers shall no longer spin out the poor man's cause in length to his undoing and the delay of justice.' The speaker, Richard Stock, demanded benefices no longer be sold, the nobility resume their neglected responsibilities to the poor, and placemen be rebuked for their 'abuse [of] the authority of his Majesty to their private gain and greatness'.[21] Ironically, the spur to these pointed demands was the recent republication of James's own book on kingship.[22] Seven copies for private circulation were published in Edinburgh, but James had thousands reprinted in London on his accession.

Human Hierarchy: The Social Pyramid of Power

Each man inhabited different hierarchies relating to 1. society in general (as above), 2. work and 3. family. It is usual nowadays to see human hierarchies as layered pyramids. This simple sociological model classifies according to priority, power and function. First you had a place in the social pyramid (better, middling or lower) and every rank (with its internal hierarchy) had its duties and its role to play. At work there was another pyramid where position depended on age, experience, seniority, qualification and success. Within the family pyramid an unmarried man was subordinate to his father and other male elders. Once married, he was still subordinate within his extended patrilineal family but ruled his nuclear family – wife, children and servants.

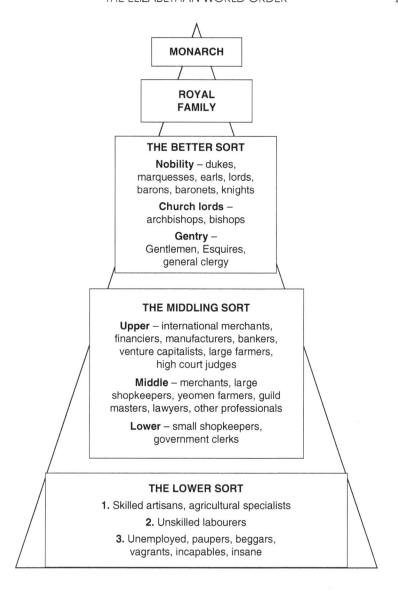

In each of these social arenas obedience to those above was paramount, resistance to change the default attitude and threats to order seen as blasphemy for defying God's arrangement. Those with most to lose were most in favour of hierarchy. In history and literature noblemen and kings promote it as God-ordained and not to be overthrown; maintaining the status quo guaranteed the perpetuation of their power and privilege. The Bible, as so often, authorizes this view: e.g., 'Remember them that have the rule over you' (Hebrews 13:7) and the Commandment 'Honour thy father and thy mother'. 'Filial ingratitude' gives a blasphemous and order-threatening edge to the central action of the main and subplots in *Lear*. Goneril, Regan and Edmund subvert normality by actively opposing their parents. It must be remembered always that the world order was 'produced by power for its own interests' (church power and state power) and predates the Jacobean reverence for hierarchy by centuries.[23]

At the pyramid's pinnacle the ruler reflected God's dominance. The idea of Divine Right is founded on the belief that kings are chosen by God as his representatives on Earth. This endows monarchs with immense psychological/superstitious influence. As God's vice-regent a king could no more be questioned, harassed, imprisoned or executed than you might think of questioning or dethroning God. The king's will was sufficient for anything to be done without question by willing/fearful courtiers. It was the magic password for absolute power, though increasingly James found his will thwarted, often because there was no money to execute it, but increasingly because Parliament opposed his policies and extravagance. Here we encounter the uneasy tension between the divine aura attributed to kings and the daily experience of their human failings. Lear behaves as an unquestionable, bullying autocrat, unused to opposition, and reacting angrily and punitively when opposed. How fallible this divine representative is. How quickly he banishes Kent, a long-term loyal counsellor, upon pain of death if he returns. The ritualistic, emotional reverence given to monarchs makes the later mistreatment of Lear all the more horrific, blasphemous and world threatening. That the treatment stems from his family makes it more barbaric. Becoming a suffering Christ, despised and rejected, stripped of power and dignity, he grows spiritually through his ordeal, learning humility, fortitude, and discovering a vein of satirical insight into society's corruptions. Below the king come his three daughters, then the earls and other knightly courtiers. The middling sort are represented physically only by Oswald, a steward in a royal palace, but there are references to beadles, justices and usurers. The only 'lower order' representatives are the servants present at Gloucester's blinding, and the old man who escorts the blinded earl to Poor Tom. But, vitally, there are descriptions of the vagabonds and beggars at the very bottom of society. This order of ranks was ordained by God, but the exhortations to 'Pomp' to empathize with the poor are clear messages to the silk-clad, ruffed and bejewelled audience.

The better sort

Below the king came his consort, the princes and princesses of the blood, then the descending ranks of the nobility (dukes, marquises, earls, viscounts, barons, baronets and knights) and gentry. This upper section included archbishops and bishops, the church's wealthy, power elite. Part of the upper sort, but untitled, was the gentry – men eligible to be called esquires and gentlemen. The gentry were ranked – upper, middle and lower – according to size of fortune, size of landholding, civic profile and ancientness of family title.

The 'better sort', the 'quality', was the governing elite, the political nation. What did they actually do? Some were ministers, privy councillors, government officers, MPs, army or navy officers (if there was a war – for there was no standing military system) and local magistrates.[24] Those with estates might manage them (though probably delegated through a steward). The rest were essentially idle, a leisured class pursuing their own pleasures (hunting, gambling, drinking, whoring, lounging about at court), a do-nothing aristocracy doing nothing and owning over 90 per cent of the land. They had clear social duties outlined in the Corporal and Spiritual Works of Mercy (see Chapter 4). Increasingly there were men who never had an estate (or had lost it through debt) but who called themselves gentlemen on the grounds of having (or having had) some sort of independent means, university education, officer rank, no need (or intention) to work for a living and a coat of arms. Impoverished gentlemen, living on the edge of high society, scrounging meals, trying to find court favour or trap an heiress, fill the City Comedies of Dekker, Middleton, Heywood and Jonson. They appear in Shakespeare too: e.g., Lucio and Froth (*Measure for Measure*), Sir Andrew Aguecheek (*Twelfth Night*).

The distinguishing material feature of the nobility and gentry was land ownership. Estates meant tenants (farmers and land workers) paying rents. Rent rolls provided the basic, unearned family income.[25] Many titled men were placemen holding sinecure government posts (requiring little actual work), enabling them to sell other places to family members, friends and political contacts who formed an obligated clientage. Nepotism (giving jobs to relatives), once a sin, had become accepted. Court and government corruption were growing political grievances. Wealth could be materially improved if the monarch gave or sold you a monopoly, giving you control of the taxes and other charges on a commodity or service, like imports of wine, tobacco, sugar or starch. This provided further opportunities for selling posts within the infrastructure. The upper sort thought themselves superior in virtue, born with innate leadership abilities, and morally better than other ranks. Noble in rank, supposedly noble, courageous and magnanimous in nature, they thought themselves deserving of respect from all below. They were the contemporary evolution of the medieval warrior class, now demilitarized and without apparent function. Many were fine and decent people, living on their estate, doing their social-moral duties. Many others were simply weak personalities whose extravagance got them into such debt they lost their estate. They were idle, sexually decadent, syphilitics, drunks, fools, inveterate gamblers and incompetent estate managers, indifferent to their role as social exemplars and leaders. James did nothing to encourage reform. Goneril's anger at the behaviour of Lear's knights and their 'rank and not-to-be-endured riots' (I. iv.) is a hit at the sort of drunken Roaring Boy rampages constantly breaking out in the taverns and streets of London in the early years of James's reign, when thousands of elite young men flocked there seeking court places.[26] Shakespeare is making a satirical point when Lear defends his retinue's behaviour:

> My train are men of choice and rarest parts,
> That all the particulars of duty know,
> And in the most exact regard support
> The worships of their name. (I. iv.)

He claims they all know exactly how to behave in accordance with the status and reputation of their family. Knowing how to behave and actually conducting themselves decorously, respectfully and modestly were different matters. Contemporary plays are full of men claiming gentlemanly status but behaving badly. Drunken, roistering, lecherous misconduct highlights serious discrepancies between the expected behaviour of aristo-gentry men and their actual comportment. Inconsistently, bad behaviour often ran parallel with oversensitivity to offences to their honour. Reacting to the slightest perceived insult to their conceived status and the respect it deserved, the response was usually angry and violent. To assert their honour they often were drawn into dishonour by inflammable temper and a readiness to commit violence. In an age when gentlemen habitually wore swords, the ready resort to arms was all too easy, especially when alcohol played its part in the constant outbreaks of street brawls. This gives a topical context to the swaggering braggadocio of the Montagu/Capulet bravo boys of *Romeo and Juliet*. Lear's comment hints at the Jacobean obsession with genealogy and proving the ancientness of your status. Many family trees, however, were fabricated, claiming descent from Norman knights, Saxon thegns, the pre-Roman Trojan origins claimed for the British nobility by pseudo-historians like Geoffrey of Monmouth, even from Old Testament kings. Suitable payment to the College of Heralds bought you an authenticated coat of arms and genealogy. The court audience knew full well that young men of titled or gentry background often behaved like rowdy boors, and that some of them were currently watching the play – though more likely ogling the court ladies. Edgar's description of himself as 'a servingman' (a species of lower courtier) portrays some of these braggart gallants precisely in a litany of sins that would make the audience squirm guiltily (III. iv.). Lear's defence of his train is necessitated after the king himself struck one of Goneril's court for reprimanding the Fool. This disproportionate, ungentlemanly act betokens a lack of emotional control. He will also strike Goneril's steward.[27] In the City Comedy *Eastward Ho!* Francis Quicksilver claims gentlemanly status because his mother was a gentlewoman and his father a senior justice of the peace. Feeling belittled by being apprenticed to a goldsmith he spends his time drinking, whoring and scamming money out of other gallants.[28] To him idleness, drunkenness, violence and carelessness over money are gentlemanly markers:

> Do nothing [...]. Be idle [...]. Wipe thy bum with testons [sixpences; approximately 5p], and make ducks and drakes with shillings [10p]. [...] As I am a gentleman born, I'll be drunk, grow valiant, and beat thee.[29]

Golding, the industrious apprentice, scorns Quicksilver as 'a drunken whore-hunting rake-hell' (I. i. 125). Sexual licence was common in the elite. A 'rake-hell' was a troublemaker and alludes to the gang mentality and hooliganism of the many unsupervised, upper-sort young men floating around London. Edgar claims these failings but adds gambling, lust, vanity, sloth, insincerity and debt.

Despite society's intense stratification, dividing lines were becoming blurred by many individual cases of social mobility, James's creation of new knights, growing bourgeois wealth and the increasing complexity of society. People became obsessively fussy about precedence, about being treated according to their rank and preserving fine differences that made them feel superior. Ambition is a subset of pride, so overambition is seen as pushy, selfish and sinful. A little ambition was proper use of your God-given talents. However, to avoid the *hubris* (presumptuous pride) of becoming too proud of advancement, you should humbly thank God for the good fortune of your rise, downplaying the extent and effect of your own efforts. Lear and Edmund both exhibit *hubris* – one too proud of his status, the other believing himself worthy of better status (like Satan). Goneril and Regan too, once elevated, behave as if they are irreproachably superior.

Political theorists and moral polemicists formulated programmes to train the upper ranks to serve both state and people. Elyot's *The Boke Named the Governour* (1531) proposed careful education combining a reverence for virtue and a readiness to assume social responsibilities. This meant residing on your estate, leading the community, helping the poor, and establishing schools and alms houses, as enshrined in the Corporal and Spiritual Works of Mercy. This philanthropy justified living comfortably off income derived from the work of tenant farmers and tenant labourers. Rank and privilege were counterbalanced by a requirement to put something back into the community, but one of the features of the growing new individualism was that civic spirit and charitable work were discarded by the elite (particularly young men). This was assisted by the growing tendency of the governing ranks to gravitate to London and become detached from their locality. A responsible role for the ruling classes, built upon a virtue-based humanist education, was promulgated by many writers throughout the decades leading to the Civil War, but the actual behaviour of many gentlemen conformed more to Viscount Conway's definition: 'We eat and drink and rise up to play and this is to live like a gentleman; for what is a gentleman but his pleasure?'[30] The main characters in *Lear* are from this ruling elite. Only some display laudable qualities. Courtiers were docile yes-men and yes-women, obsequiously bowing and scraping at the monarch's whim. They were intent upon pleasure and advancement. Advancement depended on others so they tended to be morally indifferent. To stand by principles could lose you favour and the pursuit of personal pleasures dulled the ability or willingness to make moral distinctions if they threatened enjoyment.

The middling sort

The next layer down was the newly enlarged bourgeoisie. In the Middle Ages, the feudal system included them with 'those who work' (anyone earning a living – 90 per cent). This group comprised everyone from day labourers to the wealthiest merchant. The country arrangement was village centred, with the lord of the manor (living in or near the village) governing and guarding (or exploiting and bullying) his 'flock' of farmers and labourers like a shepherd guards and guides his sheep. The workers clustered round and in the village. The priest represented 'those who pray'. The professional 'middling sort' (lawyers, doctors, produce factors, clothiers, etc.) hardly existed in country areas, and were a numerically an insignificant demographic nationally. By the Renaissance the pattern had changed. The numbers of the bourgeoisie burgeoned with the growth of commerce, the growth of towns and the expanded 'service' industries. Although 80 per cent of the population was still rural – farmers and labourers – 15 per cent were now largely a town-dwelling middle class, the remaining 5 per cent being the aristo-gentry. The latter thought the middling sort greedy, obsessed with making money, virtuous enough, but lacking taste, elegance and culture. They were mocked as 'cits' (citizens, city dwellers – i.e., not landowners), social climbers whose wives and daughters were snobbish, fashion mad, empty-headed and easy prey for lascivious, gold-digging courtiers. Some were like that, but many were educated, cultivated people, looking after their families (especially their children) better than many of the nobility. Most were hard working, eager to put a comfortable buffer between themselves and poverty, but modest in lifestyle and personal behaviour. They showed civic spirit, were pious and drove conservative church reform. A minority, however, were extravagant in displaying their wealth.

The rise of the middling sort was *the* big social change in Elizabethan-Jacobean England. Division into upper, middle and lower classifications distinguished between a very rich international merchant, the yeoman farmer with a middling thriving farm and a small shopkeeper. The upper echelons were merchant bankers, financiers, large-scale traders, major clothiers, wealthy manufacturers, along with leading lawyers, judges and large-scale farmers – men of wealth and local (and increasingly national) power. The middle 'middling sort' would be comfortably wealthy merchants and masters of guild trades, living in cathedral cities and market towns. The lower 'middling sort' were small shopkeepers, small farmers who owned a little land, and growing numbers of low-paid metropolitan-based government clerks. What differentiated them was money. More money meant access to mayorships, masterships of guilds and alderman or councillor status. Money gave the capacity to loan cash to the needy, thus becoming a sort of local banker or simply a moneylender. Usury (lending money at unreasonable rates), a sin in medieval times, was acceptable by the seventeenth century, a natural development of the growing cash richness of the expanding commercial world, though what constituted acceptable levels of interest was sharply debated. As the economy grew and fortunes were made and wasted, satire against moneylenders, money-amassing citizens and the debt-fuelled lifestyles of parasite gentlemen featured regularly in plays.

The middle ranks looked up to the aristo-gentry, showed public respect, but increasingly thought themselves morally better than the upper sort. Their markers were piety, hard work, earning a living, a moderate lifestyle, providing a disciplined, loving upbringing for their children, avoiding debt, donating to charity and doing civic duties. They saw the gentry and nobility as vain, idle, showy wastrels, parading in silks they did not pay for, gambling, drinking, acting promiscuously and demanding deference not always deserved. Yet, some merchants longed to rise and display the outer show of gentlemanly status – a fine country house, a coach and horses, fashionable clothes, and access to power, title and privilege. 'The old English gentry were powerfully reinforced [...] by an influx from the professional and mercantile classes. Lawyers, government officials, and successful merchants bought land not only to better their social standing but also to increase their incomes.'[31]

As England became a more active trading nation the middle class expanded and became wealthier and more upwardly mobile. The wealthiest could be awarded or buy titles. They tended also, with this rise in status, to move into the country, selling their business, cutting themselves off from the taint of trade. Legislation to stop bourgeois land ownership was increasingly ignored, circumvented or simply not applied. The bourgeoisie was unstoppable, buying estates, thinking themselves equal to the nobility; some even became nobility. Money power enabled such men to push out the cash-strapped yeoman farmer. Agricultural depression led to many of these freemen, who owned their own farm, selling up to opportunist incoming merchants-turned-landowners looking to add to their holdings. Small, independent farmers were also under pressure from some gentry augmenting their estate.[32] Another expanding bourgeois group was made up of top civil servants administering the growing departments of government. The three most prestigious power posts were those of Lord Treasurer, Lord Chancellor and the King's Secretary. These were political as well as royal household appointments. Below them was another internal court pyramid of power – the bureaucrats – reaching down to the lowliest 'base pen clerks'.[33] The most junior dreamed of catching the eye of a superior or a titled courtier and being promoted. Once in a higher place your future was made. You gained a place with patrimony, patronage or purchase. A poor clerk without family connections to help him advance, and without money, had to find a patron. It was difficult to penetrate 'the grand efflorescence of nepotism' if you could not buy promotion or inherit a post from your father.[34] A readiness to be 'super-serviceable' (as Kent calls Oswald, II. ii.), however dirty and underhand the deed required, could get you into a courtier's good books. After killing Oswald, Edgar describes him:

> I know thee well: a serviceable villain;
> As duteous to the vices of thy mistress
> As badness would desire. (IV. vi.)

The court was awash with idle young men seeking opportunities for advancement. In *Eastward Ho!* the idle apprentice, Quicksilver, cast off by his irate master, declares, 'I'll to the Court, another manner of place for maintenance [...] than the silly City!' (II. ii. 54–5).

If your courtier-patron had some measure of power you could advance. This is the ambition that drives Oswald to attempt to kill the blinded Gloucester and had previously shown him ready to change allegiance and serve Regan. The character and role of Oswald as obsequious underling assumes a topical contextual significance in the Jacobean court. Edmund too offers advancement to the Captain he sends to execute the king and Cordelia. The plots, counterplots and intrigues of the court provide innumerable examples of what servants (high and low) will do to get on. Such events in drama simply show art copying life.

The lower orders

The mass of the population formed the broad base of the pyramid. Skilled artisans were at the top along with specialist farm workers (shepherds, horse men, cattle men, etc.). Apprentices, learning a trade or craft, would count themselves as being in the middle of the lower orders, aspiring with industry to move into shop ownership and guild membership, thus becoming bourgeois. Below was the mass of unskilled day labourers, with the unemployed, paupers, beggars, vagrants, the insane and the incapable at the very bottom. Farm workers were severely squeezed at this time. Prices rose steeply throughout both Elizabeth's and James's reigns. Common land, where game could be caught, firewood gathered, vegetables cultivated and animals grazed, was being enclosed by greedy landowners. Thus, the opportunities to augment food and comfort were diminishing. These are the hardships from which Edgar draws his idea for disguise when he is outlawed. This part of society was growing alarmingly, not because of a high birth rate but because the changing economy caused 'casualties' that fell into unemployment. The growing unemployed poor not only drained local Poor Relief resources, but represented a dangerous underclass with the potential for social unrest and riot. A 1597 law aimed at reducing this danger by banishing vagabonds to Newfoundland and the East and West Indies, but remiss or reluctant justices of the peace meant the problem was neither reduced nor repressed.[35]

The lower orders were thought by the ranks above to be lazy, delinquent, ignorant, feckless and vicious (in the physically brutal and morally unsound senses). They often were, particularly the growing numbers of urban poor. But there were hard-working men and women living godly lives and running their households effectively despite hardships. Those living in the countryside were particularly susceptible to fluctuations in prices of produce and winter feed for livestock, and changes in land usage brought about by local enclosure. Disastrous harvests in the 1590s exacerbated matters, bringing starvation to many doors. Piety, thrift and frugality could not alter that. Nor could hard work and decent living protect you from market shifts caused by the greed of others in higher ranks. The state of the poor is raised in *Lear*. It is not a major theme, but it relates to the duty of kingship, the Christian duty of charity, the concept that we are all brothers and neighbours and should take care of one another. It is another topical feature aimed at the self-satisfied court audience, who encountered beggars thronging the streets whenever they left the comfort of Whitehall. There were about twelve thousand beggars in London in 1600. Some were indolent fraudsters preferring begging or thieving to work, but many were genuine victims of hard times.[36] All were the responsibility of those with wealth, rank and privilege. All were morally and metaphorically (some literally) sons and daughters of the nobility. It was the job of the monarch and court to look after them; most did not. Shakespeare roundly criticized the detachment of the rich from the poor in *King Lear* (1605–06) and *Measure for Measure* (1603). In the opening to *Coriolanus* (1607–09), the privileged senator Menenius and the arrogant Martius clash with the starving citizens of Rome:

> 1 *Citizen*: We are accounted poor citizens, the patricians good. What authority surfeits on would relieve us. If they would yield us but the superfluity while it were wholesome, we might guess they relieved us humanely. But they think we are too dear. The leanness that afflicts us, the object of our misery, is as an inventory to particularize their abundance. (I. i. 13–19)[37]

If the governing orders have responsibility to aid the poor, the poor have a duty of grateful, controlled conduct, and respect for those above them. Less and less was duty enacted on either's part.

The Theory of the Humours

There was a hierarchy of the inner man too. The head, like a monarch, ruled (theoretically) as a symbol of the primacy of reason. The major organs, like the nobility and gentry, came next as key to the functioning of the body. The limbs, like the commoners, were the mere labourers. This imprecise image was less important than the connection of the body to the outer world, the macrocosm. The alignment of stars, planets and the ascendant zodiac sign at the precise hour of your birth fixed your fate and personality, enabling predictions to be made concerning your future fortune. This alignment influenced your whole life. From classical times until the end of the eighteenth century people believed that the body contained four fluids (humours) influencing personality, attitude and behaviour. This had been particularly developed by the Roman physician Galen and persisted into Renaissance times, though beginning to be modified by new scientific discoveries. While your astrological sign provided the broad characteristics of your personality, the proportions of the four humours determined your temperament more precisely. Whatever these proportions were at birth defined your healthy, normal state and your psychological type. The humours were: phlegm, yellow bile (choler), blood and black bile. Four temperaments were associated with the humours. The phlegmatic person was normally easy-going and stoical, remaining calm in crises and seeking rational solutions. The choleric man was inclined to temper, was bossy, aggressive, ambitious, and liked to take charge. Lear is described as 'choleric' (I. i.) and his eldest daughters replicate this temperament. The sanguine man (in whom blood predominated) tended to be positive, active, impulsive, pleasure-seeking, self-confident, sociable, open, friendly and warm-hearted. Those in whom black bile dominated tended to be considerate of others but melancholic, negative, overly introverted and inclined towards pessimism about the imperfections of the world. Between these four cardinal types there were many permutations, explaining the huge variety of character types and the range of emotional phases to which an individual might be subject.[38] Illness was thought to be due to an increase or decrease in one fluid and led to (and explained) mood changes. The medical practices of bloodletting and purging were thought to rebalance the body, getting rid of an excess of one humour, while certain foods or drinks redressed deficiencies. Some natural philosophers (scientists and rationalists) were beginning to question this theory, believing parental attitudes, early life experiences and education formed personality. Some physicians were beginning to ascribe other causes to illnesses, though today's knowledge of chemical imbalances causing maladies and mental aberrations shows the humours theory was not entirely wrong. Belief in these characteristics led to 'humour' stereotypes in literature that were sources of comedy (grumpy fathers, shrewish wives, romantic lovers, bloodthirsty soldiers, gold-mad misers, sex-mad widows, scheming villains, etc.). The character flaws of tragic heroes and villains fall easily into these broad categories as well.[39] There were those who rejected astrological origins of personality, claiming they created their own destiny. The Machiavellian individualist Edmund rejects the idea of the stars forming personality. Conceived 'under the dragon's tail' and born 'under Ursa Major' he would be expected to be 'rough and lecherous' (I. ii.), but believes in himself as maker of his own destiny ('I should have been that I am, had the maidenliest star in the firmament twinkled at my bastardizing'). It was a minority view.

The Rest of Creation

Below humankind come the other animals – mammals, birds, fishes, insects, etc. – able to move, reproduce, experience appetites (e.g., hunger, thirst, heat, cold, sexual urges), with limited sensory responses, limited problem-solving intelligence, lacking capacity for a spiritual life, without ability to reason or make moral decisions and unaware of God. Animals were thought not to have souls, logic or language.

Animals were also ranged hierarchically though less precisely than humankind and often according to conflicting ideas about their nature. Some were highly regarded, while others were denigrated for what were thought to be their distasteful characteristics. The lion topped the animal world because of its imagined links to courage, nobility and kingship (reflected in the use of lions as royal heraldic emblems). Tigers were noted for ferocity. Mother tigers' protectiveness of their young is admired, but the 'tigers not daughters' description by Albany of Goneril and Regan's behaviour (IV. ii.) suggests an unreliable, savage aspect. After wild mammals, come the useful working or food-yielding animals and domestic pets. Dogs (useful guards and hunters), ranked with the working creatures, could be highly prized and Elizabethan-Jacobean gentlemen endlessly discussed the qualities of their hunting dogs. Canine loyalty was highly regarded, but there were negatives – a fawning, flattering nature, greediness, and readiness to follow anyone who fed them. 'Whoreson dog' is a common abusive epithet in plays. Wolves were lowly in rank because of their perceived savage, predatory nature. Lear describes Goneril as having a 'wolvish visage' (I. iv.). Foxes, wolves and dogs receive numerous negative mentions in *Lear*. Apes and goats were thought particularly lustful. Goats, associated with the Devil for their horns and cloven feet, were often described as part of black magic rituals. Reptiles were low in the hierarchy, snakes particularly being associated with evil, temptation and Original Sin in the Bible. *Lear* contains a number of pejorative references to serpents and adders. Frogs and toads had witchcraft associations. Lowest of all were rats, mice and other vermin.

Birds were highly thought of because of flight's association with air, thought to be a divine element along with fire. Birds of prey, used for the chase, were ranked according to their suitability to be linked with different social levels – an eagle for an emperor, gerfalcon for a king, peregrines for the nobility, goshawks for yeomen (small-scale landowning farmers), sparrowhawks for priests and kestrels for knaves (servants). Below the birds of prey (including the owl, synonymous with wisdom) come the carrion eaters (vultures, crows and kites), thought of as lowly scavengers, like hyenas in the mammal hierarchy. Kites (many combed the London rubbish tips) are always represented negatively, linked with the parasitical behaviour of feeders and sycophants hanging around the households of men of power.[40] Lear, angry at her demand he 'disquantity' his train (I. iv.), calls Goneril a 'detested kite'. The parasite (the yes-man toady, like Mosca in Jonson's classic play *Volpone* [1606] and Oswald in *Lear*) was a familiar figure of scornful fun on stage, originating in classical comedy and satirical poetry. Parasites attached themselves to a rich, powerful man in order to curry favour, to be rewarded for running errands (including pimping) and to flatter the master's self-esteem. They hoped at least to be invited to dinner, at most retained as a member of the household, a personal assistant-cum-fixer. Mosca, the paragon of parasites, is named after the Latin for fly, since flies feed off rotten things. Significantly, Volpone is named after the Latin for fox, since he is both devious and cunning, and the scavenging fortune hunters of the story after the allegorized animal figures of the medieval-Renaissance didactic fable – Voltore (a vulture-like advocate), Corbaccio (a raven-like miser) and Corvino (a crow-like merchant). Ravens also had occult connotations and were omens of death. Below the scavengers came the worm- and insect-eating birds and then the seed eaters. The nightingale (called Philomel[a] in one of Ovid's metamorphosis stories) represents the beauty of birdsong. The lark figures as the bird that heralds dawn.

Abusive name calling occurs plentifully in Jacobean drama, involving negative animal/avian epithets. *Lear* is full of such language. Few animal connotations are positive, but connecting negative human behaviour with animals is a reminder of man's sinful animal side – lustful, brutal, devious, greedy and slothful. The worst type of association involves monsters – unnatural, mythical, animal hybrids of nightmarish imagining. Jacobeans were horrified by and fascinated with what they called 'monstrous' births (malformed babies, abnormal facial features, bodily oddities, etc.). Broadsheets and pamphlets made much of reports of birth defects as divine punishment for sin, the Devil's work, or Catholic plotting or hoaxing.[41] Medieval and Renaissance people believed outward ugliness expressed inner deformity and sinfulness. Beauty was thought a guarantee of inner grace and purity. References to monstrous behaviour in *Lear* signify an extreme shift from what is regarded as decent, normal humanitarian relationships. The strongest occurrence comes as Albany's opposition to his wife's treatment of her father reaches crisis point:

Tigers, not daughters, what have you perform'd?
A father, and a gracious aged man,
Whose reverence even the head-lugg'd bear would lick,
Most barbarous, most degenerate! have you madded.
[...]
If that the heavens do not their visible spirits
Send quickly down to tame these vilde offences,
It will come,
Humanity must perforce prey on itself,[42]
Like monsters of the deep. (IV. ii.)

Albany foresees society collapsing into internecine destruction if the sisters persist in their brute-like irreverence. Their actions are 'barbarous', 'degenerate' and monstrous, suggesting that unnatural transgressing of the accepted norms of child–parent behaviour leads to endgame species extinction. The species in question is the civilized human who cares about others. Albany rejects selfish, ruthlessly individualistic conduct that disregards the ancient traditions of respect for the vulnerable. It is another collision of old and new philosophies.

The final groupings of animals were the fish, reptiles, amphibians, insects and sessiles (unmoving shellfish). Fish, though a common food source, were ranked low, as water was thought to be a dull heavy element like earth. Reptiles, amphibians and insects were thought of as even lower. Fleas and lice were vermin. Bees and ants were positively regarded for their industry and apparent social organization which suggested something approaching intelligence.[43] This period valued any form of corporate, civic or community co-operation as a mark of moral engagement with civilized behaviour.

Lower still, the plant world, only able to grow and reproduce, also had its hierarchy. Trees were at the top with the oak as the prime form – useful, because of its hardness, for ships and houses – associated with stability, rootedness, imperturbable fortitude and Englishness. A king was seen as a great oak, sheltering his people as the tree did birds and insects.[44] Shrubs and bushes came next, along with flowers. The rose was thought to be the most beautiful, associated with love and with the Virgin Mary (the rose without a thorn). The lily signified purity, chastity and death. There was a range of floral/herbal significations: pansies for thought, rosemary for remembrance, and so on, plus the useful plants – edible and medicinal. Ferns, weeds, moss and fungus were such basic forms they furnish pejorative metaphors for useless, troublesome, threatening humans. The rising bourgeoisie was sometimes described as 'so many early mushrooms, whose best growth sprang from a dunghill'.[45]

At the very bottom of creation even rocks and minerals were ranked by their values as gemstones, precious metals, building materials or chemical sources. Many were thought to have magical/medical powers. Pearls were much prized in the Renaissance – by Queen Elizabeth particularly – and long associated with purity. Among the metals gold was king, succeeded by silver, iron (and steel), bronze, copper and lead. Gold was imaginatively potent, the regal metal, used for crowns and sceptres, superior to silver and lowly lead. Gold also had its negative side as a symbol of man's greed, the means to suborn, seduce and corrupt. Its corrupting power is most forcibly, comically and sadly expressed in Jonson's *Volpone*, where, blasphemously, gold has become Volpone's god. Flamineo sharply describes this idolatrous blasphemy in Webster's *The White Devil* (1612):

> O gold, what a god art thou! And O man, what a devil art thou to be tempted by that cursed mineral […]. There's nothing so holy but money will corrupt and putrify it. (III. iii. 21–8)

For Romeo gold is 'saint-seducing' (*Romeo and Juliet*, I. i.) and Lear's reference to gold's power to corrupt justice, making it a buyable commodity, is particularly pointed considering the persistent contemporary pleas to reform and purify public life and James's ignoring of complaints about venial judges.

> Plate sin with gold,
> And the strong lance of justice hurtless breaks;
> Arm it in rags, a pigmy's straw does pierce it. (IV. vi.)

Gold became a Renaissance obsession. People longed for it, got it, then wanted more. Foolish speculators gave huge amounts of money and metal objects to alchemists experimenting to turn base metals into gold. Some seriously believed this possible; others used its potential for lucrative scams. This avaricious dream became the subject of Jonson's powerful satire on human greed, *The Alchemist* (1610). Exploration of America was triggered by the belief that huge amounts of gold could be found there to rival the spoils brought home by the annual Spanish treasure fleet. Balboa wrote to King Ferdinand that in Darien (in Columbia) there were rivers of gold.[46] Sir Walter Raleigh fantasized a South American kingdom – El Dorado – of limitless gold.[47] Gold thread woven into cloth, gold jewellery, gold plates and gold drinking goblets all showed off your pride in your wealth. Pride, vanity and display were regarded as sinful.

Among rocks marble was most prized (for sculpture and building), followed by granite, sandstone and limestone. Lowly chalk and clay had their uses, though clay was connected metaphorically with man's mortality. Last of all are the particle forms – sand, gravel, soil and dust. Sand and gravel represented the precariousness of man's attempts to build a solid life, earth was thought a dull, heavy element, appropriately typifying man's last state: 'earth to earth, ashes to ashes, dust to dust'.[48]

Order

Not only were human ranks given an order reflecting how they were valued, but the preservation of that order was seen as a guarantee of social harmony. Orderliness reflected, therefore affirmed, God's arrangement of the universe. The fourth line of *King Lear* introduces the first unsettling of order – dividing the kingdom. The audience would have felt uneasy at this; their position at court and in the world at large relied absolutely on preserving order. They had recently undergone the nervousness naturally accompanying a power handover. The new king calmed anxieties by decreeing all posts held under Elizabeth I would continue in the hands of current placeholders, but then (not the last time he would renege on his word) replaced with Scots all the gentlemen of his Bedchamber (responsible for organizing his bed linen, night clothes, day clothes and washing and toilet needs). These salaried posts gave the holders valuable access to the king. The increasingly elaborate ritualization of all aspects of the king's life meant nobles and titled men doing menial tasks. Some enjoyed the honour, some found it degrading but necessary to maintain their influence. Sir Philip Gawdy describes the king's dinner served not by ordinary household servants but by titled courtiers:

[The king] was serued wth great State. My Lo: of Southa [Southampton]: was caruer [carving the meat], my L. of Effingham Sewer, and my Lo: of Shrewsberry cup bearer, my poore selfe carried vp ij [2] dishes to his Maties [Majesty's] table.[49]

Courtiers struggled indecorously for these places, flattering, bribing and defaming rivals. James destabilized order by rearranging the tenancies of these posts. The tense uneasiness of Goneril's household, the conflict between her domain's order, her individual commands and her father's, was one the audience well understood. The court was a precarious world; power and place struggles were everyday happenings. Loss of post meant shame, dishonour, loss of influence with the king, loss of valuable patronage saleable to those wanting your help accessing the monarch. The disassembling order of Lear's world would have had uneasy political relevance for the audience, the feeling of a takeover of power, a new force, adding to the general mood of uneasiness in a society that believed the world was in decline. The Privy Council was expanded and among the new members were five Scots, two of whom were additionally given top legal and financial posts. New monarchs usually meant new men, but James gave unprecedented power to men regarded as foreigners. This political usurpation generated grievances to add to others accumulating around the wholesale Scots incursion into London and Whitehall. Crucial in any court was who controlled access to the ruler. The Venetian ambassador, Giovanni Scaramelli, recounted how English courtiers complained:

No Englishman, whatever his rank, can enter the Presence Chamber without being summoned, whereas the Scottish Lords have free entrée of the Privy Chamber, and more especially at the toilette; at which time they discuss proposals which, after dinner are submitted to the Council, in so high and mighty a fashion that no one has the courage to oppose them.[50]

James's desire to unify the kingdoms created much dissatisfaction and Shakespeare is able cleverly to address the problem by showing the disruption of a reverse political settlement. Sir Philip Gawdy complained that the king put Scots 'in all offices' and 'put out many English, meaning to make us all under the name of ancient Britons'.[51] This aim to return to the polity of ancient Britain may have been a spur to Shakespeare returning to the already dramatized story of Lear. James's blatant favouritism had the effect of uniting rival English courtiers and politicians. Scaramelli observed, 'The English, who were at first divided amongst themselves, begin now to make common cause against the Scots.'[52] Though James envisaged the opposite of what Lear does, most politicians and the English population in general did not want to change the way things were. England worked – up to a point. It was a viable state that had a relatively peaceful, increasingly thriving economic arrangement. But it was a conflicted culture that did not want further destabilization. Internal commerce, manufacture and foreign trade were growing rapidly, but other areas of the economy (agriculture, unemployment, monopolies, etc.) were highly problematic. Religious life was severely conflicted. The paganism of *Lear* precludes allusion to that, but presents moral issues whose bases would have been largely agreed by the various faiths. It is political and social problems that are foregrounded: the problems raised by absolutist tyranny, the split between ranks. Heinemann asserts,

> The central focus is on the horror of a society divided between extremes of rich and poor, greed and starvation, the powerful and the powerless, robes and rags, and the impossibility of real justice and security in such a world.[53]

Lear is not a play written to flatter a Scots king's favourite policy, but about poor kingship, warning against ill-considered changes made in response to anger. Lear admits that his anger 'like an engine, wrench'd my frame of nature/From the fix'd place' (I. iv.). Frustrated anger, invective and threats increasingly became tools of government for James. Acknowledgement that wrath distorts the natural state echoes Montaigne's comment, 'No passion disturbs the soundness of our judgement as anger does.'[54] Anger and its effects was a theme schoolboys studied in Seneca's *De Ira* (*On Anger*). Goneril claims, 'The best and soundest of his time hath been but rash' (I. i.). Rash, impulsive action is unwise, and when the actor is a king the consequences are national; when he is a father they can devastate private lives too. In his essay 'Of Anger', Bacon quotes Seneca: 'Anger is like ruin, which breaks itself upon that it falls.'[55] Lear's anger brings ruin to the state and to himself; his wrath initially falls on his daughters but ultimately they break him. The biblical context for Lear's fatal flaw is Ephesians 4:26: 'Be angry, but sin not' and Luke 21:19: 'In your patience possess ye your souls.' Wrath was a Deadly Sin.

As the play develops allusions to disorder and examples of its consequences proliferate and the fictional polity descends into civil war. There is collapse in

Lear's personal state (as king, father, rational being), collapse in his family, in Gloucester's family, and rumours of dissension between the two dukes. There is disorder in the ferocity of the storm. Keeping order, preserving normality, the distinctions of rank, was essential.

Orderliness is given its most famous, detailed definition in *Troilus and Cressida* (1602). Ulysses upbraids the bickering Greek leaders for neglecting the 'specialty of rule'. If the clarity of 'degree' is blurred the unworthy will appear no different from anyone else. James himself blurred degree when, relieved at the welcome of his people as he progressed south, he made hundreds of unworthy knights.[56] The specialty of rule is founded on the traditional belief that 'some things are so divided right from birth, some to rule, some to be ruled'.[57] Ulysses points out that the whole universe follows ordained rule:

> The heavens themselves, the planets, and this centre,
> Observe degree, priority, and place,
> Insisture, course, proportion, season, form,
> Office, and custom, in all line of order. (I. iii. 85–8)

If orderliness is disturbed:

> What plagues and what portents, what mutiny,
> What raging of the sea, shaking of the earth,
> Commotion in the winds. (I. iii. 96–8)

Disorder affects human society when rank is disrespected:

> O, when degree is shaked,
> Which is the ladder of all high designs,
> The enterprise is sick! How could communities,
> Degrees in schools, and brotherhoods in cities,
> Peaceful commerce from dividable shores,
> The primogenitive and due of birth,
> Prerogative of age, crowns, sceptres, laurels,
> But by degree, stand in authentic place? (I. iii. 101–8)

Order is the cement bonding human society and Ulysses warns of the consequences of disassembling order:

> Take but degree away, untune that string,
> And hark what discord follows! each thing meets
> In mere oppugnancy: the bounded waters

Should lift their bosoms higher than the shores,
And make a sop of all this solid globe;
Strength should be lord of imbecility,
And the rude son should strike the father dead. (I. iii. 109–15)

Shakespeare was always concerned with order – nationally, socially, personally and spiritually. Rebellion, usurpation and collapse are political themes found in all his history plays (including the Roman ones). Disorder, excess and misrule figure too in his tragedies and comedies. Like many writers in the early 1600s, he was preoccupied by political and social questions relating to how society should be run. Loss of 'degree' meant force would dominate society, justice would be lost, and illegitimate power, will and appetite ('an universal wolf') would rule. James warned his son, 'Beware yee wrest not the World to your owne appetite, as over many doe, making it like A Bell to sound as yee please to interpret.'[58] Ulysses uses imagery of natural order turned upside down, unnatural human behaviour and the dominance of sin. This is exactly what we see in *Lear*, in the actions represented, in the language and imagery. Ironically, history shows repeatedly that what is natural for man is that the strongest oppress the weak, the brutal take control, the ruthless rule. The need and desire to co-operate creates society and cements community, but such bonding is often weak when faced by strong men backed by pitiless, armed henchmen ready to shed blood to gain power. In *Lear* Cornwall is very ready to deconstruct the old king's power to assert and augment his own new status. Regan readily backs him and temporarily combines with Goneril to pursue their power agenda. We see how slow to recognize danger and react the decent people are. The naivety and gullibility of Lear, Gloucester, Edgar and Albany illustrates the saying 'It is necessary only for good men to do nothing for evil to triumph'. Christians believed evil was ever-present, the Devil constantly trying to tempt people into sin. Vigilance was crucial. Alertness is absent for much of *Lear*. Salvation finally becomes possible but only after horrors have been committed. By the time Edgar and Albany bestir themselves it is too late to save Cordelia, Lear or the blind earl. Lear and Gloucester deserve punishment for their transgressions as fathers, but Cordelia is the innocent victim always sacrificed when men of blood grasp for power. Arguably Cordelia too deserves punishment. She triggers Lear's anger with a too-naive, too-blunt, undiplomatic refusal to play his 'flatter me' game. A more experienced, mature person, knowing his likely response, would tell white lies to keep him calm. Tragedy lies in the extremity of her payment for a minor misjudgement.

The seventeenth century was much concerned with political theory. Playwrights, especially Shakespeare, picked up on sixteenth-century interests

in how society was best to be administered, and *Lear* owes something to
Sir Thomas Elyot's *The Boke Named the Governour* (1531) and the various
editions of *The Mirrour for Magistrates* (see Chapter 10, 'The Literary
Context'). James contributed two theoretical conduct books on kingship:
The True Law of Free Monarchies (1598) and *Basilikon Doron* (1598). There
was, however, severe discrepancy between his ideas and his actions. The
theory of order, the desire for peace and harmony, were also belied by the
actualities of life. Order seemed continually under attack and the fear of
disorder added to the Jacobean angst. Rising crime and alcoholism in the
1600s contributed to the general gloomy sense of decline and decay.[59] On
15 March 1604 James formally processed through the city to Westminster.
At one of the seven highly ornamented gates built for him to pass through,
a Latin oration (among many sycophantic speeches) spoke of 'this sixt age of
the world [...] *in the declyning age of our Kingdome*'.[60] These factors fed into
those dramas which reflected, as *Lear* does, the feeling of increased dishonesty,
licentiousness, greed and brutality. Lear has much in common with the
comedies of the time. Though the genres and outcomes differ the themes and
satirical targets are similar. City Comedies are peopled by petty criminals,
shysters, cozeners, cony catchers, usurers, legacy chasers, greedy merchants
and braggart penniless gentlemen. London itself emerges as a character in
critical dramas from the 1590s. Though foreign cities (especially Italian)
are often the pretended setting, the virulent satire, the abuses and 'ragged
follies' are transparently English and associated with London. The increase in
the crowded metropolitan population (200,000 in 1600, 575,000 in 1700)[61]
provided a huge variety of human types. Writers revelled in portraying the
seedier characters, enjoying their vitality while deprecating their dishonesty
and trickiness. *Lear* is less topically specific, but its overall mood concentrates
all those neurotic fears of collapse, order turned upside down, the family
itself threatened, evil thriving and good seemingly rare. *Lear* is driven by acts
of transgression, accepted norms subverted, by tricks, cruelty, lies, lust and
ambition. The perpetrators are members of a court and the subsidiary targets
mentioned by Lear and Edgar are types recurring in the comedies. It is also a
palimpsest of sins and broken Commandments.

The geographical arrangements of the nation reflected authority and
hierarchy. Divided into structures imposing order on what might otherwise
be, and sometimes was, a restless population, a patchwork of counties each
had a sheriff or lord lieutenant. Below him a network of estates owned
by rich, titled, powerful men imposed authority locally. Estates varied
in size, but within reach (sometimes within the perimeter) of even the
smallest would be villages, parishes and individual dwellings rented by
families dependent on the landowner's good will. Grandees often owned

several estates in different parts of the country, each providing income from rents and farm produce. Increasingly, though land gave status, such men were becoming entrepreneur-employers exploiting mineral deposits on their domains and other natural advantages like water, timber, rush for thatching and clay for bricks. Men of lesser title and less money, with smaller estates, would still have dependent tenants and a tenanted home farm to provision the family. The gentry might only own a house, maybe a fortified manor, and their land might be no more than a small acreage surrounding the house, but as part of the ruling class (magistrates, justices of the peace, chairmen of parish councils, etc.), they further imposed the values of their privileged elite. Hierarchy penetrated parish churches, where the better sort had boxed-in family pews near the pulpit, the middling sort sat on benches and the poor stood at the back. The gentry monopolized parish councils through the so-called 'select vestry' that barred lower ranks from attending. Local politics was controlled by landed families and Parliament was 88 per cent upper orders and 12 per cent merchants and civic authorities. The few large cities – London, Bristol, Norwich, York – also had their networks of power, with aldermen, beadles, mayors and the wealthy liveried companies. Richard Stock's 1603 Lent sermon in St Paul's churchyard directly addressed the Mayor of London, aldermen, nobility and privy councillors:

> You are magistrates for the good of them that are under you, not to oppress them for your own ease. I would speak to him who is chief of the city for this year. What is past cannot be remedied, but for the future, as far as lies in your power, prevent these things.[62]

With the queen close to death, the mood was anxious. 'The wealthier sort feared sudden uproars and tumults, and the needy and loose persons desired them.'[63] The gentry largely resided in the country (though sons migrated to London) while titled men spent most of their time at court and in Parliament. In a period of high produce prices and little profit to be made from agriculture by any except the great farmers, landowners raised rents, reducing the profit margins of the yeoman farmers holding leases from them and forcing many labourers into homeless unemployment. Increasingly, gentry heirs and younger sons drifted to the capital, forming a large, shifting population of troublesome young men, some hanging about the court seeking posts or heiresses. Many simply saw London as a pleasure ground, removed from immediate parental disapproval. Like Edgar's 'servingman' they were generally a nuisance, drinking, whoring, gambling, fighting, theatregoing and chasing rich merchants' daughters.

Many titled families were founded by men who came to power under Henry VIII, buying or given by the king church lands that came onto the market at the Reformation. These were now the old families of the upper ranks. A few titled men could trace their ancestry further back, even to the Conquest, but most were of relatively recent authority, paying the College of Heralds to manufacture fake genealogies that gave them more respectable and ancient descent.[64] This system of power and privilege was intended to keep the queen's or king's peace. It largely did so, despite outbursts of local unrest, but at the expense of the physical and political repression of the 'baser sort'. Generations of psychological pressure established fear of the upper ranks, a belief that, like the king, they were part of God's order and opposing them was a grave blasphemy, pitting your puny, sinful self against the divinely ordained state of creation. In 1549 Thomas Cranmer, Archbishop of Canterbury, reinforced this in upbraiding rebels: 'Though the magistrates be evil and very tyrants against the commonwealth and enemies to Christ's religion, yet the subjects must obey in all worldly things.'[65] This encouragement to submit even to injustice was repeated in the *Second Tome of Homilies* (1571). The sermon 'against disobedience and wilful rebellion' saw tyranny as divine punishment against a sinful people who should not 'shake off that curse at their owne hand'.[66] Attempting to liken hierarchical deference to submission to God is part of seeing the order of society as God's will. By making it an aspect of church doctrine, church authorities aimed to curb rebellion and maintain their own power. It worked for the mass of fearful, superstitious people, but opposition was growing.

The civil power was not the only repressive network controlling England. Hand in hand with government, often synonymous with it, the church attempted to guide conformity and forcibly dissuade dissent. Each English diocese had a bishop responsible for ensuring priests and congregations followed the Anglican form of worship. These dioceses totalled between nine and a half and ten thousand parishes each (theoretically) with a priest and an average of 300 parishioners (450 in the less controllable, expanding cities). Pluralism (holding more than one living) was a growing practice whereby already rich vicars could augment their wealth or a poorly paid vicar could augment his stipend. Either way it was a corrupt practice. Non-resident parsons employed curate substitutes, so there was religious presence to oversee the social and spiritual state of congregations. The priest, representing the church's might, was a figure to be respected, part of the ruling establishment. Part of his power aura was his education. The ability to read and write gave him special, magical status (though not all priests were highly literate). Additionally, as supposed mediator between this world and the next, he had immense psychological influence. Education enabled him to advise on moral and practical matters, his spiritual role made him a privileged mentor in matters related to living the virtuous life. Not everyone in a village would necessarily defer to the priest. Some saw him as an arrogant snob, allied to the gentry, parading his learning, an outsider speaking an incomprehensible, elite language.[67] Some vicars were ineffective – drunk, ignorant and more interested in hunting. Closet Catholics and Dissenters paid only lip service. Puritan dissidents were increasing in numbers and were increasingly vocally critical of the church. More worrying for the church's elite was the spread of vicars of Puritan sympathy. In the 1590s large numbers of progressive, radical-thinking young ordinands graduated from Cambridge, adding yet another destabilizing factor to an age already undergoing disturbing changes. Principles learned from the teachings of Cambridge don William Perkins inclined them to be less obsequious to gentry parishioners, more mindful of the hardships of the poor and determined to simplify vestments, rituals and sermons. Some gentry families, sympathetic to reform, protected Puritan-minded vicars from church persecution. This was particularly evident in the 'Pilgrim Quadrilateral' and the Boston area of Lincolnshire in the years 1600–1610.[68]

Another burgeoning force undermining the establishment was the irreverent, radically minded university-trained playwrights. Vitriolic in criticizing purse-proud citizens, their ostentatious wives, the explosion of greed, the obsession with luxury, vanity, lust, the idle and incompetent aristocracy, and particularly those many ungentlemanly gentlemen buzzing like flies around the court, they also deplored the state of the lower orders. Though set firmly in the contemporary world their work is essentially morality based, harking back to medieval values. *Lear*, though set in a timeless time, has a similar value system with its scatter of broken Commandments and sins committed.

Becoming aware of the poverty-stricken majority of the population marks a key stage in the rehabilitation of Edgar, Gloucester and Lear. The economic and political system of England was organized for the benefit of those who already had much, but noticeably, as Lear's fortunes decline he becomes more sympathetic to the oppressed. This is most tellingly expressed in his prayer before he enters the hovel:

Poor naked wretches, whereso'er you are,
That bide the pelting of this pitiless storm,
How shall your houseless heads and unfed sides,
Your looped and windowed raggedness, defend you
From seasons such as these? O! I have ta'en
Too little care of this! Take physic, Pomp;
Expose thyself to feel what wretches feel,
That thou mayst shake the superflux to them
And show the heavens more just. (III. iv.)

This reflects James I's declaration that concern for 'the well-fare and peace of his people' shows a king 'as their naturall father and kindly maister', while in 'subjecting his owne private affections and appetites to the weale and standing of his subjects' he shows himself better than the tyrannical king who 'thinketh his people ordained for him, a pray [sic] to his passions and inordinate appetites'.[69] James was soon criticized for his stand-offishness to the 'baser sort'. In a broader sense it also reflects the growth of vagrancy and homelessness, the anxiety of the authorities about the threat to public order such people posed, and the failure of successive governments to deal effectively and positively with a perennial problem. Gloucester's sufferings similarly awake charitable awareness. Giving Poor Tom his purse he says:

> Let the superfluous and lust-dieted man,
> That slaves your ordinance, that will not see
> Because he does not feel, feel your power quickly;
> So distribution should undo excess
> And each man have enough. (IV. i.)

Like Lear, his use of 'feel' suggests that the powerful and wealthy become too easily detached from thinking how life is for the poor and need to be made to experience what it is like. Lear's comment, 'The art of our necessities is strange/And can make vile things precious' (III. ii.), voices a realignment of priorities and understanding caused by a suffering that makes him feel fellowship with the oppressed. Detachment from the people bred desensitization and brutal attitudes, but experiencing major setbacks re-sensitizes Lear and Gloucester, reminds them of their duty to make charitable use of their excess money, food and goods ('the superflux'). Would the court audience have felt awkward being reminded of the rich man's duty to help the poor, to show God his gratitude for being wealthy by not wasting his excess fortune on pointless extravagances but putting it to good use in the community? The Bible is clear about this: 'For unto whomsoever much is given, of him shall be much required' (Luke 12:48). The middling and lower orders had to work to live, those with wealth and rank did not. Orthodox theory held that 'none are less exempted from a calling than great men'.[70] The bible story of Dives and Lazarus (Luke 16:19), a popular sermon text, told how the rich Dives refused to give the crumbs off his table to the poor Lazarus. Dives dies, goes to Hell and in his sufferings sees Lazarus among the elect. The rich and powerful had a duty to be fathers to their neighbours, shepherds to the flock around them. Brathwait put it starkly: 'The higher the place the heavier the charge.'[71] Many privileged lords and ladies sent to the poor unwanted food from their own table, endowed alms houses and schools and did other acts of charity. Many did nothing. Each new generation inheriting wealth needed reminding that

[...] charity [...] should flow
From every generous and noble spirit,
To orphans and to widows.[72]

The concept of *caritas* (love expressed through charity), integral to medieval church teaching, was derived from canon law's delineation of the basic duty of the rich to assist the needy. Protestant thinking endorsed it too. The Christian virtue of compassion was essential for those who had never experienced adversity or affliction. The Jacobean governing classes had detached themselves from the rest of society, living their own self-interested, selfish, narcissistic lives at court or isolated on their estates. Corrupt, ineffective, arrogant kingship was another feature of the time and the period is full of admonitions to kings and nobility. In 1609 the earl of Northumberland wrote:

There are certain works fit for every vocation; some for kings; some for noblemen; some for gentlemen; some for artificers; some for clowns [country people]; and some for beggars; [...] If everyone play his part well, that is allotted him, the commonwealth will be happy; if not then it will be deformed.[73]

God's judgement against Adam and Eve at the Fall condemned men to live by the sweat of their brow. The audience knew that. The Bible (e.g., Ezekiel, Proverbs, Ecclesiastes, Thessalonians and Timothy) strongly criticizes idleness and recommends employment. That included kings and courtiers. They too had a duty to perform, an injunction increasingly ignored. James did read state papers and attend councils – when it suited him. He might just as readily disappear suddenly on a hunting trip. His effectiveness diminished, bribery and favouritism became the norm and his court became increasingly idle and debauched in its pursuit of pleasure, increasingly corrupt and self-seeking in its administration of the realm. *Lear* is both about flawed kingship and flawed fatherhood. Significantly both Lear and Gloucester are without female (i.e., wifely) advice in their parenting.[74] Lear foolishly, rashly, refuses advice offered by Kent and the Fool on the important decisions he makes. His explosive reaction to Cordelia's 'Nothing', provokes the otherwise loyal Kent to be 'unmannerly/When Lear is mad' (I. i.), but the king is an old-fashioned autocrat, unused to anyone disagreeing with him. It is too late when he realizes he has 'let [...] folly in,/And [...] judgement out!' (I. iv.).

Chapter 3

SIN, DEATH AND THE PRINCE OF DARKNESS

Stand thou in rightwiseness and in dread, and make ready
thy soul to temptation, for temptation is a man's life on the earth.[1]

An inescapable factor in every aspect of Jacobean life was the ever-present possibility of sin. Jacobeans were neurotically alert to the temptations surrounding them. People's sinfulness was the greatest threat to order. Conflicting Christian sects shared basic beliefs when it came to right and wrong: man was perpetually open to sin and temptation was all around him, the Devil was to be defied, and Christ was man's redeemer and the way to salvation. The religions may have differed homicidally about doctrine, but the moral bases of life were agreed.

The Ten Commandments were the foundational start point for Christians:

The Ten Commandments (abridged from Exodus 20:19)

1. Thou shalt have no other gods before me.
2. Thou shalt not make unto thee any graven image.
3. Thou shalt not take the name of the Lord thy God in vain.
4. Remember the Sabbath day, to keep it holy.
5. Honour thy father and thy mother.
6. Thou shalt not kill.
7. Thou shalt not commit adultery.
8. Thou shalt not steal.
9. Thou shalt not bear false witness.
10. Thou shalt not covet […] any thing that is thy neighbour's.

They were paired inextricably with the Seven Deadly Sins to mark the way to avoid damnation and win salvation through godly living (the Seven Cardinal Virtues are discussed in Chapter 4):

The Seven Deadly Sins

1. **Pride** (arrogance, vanity, vainglory, *hubris*)
2. **Wrath** (anger, violence)
3. **Lust** (lechery, wantonness, lasciviousness)
4. **Envy** (covetousness)
5. **Greed** (avarice)
6. **Gluttony** (including drunkenness)
7. **Sloth** (laziness, despair)

Sin and Satan were as much part of religious consciousness as the desire to emulate Jesus and live virtuously. The church's cultural monopoly meant even those indifferent to religion would acknowledge that faith was the common, underlying feature of life at all levels. The passing year was marked by religious events and each day was punctuated by aspects of faith. The parish church bell indicated the times of services, pious families gathered for morning and evening prayers and individuals might well visit the church during the day too. Schoolboys had communal classroom prayers with their teacher. A master craftsman, his journeymen and apprentices might start the working day with prayers. The formal ceremonies of their guild involved prayers, readings and sermon-like addresses. Children were taught the Bible, learned texts, creeds, catechisms and prayers and would kneel by their bedside to ask for protection during the dangerous hours of darkness. The Lord's Prayer was central to ordinary belief, asking for daily bread, the forgiveness of trespasses and protection from temptation. Those of weak faith attended Sunday service rather than be fined in a church court.[2] Those not particularly pious in their everyday life had scriptural grounding as children and, like everyone else, would know how they were expected to behave as Christians, would be aware of biblical allusions, echoes and ethics in what their neighbours said and did. They would see too how stage plays displayed, reinforced and debated society's basic Christian values. The church was omnipresent. When you were born, married, committed adultery, defamed a neighbour, were rowdy, sharp tongued or shrewish, or traded on Sunday, the church was there approving or wagging its finger. You lived in public, your sins were easily made public and your punishment would be public. Your misdemeanours would be spied out by constables, beadles, the watch, servants or neighbours and dealt with in the local church court. In the

Anglican Church you were rarely left to solve a problem alone, individual conscience being too weak to deal with matters of sin and morality unaided. In times of national or personal stress, people turned to the consolations offered by being part of a communally held belief. When you were afraid of imminent disaster, the support of others was a coping mechanism, with church and priest as spiritual and physical refuge.

All Shakespeare plays allude to or echo Christian ethics. *Measure for Measure* does so abundantly, but *Lear*, rather oddly, does not – at least not explicitly. Chute claims,

> *King Lear* is the one play of Shakespeare's that seems to have no basis at all in any kind of Christian dogma, and it is significant that he chose a pre-Christian era and wrote of events that took place 'in the days when Jereboam ruled in Israel'.[3]

This ignores the second agent in the mediation of a text: the reader or viewer. The text may lack direct allusion to Christian dogma, but Shakespeare knew his audience would make the connections. Almost every line provokes a Christianity-focused judgement of what is said and done. Whatever level of engagement with faith, audiences had a Christian upbringing and conscious or subconscious religious reactions to everything. Debauched libertines or those who had lost their religion still had in the recesses of their minds the responses and values learned as children. The Bible was the standard of all conduct. Despite its pagan setting, *Lear* has an unspoken, indirect, implicit biblical context evoking Christian reactions and assessments. Responses varied according to education, upbringing, experience of and attitude to the world, rank and political or religious allegiance, but there would be broad agreement in a court sharing this common Bible-based background. The ways the characters persistently offend the Commandments or commit sins would be glaringly obvious. It is an absolutely fundamental aspect of the play and outweighs every other motif in it.

Life was seen as a journey, a pilgrim's progress towards holiness and union with God. Kent's last words refer to his approaching death and transition into the afterlife:

> I have a journey, sir, shortly to go;
> My master calls me, I must not say no. (V. iii.)

The words 'journey' and 'master' relate to imminent death and Lear, but hint too at Christ as 'master', Christian overtones spectators would spot.

From birth people were to pursue virtue, shun sin, imitate Christ, keep the soul pure and progress towards death, ready to pass through to the life everlasting. In John Ford's late Revenge Tragedy *'Tis Pity She's a Whore* (c. 1629–31), when sexual sins and violent plots begin to gather and drive the drama, the character Richardetto states the basic situation of Christian existence: 'No life is blessèd but the way to heaven' (IV. ii. 21); he then encourages his niece to flee a vile world by entering a convent: 'Who dies a virgin lives a saint on earth' (IV. ii. 28). The virtuous life gained Christ's favour and a state of grace. No advantage in the fleshly, physical world was of any value if you lacked grace. Ford presents even good looks in a religious context:

> Beauty that clothes the outside of the face
> Is cursèd if it be not clothed with grace. (V. i. 12–13)

Lear portrays a world where ruthless individualists intent on getting their own way hound and punish virtue, grace and charity. Uncontrolled appetite was something the church feared and punished. Lust was the most common everyday sin, but any of the Seven Deadly (or Mortal) Sins could damn you eternally if unrepented. The sinfulness of Lear (anger) and Gloucester (lust) trigger the tragedy. The play's pre-Christian setting shows how uncivilized and savage natural man could be. Shakespeare relied on his audience seeing the danger of this and the value of the guiding restraint Christian morality offered. He relied too on their seeing how the barbarities and failings of Lear's world were evident in Jacobean society. A Whitehall audience, possibly more attentive than the social mix at the public theatres, perhaps on their best behaviour in the king's presence, had enough biblical knowledge (even if their faith was weak) to put the actions and words before them into a moral context that reflected poorly on them.

The pervasive religious atmosphere made identifying sin instinctive. Sin was the Devil's portal, giving access to your soul to damn you. The Devil was a tangible entity to people, not a mere concept of evil, but a very real horned, cloven-hoofed, fork-tailed, sulphurous, fearsome presence. His earthly work, assisted by legions of demons, imps, goblins, incubi and succubi, was devoted to corrupting man and thwarting God's will. The Book of Revelation (increasingly the most popular book in the Bible) describes 'the great dragon' who 'was cast out, that old serpent, called the Devil and Satan, which deceiveth the whole world' (12:9). In John's Gospel he is called 'the prince of this world' (12:31), in Corinthians 'god of this world' (4:4), suggesting that the fleshly world of greed, brutality, cheating and lust (as presented in the plays of the 1600s) is the Devil's domain. Paul's Epistle to the Ephesians (2:2–3) goes further:

Wherein in time past ye walked according to the course of this world, according to the prince of the power of the air: the spirit that now worketh in the children of disobedience:
　Among whom also we had all our conversation in times past in the lusts of our flesh, fulfilling the desires of the flesh and of the mind: and were by nature the children of wrath.

This text places the Devil firmly in this world, embodied in the waywardness and violence of men. Seeing the Devil as a manifestation of human evil (as some were beginning to do in the seventeenth century) suggests why *Lear* is so disturbing. It shows how the Devil is loosed when Christian values, cultivated, civilized, sensitive and sympathetic behaviours, are ignored. The Devil, the Father of Lies, stalks the stage in *Lear* and sins permeate the play. The lying, hypocritical cruelty of Goneril, Regan, Cornwall and Edmund are emanations of the Devil in man. Viewers would understand that. It is not simply a tale of an old man having difficulties with his family, but a *psychomachia*, an allegorical drama in which the soul of humanity is assailed by evil and the virtuous qualities of understanding, repentance, forgiveness, reconciliation and salvation face defeat, but eventually salvage mankind from the wreckage. Though not written in the style of the earlier morality plays, the subject matter is the same.

Vicars loved loosing their imaginations sermonizing about the workings of the Evil One and the torments of Hell awaiting unrepentant sinners. Writers too enjoyed the fantastical opportunities offered by ideas of Hell, Sin, Death and the Devil. In *Lear* the atmosphere of evil is conjured by brutal actions but also focused graphically in the dialogue and particularly in the diabolic imaginings of Edgar in his pretended fits as Poor Tom. The names Frateretto, Modo, Mahu and the rest, Shakespeare found in Samuel Harsnett's pamphlet.[4] They represent a Christian idea inserted into a pagan setting. Such diabolic names are anachronisms imported from Christian times into pagan England, but keep viewers aware that sin is ever present, that life is a persistent battle between good and evil, that vice's lure has to be constantly avoided. Edgar 'depicts' the 'fiend' that supposedly lured Gloucester to attempt suicide, adding further to the sense of evil loosed in the play:

As I stood here below methought his eyes
Were two full moons; he had a thousand noses,
Horns whelk'd and wav'd like the enridged sea. (IV. vi.)

This emphasizes the danger his father had been in, giving way to despair and not trusting in Providence. Despair was a Deadly Sin, and Edgar encourages Gloucester to stoically accept his sufferings as part of God's plan, as Job did. As well as metaphorical expressions of their state, the gouging of Gloucester's eyes, the intense misery of Lear – likened to being 'bound upon a wheel of fire' – reference real-life tortures similar to the physical pains imagined to be suffered in Hell. It was an age when hanged bodies were routinely publicly displayed strung up in chains, heretics were burnt at the stake, and Gunpowder Plotters had their entrails cut out and burned in front of them. The rack, thumbscrew and strappado were regularly used to extract information. Noses were slit and ears cropped for criticizing royalty or church, thieves were branded, and blasphemers had their tongue pulled out or a hole bored in it. Birching, blinding and being broken on the wheel were simply part of institutionalized cruelty. The gruesome acts portrayed in plays reflect a violent culture. Sin against the state, sin against God – the painful punishments were similar. These brutal punishments reflect both the age and how people imagined the eternal tortures of Hell.

Threats of damnation and eternal torture for extreme, repeated sin, were a useful control device to frighten naughty children and a moral corrective for adults. While most believed in the physical existence of Satan there were those who cared nothing for hellfire and damnation, and those who did not believe in Hell. Marlowe's Faustus arrogantly declares that 'hell's a fable' (Scene v. 128) despite Mephistophelis asserting 'this is hell, nor am I out of it' and 'where we are is hell'.

FAUSTUS: Think'st thou that Faustus is so fond to imagine
                  That, after this life, there is any pain?
                  Tush, these are trifles and mere old wives' tales.
MEPHISTOPHELIS: But, Faustus, I am an instance to prove the contrary,
                  For I am damn'd, and am now in hell.
                  [...]
FAUSTUS: How! now in hell!
                  Nay, an this be hell, I'll willingly be damn'd here.
                  (Scene v. 134–44)

People were beginning to question Hell's existence, claiming this life was our Hell. In *'Tis Pity*, the reckless Giovanni, a scholar like Faustus, thinks reasoned argument can demolish the idea of Hell, and confidently announces to his confessor:

The hell you oft have prompted is nought else
But slavish and fond superstitious fear,
And I could prove it too. (V. iii. 19–21)

The friar replies, 'Thy blindness slays thee.' Giovanni's trust in rational arguments led him to believe sex with his sister was permissible – a moral blindness (like Gloucester's). His actions lead to spiritual death and physical slaughter. Certainly experience on Earth is a Hell-like torture for Lear and Gloucester. The court audience, if they thought about it, probably believed in both Heaven and Hell as places of reward and punishment after life. Most, except extreme libertines, believed sin was everywhere and virtue needed to be cultivated. This would not prevent them sinning or encourage living a good life. Like most people they would probably experience periods of guilt and fear in realizing their failings, resolve to improve, then relapse into their normal not-very-bad-but-not-very-good lives. An affecting play might prick their consciences – for a while at least.

In *Lear* the mad king briefly mentions Hell. Commenting on female lust he shifts from describing how from the waist down 'is all the fiend's' domain to recognizably describing the Christian idea of the Devil's kingdom:

> There's hell, there's darkness,
> There is the sulphurous pit – burning, scalding,
> Stench, consumption […]. (IV. vi.)

In *'Tis Pity* (where *Lear* and *Othello* are verbally echoed) the friar, trying to frighten Annabella into repentance for her fornication and incest, describes Hell:

> There is a place […] in a black and hollow vault,
> Where day is never seen. There shines no sun,
> But flaming horror of consuming fires,
> A lightless sulphur, choked with smoky fogs
> Of an infected darkness. In this place
> Dwell many thousand thousand sundry sorts
> Of never-dying deaths; there damned souls
> Roar without pity […]. (III. vi. 8–16)

He continues, describing the punishments fitting specific sins (see below, 52–53).

Sin and Death

The Prince of Darkness[5] was inexorably linked with temptation, reminders of what awaited after death and the very fact of death itself. In medieval and Renaissance art reminders of death are ubiquitous. Skulls and skeletons, the Grim Reaper, appear regularly in church paintings and in the funerary furniture surrounding the congregation. Sin and Death are an ugly duo in opposition to Christ and the Holy Spirit. The everyday world was a minefield for the morally unwary, full of devils waiting for any hint of ungodly, impure thought. Momentary lapses – a nasty comment, bitchy gossip, a bad-tempered, snappish reply, blasphemous expletives, gluttony, theft, the prickings of lust – these were all opportunities for 'the Enemy of Mankind'. I Peter 5:8 warned: 'Be sober, be vigilant; because your adversary the devil, as a roaring lion, walketh about, seeking whom he may devour.' Wary Christians should pray regularly for protection. Bedtime prayers were especially important, calling on guardian angels as night security. A habit grew of eventide self-examination, casting up your account of good and bad done during the day, resolving to amend, repenting and praying for salvation. It was end-of-the-day quiet time for assessing how well you had passed the day and resolving to reform if need be. James recommended to Prince Henry, 'As […] a preservative against […] letting slide your spiritual conscience':

> Remember ever once in the foure and twentie houres, either in the night, or when yee are at greatest quiet, to call yourself to account of all your last dayes actions, either wherein yee have committed things ye should not, or omitted the things yee should doe, either in your Christian or Kingly duty.[6]

He quotes I Corinthians 11:31: 'For if ye judge your selfe, ye shall not be judged.' Reflective self-judgement is something no one does in *Lear* until it is too late.

Temptation was everywhere and everyone knew 'the wages of sin is death' (Romans 6:23). Winning the gift of 'eternal life through Jesus Christ our Lord' required persistent vigilance. The difficulty was being born a sinner with the susceptibility to sin already in you. This 'Original Sin' was the curse Adam and Eve's fall brought to mankind. Their disobedience meant all successive generations were weakened by the proclivity to temptation – a weakness played upon by omnipresent devils and much utilized by playwrights. This idea provoked a rich language of condemnation among moralists – pamphleteers or preachers – and a delight in describing the pains of Hell, where

> [...] there are gluttons fed
> With toads and adders; there is burning oil
> Poured down the drunkard's throat, the usurer
> Is forced to sup whole draughts of molten gold;
> There is the murderer forever stabbed,
> Yet he can never die; there lies the wanton (lustful person)

On racks of burning steel, whiles in his soul
He feels the torment of his raging lust. (*'Tis Pity*, III. vi. 16–23)

In the turbulent times when *Lear* was written there was no shortage of targets named as the source of sin. Sin bred like disease in the growing capital. Disease was seen as God's punishment for sin – not just the usual bodily sins of lust, gluttony and sloth, but pride in rank, the vanity of fashion, the greed of obsessive money making. Society seemed to be disintegrating; crime, alcoholism and illegitimacy were all rising,[7] and heresy and religious dissent were rife. Anglicans blamed Puritans, Puritans blamed Anglicans, everyone blamed the Catholics, the Pope (the Antichrist), the French, the Spanish, the court or the king.

Life was a battle to preserve your virtue and live like Christ, cleansing sin by prayer. Prayer would involve repentance and begging forgiveness ('Forgive us our trespasses …'). Accumulated unrepented sins, particularly grave ones, could damn you when you died, though repentance (even at the last minute) could save you. About to be dragged down to Hell as payment of his side of his bargain with Satan, the terrified Faustus cries out:

See, see where Christ's blood streams in the firmament!
One drop would save my soul, half a drop. Ah, my Christ!
Ah, rend not my heart for naming of my Christ!
Yet will I call on him. (Scene xix. 146–9)

Death was never far away in those days of plague and illnesses easily brought on by a poor diet, unhealthy living conditions and ignorance of basic hygiene. Infections were a leveller making no distinction between rich or poor, though the better-off might be protected by superior food.[8] The world was an insecure place, made even more uncertain by persistent Puritan claims that epidemic and disasters were punishment for tolerating Catholicism or changing church ritual, performing plays, not keeping the Sabbath holy, a sinful court or the sinfulness of everyone in general.[9] Poverty, illness and sudden disaster were constant anxieties people lived with. As Montaigne put it, 'We do not know where death awaits us: so let us wait for it everywhere.'[10] Starting and ending the day with family prayers was part of that protection/salvation process, behaving piously during the day was another. James advised his son, 'Pray […] God would give you grace so to live, as yee may everie houre of your life be readie for death.'[11] Life, though the gift of a bountiful God, was short, merely preparation for the life eternal, spent in the torments of Hell or among the blessings of Heaven.

Small coteries of seventeenth-century scientists and intellectuals began questioning the authority and authenticity of the concepts of sin, damnation and salvation.[12] Part of a growing rationalist movement, they encouraged cynicism, secularism and individualism. Questioning the existence of God, the centrality of Christ, the rights of kings, inhabiting the border between astrology/magic and astronomy/science, they were forerunners of the Enlightenment, but did not represent the beliefs of the majority. While Dollimore claims that Jacobean tragedies display man in an existential state, redeeming himself, unsupported by Providence,[13] a Jacobean audience would be rather more traditionalist, believing there was design and purpose in the workings of nature, that man was free to make devastating mistakes, but could find redemption. Even Raleigh asserted everything that happened was the 'secret will' of God, echoing the orthodox church view voiced by Bishop Cooper: 'Fortune is nothing but the hand of God.'[14] The growing rationalist movement encouraged cynicism, secularism and individualism. The idea of the individual's responsibility for his own soul, for his personal relationship with God, was refreshing and liberating, facilitating independence from a new church already mired in old corruptions and entangled in a discredited establishment power structure. But individualism, emerging simultaneously with the capitalist practices of a profit-driven, go-getting, selfish commercial world, threatened old ideas of humble self-effacement and dedication to the community's good. This individualism prioritized your needs, discounted others, disconnected you from moral restraints and promoted a world where personal will and private appetite were the measure of actions, where villainy thrived and where the Gonerils, Regans and Edmunds made it to the top. Orthodox morality demanded the bad be punished in fiction. In real life such achievers often got away with skulduggery and dishonesty. Machiavelli was demonized because his works 'openly and unfeignedly [...] describe what men do, and not what they ought to do'.[15] Discrepancies between moral expectation and actual behaviour show that rule breakers succeed. Man's unique features – the virtues of charity, mercy, sympathy, intellectual ability and reason, and the emotional faculties of imagination and love – raised him above animals and closer to godlike status. But the pinnacle of God's creation, part divine, part animal, was too easily tempted by fleshly failings. Mankind was God's second attempt after some of his first angelic creations rebelled with Satan. Because humans had animal traits life was a constant battle between the animal promptings of appetite and passion and the angelic demands of reason and virtue. The exploration of that struggle between our baser and our better nature is the domain of literature. The Ten Commandments, the Seven Deadly Sins and the Seven Cardinal Virtues specifically address this need to fight the impulses to sin. The presence of many of these appetites gives *Lear* its religious/ethical/political context. These conduct guidelines occur in all Elizabethan-Jacobean drama. Characters can be measured against them.

The list of sins, revised by Pope Gregory I in AD 590, was tabulated hierarchically by Dante in his influential poem *The Divine Comedy* (1321). Originating in Catholicism, these mortal, capital or cardinal sins were still relevant to the sin-conscious Anglican Protestants and dissenting sectarians of Shakespeare's time. They are cardinal because they were thought grave enough to require God renew his grace to the sinner and for the sinner to show repentance before forgiveness could be shown. They are mortal or capital because they were thought serious enough to warrant death ('For the wages of sin is death'). God was thought able to strike sinners down by sudden death or use human agents. The Book of Proverbs lists as sins looking proud of yourself, lying, shedding innocent blood, having a heart ready to devise wickedness, a readiness to do mischief and stirring trouble. All appear in *Lear*. St Paul offers a longer list of sins which will lose you the kingdom of God: adultery, fornication, uncleanness, lasciviousness, idolatry, witchcraft, hatred, variance, emulations, wrath, strife, sedition, heresy, envy, murder, drunkenness, revelling and 'such like' (Galatians 5:19–21). Fornication was sex between participants not married to each other. The principle was that sex should not take place at all unless within matrimony. James's court was a hotbed of promiscuity which he did nothing to curb or punish. This is relevant in the light of Lear and Edgar's comments on lust. Venial sins, secondary negative behaviours and vices, were sinful though less serious. Casual swearing, irreverence, failing to pray daily, lack of consideration for others, gossiping, stubbornness and ingratitude are just some of the many venial failings. Committing them did not lose you God's grace, thus you could be cleansed and saved – with effort on your part.

Dante formalized the idea of Hell as below the Earth in *Inferno* (Hell) the first part of *The Divine Comedy*.[16] The hierarchy of sin was tabulated and each allocated its sector in Hell. Hell, imagined as a fiery pit like a funnel, contains nine circles. The lower Dante goes in his visit the worse the sins committed by the damned he meets. In 'Upper Hell' are sinners of incontinence, failings effected by those constant enemies of mankind, the appetites. In descending order they are: the lustful, the gluttonous, hoarders and spendthrifts, the wrathful and suicides – mainly personal failings tied to the Seven Deadly Sins. In 'Nether Hell', closer to Satan at the bottom of the pit, are sinners who committed planned transgressions – fraud or acts of malice. In descending order they are: panders and seducers (pimps and fornicators), flatterers, simoniacs (those who sold church offices), sorcerers, barrators (abusing the legal system to profit by groundless cases or false claims), hypocrites, thieves, those encouraging fraud, sowers of discord, falsifiers and traitors (to kindred, country, guests, their lord, etc.). These broad definitions comprise a number of sins against community and against probity in public office. The merest glance at these triggers connections with characters in *Lear*. Edmund is a multiple offender – proud, lecherous, hypocritical, a sower of discord, a flatterer, a traitor, wrathful.

Pride was the first sin, committed by the Devil thinking so well of himself he rebelled against God to replace him. As Lucifer ('the bright one') he was God's favourite angel, but becoming ambitious, thinking that although God favoured him above the other angels he deserved even better and higher status, he rebelled, was defeated and was cast out of Heaven. He and his co-conspirators fell through Chaos into Hell, a fiery pit full of sulphur and smoke, specially created by God. Vanity is a form of pride. At a venial level it is conceit about your looks, clothes or status. Edgar refers to himself as 'a servingman, proud in heart and mind' who 'curl'd my hair, wore gloves in my cap' (III. iv.).[17] This vanity related to appearance and fashion is relevant to a court whose wasteful extravagance on clothes was infamous. Believing yourself better than others is a small vanity until it becomes active disregard and bad treatment of others, behaving as if you were beyond reproach. Edmund displays a degree of overly high self-esteem in believing he has the right to privilege. He has the right to expect proper parenting and a lifestyle suited to the bastard son of an earl, but goes further, demanding the overturning of traditional primogeniture (the inheritance of land, estates, fortune and title by the eldest son). Pride is the besetting sin of those with power, privilege, rank and wealth (like the audience). A king is most likely to be proud, but inflated self-regard was rife in the court. The Bible required such people to disregard their advantages and humbly serve those whom it was their duty to help.

Wrath could be any tiny moment of anger flaring up and soon dying away, through a range of escalating losses of temper to the irrational rage that becomes violence against another. Edgar claims he has been 'bloody of hand [...] dog in madness' (III. iv.). This is relevant to those men in the audience ready to quarrel and fight duels. Men (not just gentlemen) wore swords, carried concealed daggers and were prepared to use them. With too much wine tempers frayed easily – over cards, dice, women or a word taken the wrong way. The key, plot-impelling wrath of *Lear* is the real, irrational, vengeful anger of the king's outbursts against his daughters. It is replicated in Regan, Goneril, Cornwall, the servant who intervenes to prevent Gloucester's blinding, in Kent's abuse of Oswald, his comments to Regan and Cornwall, and most chillingly (because it is controlled) in Edmund's plotting. The play vibrates with anger, spoken and unspoken. The combative language reflects a social phenomenon identified by numerous polemicists. William Perkins lamented 'the abuse of the tongue among all sorts and degrees of men everywhere'.[18] Socio-religious tensions were expressed in inventive invective – in Parliament, in court, in church, in the street. Campbell sees *Lear* as a tragedy of anger in old age.[19] It is more than that. The end scene, the consequence of anger, looks like universal destruction. Kent asks, 'Is this the promis'd end?' (V. iii.). The Day of Judgement (the promised end) was known as the *Dies Irae* (Day of Wrath, a term used in the Anglican Communion). Though a sin liable to occur in any rank of society, young men of rank and wealth were most susceptible to irascibility (a tendency to hot temper), believing themselves superior to others and ready to defend any perceived slur against their honour.

Lust was a universal sin, felt by both sexes, all ranks and most ages. The 'disease of lust' was to St Augustine persistently intrusive and the most destructive of the appetites.[20] The human sex drive greatly concerned all churches. Necessary for the continuation of the species, it was difficult to control. And they tried. Fornication was the sin of prohibited sex, meaning outside marriage – sex between unmarried adults was forbidden. Sex with someone other than your spouse was fornication and adultery. The intention to conceive a child was the only justification for intercourse within marriage. Sex for pleasure alone was lust and fornication. Lust comprised all unclean thoughts and unclean acts, including unnatural ones like bestiality, incest and homosexuality (condemned in Romans 1:26). Masturbation, rape and erotic thoughts were all lust. Lear in his madness and Edgar in his assumed insanity have much to say on lust. A perceived growing libidinousness in society, with increased illegal pregnancies in all ranks, concerned preachers and playwrights alike. 'In political libels, lampoons, satires, and other forms of writing and action, upper-class immorality is almost inevitably the object of sharp disapproval, reflecting the growing grip of Protestant attitudes to sin, social order, and divine vengeance.'[21] Titled men might acknowledge their 'whoresons' – as Gloucester does – but did not necessarily make suitable provision for them. Some brought them up in their own household, but others, like Gloucester, sent them 'out' (i.e., abroad, or away from the father's house).

The church's attitudes to sexuality focused on two problem areas: women as the source of sin (particularly the belief that women were naturally more lascivious than men)[22] and the principle that appetites made men more like animals than angels and needed to be controlled or suppressed. The Christian tradition of asceticism required the avoidance of any excess – simple food, simple clothes and a focus on the spiritual rather than the carnal. Every Deadly Sin was a form of appetite developed to excess. In *'Tis Pity* calm reason is recommended to a jealous, vengeful husband: 'Sir you must be ruled by your reason and not by your fury: that were unhuman and beastly' (IV. iii. 83–5). Unruly appetites were a recurrent theme in drama. Very slowly, marriage was established as a means of controlling and channelling lust. While theoretically chastity was preferable if full spiritual perfection was to be achieved, it was gradually conceded that marriage was the best course if you could not effectively control your sexual impulses.[23] Marrying was preferable to promiscuity, but even within wedlock lust had to be restrained. Lust was a major topic for admonition in sermons and religious writing. Men and women even sat separately in church. The Puritans, though in favour of marriage, had considerable difficulty with the whole area of sexuality.

Poor Tom's imagined self is guilty of various lustful acts and he finishes with a warning to all young men: '[...] keep thy foot out of brothels, thy hand out of plackets' (III. iv.).[24] Lear in his madness makes some pointed remarks about sexuality. Commonly, when the controls of consciousness are inoperative, during hypnosis, under the effects of drugs, alcohol or insanity, the human mind turns readily to thoughts about the primal drive – sex. Of Gloucester's adultery the king remarks:

> Thou shalt not die: die for adultery! No:
> The wren goes to't, and the small gilded fly
> Does lecher in my sight. Let copulation thrive
> [...]
> To't, Luxury, pell mell! (IV. vi.)[25]

He takes a traditional misogynistic stance on the hypocrisy of women who affect public virtue, disapprove of 'pleasure's name', but in private enjoy sex with as much relish as a 'fitchew' (a polecat) or 'soiled horse' (aroused sexually by rich feed).[26] Lear adopts the long-established view that women had an excessive sex drive. His concluding strictures sound as condemnatory as any Puritan preacher:

> Down from the waist they are Centaurs,
> Though women all above:
> But to the girdle do the Gods inherit,
> Beneath is all the fiends: there's hell, there's darkness,
> There is the sulphurous pit – burning, scalding,
> Stench, consumption; fie, fie, fie! pah, pah! (IV. vi.)

The image of the centaurs (mythical beasts, human to the waist, horse below), is apt, echoing the idea of humans as angel/animal hybrids. Ancient Greek stories testify to their lustful nature. Well known was that of the centaur Nessus who tried to rape Hercules' wife, a story Shakespeare would have known from Ovid (*Metamorphoses*, bk IX), his favourite Latin text. Some of the audience would have recognized the allusion from their school days, others might have squirmed with embarrassment to recognize their own pretended pious virtue and their hidden 'riotous appetite'. Metrical and syllabic irregularity in these lines reflects the emotion of the king, swinging from a practical, liberal acceptance of the strength of the sex drive ('Let copulation thrive') to violent repulsion. Either attitude is unusual in a man so old you might think him unconcerned with sex, but he displays the erratic inconsistency of mental derangement and the natural recourse of human thought to dwell upon one of its strongest impulses. *Measure for Measure*, *Hamlet*, *Othello* and *Troilus and Cressida* all express concern about the lasciviousness of both sexes and criticism of rampant lust recurs regularly in other contemporary plays.

Envy or covetousness is jealous desire for what others have, a form of mental theft and discontent with the lot God gave you. Envy drives Edmund's comparison between how he has been treated and how his brother, the heir, has been brought up. Aware of his intellectual strength but marginalized status, Edmund is bitter the 'plague of custom' excludes him. This is a mere excuse. Had he wanted he could have served his father as a personal assistant or sought Gloucester's help in gaining a post in another household or at court. Discontent is his motive for doing the evil that is natural to him. His grievance is, however, a means of highlighting the problem of younger sons and the need to find them a function in life, raising the age-old controversy of whether primogeniture was the best means of dealing with family inheritance. Most English landowners believed in primogeniture because it was traditional and kept family property intact. Edmund has been left out, ignored and neglected (the common lot of the bastard), while tradition hands everything to his brother. This theme was as old as families themselves and Shakespeare uses the sibling rivalry motif many times. Usually it demonstrates how younger sons react to the eldest getting everything, so is firmly based in material possessions, but may include the jealousy older sons feel at the second's arrival, threatening his monopoly of love and attention, and may address the problem raised when the official heir is a wastrel, a spendthrift, irresponsible, evil, mentally incapable or unsuitable some other way. The history plays address this in relation to inept kingship and questions of succession. There are few examples of the envy involving an illegitimate child's jealousy (*Much Ado About Nothing* has Don Pedro and his bastard brother Don John), but sibling rivalry between legitimate offspring is recurrent. It is doubly present in *As You Like It* with Orlando and his brother, and the exiled Duke and his brother. *Hamlet* focuses on Hamlet Senior and Claudius. Such rivalries involve deceit, cheating, attempts to oust the hated rival, an actual murder of one brother by another (*Hamlet*), and a war between siblings (*Much Ado*). In *Richard III* the Duke of Gloucester is deeply envious of his handsome, golden, successful brother Edward. In *The Taming of the Shrew* an elder sister is jealous of the younger because she is father's pet. In *Lear* the long-held grievances of childhood surface in the jealousies of the king's three daughters. It is deeply disturbing to see how little love can exist within the family, or how testing times can open cracks rather than strengthen bonds. The Fool's cruel joke about the cuckoo takes on a prophetic note as we see the manoeuvrings to outdo each other, to push each other out of the nest. In different ways, and to different degrees of seriousness, Shakespeare reworks envy as an unsettling, potentially destructive aspect of family relationships. The early Morality/Chronicle Play *Gorboduc* (1571) goes back to the Lear period of British pre-history, focusing the rivalry of two brothers who are given half the kingdom by their father, Gorboduc, who like Lear is resigning from power. (See 'The *Gorboduc* Effect' in Chapter 10.) The plot pivots on sibling rivalry and succession. The Mary Tudor/Elizabeth relationship had had its uneasy jealousies. The Mary Queen of Scots/Elizabeth cousin rivalry bedevilled English politics until the former was executed for yet another plot against the queen. Also pertinent is the support for Arbella Stuart as a more authentic claimant to the throne than James I. Plots, envious siblings and succession rivalries were all part of the ambience of court politics of the period and the internecine rivalry of Lear's daughters adds a topical frisson to the naturally upsetting spectacle of a family self-destructing.

Greed and **gluttony** are sins of excess. Avarice (greed), usually seen as excessive desire for material goods or wealth, is the miser's sin – hoarding for its own sake. It is the sin of the money maker – the financier/speculator/ entrepreneur – accumulating more than he needs, a theme much discussed in the hard times of the 1590s and 1600s. It suggests psychological insecurity, but from a religious standpoint is the sin of the man who does not 'shake the superflux' to the needy. Gluttony is a sin of bodily excess, usually applied to overindulgence in food and drink. It was believed that 'enough is as good as a feast'; if you had eaten and drunk in moderation, sufficient for bodily needs, anything more was unnecessary indulgence. Leftovers should be given to the old and poor – the Dives and Lazarus story again, reminding the rich and comfortably-off of their duty to the community. The ancient tradition of hospitality survived, but was declining. In medieval times beggars or travellers could call at a monastery or a gentleman's house and be given something to eat, even a bed for the night. Great lords with tenants and a clientage were expected to provide food and drink to any who came on business. It was all part of the harmony of society, payment for deference, putting back into the community, shaking the superflux.

Any excess was sin. The early church was built upon moderation, asceticism, fast days, a lack of material possessions – the simple life. Failing to live up to that, becoming a monolithic edifice of accumulated wealth, land, power and self-indulgence, its decadence and worldliness triggered various reformist heresies violently suppressed in the name of preserving the faith, but actually defending Catholicism's monopoly over the people of Europe. Occasionally, as in the case of St Francis, a movement towards simplicity gained support within the church. Ancient Greece's Apolline religion also had a tradition of controlled moderation. 'Nothing in excess', inscribed on Apollo's temple in Delphi, became part of essential Christian thinking, though always under pressure from human weakness. A late fourteenth-century proverb says, 'There is measure in all things.' St Augustine wisely remarked, 'To some, total abstinence is easier than perfect moderation.'[27] Puritan revitalization of the ascetic traditions led to them being called killjoys, but excess was a moral danger marker. Measure and moderation were qualities unknown at court. It is a feature of tragedy (classical and Renaissance) that once a character behaves with excess, disaster is unavoidable. In *Lear* devastation is triggered by the immoderate wrath of a king who 'hath ever but slenderly known himself' (I. i.), reacting excessively and unwisely in giving away everything. The Fool hints at his folly in the gnomic rhyme encapsulating the different types of moderation Lear lacks:

> Have more than thou showest,
> Speak less than thou knowest,
> Lend less than thou owest,
> Ride more than thou goest,
> Learn more than thou trowest,
> Set less than thou throwest;
> Leave thy drink and thy whore,
> And keep in-a-door,
> And thou shalt have more
> Than two tens to a score. (I. iv.)

When this speech is delivered it is already clear the text carries various messages. The storyline has an allegorical dimension crammed with traditional Christian values and warnings with particular relevance to a decadent, self-indulgent, excessive, luxury-loving court. Within the closed meaning of the text the Fool's rhyme is primarily a *post facto* reprimand to Lear that he should have retained his status and not given away everything. In the wider context this brief poem succinctly describes the moderate life, recommending moral behaviour eschewing drinking or whoring, adopting a humble lifestyle, not showing off your material possessions, not spending your time in public display of yourself and maintaining a quiet demeanour. The wise man listens more than he speaks and never reveals all his thoughts. While not condemning gambling this proscription warns the listener not to risk everything on one throw. Metaphorically, Lear has done this – emotionally staking everything on Cordelia's protestation of love winning the day so he could, as planned, live with her, but then, when the presumed love does not materialize, giving away everything and relying on the good will of daughters we know (by the end of I. i.) are ill-disposed towards him. Wise men live thriftily and end up with more than they began with. Lear, giving away power, status and access to regal wealth, has less than he began with. Virtuous living is its own reward and the profit gained is spiritual advantage that counts when your reckoning is made at Judgement Day. Lear's only 'credit' entry is Cordelia, but, this being a tragedy, she will be unable to save the day in any material sense. Their reconciliation is a gain (reaffirming human love within their family context) and a redemptive act for both of them. The pity of it is that salvation comes at the cost of both their lives. That is the nature of tragedy. Moderation, abstinence, chastity, renunciation and avoidance were all ways to concentrate your devotion to God and virtue, but not much practised at court.

Moderation was integral to Christian belief from its beginnings. The simple life of John the Baptist, Jesus, the hermits of the Thebaid Desert and the saints prioritized spiritual cleansing over the demands of the body. Regular fasting and frugality were practices that continued in Protestant England among the godly. Periods of contemplation and prayer were encouraged as was the rejection of luxury. Excessive, ostentatious displays of spirituality were also sinful. The aim was to put the corrupting influence of this world into perspective; diminishing its power over you helped to focus on the next world, but balance had to be kept. It was acceptable to work hard, enjoy your family, be an active, useful member of your community *and* take moderate pleasure in the good things of this world. Shakespeare is always subtextually smuggling in warnings for the audience. The court – an ostentatious, drunken, promiscuous, gambling-obsessed, garrulous, debt-ridden lot, mostly living away from home, thus neglecting their families and their local social duty – needed more instruction than most. Given the sometimes noisy, inattentive, food-munching, giggling, gossiping nature of audiences, we can only hope the Whitehall spectators were receptive to the lessons *Lear* teaches.

Sloth is another sort of excess – an overdeveloped laziness, not just disinclination to work but a psychological state of not bothering. Your duty to God was to work hard at your trade and at being virtuous. Many didactic stories and plays illustrate the spiritual and material rewards of industry. A popular motif compared two apprentices – one hard-working, who gains his master's daughter and progresses in his trade, the other idle, who falls into bad habits and ends up in prison for debt. This is demonstrated in *Eastward Ho!* (1605). Industry meant more than working at your livelihood, it meant being a committed and active Christian, helping the community and actively working at guarding and improving your own spiritual state. The Latin word for sloth, *acedia* (or *accidia*), also applies to spiritual slothfulness or despair, the state in which you lose belief that God cares for and watches over you. It was a state associated with melancholy or depression.

In relation to sin the animal imagery in *Lear* shows how much the Renaissance loved classification and symbolism. Peacocks represented pride, lions wrath, goats lust, snakes envy, toads greed, pigs gluttony, snails sloth. The play is filled with these associations. The animals are sometimes given different significances. Rats, snakes, foxes and dogs commonly occur with different pejorative meanings. An audience of the time would be of the mindset to interpret the drama before them in the light of these moral waymarkers.

Chapter 4

THE SEVEN CARDINAL VIRTUES

If the Seven Deadly Sins were the warning signs for avoiding damnation, the Seven Cardinal Virtues were signposts to salvation. The Seven Deadly Sins all had obvious opposites (pride/humility, wrath/calm forbearance, lust/abstinence or moderation, covetousness/generosity, greed/charity, gluttony/moderation, sloth/active engagement), but there was also an official list of virtues, some of which appeared as opposites to the sins, some of which related to broader matters of faith.

The Seven Cardinal Virtues

1. *Temperance* (abstinence, moderation)
2. *Prudence* (providence, foresight, circumspection, consideration, wise conduct)
3. *Justice* (justice, equity, fair judgement)
4. *Fortitude* (strength under pressure)
5. *Faith* (piety, duty to and belief in God)
6. *Hope* (hope of salvation)
7. *Charity* (love of, benevolence to, others)

A godly life won a heavenly crown. If life was a journey, each person a pilgrim on the highway, then conduct determined destination. Virtue's path was hard – steep, thorny, stony, winding and tiring. The way for the carnal man of weak character, Mr Worldly Wiseman, was easy – a 'primrose path', as Macbeth puts it – but it led to an 'everlasting bonfire' and 'sulphurous pit'. Inevitably in *Lear*, because it is a tragedy, the audience is more aware of the accumulating sins driving the inciting moments and rising action. The evils of Goneril, Regan and Edmund, their flattering misuse of misleading language and readiness to grasp power, acting in uncivilized, brutal ways and using ruthless means, naturally fascinate, holding our attention because they are clever and intriguingly horrible. We see too that their victims are not wholly pure. The two fathers have committed sins for which they will be punished. Others unwittingly commit faults without foreseeing the consequences. Cordelia's fate underlines the fact that in the tragic world, like the real world, action for good can sometimes turn out badly. When she and her father are captured after their defeat, she comments, 'We are not the first/ Who, with best meaning, have incurr'd the worst' (V. iii.). Her attempt to explain how she loves Lear is honest but creates unintended consequences. Cordelia's love, Kent's blunt loyalty, the Fool's affectionate companionship and Edgar's devotion are virtues of which audiences may only be subliminally aware much of the time. As the catastrophe approaches the goodness of the good characters emerges more visibly. Lear initially lacks justice, temperance, prudence and fortitude – recognized virtues. During his sufferings his angry despair ('I am a man more sinned against than sinning' [III. ii.]) turns slowly to stoical fortitude. By the time he is reunited with Cordelia he has also learned temperance, calmly acknowledging his failings and quietly begging forgiveness.

The centrality of virtue to living the good life was not only recognized in Christian thought. Classical writings extolled virtue, particularly Plato's Socratic dialogue *Protagoras*, Aristotle's *Nichomachean Ethics*, Cicero's *De Officiis* (*On Duty* or *Obligation*), and Seneca's *De Ira* (*On Anger*) and *De Clementia* (*On Mercy*). Each listed those qualities required to live the good (i.e., virtuous and wise) life. Plato names wisdom, courage, justice, kindness, circumspection and holiness as essential components of excellence. Aristotle identifies courage, temperance, liberality, magnanimity, proper ambition, patience, truthfulness, friendliness, modesty and righteous indignation. Cicero was studied at school as a model of the Latin style, elegant but direct. In an age when one's first duty was to others and not to selfish individual desires, *De Officiis* became the key guide to public duty and good citizenship. Studied at university as an essential guide to moral behaviour and public conduct for young men who might become active in national arenas, it advised how to discern flattery from wise counsel, something Lear and Gloucester fail to do.

These classical qualities evolved into the four virtues of Christian thinking (temperance, prudence, justice and fortitude), then extended to seven with Paul's first letter to the Corinthians (13:13): 'And now abideth faith, hope, charity, these three: but the greatest of these is charity'. Paul also says, 'The fruit of the Spirit is love, joy, peace, longsuffering, gentleness, goodness, faith, meekness, temperance' (Galatians 5:22–3). Such characteristics are part of the moral excellence constituting personal virtue. The Christian fathers St Ambrose, St Augustine and St Thomas Aquinas (*Summa Theologica*, II. i. 61), responding to and refining St Paul, discussed and detailed what became the seven key characteristics of the pious Christian and incorporated them into the main body of church teaching. By the Renaissance (with its love of classical writings) they had become an amalgamation of classical and Christian virtues and proliferated into a huge mentoring literature aimed at any sort of leader or governor. For King James, temperance was not only an opposite to gluttony but meant moderation in all things, particularly in the exercise of justice power and controlling anger – not something he actually followed himself, being an intemperate drinker, given to immoderate anger when thwarted and often inconsistent, unjust and capricious in using his power. Lear, very specifically, does not show temperance. He loses his temper (while unsuccessfully counselling himself to be patient) and threatens immoderate punishment. To Sir Thomas Elyot self-control and emotional balance were crucial qualities in someone with the immense potential for punishment available to a king.

Along with prudence or circumspection, moderation was fundamental to kingly rule. In defining the ideal courtier, Castiglione has Count Ludovico Canossa specifically pick out 'prudence, goodness, fortitude and temperance of soul' as essential to a man of 'honour and integrity'.[1] Not jumping to conclusions but carefully considering options and outcomes is a vital skill for any civic leader whose actions and judgements have widespread consequences. Lear punishes without justice, has not considered the ramifications of dividing the kingdom, does not weigh up the fallout from banishing Cordelia or Kent and fails to foresee the effects of rejecting both his other daughters and going out into a storm with just a handful of followers. He becomes a man in meltdown, a self-induced disaster zone irretrievably destroying family bonds. The one virtue he does have is fortitude, but perhaps only bears his adversities because he has already retreated into an insanity that makes him less aware of his situation. He is hardly discomfited by the storm, is neurotically alert to any stimulus reminding him of his daughters' ingratitude, yet touchingly alert to the sufferings of the Fool, Poor Tom and (abstractly) the poor. As a pagan he is without Christian faith but expresses some belief in the justice of the gods and hopes they will punish his daughters. Lear shows little love, except in his concern for the Fool, until, as a broken man recovering from a breakdown, he displays sentimental, mawkish affection for Cordelia. This looks more like self-pity after his sufferings and shame at his treatment of so loving a child. The virtues, so strikingly evident in Edgar and Cordelia's conduct, present them as Christian saints in this pagan world. James presumably approved of a play displaying the causes and consequences of bad kingship, though he may have felt awkward at seeing some of his own characteristics in Lear and how Tom's description of a courtier highlighted his own failure to set an example – all the more embarrassing having proclaimed the virtues required of a prince in 'A King's Duty in His Office', the central second part of *Basilikon Doron*. Watching *Lear*, he may have blushed in recognition of the transgressions on stage as his own failings and those of his court. Patience, perseverance, courage (to do the right thing and face evil), fairness (justice for all who deserve it), tolerance, truthfulness and honesty, respect for others, kindness, generosity and forgiveness are displayed in *Lear*; but pride, intemperance, greed, sexual licence, envy, indulgence, irreverence, dishonour, murder, violence and deceit are rather more often evident.

A cynical streak in plays from 1600 to 1606 reflects a sense of spiritual and moral decline. For an age believing everyone was a sinner to a greater or lesser degree, the corruption of man was a given. Pessimism about individual probity (personal goodness, honesty and openness) extended into the wider workings of society and government. Individuals from all ranks were thought to be corrupt in different ways, but the self-styled better sort – the supposed exemplars of good practice, the titled governing elite – were persistently shown to be selfish, indifferent and morally bankrupt. Due to the religious aspect of Elizabethan-Jacobean ethics, the Deadly Sins inevitably parade through the drama of the period, satisfying the demand for tension in the conflict between sin and virtue.

There were three other moral schemas that had become part of ethical thinking about how men should behave towards each other. All officially disappeared at the Reformation, but were still in people's heads and hearts, becoming absorbed into Protestant thinking, particularly in relation to social responsibilities:

The Seven Corporal Works of Mercy

1. To tend the sick
2. To feed the hungry
3. To give drink to the thirsty
4. To clothe the naked
5. To harbour the stranger
6. To minister to prisoners
7. To bury the dead

The Seven Spiritual Works of Mercy

1. To convert the sinner
2. To instruct the ignorant
3. To counsel those in doubt
4. To comfort those in sorrow

5. To bear wrongs patiently
6. To forgive injuries
7. To pray for the living and the dead

The Seven Gifts of the Holy Ghost

1. Counsel
2. Fear of the Lord
3. Fortitude
4. Piety
5. Understanding
6. Wisdom
7. Knowledge

These are the positives by which the characters would be judged by the contemporary audience. Like the Seven Virtues, they are scantly represented in *Lear*.

Chapter 5

KINGSHIP

Savage and relentless anger is unbecoming in a king. (Seneca, 'On Mercy', 193)

Now what shall I say about the courtiers? For the most part they are the most obsequious, servile, stupid and worthless creatures, and yet they're bent on appearing foremost in everything. (Erasmus, *Praise of Folly*, 176)

The aim of the courtier is to make his prince virtuous. (Castiglione, *The Book of the Courtier*, 320)

They do abuse the king that flatter him:
For flattery is the bellows blows up sin. (*Pericles*, I. ii. 39–40)

The question of government – of people, of self – is common to all Shakespeare's work. Lear's lack of self-control triggers the action and his inability to rein in his anger in the scenes after the banishment of Cordelia starts the tragic machine on its disastrous course. His kingship and fatherhood are seriously faulty.

Kingship is explicitly themed in the history plays. Audiences seemed insatiable for replays of the English past, displaying the fortunes of various heroes and villains, plotters arrested and executed, monarchs succeeding or failing. The stories of Henry V, King John, Richard II, Richard III and King Leir were popular subjects Shakespeare would later rework in his own way. The fall of kings was endlessly fascinating, and the history genre remained popular at the Swan and Rose Theatres even into the 1600s,[1] when writers at other venues, doubtful and discontented about the running of public affairs and the direction in which society seemed to be going, turned to topical satire to voice their anxieties. But the treatment of history changed. The patriotism of the early dramas had turned to cynicism. 'The contrast between the monarch as symbol of the independent English commonwealth, and the actual occupants of the throne, was too marked.'[2] Reading or watching the many Chronicle Plays infesting the stage leads inevitably to the conclusion that though kings are theoretically honoured as God's vice-regents on Earth, in practice history shows them persistently opposed, plotted against, harried from battle to battle, disrespected, forcibly removed from the throne and violently disposed of. Tragedies and histories rehearse virtue, but perhaps also mask a love of seeing the great assailed and destroyed. From 1599 the writing of academic history came under the paranoid scrutiny of the authorities. As all plays had to be approved by the Revels Office and be registered, so history books had to have the authorization of a privy councillor.[3]

Good kings are undermined by evil men. Bad kings, unworthy of their role either on personal or political grounds, have nasty ends. The occasional charismatic king generated patriotic loyalty and provoked a similar response in audiences when their stories were dramatized, but by the end of Elizabeth I's life a general cynicism about real-life leaders (nobles and monarchs) seemed to have pervaded public opinion. The decline of a strong leader opens up consideration of failings that would otherwise have been diplomatically ignored while the ruler's strength was feared. Elizabeth's death precipitated open discussion of many long-repressed anxieties. The chronicles crowding the early public stage reflected an interest in revisiting and rethinking the nation's past and sublimated contemporary anxieties about stability, masked and made palatable by dead personae and long-gone events. The inexorable approach of the end of the century released many superstitious fears of the Apocalypse and gloomy anticipation of the new era. These fears transferred into negative representations of magistrate figures. Jonson's *Sejanus* and the numerous Revenge Tragedies do not portray leaders as divine or their courts and advisers as anything other than basely human, grasping and unscrupulous. Roman history and recent Italian city-state politics afforded a useful means of dealing with current English concerns under the mask of foreign settings.

The question of government is present too in the four Great Tragedies, focusing the qualities that assist/impede proper/improper governorship of self or *polis*.[4] That *polis* may be a household, a city or a nation, but one way or another, control of emotions, appetites and vices (and the consequences of not doing so) is at the heart of Shakespearean drama. With restrictions on what aspects of contemporary life could be presented and portrayal of the monarch prohibited, indirection was the only means. As unlikely a piece for Christmas festivities as it is, *Lear*'s study of faulty governorship and faulty parenthood, its exposure of personal and political ambitions, and its satire on authority and power, the corruption of courtiers and the ruling infrastructure in general would have been of great interest to a king who had contributed to the literature relating to the education of a prince, even if he might have been thought an unacknowledged target.

Tudor conceptions of preparation for rule were dominated by Sir Thomas Elyot's *The Boke Named the Governour* (1531). Elyot echoes much of the thinking promulgated in Castiglione. He had probably read it, but, in any case, they shared a long tradition of works acting as *speculum principis* (a mirror for princes), defining the personality and conduct required to make a good ruler.[5] Elyot asserts the need of 'one souerayne gouernour […] in a publike weale', but acknowledges the need for councillors and a nationwide group of 'inferior governours called magistratis'.[6] Virtuous leadership is based on the proper upbringing of 'the chylde of a gentilman which is to have auctorite in the publike weale'. He discusses lengthily the curriculum for this education because 'gentyllmen in this present time be not equall in doctrine to th'ancient noble men' due to 'the pride, avarice, and negligence of parentes', snobbery and a lack of teachers. Elyot complains that gentlemen believe 'it is a notable reproche to be well lerned'. The better sort of families paid high wages for skilled cooks or falconers, but not for a tutor to educate their child and inculcate virtue. General qualities identified by Elyot for any man destined to govern at any level were prudence, industry, circumspection and modesty. Monarchs required comeliness in language and gesture, dignity in deportment and behaviour, a demeanour of honour and sobriety, affability, mercifulness, placability, humanity, benevolence and liberality, well-selected friends, sharp discernment of the 'diversity of flatterers', a sense of justice, personal fortitude and 'the faire vertu pacience'. Lear eminently lacks these qualities. Elyot sees obstinacy as 'a familiare vice' and recommends a set of virtues for controlling passion: abstinence, continence, temperance, moderation, sobriety, sapience (wisdom) and understanding. These requirements, echoing the Seven Virtues and the Works of Mercy, are demanding and Lear clearly falls short. Yet he has what Elyot calls 'the exposition of maiestie' and Kent calls 'authority' (I. iv.), and generates loyalty and love – witness the allegiance of those who remain loyal and Cordelia's words and tone in handling him when they are reconciled. The ability to inspire subjects with loyalty is crucial to kingship. It was one Elizabeth possessed pre-eminently and James did not. Elizabeth, for all her faults, was adored and allowed her subjects to approach her. James, though he enjoyed their enthusiastic welcome of him to the throne, had little sympathy for his new people, was sarcastic about them, and kept them at bay whenever possible.

The governor's role is keeping just harmony between the 'comunaltie' ('the base and vulgare') and those with honour and dignities (titled men with responsibilities). Maintaining order is vital. The 'discrepance of degrees' (differences of ranks) is part of 'the incomprehensible maiestie of

God': 'Take away ordre [...] what shulde then remayne? [...] Chaos [...] perpetyuall conflicte [...] vniuersall dissolution.' We see here the ideological similarity to Ulysses's speech on degree in *Troilus and Cressida*. Elyot asserts that the hierarchies of Heaven are reflected on Earth – the elements have their 'spheris' and men do not all have the same gifts from God. Potters cannot administer justice, ploughmen and carters 'shall make but an feble answere to an ambassadour'.

Key to educating men born to authority is that their early years be lived in a milieu of virtue, that the language and behaviour of mothers, nurses and maids be irreproachable. At the age of 7 boys should be removed from 'the company of women' and tutored by 'an auncient & worshipfull man' with grave demeanour, gentle manners and impeccable morality. Then began a course in the classics that would develop their rhetorical skills, improve their Latin and perfect the fluency and accuracy of their English. Elyot does not preclude physical exercise in his regimen, recommending hunting, hawking, dancing, wrestling, running, swimming and weapons training – in moderation. This is standard Renaissance elite education.[7] He deplores the tendency of noble families to halt their children's education at 14 and 'sufre them to live in idelnes'.[8] He believes education is a lifelong process and that this is essential for the production of governors if they are to resemble Plato's philosopher king. Edgar[9] is the only character in *Lear* displaying any of the virtues Elyot applauds. We do not know what sort of education Edgar or Edmund received and only see Edgar in adversity. Did his virtues exist before or were they discovered only through suffering? Was he 'trayned in the way of vertue' as Elyot intended or did he as an idle young gentleman find, as Elyot warned, 'the tediousness' of virtue lured him to gluttony, avarice, lechery, swearing, staying up late and dicing? These diversions, the pastimes and temptations of those with nothing to do, develop if 'children of gentill nature' are not kept to continued education and exercise and given responsibility. Edgar, as Poor Tom, admits to these vices. Elyot puts them into a wider context: 'Howe many gentilmen, howe many marchauntes, have in this damnable passé tyme (dicing) consumed their substaunce [...] and fynisshed their lyfes in dette and penurie.'

Elyot exhorts young men to 'lerne wisdom & fal nat [i.e., do not fall into sin]' and abide by Christian precepts of behaviour, for 'from god only procedeth all honour' and God 'shal examine your dedes & serch your thoughtes'. Since no one man can know all that is happening in a realm, a king needs reliable deputies to act as his eyes, ears, hands and legs. The body image was often invoked. The nation was 'the body politic', head and heart were the monarch, the major organs the nobility, and the hands, legs and muscles were the labouring part of society. All had a job to do and if one part did not work properly the whole became less effective. Such subsidiary governors (courtiers, councillors/counsellors, etc.) should be men 'superiour in condition or haviour [and] vertue'. He is adamant they have 'their owne reuenues certeine, wherby they have competent substance to lyve without taking rewardes: it is likely that they wyll not be so desirous of lucre'. This anti-bribery defence had disappeared by James's time. Jobbery, corruption and greed were standard at court. Two generations of extravagant living left many high-end families financially embarrassed. An unseemly scrabble for lucrative posts, lobbying for monopolies and a readiness to accept bribes were ways to recoup family fortunes. A profitable marriage was another. In the sixteenth century, marriage for mainly monetary reasons stood at 20 per cent among titled families, rising steadily and reaching 34 per cent by 1660.[10]

A King's View of His Office

The new king's contribution to conduct literature focused the role and nature of kingship. *Basilikon Doron*, an advice book to his son, Henry, Prince of Wales, is structured in three parts: 'Of a King's Christian Duty towards God', 'Of a King's Duty in His Office' and 'Of a King's Behaviour in Indifferent Things' ('indifferent' meaning matters relating to leisure time). The first section is very clear about a king's duty to follow the tenets of Christianity, strongly establishing the idea of a king as God's representative. This becomes a running motif throughout. Many ideas parallel Elyot and there are verbal echoes of him. Marginal notes indicate James's debt to Plato's *Republic* and Cicero's seminal *De Officiis*, the common source for books on the perpetually vexing necessity of reminding the governing ranks just what their function in society was.

The key interests of *Basilikon Doron* in relation to *King Lear* are threefold: 1. establishing the criteria by which to measure Lear against the idealized monarch presented in *Basilikon*, 2. as an ironic reflection of the discrepancy between James's theory and practice, 3. as a topical-satirical mirror reflecting how the Jacobean court fails to live up to its monarch's precepts. The play is not a thoroughgoing 'Mirror for Miscreants', but Lear's behaviour is at times so contrary to James's ideal it looks as if Shakespeare is using *Basilikon* as a countertext. Other characters' conduct and the portrait of society emerging reflect some of the critical remarks made by James. *Lear* acts as a mirror to the court. The book begins with an abstract of the 'Argument' in sonnet form:

GOD giues not Kings the stile of Gods in vaine,
For on his throne his sceptre doe they swey:
And as their subjects ought them to obey,

So Kings should feare and serve their God againe.
If then ye would enjoy a happy raigne,
Obserue the statutes of your heauenly King,
And from his Law, make all your Lawes to spring:
Since his Lieutenant here ye should remaine,
Reward the iust, be steadfast, true, and plaine,
Represse the proud, maintaining aye the right,
Walk always so, as euer in his sight,
Who guards the godly, plaguing the prophane:
And so ye shall in Princely vertue shine,
Resembling right your mightie King Diuine.

James overlaps the belief that kingship was divinely sanctioned with the image of God's 'lieutenant here' until kings almost become divine. Few Jacobeans questioned that rule should be monarchical or doubted that the English system should have a one-person government, but increasingly they questioned kingship's divinity, the relationship between ruler and ruled and the limits to princely authority. It is often assumed Divine Right was universally accepted; it was and was not. More and more voices questioned the manner of kingship as exercised by Elizabeth and James.[11] The unthinking mass accepted that the king – a distant figure of power and awe – was like a god on Earth. Largely they were voiceless, but others spoke for traditional beliefs. Robert Filmer formalized these in *Patriarcha* (written in the 1620s, published posthumously in 1680), summarizing the accumulated ideology of Divine Right. Filmer believes the model monarchical state is founded on the idea of familial patriarchy, quoting the Adamic dominion established by God (in Genesis) as the origin of patriarchy and kingship. As fathers rule the domestic *polis*, so the king (father of the nation) rules the state. Elizabeth's death foregrounded discussions increasingly focused on the complex concept of Divine Right and how kings should govern. The justificatory line of argument was that God made Adam lord of all creation, with dominion over his wife, family and the fruits of the Earth. The male therefore had divine sanction for his rule. Kings had similar incontrovertible, unopposable rule. Disagreement seriously sinned against God, against nature. Thus bulwarked against opposition, monarchy and patriarchy became firmly embedded in society. Kings had absolute power over life and property, could have people executed or pardoned, declare war, make peace, levy taxes, regulate trade, charter markets, issue licenses for manufacture, legitimize bastards or send people to the Tower. Their will was law and the law bent to their will. Regal proclamations were made with the mantra 'Le roi le veult' (The king wills it). Laws were only passed if similarly authenticated. He nominated government officers, bishops, judges and peers. His power was absolute, his favour vital. James declared of kings that 'even by God himself they are called gods'.[12] One might ask how he knew this.

The first book of *Basilikon Doron* opens with an orthodox declaration that immediately places Lear in the wrong:

> He cannot bee thought worthie to rule and commaund others, that cannot rule [...] his owne proper affections and unreasonable appetites, so can he not be thought worthie to governe a Christian People [that] feareth not and loveth not the Divine Majestie. Neither can [...] his Government succeed well with him [...] as coming from a filthie spring, if his person be unsanctified. (1)

That *Lear* is not set in a Christian era is irrelevant, for the audience was and would judge accordingly. James stresses the need for piety in a king and a life lived according to the demands of Christianity (as an example to his court and his people): virtue, self-control, respect for and obedience to scripture, conscience and faith ('the Golden Chaine that linketh the Faithfull Soule to Christ' [9]). The summative precepts offered are relevant to *Lear*: 'wrest not the World to your owne appetite' (4); 'The summe of the Law is the Tenne Commandements' (6); 'wisely [...] discerne [...] betwixt the expres Commaundment and Will of God in his Word and the invention and ordinance of Man' (15); 'kythe [show] more by your deedes than by your wordes the love of Vertue and hatred of Vice' (16).

The second book, 'A King's Duty in His Office', links the lesson of the first to the prince's second calling: being a good king. This office is discharged through 'justice and equitie [fairness]' and they are achieved by 'establishing and executing good lawes' and 'by your behaviour in your own person, and with your servants, to teach your people by your example: for people are naturally inclined to counterfaite (like Apes) their Princes manners' (17–18). This immediately triggers comparisons with Lear's unjust behaviour, raising the question whether his dogmatic, dictatorial manner is ingrained or a recent development stemming from age and encroaching senility. The former suggests Goneril and Regan's coldly autocratic behaviour, their lack of sympathy or understanding, were learned from Lear. James defines the difference between a true king ('ordained for his people') and a tyrant who 'thinketh his people ordained for him, a prey to his passions and inordinate appetites' (18). A good king 'employeth all his studie and paines, to procure and maintaine [...] the well-fare and peace of his people [...] as their naturall father and kindly maister [...], subjecting his owne private affections and appetites to the weale and standing of his subjects' (18–19). Lear's 'Take physic, Pomp' speech indicates his previous lack of concern for the 'weale and standing' of part of his people.

James warns that new laws are always needed to deal with 'new rising corruptions' (20) and that 'a Parliament is the honourablest and highest judgement [...] as being the Kings heade Courte' (21). His next comment seems to indicate a limited view of what a parliament was for: 'Hold no Parliaments but for necessity of new lawes' (21). Of Parliament he once told an ambassador, 'I am surprised that my ancestors should ever have permitted such an institution to come into existence.'[13] He repeatedly called Parliament when he needed money but regularly left the country in the charge of his Privy Council while he gallivanted off hunting for days on end. James did not deal with the old or new corruptions that surrounded him, did not settle the country 'by the severitie of justice' (22), but left in place the endemic institutional corruption. He did not 'embrace the quarrel of the poore and distressed' (26). His view that as a king you should 'governe your subjects, by knowing what vices they are naturally most inclined to, as a good Physician' (27), gives an edge to Lear's comments upon the moral failings he has seen.

Both fictional and real king bear responsibility for their failure to correct such corruption. It is probable James found the English situation too complex and ingrained, gave up trying to reform either court or country on *Basilikon* lines and, having attained the crown, became too hypnotized by the immensely increased disposable income it gave him, stopped bothering to be a good king and enjoyed the ritual, the status, the luxury. James never got to grips with any of the underlying social problems, seemingly letting the nobility act much as they pleased, despite his admonitions in *Basilikon* about repressing pride and supporting the poor.

The Scottish and English nobility were similar; 'although second in ranke, yet over-farre first in greatnes and power, either to do good or evill', with a 'fectlesse arrogant conceit of their greatnes and power', tending 'to thrall, by oppression, the meaner sort', 'maintaine their servants and dependers in any wrong' and run to the law 'for any displeasure' (33). James advises taming arrogant nobles; a governor must 'teache' them 'to keepe [the] lawes as precisely as the meanest' (34). Echoing Elyot he says, 'Acquaint your selfe [...] with all the honest men of your Barrones and Gentlemen' (34) for 'vertue followeth oftest noble blood' (35) and such men 'must be your armes and executers of your lawes' (35). We see little of Lear's court in formal action, but there is moral cowardice in its general readiness to accede to unjust actions and say nothing. There is Goneril using Oswald to destabilize the king, Edgar's depiction of a servingman's life, the disguised Kent's undiplomatic irritation of Cornwall and Regan and their spiteful retaliation. Kent is loyal, good, but lacks social skills – in defending Cordelia and abusing Oswald and the

Cornwalls. It is an unsophisticated court. James repeatedly emphasizes that the king is an example to his courtiers; Kent's blunt behaviour and plain speaking are perhaps learned from his master.

James's recommendation to 'bee well acquainted with the nature and humours of all your subjects' and 'once in the yeare [...] visit the principall parts of the country' (40) was not something he did and clearly Lear had no 'meet the people' policy or he would not, after wondering how the homeless would cope with the storm that soaked him, say 'O! I have ta'en/ Too little care of this' (III. iv.). James agrees, after reading Polydore Vergil's *Anglica Historia* (*A History of England*), that a king's actions were key in determining his country's fate.[14] Sadly true of Lear. The image of a 'filthie spring' polluting the stream (a ruler's corruption corrupting the country) occurs frequently in contemporary drama.[15] The gap between precept and practice is made wider and more ironic in James's discussion of a prince and his court as exemplars:

> It is not enough to a good King, by the sceptre of good lawes well excute to governe, and by force of armes to protect his people; if he joyne not therewith his virtuous life in his owne person, and in the person of his Court and companie: by good example alluring his subjects to the love of vertue, and hatred of vice. [...] All people are naturally inclined to followe their Princes example [...]. Let your owne life be a law-book and a mirrour to your people. (45)

This was to be achieved 'in the governement of your Court and followers' and

> in having your minde decked and enriched so with all virtuous qualities, that there-with ye may worthilie rule your people. For it is not enough that yr [sic] have and retaine [...] within your selfe never so many good qualities and virtues, except ye imploy them, and set them on worke, for the weale of them that are committed to your charge. (45)

Courtiers and servants should be 'of a good fame, and without blemish' (48). Care was crucial when appointing public officers who had responsibility for 'the weale of your people' (50). They should be men 'of knowne wisdome, honestie, and good conference [...], free of all factions and partialities: but specially free of that filthie vice of Flattery, the pest of all Princes' (51). James recommends: 'Commaund a hartly and brotherly love among them that serve you. [...] Maintaine peace in your Court, banish envie, cherish modestie, banish deboshed insolence, foster humility, and represse pride' (53–4).

Brotherly love, modesty, banished insolence, repressed pride – the opposite of Lear's court (and Whitehall).

As regards personal kingly qualities, James echoes much of what Elyot recommended, highlighting how far short of the ideal Lear falls. A prince should follow the four cardinal virtues with 'Temperance, Queene of all the rest' (62). The synonym for temperance used by both Elyot and James is moderation. A king needs 'wise moderation [...] first commanding your selfe [...] in all your affections and passions, [...] even in your most virtuous actions, [so you] make ever moderation to bee the chief ruler' (63). Lear lacks self-command and moderation. After temperance comes justice, 'the greatest vertue, that properly belongeth to a Kings office [...]. Use Justice [...] with such moderation as it turne not in Tyrannie' (63).[16] Lear's behaviour in the first two acts often resembles tyranny – peremptory, overly strict, inflexible, not unlike the old queen. James picked out the 'difference [...] betwixt extreame tyrannie [...] and extreame slacknesse of punishment' (64–5). The unspoken question of the play is, should a king be obeyed when behaving tyrannically? Shakespeare explores tyranny in *Lear*, weak government in *Measure for Measure*. With typical Shakespearean ambiguity, Lear's heavy-handed, high-handed style of rule is counterbalanced by the audience's growing sympathy for him as he becomes 'more sinned against than sinning'. James specifies 'Clemencie, Magnanimitie, Liberalitie, Constancie, Humilitie, and all other Princely vertues' (64) as essential. Another recommendation not followed by James was the encouragement to 'haunt your Sessions [court hearings], and spie carefullie their proceedings' (67). He advocates 'reading of authenticke histories and Chronicles [...] applying [...] by-past things to the present estate' (69), yet learned nothing from history, seeming swamped by the complexity of English society's problems and the immoveable corruption of a court and government he could never fully control. How, why and by whom *Lear* was selected for performance is unknown. Perhaps by James as a sharp reminder to his court. He knew the chronicle story, but probably did not know Shakespeare had amended it.[17] In the event it acts as an embarrassing exposure of failing to live up to declared principles.

The important second book of *Basilikon Doron* finishes with a series of precepts highly pertinent to Lear: 'Embrace true Magnanimitie [...] thinking your offender not worthie your wrath, empyring over your owne passion, and triumphing in the commanding your selfe to forgive [...]. Foster true Humility [...] banishing pride' (71; relevant to a number of major characters). He warns, 'Beginne not, like the young Lords [...], your first warres upon your Mother [...]. O invert not the order of nature, by judging your superiours' (72). *Lear* is much concerned with unnatural behaviour, nature perverted/inverted, the world turned upside down, most potently expressed through the family 'warres' that are the play's focus. James concludes with an admonition to 'exercise true Wisedome; in discerning wisely betwixt true and false reports' (74), reminiscent of Montaigne's comments on the misuse of words. Lear's problems stem from others' misuse of words and his inability to read them correctly. Lear is a victim of flattery and rhetoric's ploys. Montaigne deplored the art of fine speaking as 'deceiving not our eyes but our judgement, bastardizing and corrupting things in their very essence' so that feelings are 'inflated with rich and magnificent words'.[18] Cordelia's reactions to the 'glib and oily' rhetoric of Goneril and Regan's flatteries are mostly given as asides only we hear. Kent's reactions, more direct, condemning power bowing to flattery, are disregarded. James's final dictum resonates with the ironies of his own failings and Lear's:

> Consider that God is the author of all vertue, having imprinted in men's mindes by the very light of nature, the love of all morall virtues; [...] preasse then to shine as farre before your people, in all vertue and honestie; as in greatnesse of ranke [...] as by their hearing of your lawes, both their eyes and their eares, may leade [...] them to the love of vertue, and hatred of vice. (75)

King Lear and King James

Lear is not James I fictionalized, but gets very close. Exploring the consequences of absolute power in the hands of a temperamental, erratic, obstinate old monarch could as easily be identified with Elizabeth I. Lear's court is not Whitehall; that would not be allowed. All plays were licensed by the Revels Office and registered at the Stationers' Office only once government officials were sure nothing in the work was treasonable or heretical. The meaning of treasonable was elastically expanded to mean any criticism of the monarch. Direct representation of or critical reference to a reigning monarch was prohibited and would be removed from the script. The author could face imprisonment and James had already shown a readiness to do that.[19] A marginal note in Basilikon – 'Witnesse the experience of the late house of Gowrie' (47) – alludes to the 1600 plot by the Earl of Gowrie to kidnap James.[20] In 1604 the King's Men rehearsed a new play, The Tragedy of the Gowrie, for the court Christmas celebrations. Politically sensitive, it necessitated an actor playing the king and represented an incident from his life. The play was suppressed.[21] Shakespeare, however, knew how to cloak his concerns by indirection, smuggling in themes, presenting them in such a way as to not appear overtly critical of particular persons. As one of the leading King's Men he could ill afford to upset his employer, but from inside the establishment, with insider knowledge, he covertly raised controversial contemporary issues, resonantly relevant to the court, but conveniently distanced and disguised them to avert suspicion. *Measure for Measure*, another political play about misruling a state, but less sensitive because it was not blatantly personal, was performed at court on 26 December 1604. Satire of flawed leadership and the corrupt ruling classes is evident in all the last plays: *Measure* is set in Vienna, *Lear* in pagan times, *Macbeth* in the relatively recent past (but showing the restoration of a legitimate line from which James was descended), *Antony and Cleopatra* in the Roman era, *Timon of Athens* in Athens, *Coriolanus* in Rome, *Cymbeline* in pre-Christian Britain, *The Winter's Tale* in Sicily and Bohemia, and *The Tempest* on a Mediterranean island. Whatever the locational or periodic indirection, the themes were resonantly contemporary.

At the same time, Lear's court *is* Whitehall, but oblique enough to be impossible for government censors to pin down definitively. The sustained critique of kingship and court behaviour presents neither as acceptable. Aiming to prick the conscience of the guilty it provokes the rethinking of one's moral status, an adjustment of values. It achieves this by indirection. Setting the action in a past so distant few knew about it, Shakespeare raises innumerable questions about reprehensible court behaviour as a device for making his audience think about current court behaviour.[22] His defence might be: 'This is history. If you think I am talking about today or anyone particular you have seen parallels I didn't intend.'

James looked a very promising replacement as ruler of England: experienced as ruler of Scotland, something of a philosopher-king, authoring books on witchcraft and smoking in addition to two kingship studies. *The True Law of Free Monarchies* (1598) gives a clear statement of his belief in Divine Right absolutism. Its subtitle 'Or the Reciprocal and Mutual Duty Betwixt a Free King and His Natural Subjects' suggests belief in rule involving a contract between king and people. There is an unresolved contradiction here. A contractual relationship suggests that both sides agree to organize matters through discussion and compromise, and that one (the king) acts as the public voice for those he represents. James's actual style of rule, once in power, betrayed him as wilfully absolutist. *The True Law* (1598) demonstrated (somewhat tenuously) that kings derived power from God, that their authority was 'the true pattern of divinity' and, like God's, kingly authority was part of the laws of nature and the customs of the realm. There were already those supporting the contract idea tying people and ruler together in a liaison of mutual responsibilities, but James's practice took less notice of the customs of his realm than of his own will and needs. Quoting the Book of Samuel he repeated the idea that all subjects' property was the king's to use as he chose. This was not well received by the Commons, whom he lectured on the subject, for they were all men of property. The great obstacle was the traditional claim that as God's deputy, no one could judge him but God. Putting him above the law, blocking any suggestion he could ever be judged by his people, diametrically opposed the view of his one-time tutor George Buchanan. Buchanan's *De Jure Regni apud Scotos Dialogus* (*Dialogue on the Rule of Kings in Scotland*, 1579) contributed importantly to the contractarian debate, proposing that royal power originates from the agreement of the people, that kings hold power only as long as they conform to the terms by which power was given them by the people, and that a people may resist, depose and punish a king breaking his contract by becoming tyrannical.[23] James's belief in his divine mission was well established by his accession but endorsed by fawning verses, flattering speeches and obsequious courtiers. During his March 1604 procession through the city he heard an address at the Fenchurch Street gate in which a character, Theosophia (Divine Wisdom), announced '*Per me reges regnant*' (By me do all kings govern).[24] It was not long before people doubted James's will was identical to God's.

At his accession James promised to act 'like a good physician'. He immediately set up the Hampton Court Conference to deal with the 'millenary petition' he had been given coming south, a plea from the puritanical wing of the church for more tolerance of church reform. The conference looked promising, but it was a blind. James listened without ever intending to make any concessions. The philosopher-king persona was a mask only. The real James wanted his way and was fairly uninterested in debate, preferring to hector and lecture. He disappointed Catholics hoping for toleration, making clear he intended, like Elizabeth, not to permit two forms of faith in his kingdom. He also promised to consider the supplication made by poor petitioners against Cecil's and other landowners' increasing enclosure of common lands, fobbed them off with promises to consider their cases, then did nothing once installed in Whitehall.

Chapter 6

PATRIARCHY, FAMILY AUTHORITY AND GENDER RELATIONSHIPS

Yet will not I forget what I should be
And what I am, a husband: in that name
Is hid divinity. (*'Tis Pity She's a Whore*, IV. iii. 135–7)

The matter of gender relationships is full of ambiguities, prejudices, contradictions and inconsistencies, from both sides. Two features are definite: theoretically men ruled, and women often subverted male domination. Custom, doctrine and law made fathers heads of families. God ruled creation, kings ruled nations, fathers ruled families. God could punish sin, kings could punish crime, and a man could beat his wife, his children and his servants (Lear warns the Fool, 'Take heed, sirrah; the whip' [I. iv.]). Custom recommended moderation in corporal punishment, advocating its avoidance if possible, but its support in law meant it could happen. Beating causing bodily harm was not allowed. No doubt there were abusive and violent men who caused serious injury, but they were protected by an all-male legal system. A husband was an authoritarian figure whose word was law and the law supported men. Patriarchy ruled. St Paul authorized male dominance in the New Testament, *the* primary conduct book: 'Wives, submit yourselves unto your own husbands, as unto the Lord. For the husband is the head of the wife, even as Christ is the head of the church.'[1] Supposedly, husbands were dominant and wives subordinate in all things – legal status, physical strength, intelligence and virtue.

Patriarchy originates in Genesis when God makes man first, gives Adam dominion over all animals, then makes Eve out of Adam's rib and gives him rule over her. She is designed as 'an help meet' (Genesis 2:18) – a companion and assistant. When Adam is tempted by Eve to eat the apple God upbraids him for listening to his wife and acting according to her encouragement rather than God's command against eating of the forbidden tree. This story, written by men, endorsing male superiority and rule, an extension of the hierarchy of the chain of creation, reflects how society was organized and was reinforced by a misogynistic Catholic Church deeply suspicious of women. To the fallen Eve God says, 'I will greatly multiply thy sorrow [...]. In sorrow thou shalt bring forth children: and thy desire shall be to thy husband, and he shall rule over thee.'[2] Thus the pains of childbirth are annexed as punishment for Eve's sin and misogyny given divine authority. The seventeenth century saw female inferiority as pre-dating the Fall. Made after Adam, Eve was always secondary, so were all women to men. The poet-satirist George Wither summed this up: 'The woman for the man was made/And not the man for her.'[3]

Advising his son about marriage, James I quoted Genesis 2:23 (where Adam claims Eve is 'bone of my bone, and flesh of my flesh'), commenting on the institution as 'the greatest earthly felicite or miserie, that can come to a man, according as it pleaseth God to blesse or cursse the same'.[4] His advice is orthodox. He tells Henry to 'marrie one [...] of your own Religion; her ranke and other qualities being agreeable to your estate'.[5] There is awareness of the partnership aspect of marriage but it is patriarchally slanted:

> Treate her as your owne flesh, commaund her as her Lord, cherish her as your helper, rule her as your pupil, and please her in all things reasonable [...]. Ye are the head, as she is your body: [...] your office to commaund, [...] hers to obey; but yet with such a sweete harmonie, as shee should be as readie to obey, as yee to commaund [...]. Suffer her never to medle with the politick government of the common-weale, but hold her at the Oeconomick rule of the house; [...] yet all to be subject to your direction: keepe carefullie good and chaste companie about her; for women are the frailest sexe.[6]

Publicly, it was a man's world. Regardless of theory, whatever the biblical and legal support, private reality varied greatly. In defining gender roles and attitudes it is always important to remember, whatever the stereotypes, in practice matters could be different and women subverted patriarchy in many ways and in many arenas.

The long-established medieval position on women still persisted, but there had been changes. Orthodoxy saw women as the origin of sin, the source of temptation, taking its authority from the Bible. Paul told wives to submit to their husbands and keep silent in church (Colossians 3:18). In I Timothy (2:8–12) he wrote: 'I will therefore that the men pray [...]. Let the women learn in silence with all subjection. I permit not a woman to teach, neither to usurp authority over the man, but to be in silence.' The Bible's good women, the Virgin Mary and an array of female saints, were outweighed by evil women in scripture, in history and in the diatribes of the church fathers.[7] Biased selection of biased texts built up formidable prejudice against the sex. Tertullian (AD c. 160–c. 225) saw women as 'the devil's gateway'.[8] St John Chrysostom (AD c. 347–407) exclaimed: 'How often do we, from beholding a woman, suffer a thousand evils; [...] entertaining an inordinate desire, and experiencing anguish for many days [...]. The beauty of woman is the greatest snare.'[9] Clement of Alexandria (AD c. 150–c. 215), went further: 'Every woman should be ashamed that she is a woman' for they are 'the confusion of men, an insatiable animal [...], an eternal ruin'.[10] Male mistrust of female sexuality underlies much of the patriarchal system. It was a factor in the intermittent waves of witch trials and executions. The *Malleus Maleficarum* (*The Hammer of Witches*, 1496) declared, 'All witchcraft comes from carnal lust, which in women is insatiable.'[11] Women are commonly accused of sex with the Devil in accounts of witches' covens and other black mass rituals.

Women's main role was keeping the house and largely keeping to the house, though urban middling sort wives had, according to foreign observers, considerable freedom to move outside the home. In the agricultural world women helped in the fields, but many of their tasks were home based – cooking, feeding poultry, tending vegetable gardens, cleaning and making clothes. A shopkeeper's wife or daughter might help behind the counter, but making saleable products (pastry, clothes, crafted items, etc.) was done by men (apprentices, journeymen and masters) and shop assistants were largely men. Women were barred from the professions, public life and higher education. The standard view was that women were intellectually feeble, unreliable, shrewish, gossips, spendthrifts, bad tempered, endlessly demanding, and if given rein would monopolize any public/social meeting. There were dissenting voices, but it was a well-entrenched view that women were overemotional and easily overheated sexually. Belief in women's sexual insatiability reflected male insecurity and a man's uncertainty whether the child he was paying to bring up was indeed his own – fears related to questions of inheritance and keeping the family bloodline pure. It explains the obsession with the chastity of daughters and wives. Tainted daughters with little value in the marriage market remained a drain on family finances. A wife who was 'loose i'the hilts' degraded the husband's public reputation and honour, wounded his personal esteem, cast doubt on his children's legitimacy, and made him the butt of jokes about cuckolds and horns.[12] Proverbs 12:4 put it thus: 'A virtuous woman is a crown to her husband: but she that maketh ashamed is as rottenness in his bones.' Illegitimacy stemming from male adultery could have disastrous psychological outcomes, as witness Gloucester's case, but was often smiled at.

Patriarchy's dominance explains why so many men had such low opinions of women, treating them unsympathetically and as sex objects. Such views are voiced frequently by rakish male characters crowding Elizabethan-Jacobean comedies, though Hamlet and Iago are misogynistic too. This loose-living, loose-tongued, bawdy, joking brotherhood stretches from Lucio (*Measure for Measure*, 1604) through Willmore (Aphra Behn's *The Rover*, 1677) to innumerable libertines in later drama and novels. A counterbalancing philosophy offers the *gentils domna* (gentle lady) of Courtly Love, the beautiful but virtuous woman whose example civilizes brutish men. She has the self-effacing quiet of the confident but restrained woman, not the silence of the repressed and downtrodden creature. Cordelia has something of this quality as opposed to her ruthless virago sisters.

The 1571 *Second Book of Homilies* (XVIII, 'Of the State of Matrimony') declared woman 'a weak creature, prone to all weak affections and dispositions of the mind', indicating the Church of England was essentially little different from Rome. Greater respect for women, though still wary, emerged among the Puritans, who demanded abstinence from both sexes outside marriage and continence within. Puritanism was still, however, a minority sect. Cordelia's reputation for virtue elevates her in France's eyes, while Goneril and Regan exhibit signs of the sexuality misogynists expected – Goneril contemplating adultery with Edmund (hinting a readiness to have Albany conveniently killed), Regan targeting Gloucester's bastard almost immediately after Cornwall's death. In this she represents another stock character from drama – the widow either rampantly free or easily victimized, reflecting the standard view of predatory female sexuality and echoing anxieties about overhasty second marriage for women. Dynastic and financial concerns are involved. Family fortunes could quickly be lost to mercenary second husbands and the children of the first union married off or simply sent to a faraway estate and neglected. The 'merry widow' was not just a comic figure. *Hamlet* and *The Duchess of Malfi* present tragic examples of the difficulties second marriage could bring. In practice second marriages were common among both sexes and all classes. Moralists admitted that humankind was inordinately lustful, but since most moralists were male they tended to be more tolerant of male libidinousness and more critical of female failings. Neither the wildfire spread of syphilis nor the widespread ecclesiastical condemnation of sex outside marriage for both sexes as a Deadly Sin curbed the natural lustfulness of either. With the blatant hypocrisy, chauvinism and prejudice that each sex brings to stereotyping the other, there was, on the male side, a double standard in accepting young men fornicating indiscriminately and regarding having a mistress as a sign of manhood, while demanding chaste behaviour among their women.

The orthodox husband–wife relationship is defined in Shakespeare's early 'sex war' comedy *The Taming of the Shrew* (1593–94). Petruchio, seeking a wife to refill his coffers (as many of both sexes did), announces to the assembled wedding guests:

I will be master of what is mine own.
She is my goods, my chattels: she is my house,
My household stuff, my field, my barn,
My horse, my ox, my ass, my anything. (III. ii. 229–32)

At the end of the play, Kate supposedly defines the theoretically submissive role of the wife:

Thy husband is thy lord, thy life, thy keeper,
Thy head, thy sovereign – one that cares for thee,
And for thy maintenance commits his body
To painful labour both by sea and land,
To watch the night in storms, the day in cold,
Whilst thou li'st warm at home, secure and safe. (V. ii. 146–51)[13]

She sees wifely 'love, fair looks, and true obedience' as a duty like that 'the subject owes the prince' and deprecates the rebellious wife seeking 'rule, supremacy, and sway'. Is this sincere or has she discovered that, like women before and after, she can get all she wants by appearing submissive while secretly gaining control of household and husband? This is the comic discrepancy inherent in the gender relationship. Man plays the master publicly while woman pulls his strings behind the scenes.

Manipulation, deviousness, sheer bloody-mindedness and simple evil (their weapons of mass subversion in the sex war) were attributed to women in the social comedies of the 1600s. While female tenderness and sensitivity are acknowledged, misogyny is accurate in its definitions too. In Middleton's *A Mad World My Masters* a country gentleman, surreally named Penitent Brothel, admits the superior acumen of the courtesan Frank (Frances) Gullman and associates it with inventive, devious female resourcefulness:

The wit of man wanes and decreases soon,
But women's wit is ever at full moon. (III. ii. 159–160)

He later comments:

When plots are e'en past hope and hang their head,
Set with a woman's hand, they thrive and spread. (III. ii. 246–7)

He is proved correct when the aptly named Gullman ('man fooler')[14] successfully gulls into marriage Follywit, the heir of Sir Bounteous Plenty. Shakespeare's comic heroines (e.g., Beatrice, Rosalind, Viola and Portia) are similarly clever, inventive and resourceful. Their virtue prevents them intending or doing evil, but they are irrepressibly wilful. There are devious women with ruthless and destructive ambitions. Lady Macbeth, Goneril and Regan are prime examples.

In the real world theory and practice diverge and diversify into a variety of relationships. Every marriage was unique – some paralleled the orthodox model, in some the woman ruled unopposed, in many there was a compromise negotiated or appropriated. There were happy marriages, arranged or not. In the upper and middle ranks many men and women married for fiscal or dynastic reasons. This did not always make for easy relationships, but neither did it preclude love, companionship and happiness. A slow shift evolved marriage into a partnership of physical and spiritual companions. Lord Montagu advised his son, 'In your marriage looke after goodness rather than goodes.'[15] Traditionally men sought love and sexual relief outside marriage. This was the negative aspect of arranged marriages where there was no initial attraction and none developed afterwards. The Earl of Northumberland advised his son, 'As you must love, love a mistress for her flesh and a wife for her virtues.'[16] Women took lovers less openly than men, though in the court they were more blatant. Some women sublimated their emotional needs through running estates and raising children, while their husbands attended court or Parliament, joined the army or indulged in usual male activities – hunting, gambling, drinking, theatregoing, whoring, etc. Many elite marriages were based on separate lives, but many thrived on the love and respect that formed the new companionate marriage. Puritan pamphlet/sermon input to the marriage debate promoted the development of the helpmeet/companion element.[17]

A play marking the emergence of the strong, independent woman is Fletcher's *The Woman's Prize, or The Tamer Tamed* (1610). Appropriating Shakespeare's Petruchio, the shrew tamer, Fletcher has him tamed (or humanized) by his second wife, Maria, who outwits standard male chauvinism. No longer 'gentle' or 'tame', her 'new soul' is

> Made of a north wind, nothing but tempest,
> And like a tempest shall it make all ruins
> Till I have run my will out. (I. ii. 77–9)

Her sister advises her to abandon her plans and accept her expected sexual destiny. Maria is implacable:

> To bed? No, Livia, there be comets yet hang
> Prodigious over that yet. There is a fellow [Petruchio]

Must yet before I know that heat – ne'er start wench –
Be made a man, for yet he is a monster;
Here must his head be […]. (I. ii. 101–5)

No stage direction indicates where she points – to herself (as his head),
her breast (where his head must rest lovingly), or under her foot? Her
transgressiveness expresses something of the rebalancing of the gender roles
of the time. Her cousin Bianca contextualizes Maria's stand:

All the several wrongs
Done by imperious husbands to their wives
These thousand years and upwards strengthen thee!
Thou hast a brave cause. (I. ii. 122–5)

Maria's apparent goal is equality in marriage, declaring:

[…] That childish woman
That lives a prisoner to her husband's pleasure
Has lost her making and becomes a beast
Created for his use, not fellowship. (I. ii. 137–40)

This play contributes to the lively late sixteenth-/early seventeenth-century
debate about women's nature and what their place in society should be.
Opinion was mounting against arranged marriages forced for dynastic and
material reasons (characteristic of royal and aristocratic unions) where there
was no attraction or love. Cordelia is disposed of at Lear's whim though
accepted by France on the grounds of her virtue and with apparent attraction
to her personality. Arranged royal marriages were traditionally a façade only,
sometimes fruitful, sometimes not, often becoming a union of separateness
masked by ritual and splendour. France represents the new affective
approach. He and Burgundy have 'long […] made their amorous sojourn' at
court so have had time to assess her character. France is content she is 'rich
[in qualities, not wealth] […] choice […] lov'd […]' and has 'virtues'. His
feelings of love 'kindle to inflam'd respect' for 'this unpriz'd precious maid'.
Cordelia accepts him too.[18] We see nothing of this marriage though the
sources all agree it was happy. The unions we do see are without obvious
affection. In the source play, *The True Chronicle History of King Leir*, the elder
sisters are attracted to the husbands selected for them and marry according to
paternal wishes and their own. Shakespeare reveals much about these unions.
Goneril uses a servant to provoke confrontation with her father, without
discussion, presumably knowing Albany would not approve. She is therefore

acting unilaterally and transgressively – an example of independent decision making and action unacceptable in a wife. Regan and Cordelia (to different ends) work in conjunction with their respective spouses. Goneril despises her husband, subversively assumes the dominant role, makes decisions, 'is the better soldier' (IV. v.). Regan shares power ambition with Cornwall, but there is no show of affection or grief when he is killed. Thomas Becon, in his *Golden Boke of Christen Matrimonie* (1542), describes couples trapped unhappily in arranged/forced marriages cursing 'their parents even unto the pit of hell for coupling them together', though there were also many who coped or even found happiness. Dekker asks gentlefolk who are so careful matching their coach horses, why 'will you be carelesse in coupling your children?'[19] Unhappy elite couples could more easily afford to live separate lives. Among the middling sort this was less possible. In these two ranks forced/arranged marriages occurred more frequently, but the men customarily spent much more time with other men in business or leisure. Evidence for marriage practices and experience of married life among the common sort is scanty, but both in drama and in documentary sources it is also clear that there were many loving and happy unions at all levels.[20]

The increasing vocal presence of women in society and at court combined with their increased presence in print ratcheted up the gender discourse. Though women were beginning to record their lives in private journals and letters, few are represented in print, but that was changing rapidly. Gender issues were addressed mainly through male dramatists. The public dimension of theatre and the growth in the practice of printing play texts for commercial sale foregrounded this perennial concern. But in privately circulated manuscripts and in occasional printed texts, women were emerging as authors and were raising gender issues.[21] *The Memorandum of Martha Moulsworth, Widow* (1632) offers a touching verse account of her life and three happy marriages. A loving father brought her up 'in godlie pietie' and 'in modest chearfullnes & sad sobrietie'. Unusually, for her sex and rank (rural gentry), she was taught Latin, but lamented, 'Two universities we have of men/O that we had but one of women then!' (lines 33–4).[22] Married at 21, widowed after five years, she mourned a year, then remarried. Ten years later she was widowed again. After nearly four years she married a third time. Of this last relationship she writes:

> The third I tooke a lovely man, & kind
> such comlines in age we seldom find
> [...]
> was never man so Buxome to his wife
> with him I led an easie darlings life

I had my will in house, in purse in Store
what would a women old or yong have more? (Lines 57–68)

She declares she loved all her partners, was very happy with them and enjoyed domestic responsibility: 'I had my will in house, in purse, in store'. She completes her autobiography with a neat and witty couplet in keeping with her sense of satisfaction in marriage:

the Virgins life is gold, as Clarks us tell
the Widowes silvar, I love silvar well. (Lines 109–10)

There is insufficient evidence to form any distinct pattern or profile showing how widespread such education was for girls or how common such happiness was in marriage.[23] Martha is a positive example of a woman living in the provinces – her education makes her an exception. Reading, writing and enjoyment of literature was largely confined to small groups of gentlewomen housed with an aristocratic mistress whom they served. Martha is not unique, but the bulk of women (and men) had little learning. How much love they found within arranged unions is impossible to tell.

If work, running the estate or pursuing pleasure was a man's life, family tended to be the major part of the female sphere, along with overseeing the household economy (though a wife was responsible to her husband for expenditure in both areas). Traditionally women were thought more naturally inclined to be loving and nurturing, while fathers were distant, even when at home. King James warned his son that when he had 'succession' (children) he should 'bee carefull for their virtuous education: love them as yee ought', but 'contayning them ever in a reverent love and feare of you'. As regards inheritance:

Make your eldest sonne Isaac, leaving him all your kingdoms; and provide the rest with private possessions. Otherwaies by dividing your kingdoms, ye shall leave the seede of division and discorde among your posteritie: as befell to this Ile, by the division and assignment thereof, to the three sonnes of Brutus, Locrine, Albanact, and Camber.[24]

Some mothers too were distant (especially court ladies) and noble offspring were largely reared by nurses and maids. Fathers tended to be strict, concerned to discipline children to conform to society's expectations of their gender role and attitudes. Formality and ritual deference were more common among the elite. In their parents' presence children stood in silence, speaking only when spoken to. In very strict aristocratic families they knelt. Even bourgeois children asked father's permission and blessing before beginning any undertaking – a journey, going to university, leaving home to marry, leaving the table, going to bed, etc. Lear's last words to the banished Cordelia, 'be gone/Without our grace, our love, our benison' (I. i.), distinctly marks her rejection. When reunited she asks, 'hold your hand in benediction o'er me' – showing reacceptance of her as his child (IV. vii.). Shakespeare and the source play have reconciled daughter and father kneel to each other. Lear's kneeling signifies asking forgiveness, an unusual act marked by the oddity of a father/king kneeling to his daughter. Her kneeling signifies asking forgiveness and her readiness to be readmitted to his family and rule. Addressing a father or mother could be very formal – using their title or calling them 'Sir' and 'Madam'. Lear's daughters only call him father in moments of high emotion – positive or negative. Otherwise he is addressed as 'Sir' or 'your Majesty'. Cordelia uses the affectionate form more often and more sincerely than the other two. Edmund, to convince Gloucester of his loyalty and proper respect, calls him 'my Lord' six times and 'your Lordship' once, as he plants seeds of doubt about Edgar (I. ii.). Similar formality could apply between husband and wife. That said, in many families there was affectionate informality. Lear says of Cordelia:

> Her voice was ever soft,
> Gentle and low, an excellent thing in woman. (V. iii.)

This suggests she had always been quietly spoken, not brashly forward. He had loved her, perhaps as the baby of the family, the last bond between him and his dead wife, perhaps because she was more lovable than her sisters. Whether her sisters had a history of being demanding and peremptory is not revealed, but they emerge as such in the play. Humility was valued as a form of personal modesty. It was equally prized in men and was not merely a chauvinistic desire for quietly deferential women. Talkative, overwhelming, gossipy adults were unacceptable whatever their sex. There are blabbermouth males in the works of Shakespeare and other dramatists, but at least since the rise of medieval misogyny there was a belief that, given their head, many women would talk and talk. The terms gossip, flibbertigibbet, scold and shrew range through the types of more ready female verbalizing. If women stereotype men as talking too little, men stereotype women as talking too much. The implication is that female vocalization is silly, pointless, idle gossip. As the saying has it, 'Every ass loves to hear himself bray'. Or herself. Gratiano (*The Merchant of Venice*) and Lady Would-Be (*Volpone*) are a male and female example of the comic figure of the ceaseless chatterer who makes little sense. Even Benedick, fairly vocal himself, expresses frustration at Beatrice being 'possessed with a fury' (*Much Ado*, I. i. 160), 'huddling jest upon jest' (II. i. 214), nominating her 'my Lady Tongue' (II. i. 240). Knowing when to voice opinions and give them inoffensively and courteously was a social skill prized among cultured people. It is a quality not displayed by Goneril, Regan or Kent. The quiet-spoken manner of Cordelia is defined by Dusinberre as 'the intractability of [...] silence in a world where silence in women spells submission'.[25] Female quietness may sometimes be enforced conformity to male repression, but may also be a courteous and cultured wisdom, guarding your views when there were others ready to talk nonsense. Goneril and Regan exemplify the consequences of encouraging or allowing to talk those whose language is lies, who aim to flatter and impress for their own gain and insist on voicing their views and pushing themselves forward, taking command. Only speaking when you have something worth saying was regarded as a strength and a virtue, but Goneril and Regan speak to show they have broken free of their father's shackles. They speak, order and demand, to demonstrate their autonomy. Apart from the contrast with Cordelia, a counterargument to their overcompensation for what may have been years of repression comes from another female who is never at a loss for words. Isabella condemns arbitrary and unnecessary displays of power:

> O, it is excellent
> To have a giant's strength, but it is tyrannous
> To use it like a giant. (*Measure for Measure*, II. i. 108–110)

Lear has been a giant and the elder daughters may have learnt their ruthless authoritarianism from him. Dusinberre sees their 'glib and oily' flattery in Act I as 'self selling', as if they saw themselves as commodities (the property of the king/father) or courtesans selling themselves, advertising their attractions through the flattering misuse of words, and foreshadowing their readiness to become available to Edmund.[26] They demean themselves by playing Lear's love test game. Cordelia holds herself aloof from it. They gain power – and then misuse it horrifically. They 'manifest human nature reduced to the predatory with none of the grandeur'.[27] When Regan and Goneril's support is offered under unacceptable terms Lear storms out into a real storm. Close to tears of frustration and impotence, having given away his manhood with his power, he declares he will not weep (II. iv.). He did cry in front of Goneril as he quitted her castle. It would be a very awkward moment. A grown man, a king, shedding tears – in anger, frustration and self-pity. It would be a reverse of expected behavioural and gender stereotypes. Dusinberre asserts, 'A woman suffers continually from the impotence which is exceptional in a man.'[28] Shakespeare's impotent women are far outnumbered by his resourceful, independent ones, reflecting perhaps his perception that despite patriarchy, despite the public limitations of their horizons, women did achieve more than might be assumed if theory and orthodoxy alone are considered.

Legal and biblical authority made man the head of the woman and the family. His wife's money and property became his, his claim to custody of the children took precedence over hers and theoretically he had the final say in all things. In practice many different arrangements were negotiated by individual couples. Some women were independent, bossy termagants.[29] Some efficiently ran households with the power of decision over menus, furnishings, hiring and firing servants and the education of the younger children. Some were docile shadows. There was an immense range of different male familial profiles too, from the ultra-chauvinist patriarch, through the liberal, kindly, affectionate, caring father, to the weak or indifferent nonentity. Albany is passive and wife-dominated. He is awkwardly situated – a duke married to a king's daughter. Lear – apparently too strong, too dominating – creates a backlash from the two eldest daughters by foolishly giving them independence without conserving his own power. Gloucester has been too weak and thoughtless in the unequal upbringing of his sons.

There was considerable debate about how fathers should behave to their children and how best children should be brought up. Montaigne and Bacon have much to say on the subject (see 'The Montaigne Effect' in Chapter 10). Largely, fathers were stern, distant and formal, partly because high infant/teenage mortality discouraged too close and affectionate a relationship developing, partly because strict fathers were thought better teachers of respect and discipline.[30] Mothers were thought too indulgent. Fathers reflected the loving sternness of God. Children were thought to be wild creatures needing taming and training if they were to be self-disciplined in later life and cope with the customs and practices of a highly stratified, ritual-conscious, traditionalist society. The entrenched suspicions men had of female irrationality, unreliability and emotional instability transferred into their attitude towards a mother's relationships with her children. In elite families boys were removed from female control at age 7, breeched and put under a tutor until ready to be sent away to complete their education.

Affective family relations did exist as did companionate marriages. Not all was male chauvinism, female submission and conflict. Widows took on the running of estates and businesses, did so very effectively and were accepted. There were many more of these than one might think since men tended to marry later than women and die earlier. It was not unusual or unexpected for a woman to remarry. In business a widow commonly married one of the journeymen or a senior apprentice. A journeyman was a skilled worker who had completed his seven-year apprenticeship. He was not yet a master of his craft, but was sufficiently skilled and experienced for it to be a practical union keeping the business going and money coming in. Among high-status families marriage and family relationships were often thought of not as loving support networks developing within a sheltered environment, but as units of child production enabling the family title, status, money and property to be kept together and handed on. It is a chilling fact that one-third of marriages did not last longer than 15 years, old husbands died and many women did not survive childbirth. Remarriage was common, often swiftly following the funeral. These dynastic concerns seem inhumanly disagreeable to modern minds, but in an age when death was a constantly imminent possibility such severe considerations were crucial at every level of society where property (however minor) was held. At stake might be the tenure of thousands of acres and a place at court, or simply the hedging tools of a farm labourer and the lease on his cottage. Apart from biblical authority for patriarchy there were practical reasons for it. Among the aristo-gentry, emerging from the violence and precariousness of the Wars of the Roses, men needed large families in the hope at least one male would survive. This required a fertile wife, based at home to rear the offspring. Stone puts it thus:

> Among the landed classes in pre-Reformation England [the] objectives of family planning were the continuity of the male line, the preservation intact of the inherited property, and the acquisition of further property or useful political alliances.[31]

Feminist historians and literary critics have drawn attention to the marginalized role and restricted potential of women throughout the ages.[32] This has been useful to counterbalance the male-dominated view of social history, but has simultaneously overemphasized the degree of male domination and underemphasized the strength and sometimes negative aspects of covert petticoat power. The behind-the-scenes and in-the-bedroom influence of women at court is an acknowledged but underexplored factor. Because women had no official political role, it has been assumed they had no power, yet literature shows their incitement and complicity in tragic and comic plots and history increasingly reveals the influence they wielded in the arenas of power. The most material sign of male dominance was appropriation of his wife's property and money to do with as he wished, though sometimes family wealth could be held combined and administered jointly. Some husbands let their wife keep her money or land or both.[33] Less publicized is the jointure arranged by parents and lawyers. This agreed annuity, payable if the husband predeceased his wife, could represent a considerable sum if it had to be paid over a long period. Debts accrued by a wife were legally payable by the husband and extravagant female spending, a traditional feature of satire, is frequently referenced in Jacobean drama and particularly targeted at women of the better sort and citizens' wives. Materially and emotionally every arranged union had two potential victims. The patriarch kept family property intact through primogeniture, but may himself have been forced into marriage with an old, ugly or ill-tempered woman. Younger offspring had to be found appropriate partners as much as the heir. Sons were a problem, tending to drift into similarly cash-strapped homosocial groups in London, unsupervised, uncivilized and antisocial. They were increasingly pushed into high-status professions – the church, law, government service, the army, etc. – but often dropped out. Daughters had to be found dowries, though many young high-status women remained unmarried, without a vocation, without the chance to work other than at relatively trivial domestic and social accomplishments (sewing, embroidery, music, etc.). Some upper-rank gentlewomen serving an aristocratic lady had leisure time for reading, thinking, writing and consensual discourse.[34] These cultured coteries tended to be located in the more splendid country mansions. Those daughters who did marry, even if they wed a rich man, had to be provided with a dowry. This could represent a cripplingly difficult sum to find.

While parental wishes, much influenced by financial, hierarchical or political interests, were dominant in choosing a partner, increasingly the child's consent was sought. This approach was particularly evident in the wealthy upper-middle ranks. If a child did not like and was not attracted to a possible partner, that could end negotiations. In *'Tis Pity She's a Whore* a fellow citizen seeks Florio's daughter as wife for his booby fop of a nephew. Florio tells him:

> My care is how to match her to her liking:
> I would not have her marry wealth, but love;
> And if she like your nephew, let him have her. (I. iii. 10–12)

Ironically, this liberal approach is voiced while Annabella is in bed with her chosen lover – her brother.[35] Drama presents the mass of different conflicts over courtship and marriage because they offer excitement and more plot possibilities than demure agreement. Largely, however, in real life, it seemed that parents commonly chose a suitor or bride if there was already an attraction. In the case of a candidate picked by the parents but unknown to the prospective bride/groom, proposed by the suitor/bride's family or self-presented by a free bachelor, the child's response was taken into account. But if a candidate was strongly preferred by the parents on material grounds and rejected by the son or daughter, then parental pressure and patriarchal weight (threats of disinheritance and other punishments) could be applied. Marriage without parental consent was illegal, which puts the archetypal romantic lovers, Romeo and Juliet, outside the law. Prospero (*The Tempest*), a more caring father, approves of the mutual attraction between his daughter and future son-in-law. King Lear, in his anger, disposes of Cordelia to the lowest bidder without her say.

Though the odds were often against it, there is evidence of loving marriages and of happy families 'long before the eighteenth century'.[36] Studies show that 'patriarchal authority applied in theory to this period, but could be modified in practice, by illustrating the range of experiences of married couples in which much depended upon factors such as the personality and relative status of the husband and wife'.[37] More importantly, as a counterbalance to the idea of women being completely dominated, 'Far from being passive subordinates, some women developed strategies to modify or resist patriarchal authority, including marshalling support through friends, neighbours and kin to circumvent their putative subordination to their husbands.'[38]

Patriarchy and a Woman's Place

Deep-seated institutional misogyny persisted through the 1600s. Though the Catholic Church no longer held sway in England, its ideas had bitten deep into the male psyche, and suspicion of women was endemic in masculine thinking. The Church of Rome, systemically misogynistic in its doctrines, saw women's secondary role as part of God's plan. The Church of England was more of the mind that men and women should respect one another, that husbands and wives should work in harmony, but was clear that ultimately the man was in charge. As descendants of Eve, women were thought more inclined to sin. Men too were sinners but a neat argument mitigated that: 'though an husband in regard of evil qualities may carry the image of the devil, yet in regard to his place and office, he beareth the image of God'.[39]

No one statement or view can be universally true of the complexities of male–female relationships, but in general a woman's place was subordinate to the males within her family and social sphere. Women did have some status: a mother had authority over her children (in the father's absence); a housewife had authority over her servants (in the master's absence); the wife of a guild master, a titled lady or a shop owner's wife was superior to anyone of an inferior station (male or female), but within their own rank was secondary to any adult male, subordinate even to a son of age if he had just inherited from a dead father and was the head of the family. Respect for her as a woman, as a mother and as dowager (widow of a titled/propertied man) would partially mitigate his authority. There would also be families where a naturally aggressive and dominating widow would hold on to power and influence. It is clear Lear regards his daughters as very much his property, both as father and king, disposing of them as he sees fit. Once free of him, with his power diminished to a level where only affection might work in his favour, the two older daughters display a barbaric cruelty transgressing custom and civilized behaviour.

The subordination of women was part of an unfair hierarchical system within a social structure that designated a place for everyone and in which most people (men included) were subordinate to someone. It was unjust but most of the social and legal structure was unfairly organized in favour of the rich over the poor and men over women.

In 1558, the year of Elizabeth I's accession, the most strident statement of female inferiority was made by the Scottish radical Protestant John Knox from his exile in Geneva:

> To promote a woman to bear rule, superiority, dominion or empire above any realm, nation or city is repugnant to nature, contumely to God, a thing most contrarious to his revealed will and approved ordinance, and finally it is the subversion of good order, of all equity and justice.[40]

Knox's views resonate with the fear that transgressing social, familial or gender order would herald anarchy and collapse. Even Montaigne, usually liberal and fair, expresses this orthodox view of females:

> Women should have no mastery over men save only the natural one of motherhood [...]. It is dangerous to leave the superintendence of our succession to the judgement of our wives and to their choice between our sons, which over and over again is iniquitous and fantastic. For those unruly tastes and physical cravings which they experience during pregnancy are ever-present in their souls.[41]

This fails to take account of the fact that people in restricted situations generally find ways of subverting the limitations put upon them and that some women have always tended to: 1. oppose by a variety of means attempts by males to repress them, and 2. achieve some independence for themselves by negotiation, by clandestine action or by default. Plays are full of female rule breakers. Some women failed to win any area of domination. Some ruled every area of family life, some a limited area. Some said 'Yes, dear', 'No, dear' and then secretly did what they wished. Some men were indifferent to household matters or child rearing, so the wife/mother ruled by default.

Some women gained rule of estates or businesses through their husband's decease, some inherited in default of male heirs. But largely Heaven's hierarchy was reflected on Earth and backed by religion. Thus, 'By marriage, the husband and wife became one person in law – and that person was the husband.'[42]

Just where women were placed in day-to-day reality is problematic. The bulk of ordinary people were voiceless. Women provide even less evidence of their existence than men. Documents profiling actual relationships are scarce and differ between court and country and between the aristo-gentry and other ranks. The lower down the social scale the less material is available. The few remaining personal diaries and letters by women are held in archives, though probably more await discovery. It was a period in which few people committed personal feelings to paper. Cost of materials was one factor, but the culture was only slowly coming to accept that an individual's thoughts and feelings were of value. The various intersecting seventeenth-century conflicts encouraged more people to put pen to paper to express their views. The 80 per cent male literacy rate in London effectively boosted this. Urban trading families needed literate heirs and dissenting groups began establishing their own small local schools. From the mid-seventeenth century, Dissenting Academies provided excellent broad education, more liberal, practical and extensive than the limited classical studies of high-end families. There were many grammar schools and these often had endowments, bursaries and scholarships that enabled boys from poor families to gain formal education. Little formal schooling was given to girls, even from high-status families (apart from the royal family and a few cultured aristocratic households). Literacy and numeracy, taught at home, was often the only scope for girls. Individual tutors in individual households did provide more liberal studies and there were some institutions for girls set up by Puritans, but these were the exception to the rule.

It was common (among Dissenters particularly) for Christians to make personal daily examination of their lives. In time this came to be written down in a spiritual journal, and subsequently more material is available. The 1600s saw an increasing number of pamphlets (many by women) offering opinions on everything from politics to horticulture to horoscopes. By the Restoration (1660), a slightly higher proportion of female-to-male professional writers reflected some easing of male repressiveness, but as a demographic percentage figures for female writing are small. There are more questions than evidence to answer them. Did women write but not publish? Did women just not write much? Were they unable to access reading material that triggered their own writing? Was female literacy just too low to make a showing? Much female-authored fictional work circulated in manuscript among social networks like the court, London-based writers and literate and literary families and their friends. Prohibited from acting, women seem not to have written for the public stage until Aphra Behn, but many translated foreign plays or wrote their own for private circulation.[43] Any assessment of women in the period 1600–1620 will largely be constructed from male perspectives, though a number of recent studies (like Schleiner's) are revealing the hidden archaeology of women's literary creation. This is confined to privileged groups. The general picture seems to be that private individuals (male and female) were increasingly writing about their lives, opinions and personal struggles. This accelerated in the Civil War and afterwards. But most of this manuscript material is locked away in scattered archives, public and private, awaiting analysis and publication.

The late Stuart period provides many spiritual autobiographies. An interesting early exception, giving insight into provincial life, comes from Lady Margaret Hoby's diary of 1599–1605. A Yorkshire heiress, educated in a Puritan school for gentlewomen run by the Countess of Huntingdon, she married three times, making alliances with high-profile court dynasties (the Devereux, Sidneys and Hobys). Her life was spent in Hackness near Scarborough, with only few visits to London. Her diary, the earliest known by an English woman, records her local charity work, her running of the household and estate, and her domestic activities – managing servants, paying them, mundane activities like gardening, arranging the washing and ironing, preparing medicines, and her contacts with neighbours and estate tenants. It recounts her outer spiritual life – organizing household prayers, listing her personal devotions and reading – but does not delve into her inner feelings.

At every stage of life a woman was expected to be deferential, submissive and aware constantly of her different and separate expectations. Her infant education (if she received one) would be at home and limited to letters and figures, while her brothers attended school (or were home tutored) and then, once literate and numerate, moved on to Greek, Latin, mathematics, history and geography, followed by university. In the lower ranks a schooled boy might be apprenticed or simply join his father in the family business. A girl stayed at home and learned housecraft and needlework skills. Farmers' daughters joined women labourers in planting, harvesting and tending animals, but joined her mother spinning, cooking and nursing younger siblings, while brothers ploughed, reaped, herded animals, made and used tools, went to market and met the world. Once of marriageable age, whatever her rank, she might be contracted to a man of her father's choosing if profitable to the family, or remain at home unmarried as general help (i.e., an unpaid servant). If lucky she might go into service. While exposing her to innumerable risks, this could open up better prospects, allowing her to climb the ladder of service from housemaid to housekeeper. A prime fantasy was that she might attract her master's eldest son and marry him. In practice most parents were horrified at a son wishing to unite himself to a maidservant and gentry sons tended to see female servants as sexual provender, not marriage material. Girls from the governing ranks and bourgeoisie had fewer opportunities, so simply waited to be courted. Numbers from all ranks simply never married.

The tediousness of such limited horizons is well detailed in the eighteenth and nineteenth centuries, but the bored girls of the sixteenth and seventeenth centuries are relatively silent. Like their brothers, however, they had virtues to cultivate: piety, chastity, discretion, modesty, gentleness, decorum, prudence, diligence and industry. If from a comfortably-off family, she was expected to join her mother in charity visits to the poor and other almsgiving. Lower down the social ladder things were better as regards active occupation, for you were expected to work and earn money to contribute to the family income. Middle- and upper-rank girls had to do much sewing, embroidery, cutting out and assembling of clothes for younger siblings or for charity children. Thousands upon thousands must have agreed to marry the first man who offered, simply to escape to another life and a home of their own to run. There were differences between how the court treated women and how they were expected to behave elsewhere. Court women were perceived (often correctly) to be promiscuous, flattering, fawning (therefore manipulative and devious hypocrites), overly interested in clothes and show, given to gossip and rumour mongering, and generally flirtatious and frivolous. Aristo-gentry young women serving a country-based aristocratic lady had more chance to form reading/discussion groups.

There were differences in how men regarded and treated women and what was expected of them according to their rank. Common girls were regarded as skivvies and sexual prey, middling ones as sexual prey and sources of fortune. A girl from a titled family could not easily be predated sexually if she had kinsmen to take revenge, but she could be courted for her money, married and left at home to nurture the offspring. Many girls in the two upper tiers did receive a good education, depending as always on parental attitudes (the father particularly) and there was a swing towards humanist ideals that saw female education as essential for the next generation of wives and mothers.

Renaissance Improvements

Richard Mulcaster, first headmaster of Merchant Taylors' School, then high master of St Paul's School, strongly supported female education. His book, *Positions* (1581), declares that as 'our' closest 'companions', women should be 'well furnished in mind' and 'well strengthened in body'. Fathers have a 'duty' to educate their daughters. God 'require[s] an account for natural talents of both the parties, us for directing them; them for performance of our direction'. This alludes to the parable of the talents (Matthew 25:13–40; Luke 19:12–27) concerning one's God-given abilities. Mulcaster believed women's education should be selectively targeted towards strengthening virtue. He emphasized four essential skills: 'reading well, writing faire, singing sweet, playing fine', plus languages and drawing. Maths, science and divinity were less useful but not excluded. Women, he felt, were weak by nature, but education could strengthen the intellect and soul. Men should be educated 'without restraint for either matter or manner'. Countering the stereotypical view that women's education was neglected he asks:

> Do we not see in our country some of that sex so excellently well trained and so rarely qualified in regard both to the tongues themselves and to the subject matter contained in them, that they may be placed along with, or even above, the most vaunted paragons of Greece or Rome?[44]

How broadly spread was the education of girls in the upper and middling ranks is unquantifiable. While masses of boys went to grammar school then university, and scholarships, bursaries and endowments enabled poor scholars to receive an education otherwise beyond their reach, such institutional learning was generally unavailable to girls, and such home tutoring as was provided has left few examples of its existence except among high-status ladies of evident learning.

Henry VIII's daughters, Mary and Elizabeth, were naturally very well taught. Elizabeth, with her Latin, Greek, Hebrew, Italian and French, was one of the most learned rulers in Europe. Her speeches use rhetorical devices that display her classical learning, but she insisted that a prince's education should be useful to ruling the nation. The princesses were tutored by leading scholars, including Juan Vives, the Spanish humanist. Vives – conservative, wary of a classical education because some political-historical material was not suitable and the poetry of Ovid and Catullus immoral – based their curriculum on his *Instruction of a Christian Woman* (1524), broadened to include Erasmus's *Paraphrases* (1517–24) and More's *Utopia* (1516). He believed 'most of the vices of women [...] are the products of ignorance, whence they never read nor heard those excellent sayings and monitions of the Holy Fathers about chastity, about obedience, about silence, women's adornments and treasures'. Women had to be obedient to their duties, needed their morals shaped and their virtues developed – as did men. Only 'a little learning is required of women', while 'men must do many things in the world and must be broadly educated'.[45] Women should confine their reading to works on chastity. This betrays the anxiety about female sexuality. Men felt that independent female sexuality would lead to increased illegitimacy thus obscuring the fatherhood and confusing matters of inheritance, the central concern of patriarchally controlled marriage. Erasmus (*The Institution of Marriage*, 1526), friend of Sir Thomas More and key figure in developing Renaissance ideas, suggests education is more effective than needlework in banishing idleness, preserving virginity and enhancing matrimonial relationships.

It should not be assumed that humanist ideas greatly influenced James's court or spread very far outside. Young women attending court, already past the education stage, personalities and tastes already formed, usually had more worldly matters on their minds. Away from court there was a huge variety of attitudes among the country aristo-gentry as regards rearing and educating daughters. Learned education (Greek and Latin) was briefly fashionable for aristocratic girls from 1520–1560.[46] Thereafter it waned. Other positive influences did emerge, though again it is impossible to chart their influence. One was Castiglione's *Il Cortegiano* (1528; *The Courtier*, trans. Thomas Hoby, 1561). This important handbook suggested a little knowledge of 'letters' (classics, modern languages, history and literature) was acceptable for women, but that the social graces (playing music, singing, dancing, drawing/painting and needlework) were more civilized and made them more marriageable. Hoby claimed the book was 'to Ladies and Gentlewomen, a mirrour to decke and trimme themselves with vertuous conditions, comeley behaviours and honest entertainment toward all men'.[47] Castiglione also acknowledged, in some detail, that cultured education should be more than a mere social ornament for women. He strongly endorses their virtue and their potential for positive influence in a court. This new courtly ideal promoted the self-effacing but socially agreeable woman – witty, culture and, chaste. Renaissance courts could be centres of high culture but were also death traps of intrigue, plotting, power struggles, assassinations, political coups, rape and seduction . History evidenced this double-sidedness of culture and killing: for all the poetry, madrigals and dancing, executions, torture, the rise and fall of favourites, hothouse animosities and sexual intrigues made the English court (from Henry VIII to Charles I) like the set of a bloody play. Such events were too close to home for staging. Foreign settings or past history were protective masks, but the lessons were the same.

As evidence of some shift in attitudes to women, Thomas Campion (1567–1620) in his lyrical poems explores how restricted social opportunities encouraged a vigorous inner life, while men are easily distracted by the world's superficialities:

Women are confined to silence,
Loosing wisht occasion.
Yet our tongues then theirs, men,
Are apter to be moving,
Women are more dumbe then they,
But in their thoughts more roving.[48]

Female-authored literature was beginning to emerge. Lady Mary Wroth (c. 1586–c. 1651), from the high-status, literary Sidney family, wrote a sonnet sequence and the first known prose romance by an English woman. Both texts engage with the ongoing gender discourse. Elizabeth Carey (1585–1639), the first woman to write a history (of Edward II), also wrote the first female-authored tragedy. *The Tragedy of Mariam* (written 1602–04, published 1613), not intended for the commercial theatre but as a 'closet drama' to be read in domestic surroundings, contributes to the gender debate in contrasting the honest, principled Queen Mariam with the devious, promiscuous Princess Salome and presenting the violent absolutist patriarch King Herod. Another contributor to the man–woman question was Rachel Speght (c. 1597–?). A Calvinist minister's daughter, she entered the literary world with panache, stepping straight into gender discourse controversy. Aged 19, with her name boldly attached, scorning anonymity, she published *A Mouzell for Melastomus* (*A Muzzle for Blackmouth*, 1617), an articulate, spirited, clearly and logically argued attack on the bigoted misogyny of Joseph Swetnam's *Araignment of Lewde, Idle, Froward, and Unconstant Women* (1615). Biblical and classical references evince her religious background and education. Living at the centre of London commercial and clerical debate, she knew well the current polemical climate and had seen many examples of husband–wife co-operation among merchant families. She claims respect is due to women as children of God and sees the possibilities for companionate relationships between men and women. Her lively style, often akin to the acerbic, insulting, combative language of male pamphlet polemics, makes her work readable, while her ideas make it convincingly sympathetic and reasonable. Marriage is a true union and married couples 'as yoake-fellowes are to sustayne part of each others cares, griefs, and calamities'. 'Marriage is a merri-age, and this worlds Paradise, where there is mutuall love [...] husbands should not account their wives as vassals, but as those that are heires together of the grace of life.' As 'head' of his wife, the husband must protect her and lead her to Christ. To 'exclaime against Woman' is ingratitude to God.[49] Swetnam focuses on female vanity and lechery (traditional targets); Speght voices a new mood of companionship, shared piety and compromise between gender egotisms.

The entrenched history and literature of Catholic misogyny, with its horror of the physical filthiness (i.e., menstruation and childbirth) and spiritual sinfulness of women, passed into male thinking and persisted after the Reformation. In religious thought the body (a temporary house for the soul) was considered corrupt and its sinful needs and dirty functions were to be minimized so the spirit could be kept pure and nourished. Subject to fleshly temptations and the vagaries of emotion, human beings were a comic treasure. One of Castiglione's disputants says, 'In each one of us there is some seed of folly which, once it is stirred, can grow indefinitely.' Another remarks, 'Our bodily senses are so untrustworthy that they often confuse our judgement as well.'[50] Folly, the senses, unreliable judgement – in these are the sources of tragedy.

The virtue/sin, duty/desire conflicts produced a body of 'sex war' literature focusing on the persistent hostility between men and women – men as bullying, lascivious brutes (or gullible weaklings), women as devious, unreliable, bullying (shrewish) in their own way (or innocent victims). Shakespeare addresses the virago–virgin polarity in *The Comedy of Errors* (Adriana and Luciana), *The Taming of the Shrew* (Katherine and Bianca) and *Much Ado About Nothing* (Beatrice and Hero). The trickiness of women sources comedy, while their evil is fitting for tragedy. The polarities are clear in the kite/tiger/wolf/monster sisters and the gentle sensitivity of Cordelia. *King Lear* says little of gender directly, but many negative implications resonate round the words and actions of Goneril and Regan. Both sisters are white devils – a common metaphor for hypocrites who disguised their evil. Though their flattery, their 'glib and oily art', is pointed out to the king by Kent and Cordelia, he is too angry (and too foolish) to recognize it. Their pretended love triggers the action and they quickly reveal their true selves in the ensuing scenes in horrific behaviour that pushes Lear past the emotional limits of sanity. The sisters are a study in the evil that females can perform. Shakespeare had often presented the failings of women, but deep evil had only been explored through Queen Tamora's cruelty (*Titus Andronicus*, c. 1588–93) and Queen Margaret, a 'she-wolf' with a 'tiger's heart wrapp'd in a woman's hide' (*Henry VI*, 1590–1592). His other great study of female evil, Lady Macbeth, appeared contemporaneously with *Lear*. His last plays project more positive, romantically idealized images of women through Hermione, Paulina and Perdita (*The Winter's Tale*), Imogen (*Cymbeline*), Thaisa and Marina (*Pericles*) and Miranda (*The Tempest*).

Men had ambivalent, contradictory views of women. As the source of human sin they needed controlling to minimize their opportunities for tempting men. A multiplicity of pejorative terms – virago, termagant, shrew, Whore of Babylon, hussy, wagtail, punk and more – provides the lexical markers of male suspicion. In opposition to the Eve/Delilah/Jezebel image, medieval Courtly Love projected an idealized woman of beauty, intelligence, elegance and chastity, while Mariolatry raised the Virgin Mary to an archetype of gentle, sympathetic womanhood and loving, nurturing motherhood, partially redeeming women. Mary became a key human intercessor in approaching Christ, an icon of the respect men should have for women. In loving a woman you re-expressed your love and respect for your mother, showing the love you first learned from her. Martin Luther asserted Mary was 'the highest woman' and 'we can never honour her enough [...].

The veneration of Mary is inscribed in the very depths of the human heart.'[51] While lauding Mary's model status, Luther made very derogatory remarks about women in general.[52] Despite some easing of extreme patriarchy and improvements in the status of women, negative views persisted and progress was slow.

Medieval hagiographies (lives of saints) celebrated the virtues of women martyrs, but Protestantism banned statues, days, prayers, oaths and relics associated with saints. Mary too was downgraded so that faith could focus on Christ. This hampered the assimilation into Protestant doctrine of any ideology applauding women, though veneration of Mary persisted in people's private faith.[53] A small amount of literature iconized particularly virtuous women and applauded romantic, reasonable and affectionate relationships. From the medieval period there are Chaucer's *Legend of Good Women* and *The Book of the Duchesse*,[54] and more recently Sir Thomas Elyot's *The Defence of Good Women* (1540) and Spenser's *The Faerie Queene* (1590 and 1596). Notable continental contributions include Boccaccio's *De Mulieribus Claris* (*Of Famous Women*, 1374) and Castiglione's *Il Cortegiano*, where, despite sharp misogynistic interruptions, Guiliano de Medici constructs the idealized court lady, ably acknowledges female capacity for virtue and illustrates his case with classical and contemporary examples. There are the scattered references to courageous, faithful women in the Bible, but generally all churches were suspicious of sex and passion, encouraged men to control their own and female appetites and warned them against women as provokers of lust. Men were thought to be more rational, while women were more emotional and vulnerable to fleshly temptations. Polemic writing tended to highlight female failings. Literature uses the constant interplay of tension between the positive aspects (affection and love) of the appetites and the dangers of following them to excessive lengths. Love was seen as a madness, an illness caught from women. For Castiglione, 'The emotions of love provide excuse for every kind of fault.'[55] In *A Midsummer Night's Dream*, Theseus describes love's insanity:

> Lovers and madmen have such seething brains,
> Such shaping fantasies, that apprehend
> More than cool reason ever comprehends. (V. i. 4–5)

Burton has much to say of the dangers of love:

> If it rage, it is no more Love, but burning Lust, a Disease, Phrensy, Madness, Hell. 'Tis death, 'tis an immedicable calamity, 'tis a raging madness, 'tis no virtuous habit this, but a vehement perturbation of the mind, a monster of nature, wit, and art.[56]

The Church of England's *Second Book of Homilies* (1571), which vicars used for sermons, included 'On the State of Matrimony', defining the church's views on women and how fathers and husbands, being in authority over them and being more rational beings, should approach them:

The woman is a weak creature not endued with like strength and constancy of mind; therefore, they be the sooner disquieted, and they be the more prone to all weak affections and dispositions of mind, more than men be; and lighter they be, and more vain in their fantasies and opinions.

They were 'the weaker vessell, of a frail heart, inconstant, and with a word soon stirred to wrath'. A commentary in Matthew's Bible (1537) says that men, being intellectually stronger and in authority, had a duty to ensure their women conformed to the demand for chastity and modest behaviour. If a woman was 'not obedient and helpful to him, [he may] beat the fear of God into her head, and that thereby she may be compelled to learn her duty and do it'. Corporal punishment was common in the Renaissance. Whores and criminals were publicly whipped, children caned at home and school, wives and servants beaten.[57] The Bible exhorts wives to be in subjection to their husbands, counterbalancing this by requiring that the husband should honour the wife and that they should have 'compassion one of another' (I Peter 3:8). Bishop Aylmer gave a sermon before Queen Elizabeth, outlining the best and worst aspects of women, in polarities evident in Shakespeare and most other dramatists:

Women are of two sorts: some of them are wiser, better learned, discreeter, and more constant than a number of men; but another and worse sort of them are fond (simple), foolish, wanton, flibbergibs, tattlers, triflers, wavering, witless, without council, feeble, careless, rash, proud, dainty (fussy), tale-bearers, eavesdroppers, rumour-raisers, evil-tongued, worse-minded, and in every way doltified with the dregs of the devil's dunghill.[58]

Legally women had few rights. Neither did most ordinary men, but they had the key ones.

There were some shifts in behaviour, but how far they penetrated society as a whole is unclear. The sixteenth century saw an increase in stern patriarchy as regards marital and parental relations. In the seventeenth century there were countermovements against both. Imperceptibly slowly, the stern, patriarchal, authoritarian father became more affectionate and considerate.

Stone charts the gradual emergence of the more companionate marriage and more affective family relations: 'For a considerable period, two conflicting trends were at work at the same time, and the growing authority of the husband can only be seen in a relatively pure form during the first half of the sixteenth century.'[59]

Playwrights hint at the hope for harmonious, loving marriages at the end of comedies, but within them tend to use the dramatic possibilities of conflict between the sexes. Offering more opportunities for humour, tension and the exploration of violent emotions, it is better theatre. In George Wilkins's *The Miseries of Enforced Marriage* (1607), the character Ilford captures the dramatic potential of the sex war: 'Women are the purgatory of men's purses, the paradise of their bodies, and the hell of their minds: marry none of them. Women are in churches saints, abroad angels, at home devils.'[60]

Romeo and Juliet, widely regarded as the archetypal romance, shows the dangers of transgressing normative behaviour. Rejecting parental wishes and the tribal allegiances demanded of a male-originated interfamily feud, they are punished for taking secret actions that break the law. Juliet transgresses by disobedience (rejecting her father's marriage plans), then illegally marries without parental consent. Following her own will she suffers the consequences. Conversely, the Capulet parents are punished for failing to take into consideration their daughter's rejection of their choice of husband. Undeservedly the lovers fall victims of a climate of hate and violence. Cordelia transgresses the normative expectation of obedience to her father. Her rationale is clear to Kent (and the audience), but to her father her frank realism is disobedience that publicly humiliates him.

John Marston, part of Shakespeare's circle, worked in the same areas of problematic moral ambivalence central to *Measure for Measure* and touched on in *Lear*. In *The Dutch Courtesan* (1604), Freevill (his name conflating evil/freedom/free will), a libertine, tries to terminate his relationship with the courtesan Franceschina so he can marry Beatrice, a respectable, wealthy heiress. He passes the whore to his friend Malheureux ('the misfortunate one'), who tries to repress his powerful sexual feelings. Freevill and Malheureux represent two significant forces in contemporary society: traditional male unfettered sexuality and the newer moral code of Puritanism attempting to control the sex impulse. The tension between these and the ambiguities clustered round them (including the hypocrisy of appearing virtuous while hiding immorality) are subjects Lear is drawn to in his madness. Franceschina admits, 'Woman corrupted is the worst of devils' (*The Dutch Courtesan*, II. ii. 201). Her remark has relevance wider than London's sex trade and applies to Goneril's behaviour and male demonizing of women. Shakespeare presents the other side of this argument when the hitherto strict Angelo, feeling the prickings of lust, asks, 'The tempter, or the tempted, who sins most, ha?' (*Measure for Measure*, II. ii. 164). Lear's comments on female sexuality, Gloucester's adultery and the ubiquity of sexual activity ('Let copulation thrive'), glance at the natural transgressiveness of the human sex drive, coalescing relevantly within the context of how a rule once broken opens the potential for moral mayhem. Goneril and Regan, having once committed sin, find it easy to commit others. After public lies, dishonouring their father, a cruel maiming, contemplation of adultery and murder follow easily. The degree of transgression against Christian ethics and common decency is summed up in Cordelia's simple, heartfelt comments as she surveys the sleeping Lear:

> Was this a face
> To be oppos'd against the warring winds?
> [...]
> Mine enemy's dog,
> Though he had bit me, should have stood that night
> Against my fire. (IV. vii.)

In different ways Marston, Jonson, Shakespeare and others explored the difficulties of trying to avoid sin and keep to the path of good. While others mocked the pretensions and greed of contemporary London through their theatrical satires, Shakespeare dives deep into human depravity and cruelty in a setting that is universal, removed from identifiable topical references, but still with targets that relate to his time and his audience.

Men could be victims too. George Wilkins's play *The Miseries of Enforced Marriage* (1607) uses the true story of William Calverley, who, provoked by his wife's denying he was their children's father and the fear she was planning his death, severely wounded her and murdered two of his three children. This play, like *Lear*, shows that women are supremely capable of verbal and psychological abuse and not incapable of committing or commissioning murder. *Arden of Faversham* (1592) is an early example and Lady Macbeth a powerful later one.

While Elizabethan-Jacobean dramatists display considerable sympathy for women in a male-dominated world and present their wit, virtue and sprightliness, they are also alert to women's fierce brutality and display how disturbingly similar it is to men's.

Chapter 7

MAN IN HIS PLACE

First walk in thy vocation,
And do not seek thy lot to change.[1]

By God's will you were born into a particular rank (your 'lot' in life). You were expected to know your place, keep it and work at whatever calling came within the scope of your family's position. Any family might rise, through hard work and God's grace. Small status improvements were not too disturbing for one's neighbours, but great success would provoke envious suspicion of overreaching ambition. Doubts about the means by which you rose might arouse accusations of bribery, magic or devilish assistance, people being all too ready to take the Bible's point of view: 'He that maketh haste to be rich shall not be innocent' (Proverbs 28:20). The industrious, careful man, slowly improving his position, was safe from negative gossip: 'Wealth gotten by vanity shall be diminished: but he that gathereth by labour shall increase' (Proverbs 13:11). The rapid increase in bourgeois wealth created an interplay between envy, condemnation of luxury, suspicion of avarice and dishonesty, and fears of an upstart, ambitiously aspirational group rivalling the traditional ruling class.

Elizabethans and Jacobeans were highly suspicious of social movement. If God made the world, putting each man in his place, to alter your standing was to defy God's will. A poor man becoming poorer was thought punished for some unnamed sin and becoming richer could be a reward for hard work, but becoming very rich (and amassing huge fortunes) displayed greed and probable dishonesty. Some argued that God gave men abilities or talents and expected men to use them. If you climbed out of your birth rank and bettered yourself then you were doing God's will and worshipping him by developing the talents he gave you. This was a popular view among the Non-conformists for whom the work ethic was central. They believed in hard work and thrift, and accepted the idea of making money. But a rise in fortunes, place and public status should not be accompanied by a complacent attitude to making money at any cost. It had to be ethical and the amounts within reason. Excessive gains should be redistributed through charities and the moneymaker and his family should avoid arrogance, ostentation and snobbery – in theory.[2] A hard-working shop assistant might marry the shopkeeper's daughter or his widow, he might rise to wealth and become master of his guild or a town councillor, but he was expected to give thanks by charitable donations and to remain humble. Education could help a poor man's son to a government clerkship. Talented, active men could rise, particularly if they earned the patronage of someone of note and power. They could fall too if they became too grasping or followed a favourite who fell out of favour. As the Fool counsels Kent: 'Let go thy hold when a great wheel runs down a hill, lest it break thy neck with following it. But the great one that goes up the hill, let him draw thee after' (II. iv.)

Nevertheless, conservative thinking was uneasy about social mobility and extreme reversals (*peripeteia* and *nemesis*) or improvements (*hubris*) in rank portrayed onstage were seen as omens of impending disaster and social implosion might engulf everyone.[3] In *Lear* we see such subversive moves, and pushy ambition is seen as sin. Central to the disasters is the king's unclear status once he has shaken off 'all cares and business'. This uncertainty encourages Goneril and Regan's transgressive assumption of superiority over Lear. The Fool alludes to this subversion of the normal order numerous times in terms starkly expressing its unnaturalness: 'Thou mad'st thy daughters thy mothers […] gav'st them the rod and putt'st down thine own breeches' (I. iv.). The Elizabethan-Jacobean fear of such disorders spreading is an essential part of the imagery and meaning of *Lear*. Oswald's ambitions follow Goneril's lead. There is Edmund's plot to topple his legitimate brother, Kent's role as royal messenger disrespected, a servant killing a duke, a duke torturing and maiming another nobleman, a steward contemplating murdering an earl, a captain hanging a princess. Though some followers remain loyal to Lear, others leave him. The orderliness of society is being shattered.

Traditional family order being destroyed through subversion of hierarchy is echoed elsewhere. In *Eastward Ho!* the goldsmith's daughter, obsessed with becoming a knight's wife, contemplates the pleasure of superiority over her father: 'He must call me daughter no more now; but "Madam", and, "please you Madam", and, "please your worship, Madam", indeed' (III. ii. 63–5). Gertrude's subversiveness is suitably punished. She marries Sir Petronel Flash for title and property, but finds he resembles his name – all show, no substance, no castle, no money. He marries her for her wealth. Each has cheated the other and their pride is humbled. In addition to pride and ambition, Gertrude and Goneril show extreme disrespect to their fathers, thus striking at the very root of social order and breaking a Commandment.

Movement was not always upward. In the seventeenth century a third to a half of the population existed at subsistence level and suffered acute unemployment. The majority of the lower sort suffered hardship relatively stoically, but the urban underclass was always a worrying barrel of gunpowder easily ignited. Regular outbreaks of riot occurred, in London particularly. At the other end of the scale increasing numbers of merchants, financiers, manufacturers and industrialists were becoming wealthier than some established aristo-gentry families, copying elite cultural habits, seeking titles, estates and political power.[4] This aspiration frightened the ruling ranks. The bourgeois elite was well educated, and with male literacy improving life-enhancement possibilities expanded. The middling sort was unstoppably on the move. Though the very poorest remained poor, their numbers increasing due to enclosures and inflation, those able to struggle upwards to literacy, and thereby to effective commercial activity, were also increasing. This widened the divide between those succeeding and the underclass in an irreversible downward spiral. Capitalism's growth created many different new levels of social sophistication and increased the need for minutely observed differentiations to distinguish between people. A merchant's wife affording to dress as well and in the same fashions as a lady at court triggered the normal responses – anger, contempt and the search for finer status identifiers to enable those with established rank to feel superior to upstarts.

Lear is largely concerned with the upper echelons. There is opposition between the old order (Gloucester and Kent) rallying to the king and the new (Goneril, Cornwall, Edmund) briefly cohering to destroy the king's power. In Oswald we have a social climber prepared to behave badly in order to gain advancement from the upcoming power. There is criticism of abuses by established powerbrokers – justices, beadles, usurers, lawyers (the 'furred robes and gowns') – and a proto-socialist concern for the 'poor naked wretches' of the underclass. In the real world of the 1600s voices were beginning to speak for the lower orders. At the end of his progress south James I arrived at Theobalds, Robert Cecil's magnificent palace north of London. There he was handed the 'Poor Man's Petition'. Demanding the new king promise religious uniformity and purify public life, it particularly attacks the legal profession: 'A pox take the proud covetous Attorney and merciless lawyer! […] Fye upon all close biting knaverie!'[5]

Successful men, their wives and their families tended to display their newfound luxury in extravagant dress and lavishly decorated houses. Conspicuous consumption and ostentatious showing-off through clothes, carriages, horses, furniture and expensive banquets were all forms of vanity.

The many mocking representations onstage of the purse-proud *nouveaux riches* had little effect. Sumptuary laws to control expenditure and regulate the types of clothing worn and the amounts/types of food consumed by the different ranks were established in the Middle Ages, updated by Henry VIII and extended by Elizabeth I. Officially claiming to restrain vain, wasteful habits and protect English trade, they were also an attempt to maintain the visual differences of rank. A titled lady felt angrily diminished if a citizen's wife wore as costly an outfit as she. A citizen's wife felt angrily diminished if her maid sported ruffs and rings like herself. As everywhere else, there was hierarchy – in the fur trimming permitted for your level in society, in the fabric you could wear, in the headgear and the jewellery. Dressing 'above your station' looked like pride. The laws were designed to discourage someone from one station imitating the manners and appearance of another, but were frankly a form of social control and means of identifying a person's rank, reinforcing the distinctions between the nobility and the up-and-coming entrepreneurial groups. Women and the lower orders were the main targets. Attempts to regulate extravagant expenditure on clothes by aspiring, fashion- and status-conscious bourgeois women were put in moral terms stressing restraint and humility. The regulation of the working man's clothing was meant to reinforce his awareness of his lowly status. Elizabeth I's 1574 law described the craze for fine show as

> the wasting and undoing of a great number of young gentlemen, otherwise serviceable, and others seeking by show of apparel to be esteemed as gentlemen, who, allured by the vain show of those things, do not only consume themselves, their goods, and lands which their parents left unto them, but also run into such debts and shifts as they cannot live out of danger of laws without attempting unlawful acts.

The terms 'show', 'vain', 'consume' and 'debts' suggest disapproval based on medieval ideas of moderation and evoke the Deadly Sins and stereotypes linking suitability of behaviour to rank. Gender, income and rank were the criteria that decided what you could wear. Thus dress signifiers identified social rank and preserved 'degree'. But the harsh punishments for infringements were largely ignored and, being simply unenforceable, the Sumptuary Laws were repealed in 1603–04. This is the context for Kent's complaint that 'such a slave should wear a sword,/Who wears no honesty' (II. ii.). Wearing a sword was the prerogative of gentlemen and gentlemen were supposed to be open, honest and respectful. Oswald is none of these. Kent calls him a 'knave' who knows 'no reverence' (respect), thus condemning him as a low servant and dishonest rogue. This is part of the play's matrix of good and bad characters, the confrontation between old values and new, and the transgression of established 'degree'. It also snipes at the sham gentlefolk in the audience, whose money, clothes and flattery had gained them an entrée to court circles. In 1583 Philip Stubbes remarked on:

> such a confused mingle mangle of apparel [...] that it is verie hard to know who is noble, who is worshipful, who is a gentleman, who is not; for you shall have those [...] go daylie in silkes, velvets, satens, damasks, taffeties and suchlike, notwithstanding that they be both base by byrthe, meane by estate & servile by calling. This is a great confusion & a general disorder, God be mercifull unto us.[6]

King Lear, a play about barriers being crossed, is full of references to clothing as both social marker and means of disguise, hiding the truth of what you are, but also a means of finding out what other people truly are. Edgar's disguise enables him to learn of his father's love for him and strengthen his own spirit through adversity. The king's madness is a sort of disguise too, as are the flowers in which he later decks himself, hiding his outer self and letting the subconscious emerge. The process allows him to express previously unacknowledged assessments of the society round him and see it for what it corruptly is. Apart from his comment on Oswald's filthy worsted (not silk) stockings, Kent's declaration that 'a tailor made thee' directly hits at the tendency of non-gentlemen to buy a suit to make them look like a gentleman courtier. Such clothing charades could gull a young heiress's family (bourgeois or titled) into accepting you as a son-in-law, as with Sir Petronel Flash. Misleading appearance applied higher up the power pyramid. Brachiano in *The White Devil* suggests the Duke of Florence is all show:

> [...] all his reverend wit
> Lies in his wardrobe; he's a discreet fellow
> When he's made up in his robes of state. (II. i. 189–91)

This reminds us of Lear's remark, 'A dog's obey'd in office' (IV. vi.). People perceive and treat you according to your robes and accoutrements of office, regardless of the fool or knave you might actually be: 'Robes and furr'd gowns hide all' (IV. vi.). From earl's son, courtier, possible companion to the king, Edgar transforms himself into a near-naked beggar, then a peasant, then an armed warrior, then back to himself. His speech changes, using different lexical patterns and registers to mark his gradual resurrection. These devices keep him hidden. His admission, 'in nothing am I chang'd/But in my garments', superficially to reassure Gloucester that he is still Poor Tom, is a declaration to the audience that his essential goodness is unchanged despite his beggar's clothing. The kindness of the poor is presented through a servant intervening to prevent Gloucester's blinding and two more binding his wounds and arranging for an old man to put him in the care of 'the Bedlam'. Low status does not prevent you being virtuous. Castiglione remarks that while some 'of the most noble blood, have been wicked in the extreme' there were 'many of humble birth, who, through their virtues, have won glory for their descendants'.[7]

Each man was guardian of his own soul, his own virtues, and responsible for his own sins. But he was a member of other associations to whom he owed loyalty and responsibility – his family, village, trade or craft, county, nation, church humanity and the whole of human creation. Family and community were the strongest bonds, though faith might take precedence and separate him from these commitments. Each man, from king to pauper, occupied a place in the detailed stratification of society. The whole theory of natural order was based on harmony. Each rank, whether high or low, had its part to play if concord and perfect working were to be achieved.

> This is the true ordering of the state of a well-fashioned commonwealth, that every part do obey one head, or governor, one law, as all parts of the body obey the head, agree among themselves, and one not to eat up the other through greediness, but that we see order, moderation, and reason bridle the affections.[8]

This theory of order and orderliness was conceived by those who gave the orders and wished to preserve degree. Rulers were the brains and heart, the nobles the important organs. The others – the limbs – had little else to do but obey. But the analogy is false. Society is not a body. Cut off the head, the body dies. Cut off the king's head or remove the aristocracy, society continues with a new political settlement. The Civil War would show that.

Chapter 8

IMAGES OF DISORDER:
THE RELIGIOUS CONTEXT

The sixteenth and seventeenth centuries were undeniably religious ages. Religion impacted all lives to varying degrees. The Church of England, present in everyone's life, was an arm of the established power that ruled England. The parish church, often on the edge of the village green (with the inn and the local lord or gentleman's manor house), was visible from the fields as you worked. Its bells punctuated your day. In the city your parish church was likewise nearby. The priest would be visibly haggling in the market like anyone else, perhaps occupying a corner of the local tavern. He was part of the civic power structure as well as sitting in judgement over your spiritual life. He reported your civil and moral misdemeanours, convened and presided over the church court, arranged poor relief and preached. One form of socio-moral reinforcement was the homily the priest was obliged by his superiors to read out every Sunday. The *Book of Homilies* (the first published 1547, the second in 1571) had 33 homilies intended to bed in the ideas of the new reformed Church of England, to educate the masses and to assist conformity. They covered doctrinal and liturgical subjects but included moral sermons: 'Against Peril of Idolatry', 'Against Gluttony and Drunkenness', 'Against Excess of Apparel', 'Of Alms [charity] Deeds', 'Of the State of Matrimony', 'Against Idleness', 'Against Disobedience and Wilful Rebellion'.

Religion meant much to the Jacobeans, but not all those who attended church did so in a spirit of devotion. Many went simply to avoid the various punishments meted out for non-attendance, but 'there was no escaping the rhythms of the Prayer Book or the barrage of catechisms and sermons'.[1] This was a largely churchgoing society, though there had always been those who claimed (and believed) they needed no church or priest to intercede between them and God. Increasingly, Dissenters were resisting enforced church attendance, declaring they could worship in the field, the workshop or their home. One sailor asserted in 1581, 'It was never merry England since we were impressed to come to church.'[2] It was a criminal offence to not attend on Sunday, though pursuit and prosecution of absentees depended on the zeal of the vicar. In London, large and anonymous, it was more difficult for parish officers to keep checks on local inhabitants, especially the constantly changing lodgers in the crowded tenements. Sunday worship was theoretically a time of communal affirmation of shared beliefs and values. That excludes those parishioners with rather different thoughts in their heads while the parson exhorted them to virtue and led their mumbled responses. There would always be some doctrinally opposed to Anglicanism. Though everyone was nominally Church of England, some in the congregation would be Catholics conforming to the law, others Puritans passively conforming while having more radical and aggressive beliefs about which they were mostly, but not always, quiet. Increasingly there were hostile interactions in the church that created simmering grievances in the outside community. Some vicars were too zealously reformist, some too lazily traditionalist.[3] Some Dissenters separated from the official church and formed their own unofficial congregations. These were illegal and the congregants subject to dispersal, fines or arrest.[4] There were those who, indifferent to religion, called themselves Christian but did not allow faith to interfere with life more than necessary. There were atheists, though they tended to keep their views to themselves (or share them only with likeminded others); denial of God was punishable by arrest, interrogation, torture and imprisonment.[5] Some there would always be more concerned with the pint of ale in the inn after the boredom of the sermon was over. Some chatted, snoozed, made mocking comments on the priest and his sermon, laughed aloud, flirted or transacted business.[6] Others would be more preoccupied with thoughts about the opposite sex seated across the aisle. Finally, there were those who had genuine faith in the Anglican Church and lived their lives in as holy and virtuous a way as possible. It is impossible to say what proportion of the population at any one time fell into these categories. The parish church was a place where the community's social and religious differences were reinforced as much as the shared Christianity.

The arrangement, style and comfort of the pews reflected hierarchy. Finely decorated, cushioned box pews with carved coats of arms on the door were for the squire's family who owned it. The rich and powerful sat near the front, the poor at the very back on benches or standing. The arrival of the gentry might even be accompanied by the congregation standing and bowing as they passed. But the pernickety niceties of snobbery aside, the service was intended as a celebration of solidarity and a reminder of the demands and sacrifices faith and virtue required. There overarching zeitgeist was religious, though like a rainbow it was of many colours. Despite the various forms of internal, external, silent and vocal opposition to imposed worship, most English men and women were regular churchgoers and those who were not, those who moved away from their village community to the anonymity of the city, would nevertheless have the vestiges of religious upbringing and the remnants of biblical teachings still in their memories. Bacon identified the causes of troubles in states:

[…] innovation in religion, taxes, alteration of laws and customs, breaking of privileges, general oppression, advancement of unworthy persons, strangers, dearths, disbanded soldiers, factions grown desperate, and whatsoever in offending people joineth and knitteth them in common cause.[7]

All of these and more were operative in James's England. Some are present in *Lear*.

Another part of this systematic structure under attack in *Lear* was the orderliness of nature. Psalm 19, 'The heavens declare the Glory of God and the firmament showeth his handiwork', expresses the idea that the natural world and cosmos are fantastically complex yet orderly, with each part of the system working and doing its allotted job, and that all this is God's doing. In *Lear* not only do the human young turn upon the old, a savage enough act overturning established order, but the old too display transgressive traits, and nature itself turns rebel. The unusually violent storm reminds men how fragile are their lives, how vulnerable their bodies, how precarious their security. There is savagery in the animal images that abound in the play and many metaphors of animal cruelty and references to monsters rise from the psyche to haunt the imagination and disturb one's peace of mind. This creates a mood of wildness and disorder, a lack of harmony that disrupts the peacefulness of each creature in its place – a reminder that the world of men is little different from the brutal and sometimes excessively bloodthirsty animal world.

Unsettling Questions

Astronomers contributed to the gradual dismantling of the Ptolemaic system, but plays too could unsettle. Audiences watching the Admiral's Men perform Marlowe's *Tamburlaine the Great* (1587) at the Rose would have heard Alleyne declaim:

Our souls, whose faculties can comprehend
The wondrous architecture of the world
And measure every wand'ring planet's course,

Still climbing after knowledge infinite
And always moving as the restless spheres,
Wills us to wear ourselves and never rest
Until we reach the ripest fruit of all,
That perfect bliss and sole felicity,
The sweet fruition of an earthly crown. (Part I. II. vii. 21–9)

This combines traditional views – man's distinguishing faculties of understanding that separate him from the animals, the glory of God's creation (the 'always moving [...] restless spheres') – with progressive, dangerously blasphemous views on man's restless search for knowledge that trespassed into the secrets of the divine. The final idea is unusual, for instead of seeing 'perfect bliss and sole felicity' as spiritual, a heavenly crown, Tamburlaine's goal is the 'earthly crown' of supreme material power – a very Renaissance ambition. This is the work of a restless, enquiring, turbulent young university man writing for an audience that would include some fairly sophisticated members. But most of England's population was rural – landless farmworkers and small subsistence farmers with beliefs still primitive, basic and medieval. Many large-scale landholders, farmers and nobles were similar. Centuries of Catholicism could not be erased overnight. Changes of thinking take several generations when few people can read, do not have access to academic research, and in any case have closed minds. There was no organized dissemination of news; regular newspapers did not appear until the Civil War. New ideas in medicine, politics and science always provoked opposition and the church always stood in the way of the free sharing of intellectual ideas, especially if they threatened orthodoxy. There was also the normal monumental public resistance to change. Most of the population was exceptionally conservative. Ignorance, fear and intellectual inertia played their parts as always. The Reformation changed the official outer world, but the private inner world of daily life and its cluster of beliefs lagged far behind. The Reformation had many fervent supporters, but was grafted onto a residue of long-ingrained beliefs and practices. Individuals, devoted to their faith, might publicly conform to the new rites and liturgy of Anglicanism while still privately crossing themselves, praying to a favourite saint or performing little acts of superstition.

The lines between magic and acceptable doctrine remained as blurred as they ever had been, but, given the growing print culture, and the spread of verbatim knowledge of what the Bible said, controversial debates sprang up as to what was orthodox and what was heresy, iconoclasm, superstition, idolatry, papist mumbo-jumbo or diabolic magic. Services in English made doctrine more accessible, and as Anglicanism settled, versions of the translated Bible became more readily available and individuals could read for themselves the words that were the basis of a priest's hitherto unique quasi-mystical interaction with his congregation. This newfound capacity for personal interpretation allowed many doctrinally divergent views to spring up and worry the Anglican hierarchy. In response bishops became more repressive, demanding greater conformity from vicars and parishioners. Episcopal repression only hardened Non-conformists' determination, though Puritanism's rise was slow. The Puritan drive to change religious thinking was regarded with irritation and new ideas in medicine, politics and science always provoked opposition. Puritans are almost always figures of fun and derided as hypocrites in plays. The mass of people just wanted to continue living as they had always done. Regardless of this conservatism, seismic shifts were rumbling in many aspects of life. John Donne in 'An Anatomy of the World' (1611) declares:

[…] new Philosophy calls all in doubt,
The Element of fire is quite put out;
The Sun is lost, and th'earth, and no man's wit
Can well direct him where to look for it.
And freely men confess that this world's spent,
When in the Planets, and the Firmament
They seek so many new; then see that this
Is crumbled out again to his Atomies.
'Tis all in pieces, all coherence gone;
All just supply, and all Relation:
Prince, Subject, Father, Son, are things forgot.

The Ptolemaic system represented to people the order of God, a divine harmony, a reassuring coherence. To hear it questioned, to hear of old beliefs discarded by new science, was destabilizing. Forcing doubts into people's heads took them out of their comfort zone, in an age already full of changes, with a new religion, a new king, new worlds being discovered, new economic practices, new towns growing (and creating new problems), and old feudal relationships breaking down. These are the undercurrents which would feed the audience's responses to *Lear*, even when that audience was an elite, cocooned, wealthy gathering. To see a kingdom and its king crumble (with a king present), two families tearing themselves apart, was disturbing. Family was the commonest, closest bond for everyone. Family history, family honour and family loyalty were central to the thinking and feeling of those watching. The tearing apart of accepted family bonds, the vile cruelty released within two families, the toppling of the throne, might partially explain why *Lear* has never been a popular play. It is too painful to see taken-for-granted relationships called into question, especially if the questions suggest family love is a thin veneer of pretence.

By the end of the play Lear's world is in pieces. There is a hint that normality and order will return and society be reassembled. But with the king, Gloucester, Kent and Cordelia dead will it ever be the same? Albany, who finally finds a voice to condemn her behaviour, responds to his wife's death:

> This judgement of the heavens, that makes us tremble,
> Touches us not with pity. (V. iii.)

The Aristotelian requirement that tragedy evoke pity means pity for Lear and Cordelia, not the evildoers. Albany suggests to Kent and Edgar:

> Friends of my soul, you twain
> Rule in this realm, and the gor'd state sustain. (V. iii.)

Kent rules himself out and it is Edgar who, despite the simple platitudes of his closing speech, seems to be assuming the crown. 'The king is dead, long live the king' was the age-old cry whenever a monarch died, expressing the urgent need to feel continuity, rule and unbroken order. Those who knew Holinshed's *Chronicles* knew that breaks in the smooth running of royal power meant danger, and handovers or takeovers by new dynasties meant difficult times. Though not written in historically chronological order, the sequence of Shakespeare's history plays amply displayed the almost neurotic, natural desire for order and peace. Political vacuums were dangerous, usually bloody and put into perspective the desperate anxieties surrounding a queen's pregnancy and the nervous wait for a hoped-for male heir. With no son the succession question would have seemed unclear even if Cordelia had not said 'Nothing'. Some audience members had experienced the traumas of the Tudor continuities and discontinuities. All remembered the recent shift into the Stuart line. Change was disturbing. From God to Earth's dust, everything had its place. Man, his communities and states, were part of that orderliness. The fast-changing, apparently disintegrating world was disorientating to Jacobeans, and the court was an increasing source of order-threatening discontent.

The court audience collided with the difference between theory and reality, the discrepancy between what we would like to think and what we know is the truth. 'The great and the good' is how assemblies of various leaders were described. Yet we know that most of those so called were neither great nor good because they were morally compromised – flattering, lying, cheating, sleeping or buying their way to the top – and were as susceptible to vice's temptations as the lowest in society. Peck states, 'Appointments to office and promotion were made through patronage and connections; officeholders were paid by those requiring their services. [...] An informal market grew up for the buying and selling of offices and their reversions, with the profits going to the officeholders, not the Crown.'[8]

Rats had got into the corn store. These are the 'simulars of virtue' who could 'plate' their 'sin with gold'. A disturbing feature of *Lear* is the series of speeches that undermine belief in the leaders of society. The seer-king, wisely mad, penetrates the disguises by which sinners in positions of power hide their faults while acting as exemplars of right conduct.

> [...] see how yond justice rails upon yond simple thief. [...] change places,
> and handy-dandy, which is the justice, which is the thief?
> [...]
> Thou rascal beadle, hold thy bloody hand!
> Why doest thou lash that whore? Strip thine own back.
> Thou hotly lusts to use her in that kind
> For which thou whipp'st her. The usurer hangs the cozener.
> Through tattered clothes small vices do appear;
> Robes and furr'd gowns hide all. (IV. vi.)

The disorderliness of courtiers was a common cause for concern, as was the unprofessional conduct of judges and justices of the peace. On 11 July 1604, Sir Philip Gawdy, MP described the Commons Speaker addressing the problem of

> Justices of Peace of wch ther wer two kyndes he founde great fault withal, the one wer such as go downe into the country, and presently fall to hawking, and other sportes, and yf any man comme about Justice, they sende him to their next neybur Justice; the others be suche as put downe one alehouse, and set vp two for it, set up one constable, and put down an other, and yf any matter be stirring whatsoeuer he must haue an ore in it.[9]

There was no shortage of examples of hypocrisy to draw upon but the double standard of the apparently virtuous public man whose personal life is vicious may have been suggested by a Stratford incident involving the town bailiff. Daniel Baker, a prominent Puritan, was excommunicated by the town's church court for failing to attend a hearing to answer the charge of getting a woman pregnant then breaching his promise to marry her.[10] Apparent probity masking private corruption is a recurrent theme in drama, in the court and in real life. Part of the play's development is stripping back appearances and exposing the realities hidden beneath. Many ladies would have felt embarrassed awkwardness at his comment:

> Behold yond simpering dame,
> Whose face between her forks presages snow;
> That minces virtue, and does shake the head
> To hear of pleasure's name.
> The fitchew nor the soiled horse goes to't
> With more riotous appetite. (IV. vi.)

Court ladies were not well known for their purity. Did Burbage's eyes or finger fix on anyone in particular as he declaimed the word 'Behold'? False virtue is part of that long list of hypocrisies that contemporary dramas attacked. Middleton's 1605 City Comedy *A Mad World, My Masters*, has the mother of the courtesan Frank Gullman declare the neat epigram:

> Who gets th'opinion for a virtuous name,
> May sin at pleasure and ne'er think of shame. (I. i. 164–5)

Middleton, a member of the Mermaid Tavern group, possibly collaborated with Shakespeare in writing *Timon of Athens*, where sham virtue was exposed as it is in *Measure for Measure* and *King Lear*.

Chapter 9

THE CONTEMPORARY POLITICAL CONTEXT

In the month progressing from Edinburgh to London and the month following arrival, James created as many new knights as Elizabeth had done in her last 10 years as queen. He elevated so many of the gentry (and non-gentry) swarming to see him and parade their loyalty (a meet-and-greet ploy that might lead to profit later) that Francis Bacon called knighthood 'this almost prostituted title'.[1] On 23 July 1603 the king dubbed 300 new knights in the palace gardens at Whitehall. Gawdy, revolted by this debasement of the title, described the recipients as 'a scum' enough to 'make a man sick to think of them'.[2] Such recipients were called 'carpet knights' for they were not knighted on the battlefield for valour, but dubbed on a carpet for often trivial assistance to the monarch.[3] Many new promotions were from the Scottish horde accompanying his removal to the wealthy milch cow of England. This tendency to favour his compatriots regardless of merit caused friction and disgruntlement among the English nobility, who described the newcomers as devouring and devastating the land like wild boar.[4] It is this blurring of distinctions between the ranks that Kent is referring to when he complains that baseborn men like Oswald should carry a sword.

Coupled with the king's persistent attempts to effect union between the two realms, the Scottish dimension provoked resistance from the Commons, the Lords and the powerful city merchant community. Other conflicts with Parliament began early too. Increasingly Puritan in its thinking, the Commons was alienated when James ridiculed them as constantly discontented, factious and quarrelsome. Hoping for some relaxation of the stringent restrictions on their freedom to worship, they found James all too ready to ban Presbyterianism and expel the more extreme Puritan reformers. Catholics too anticipated greater freedom for their practices and were disappointed.

The disaffection and discontent that bred the Bye Plot and the Gunpowder Plot led only to further repression. The appalling shock of the Gunpowder Plot is a major feature of the political context, resonating in the background as the audience watched a play full of treasonable conspiracies. The 'honeymoon' period quickly ended. James's assumed liberal attitudes and behaviour soon altered. His speech from the throne in 1606 informed the Commons that kings were God's vice-regents on Earth, 'adorned and furnished with some sparkle of Divinitie'.[5] James's 'sparkle' rapidly dimmed. His extravagance emerged immediately in his demand for £5,000 for his progress south. James regarded England 'like a man that hath been wandering in the wilderness for forty years and hath at last come within sight of the Land of Promise'.[6] Court expenses for personnel, promotions and festivities rose rapidly. Surrounding himself with handsome young men who willingly flattered him, he became infatuated with a succession of favourites who, puffed up with pride and the confidence that came from royal protection, were domineering and obnoxious. The homoerotic aspect of his attachments (sodomy was a capital offence) aroused violent reactions. The king himself, from apparent initial affable openness, became withdrawn, disliking crowds and looking with contempt on the thriving, rising middling sort, though his privy councillors increasingly used the expertise of selected merchants. On ceremonial occasions he never acted with kinglike dignity. His leisure interests did not endear him to the pious, for he loved horse racing, bear baiting and hunting, and sanctioned dancing and the playing of games on Sundays. The latter angered the Puritans particularly, but Anglicans too disapproved of breaking the Commandment to keep the Sabbath holy. It was only a matter of months before people began to talk nostalgically of the old queen – the relative decorousness of her court, the human touch displayed in her public appearances, when her love of her subjects, her approachability, were manifestly sincere. Her failings were forgotten in a wave of longing for times past that says more about the current incumbent and the nation's capacity for sentimental fantasizing than about the true nature of the old queen and her neglect of many crucial problems. In December 1602 Sir John Harington's *Tract on the Succession* complained how Elizabeth had let slide many urgent matters. By 1606 he was bemoaning the Jacobean court's excesses, saying that 'the ladies roll[ed] about in intoxication' and the men behaved in 'wild riot, excess, and devastation of time and temperance'.[7] Hunting, the traditional gentry and aristocratic pastime, was an obsession with James. It was noted how the decorous progresses of Elizabeth were replaced by the king's spontaneous hunting parties accompanied by a huge field of young nobles. This comes close to linking Lear with James. In his madness Lear gives hunting calls and imagines himself hawking. There are many references to dogs and there is the flashpoint with Goneril that follows the old man's rumbustious explosion onto stage with his entourage (I. iv). Accompanied possibly by horns[8] Lear struts in with his knights, peremptorily calling, 'Let me not stay a jot for dinner.' He shows little sensitivity as a guest and clearly a large group of young men, returning excited from a day's hunting, high on adrenaline, probably fuelled by alcohol, will be noisy and disruptive. James's neglect of political duties for impromptu hunting trips, absent for days at a time at Theobalds or Royston, soon provoked comment.[9] The Venetian ambassador reported the escalating problems James was creating:

> *Many members openly declare* that as there is no war with Spain, no war with Holland, no army on the Scottish border [...]. They cannot understand why the king, who has the revenues of Scotland should want money. They add that the people are far more heavily burdened [...] for the king stays so continually and so long in the country [...] and whenever he goes a-hunting the crops are ruined.[10]

Eager to bring matters to a head after Lear has struck one of her gentlemen, Goneril encourages her steward to become impudent rather than respectful. This is doubly transgressive. Oswald should be deferential to Lear whatever the provocation, but chooses to flatter his mistress at the expense of doing wrong. Goneril again disobeys the Commandment to honour your parents.

No hint is given of Lear's past history as an administrator. The sources say little either other than that he ruled well. Goneril angrily confronts him, keen to create a rift, calling his followers an 'insolent retinue' that

> Do hourly carp and quarrel, breaking forth
> In rank and not-to-be-endured riots. (I. iv.)

She goes further:

> Here do you keep a hundred knights and squires;
> Men so disorder'd, so deboshed, and bold,
> That this our court, infected with their manners,
> Shows like a riotous inn: epicurism and lust
> Makes it more like a tavern or brothel
> Than a grac'd palace. (I. iv.)

Lear avoids answering but claims his men are of 'choice and rarest parts' who know how to behave according to their rank. Who is telling the truth? Are both exaggerating? We can imagine the embarrassment of the members of the court (and the king too perhaps). Lear's behaviour returning to the palace and his encouraging Kent's belligerence to Oswald are not likely to create sympathy in an audience, but the viewers would be in a bind, reacting negatively to Lear, but awkwardly aware of the similarity to James's conduct and knowing how 'like a tavern or brothel' their own conduct made the palace. Those gallants watching who behaved riotously might feel ashamed, but, like brash young men the world over, would laugh to brave out their wrongdoing. Some might pretend not to care. Many would feel their rank put them above the law, above good taste, and they could do as they liked. The court was not known for being sedate, decorous or free of moral or material corruption. The older men, the powerbrokers of the state, men of high position, might be more chastened, remembering their own hot youth. Both groups would hear some sharp exposures of double standards from Lear, Gloucester, the Fool and Edgar, and witness embarrassing examples of the lies and deceptions of power seekers. Some may have cared and vowed to mend their ways. Probably others cared no more than the Roaring Boy gangs who ransacked taverns, beat up innocent passers-by, molested women and mugged anyone who might have money. King Lear might not be King James, but some interesting hints of affinity make *Lear* more than a tragedy. It has a topical socio-political edge.

In considering some of the views and values that comprise the contexts of the play and underpin the theoretical views and values of the court audience, it is well to remember what interesting possibilities for tension and drama come from the discrepancy between morality's expectation of people's conduct and how they actually behave. This applies to the real king, the stage king and the audience.

Lear's behaviour may seem to conform to both familial and national views of fatherly and kingly authority. Except that not everyone in the 1600s agreed with absolutism or rampant patriarchalism. Both inside and outside the Commons, men were beginning to believe that regulated co-operation between ruler and ruled was rational, workable and desirable. No such constitutional monarchy is part of Lear's world – or fitted James's thinking.[11]

The customary idea was that by being anointed during the coronation ceremony monarchs magically took on godlike qualities as if transubstantiated like the wine and the bread in communion. Many disputed the doctrine that wine and bread turned into the blood and flesh of Christ and many were beginning to dispute that 'divinity doth hedge a king' (*Hamlet*, V. v.). Despite the adulation of Gloriana as saviour of the nation against the Spanish Armada, her limitations were becoming obvious by the end of her reign. Obstinate, wilful, sometimes irrational, her motto, *Semper eadem* (Always the same), could be Lear's. He implies it is a virtue to never reverse decisions once made, berating Kent for trying to make 'us break our vows,/Which we durst never yet [...]' (I. i.). Lear's immovability is a mark of consistency, but also of obstinacy precluding adjusting to advice. A wise king has counsellors and considers a range of actions. Lear refuses Kent's advice and forces him to obey by calling on his oath of allegiance sworn at Lear's accession. James had introduced a law in June 1606 establishing an oath of allegiance, in response to the 'Powder Plot'. Lear's line 'Hear me, recreant! [someone disloyal] On thine allegiance, hear me!' would resonate with shocking topicality. Did the audience freeze in their seats? Did some steal glances at the king? He was notoriously difficult to shift in his views, partly due to his unshakeable belief in his Divine Right. Ironically his motto was *Beati pacifici* (Blessed are the peacemakers) yet his every action stirred trouble. Elizabeth was equally immovable. Her persistent refusal to face the succession problem, strengthened by legislation making discussion of the succession treasonable (the 1571 Treason Act and its reinforcement in 1581), began to look like a very human failure to acknowledge, address and resolve a serious matter for fear of contemplating her own mortality. The anxiety this generated merely added to accumulating unaddressed problems. Her refusal to allow much authority to the House of Commons delayed resolution of constitutional difficulties that would plague James I and Charles I and would lead to civil war. While Elizabeth's failings made a new man welcome, her strengths and people's natural resistance to change made the role of new king particularly challenging. James was not up to that challenge and disillusion very quickly followed the euphoria of his peaceful succession.

The Jacobean world was still essentially Elizabethan but with discernible changes stemming from a darkening *zeitgeist*. The new reign opened with eclipses, storms, gruesome murders, plots, freakish births and an outbreak of plague that killed 30,000 people in London. For an age believing in omens and seeing God's hand in everything, the signs were frightening. For an age believing in hierarchies and that order reflected God's harmonious design, disorder, treason, the decay of old certainties, the debasement of the nobility, the greed of society, the callousness of parents and the irreverence of children, all promised a dismal future, even perhaps the approach of the Apocalypse. God punished sinful nations and it looked as if he had withdrawn his favour from his chosen people. The Jacobean theatre reflected this dark mood. Tragedies became more bloodthirsty, their plots more devious and intricate, presenting ever more ingeniously nasty ways of killing people. They presented too a world where no one is what they appear to be and all are corrupt. Shakespeare's work alone – omitting *Much Ado*, *Twelfth Night*, *As You Like It*, heartening comedies as they are – has a string of plays from *Hamlet* to *Cymbeline* grimly depicting human duplicity and cruelty. The cynical tone, the jaded view of society, the scenes of destruction and despair, with thieves, liars, lechers, hypocrites, knaves and fools, is of a piece with other contemporary writers. Gloucester's litany of social disarray ('Love cools, friendship falls off, brothers divide: [...] mutinies [...] discord [...] treason [...] machinations, hollowness, [...] all ruinous disasters' [I. ii.]) echoes how people felt. 1606 was dubbed 'The Black Year' in Anthony Nixon's book of the same name. He comments on the extreme weather and social matters:

> The fruitfulness of the fields is not such as it hath been before time. Lords and great men bend their cogitations to the oppressing of their poor tenants, and by often fines and exactions, bring honest men to beggary, and by example of Pharaoh make slaves of their servants and subjects.[12]

The oppressiveness of 'great men' (aristo-gentry landowners) and the increase of beggary brings *Lear* immediately into focus and references growing tensions and grievances between the ranks of society. There were many other sources of anxiety, but what made them worrisome to the general public and particularly to dramatists and moralists was that they betokened a threat to order, disturbing people's need to feel that all was well.

The First Audience

Lear was registered, as it had to be by law, at the Stationers' Office on 26 November 1607:

> Mr William Shakespeare his historye of Kynge Lear as yt was played before the kings maiestie at Whitehall vppon St Stephans night at Christmas Last by his maiesties servants playing usually at the globe on the Banksyde.

This dates the first recorded performance to 26 December 1606. It was common for many plays to be performed at court around Christmas, particularly on St Stephen's Day (26 December), St John's (27), the Feast of the Innocents (28), New Year's Day and Twelfth Night (5 January). The newly named King's Men performed much of Shakespeare's already-existing *oeuvre* at court.[13] The 1605 Yuletide festivities had included a new play, *Measure for Measure*, which had thematic and political links to *Lear*. Perhaps, hearing of the new piece, James requested it as a didactic experience rather than merely entertainment. It is highly unlikely the king commissioned the work, though he certainly knew the Lear story. In 1608 the text was printed as a quarto volume for Nathaniel

Butler 'to be sold at his shop in *Pauls*/Church-yard at the signe of the Pide Bull neere/St. *Austin's* Gate'. The title page announces:

> Mr William Shakespeare his true chronicle history of the life and death of King Lear and his three daughters, with the unfortunate life of Edgar, son and heir to the Earl of Gloucester, and his sullen and assumed humour of Tom of Bedlam. As it was played before the King's majesty at Whitehall upon St. Stephen's night in Christmas holidays, by his majesty's servants usually at the Globe on Bankside.

That both the Stationers' Register and the book use the same phrase, 'usually at the Globe', implies that the piece had not already been presented to the public. There is no evidence of *Lear* being performed initially at the Bankside venue. Most entries in the register record where a piece was initially played. Apart from a 1610 performance in a private house there is no evidence of any public showing of *Lear*. James did not particularly like plays though many were performed at court, probably more to entertain others than the king. He lacked his wife's enthusiasm for masques, but did not stop them.[14] On 15 January 1604, less than a year after his accession, a courtier's letter reveals:

> We had every night a publicke play in the great hale, at which the king was ever present [...] but it seems he takes no extraordinary pleasure in them. The Queen and Prince were more the players frends, for on other nights they had them privately, and hath since taken them to theyr protection.[15]

The first Christmas of his reign we learn that 'the Queen intendeth to make a mask' and 'it is said that there shall be thirty plays'. On Twelfth Night 1604 there was another queen's masque, and before Christmas 'the ladies in the Court prepare to solemnize the Christmas with a gallant Masque which doth cost the Exchequer £3,000'.[16] By 17 December the cost had risen to £4,000 and the Council wanted to halt it. Ultimately it was performed because withdrawal would look to foreign ambassadors present at court as if the royal family could not afford it. On 6 January 1605 the notorious *Masque of Blacknesse* was performed, much criticized on account of the court ladies blacking up as moors and wearing revealing diaphanous costumes. Those Christmas festivities also included Shakespeare's company showing five plays (four comedies and the ever-popular *Henry V*). The Boys of the Chapel and the Queen's Players each performed a comedy. More masques were presented in January 1606. During James's time court performances trebled.

Then came the oddity of *Lear* at Christmas 1606. Hardly the sort of fare for such celebrations. It seems unlikely the queen was keen to have the play. Not her type of entertainment. Possibly the king, knowing the general subject of the plot, saw it as a chance to back his oft-mentioned desire to unite England and Scotland by showing the effects of a monarch dividing a realm.[17] He tended to preach to the Commons and to the court and might have wished to show the court a play about a foolish king. His favourite topic (apart from unification) was the obedience subjects owed a king as God's representative on Earth and how such exalted beings had Divine Right. James might have felt that a play about bad kingship would be timely and instructive. It is unlikely he knew much more about *Lear* than the outline of the original story. He was probably unaware Shakespeare had made crucial narrative changes and added much criticism of the behaviour of the 'great and the good' – or rather the great who abused their power and the supposedly good who were not so virtuous. Apart from foolish kingship and harrowing scenes, embedded in the piece are awkward exposures of hypocrisy among the privileged classes. These would not have been known until the performance. Focusing rule, courts, courtiers, loyalty, disloyalty, flattery and telling the truth, it is a very audience-specific play for a more socially narrow group than at the Globe. James may have felt he got more than he thought he had bargained for if he short-sightedly saw the work only as a lesson in conduct for his less than well-behaved younger courtiers.

What exactly was the court? It was composed of three layers – the Household (the 'Board of Greencloth') under the Lord Steward, the Chamber (under the Chamberlain) and the Bedchamber (under the Groom of the Stool, responsible for arranging the monarch's toilet procedures). The Household comprised all indoor and outdoor servants – cooks, footmen, chambermaids, cleaners, gardeners, soldiers, officers of the guard, a butler in charge of those who served food, clerks dealing with the paperwork (orders for food and materials) – the workers keeping a palace running. None of these would be watching – officially. The Bedchamber was the cadre of personal body servants (mostly Scots) who dressed the king and served his washing/toilet/clothing needs. The Chamber was a mix of true courtiers and an amorphous mass of hangers-on. The inner-circle courtiers (many from old-established titled families) were the king's friends and closest companions. Many had specific roles as waiting gentlemen and gentlewomen of the king and queen, direct servants (with petty responsibilities like placing the king's cutlery, carving his meat), more general persons available to escort visiting ambassadors, run errands or chat with the king and great lords and ladies attending on the king. The latter provided the polished, elegant public face of the English court. Then there were government officials and the elite group of the Privy Council – a board of top advisors. The audience would comprise these true courtiers but be bulked out with the hangers-on (often relatives of someone in an actual post, hoping to catch the eye of someone of power to help them get on the payroll). Hangers-on were invited to make up numbers at festive and official events. Many were chancers. In Jonson's satire *Every Man out of His Humour* the vitriolic Macilente (played by Asper, meaning rough, biting, critical) criticizes 'these mushroom gentlemen,/That shoot up in a night to place and worship' (I. i). Some were petty country gentlemen come to town to make their fortune, others newly raised to gentry status by payment to the College of Heralds or recently dubbed by the king. Such a one is the aspiring Sogliardo, announcing, 'I can write myself gentleman now; here's my patent, it cost me thirty pounds' (III. i.). He declares, 'I have land and money, my friends left me well, and I will be a gentleman whatsoever it cost me.' A wealthy farmer (his name signifies manure), he is one of the upwardly mobile middle class buying their way into the gentry. His lifestyle mentor is a conman, Carlo Buffone (a Falstaff/ Sir Toby Belch character). He instructs Sogliardo:

> To be an accomplished gentleman [...] you must give over housekeeping in the country, and live altogether in the city amongst gallants: where, at your first appearance, 'twere good you turn'd four or five hundred acres of your best land into two or three trunks of apparel [...] mix yourself still with such as flourish in the spring of fashion [...] study their carriage and behaviour in all; learn to play at primero [a card game], [...] and when you come to plays, be humorous [severe looking], look with a good starch'd face [...] and sit on the stage and flout, provided you have a good suit. (I. i.)

The going rate was £30 for a gentleman's patent and coat of arms and £40 for a knighthood. In *Eastward Ho!* Sir Petronel Flash is 'one of these forty-pound Knights'.[18] James, having debased the knightly rank, later augmented the Crown's income by also selling peerages. Oswald, a 'serviceable villain' on the make, is of indeterminate status – he is a servant, but is steward to a duchess/princess. He might wear a gold chain, and be called the mistress's 'chief gentleman'. He was of some count in the household, liaising between the family and the lower servants, not of gentry stock, but aspiring to rise. Kent calls him a 'three-suited, hundred pound [presumably his salary], filthy worsted-stocking knave; a lily-livered, action-taking, whoreson, glass-gazing, super-serviceable, finical rogue' (II. ii.).[19] He has no land (unlike Sogliardo) but, like many at court, plans to rise through service. The aspiration of stewards was proverbial. The arch-upstart Malvolio (*Twelfth Night*) wears a chain (which Sir Toby tells him to 'go rub' rather than harassing his superiors) and is reminded, 'Art any more than a steward?' when he becomes too overbearing. In a high-status household the steward might well be a cultivated and educated man. Antonio de Bologna, the Duchess of Malfi's 'chief gentleman', has travelled, attended the French court and is cultured after Castiglione's model. Oswald has neither class nor delicacy. His position of status encourages him to think of himself as a gentleman since a royal steward would usually be that if not something higher. Goneril confides in him on personal matters regarding the 'great abatement of kindness' (I. iv.), the slackening 'of former services', the 'weary negligence' (I. iii.) she wishes shown to the king and his train. His readiness to behave with less than the decorum required of a gentleman exposes his base origins or at least his base nature. He is cowardly when he meets Kent at Gloucester's castle, lies about his own behaviour in order to look the injured party, but betrays his true low character in his readiness to slaughter the blind, unarmed, broken Gloucester, crying, 'A most proclaim'd prize!' as he comes upon him and Edgar, the latter disregarded as appearing to be only a peasant. Oswald imagines promotion to gentlemanly status following his murder of the old man.

> That eyeless head of thine was first fram'd flesh
> To raise my fortunes. Thou old unhappy traitor,
> Briefly thyself remember: the sword is out
> That must destroy thee. (IV. vi.)

Ambition lures him to contemplate a Deadly Sin and ignore the considerations of chivalry, religion, even basic human kindness, transgressing into pride, intended murder and social subversion; Gloucester, an obvious object of sympathy and help in line with the traditional respect for the old and infirm, is also an earl, only one step down from a duke. Oswald is justly killed by Edgar, who even in his degraded physical state retains the key elements of decency, gentlemanliness and chivalric protection of the oppressed, including the father who outlawed him. Edgar, as Poor Tom, claims to have 'had three suits to his back, six shirts to his body' (III. iv.). As an earl's son his wardrobe would be extensive but he pretends to have been a gentleman/servingman.

In the plays of the 1600s, among the pretentious, crooked scamsters pilloried for the amusement and instruction of playgoers, courtiers are the commonest target for mockery. If sufficiently well dressed you could gain entry to the court and attach yourself to whoever looked to be rising. If you looked the part you were mostly taken for being it, appearance appearing real. Clothes were the key first step in the charade and many young men found themselves heavily in debt with tailors, ruff makers, shoemakers, hatters and jewellers, just to dress themselves correctly. These were often debts they did not pay, adding fraud to the vain masquerade of their clothes. While seeking someone who could become a patron, they were also hunting an heiress. An opportune wealthy marriage would make them. City Comedies present many such peacocks and mock their shady pretensions. The first spectators of *Lear* would have been just such a royal entourage of titled aristocrats, their ladies, mistresses, hangers-on, parasites, yes-men on the make and government placemen partly reflecting the *dramatis personae* of the play they gathered to watch – a fictional mirror for these 'magistrates'. The court was 'extravagant and disorderly, frivolous and indecorous, with hard drinking common and immorality winked at'.[20] There was, as is normal among all groups of human beings, constant falling out, making up, allegiances formed, loyalties betrayed, sexual rivalries, status rivalries and duels. The Earl of Worcester complained, 'There is much plotting and malice among the ladies of the court striving for the offices of honour about the Queen.' So virulent was it, 'I think envy hath tied an invisible snake around their necks, to sting each other to death.'[21] The standard court ambience was a hothouse of some celebrities and many non-entities, all thinking they were at the centre of the world, the focus of all attention, the source of all that was chic and all that counted. As king, James was responsible for this toxic charade.

The Wise Man and the Fool

Between man's capacity for sensible decisions and actions and his infinite ability for foolishness lies the potential for tragedy and comedy that is Shakespeare's arena. The interface between reason and feeling was the spark between steel and flint.

Lucifer's rebellion proving his first creation imperfect, the Almighty made a second attempt, creating Earth and man. The human 'angel' had a tragic flaw. Because man, though endowed with the ability to think calmly and decide rationally, was open to the weakening working of passions, this world was corrupted by the Devil and by his spawn, Sin and Death. As Genesis tells, this flaw resulted in disobedience to God's command (not to eat of the fruit of the forbidden Tree of Knowledge) and in listening to Eve and acting on her encouragement rather than abiding by the diktat of God. Adam faced the age-old conflict between the stringent demands of religion and the human tendency to do what is easier. This foundation story of Christianity, a prophetic allegory of the difficulties man makes for himself, encapsulates the idea that the Almighty's way is hard and involves restraining natural instincts that draw us towards self-indulgence, comfort, the easy life. This embodies the tension between good and evil that was seen as ever-present in human life.

Man had two qualities that none of the rest of creation shared: sensibilities and reason. Altruistic feelings of kindness and caring led to charity, showed in family love and in community care which rationally accepted that some loss of self-will was needed if the benefits of group co-operation were to be accrued. Such sensibilities were positive, but other feelings lured men into folly. Folly was the first step towards sin. It was, however, his ability to reason that raised him above the animal world and drew him closer to the angels – the capacity to postulate action, speculate upon causes, effects and consequences and then decide what course to take. Hamlet sums this up:

What a piece of work is a man! How noble in reason! how infinite in faculty! in form, in moving, how express and admirable! in action how like an angel! in apprehension how like a god! the beauty of the world! the paragon of animals! (II. ii. 303–7)

This ideal Renaissance man could play and write music, write poems, dance well, converse easily and fluently with all ranks and conditions and on a wide range of topics. He was learned, had impeccable manners, was cultivated and cultured. All very possible if you had position and money. Lear, as his enlightenment dawns, sees that for most men life is a struggle, that the ordinary creature, without education and riches, had a hard time of it and that it was the duty of those born to comfort to 'shake the superflux' to those in need. Man is not well equipped to face the natural world, being weak, naked and vulnerable, like the 'houseless poverty' crowding the roads of England.[22] Strip away the fine clothes and airs of the man of rank, remove the money and power, and he is a 'bare, forked animal'. *Lear* displays this process of stripping away the fine-looking veneer of power and wealth; the king is stripped of his position, stripped of family support. We see the heir to an earldom stripped of his comforts, forced to flee like a criminal and disguise himself as a filthy near-naked beggar:

To take the basest and most poorest shape
That ever penury, in contempt of man,
Brought near to beast [...]. (II. iii.)

This prick to the consciences of the fur-robed, silk-attired audience, reproaches those who, failing to give alms, ordered the coachman to drive past beggars. Through Edgar's enforced experience of poverty and Lear's partially self-induced descent into madness (another form of isolation), the comfortably-off court audience is made to watch what they would probably prefer to ignore. They would readily recognize the stripping away of those rules of behaviour that keep men civilized, the exposure of the selfish savagery that lurks not too far below the polished surface, a barbarity that can emerge within the supposed loving and supportive arena of the family. They would be reminded of the fierce rivalries and jealousies that seethed under the surface of supposedly orderly and cultured court life. This natural state of greedy striving, conflicting with Christian values of love, co-operation and brotherhood, was a view of life Shakespeare found reinforced in Montaigne's essay 'Apology of Raymond Sebond'. That he read it is evidenced by verbal echoes in Lear's 'unaccommodated man' speech. Montaigne offers a counter to Hamlet's view of man's superiority:

> When I consider man all naked [...] and view his defects, his natural subjection, and manifold imperfections; I find we have had much more reason to hide and cover our nakedness, than any creature else. We may be excused for borrowing their spoils of wool, of hair, of feathers, and of silk to shroud us.[23]

History and countless plays showed repeatedly the fall of powerful men from unbelievable luxury to the broken wreck – kneeling, head bent for the axe or writhing in agony from the assassin's knife. Lear's enlightenment warns that without wealth and position, you are no more than a weak and shivering creature:

> Is man no more than this? Consider him well. Thou ow'st the worm no silk, the beast no hide, the sheep no wool, the cat no perfume. Ha! here's three on's are sophisticated; thou art the thing itself; unaccommodated man is no more but such a poor, bare, forked animal as thou art. (III. iv.)

Shakespeare keeps Montaigne's idea of man protecting his feeble body with silk and wool, rejects hair and feathers, but inserts hide and perfume. He elaborates the image by mentioning the silkworm, the beast providing leather, the sheep and the cat. Silk, wool and hide might indicate the three main ranks but the addition of the civet cat's perfume (along with silk) focuses the description more on the courtly audience, for whom silk and perfume were common rank signifiers. Montaigne is contemptuous of man's claim to superiority, while Shakespeare maintains a more general deployment of the idea of humanity's lack of humanity.

Jacobeans were graphically aware of how fortunes turn, how poverty, sickness and sudden disaster can turn the world upside down, however virtuous you are. Those body servants who dressed and undressed them knew how poxed, scabbed and stinking their master or mistress might be under their doublet, their farthingale, their wig. Under showy tinsel and gorgeous stuff the lord might be as much of a conniving knave as the pickpocket, but worse for pretending to be better and demanding respect for the position he occupied. The bejewelled duchess might be as wanton as a Bankside twopenny whore – and as diseased. The three 'sophisticated' men in the hovel, Lear, Kent and the Fool, are artificial, impure, fabrications relying on clothing and rank for the position and deference they have. A pointed remark to make in front of an audience dressed in the costliest fashions of the day. It is a view repeated:

Thorough tatter'd clothes small vices do appear;
Robes and furr'd gowns hide all. (IV. vi.)

Across the texture of the play, from the spectacle of the king's entry to his appearance 'fantastically dressed with wild flowers', clothing imagery symbolizes the way dress disguises what people really are or intend. Appearance is stripped away metaphorically from Goneril, Regan and Edmund, and literally from Lear and Edgar. Clothes were a political statement in Shakespeare's time. The Sumptuary Laws defined the types of cloth appropriate to people's place in the hierarchy. A law of 1571 required all males over the age of 6 to wear a woollen cap on Sundays. The statute cap was only for the lower sort, a badge of rank. The gentry and nobility, of course, continued to wear silk or velvet caps. Snobbish aspirants constantly subverted these categories, aping in borrowed styles those above them. The maid on holiday, decked in her mistress's cast-offs might masquerade as a fine lady. Merchants' wives were perpetually criticized for parading in the silks and satins designated for their superiors. The gentry aped the aristocracy and the aristocracy kept adopting more and more outrageous fashions to preserve the differences marking them as leaders of style. Trends in dress became more sexually explicit. Male hose became tighter, court ladies wore lower and lower necklines. *The Masque of Blacknesse* provoked the comment, 'Their apparel was rich but, some said, too light and courtesan-like for such great ones.'[24] Lear makes the point to Regan:

Thou art a lady;
If only to go warm were gorgeous,
Why, nature needs not what thou gorgeous wear'st,
Which scarcely keeps thee warm. (II. iv.)

This criticism of wearing luxurious material that offers scant warmth Shakespeare carried over from the original *Leir* where the king's complaints about his eldest daughter's extravagant spending on clothes is one of her reasons for turning against him. In drama costume becomes a marker of moral state. Overdependence on show and the trappings of power indicates moral aberration. In *Measure for Measure*, Isabella reminds the self-righteous Angelo:

No ceremony that to great ones longs,
Not the king's crown, nor the deputed sword,
The marshal's truncheon, nor the judge's robe,
Become them with one half so good a grace
As mercy does. (II. ii. 59–63)

She further remarks on how 'man, proud man, Dress'd in a little brief authority':

like an angry ape
Plays such fantastic tricks before high heaven
As makes the angels weep […]. (II. ii. 121–3)

The image of an ape in power clothing reflecting a man of authority overproud of himself is not dissimilar to that of Lear's mocking gloss on 'the great image Authority': 'A dog's obey'd in office'. Some at court clearly would bow and scrape to a dog if he wore a badge of office. However inefficient, useless or tyrannical a judge, state councillor, general or king might be, some would still hurry to obey his orders. How many in the audience would see themselves as 'silly ducking observants'? Some would readily identify others as official 'dogs', but fail to include themselves. Others would miss the comment as they chattered about Lady Beville's diamonds or Susan Herbert's hairstyle.

The year *Hamlet* described man's perfectibility, another picture of what man could be (and generally was) is voiced by the jester Feste (*Twelfth Night*, 1601) telling Viola/Cesario, 'Foolery Sir, does walk about the Orb like the Sun, it shines everywhere' (III. i. 39–40). In theory rational, in practice foolish, is Shakespeare's presentation of mankind. Everyone acknowledged man at his best – planning ahead, commonsensical, reasonable, adjusting to changed circumstances, doing what was just and kind, constructing social agencies to fit the needs of a community, sympathetically desiring to redress imbalances of food, wealth and power and formulating this into a judicial system, and developing a power hierarchy that enabled society to work effectively. It was the other aspect, the failure to achieve perfect social harmony and perfect personal government, that most exercised the pens and tongues of satirists and moralists. Acts of folly, the first steps on the road to sin, provided a limitless, rich ground for descriptions of failure and prescriptions for improvement. Man's infinite capacity for spoiling things was a much more exciting, titillating, sensational and fruitful subject for dramatists and religious polemicists than theorizing about ideal socio-political-personal structures. Silly judgements, making a fool of oneself, deceiving others, self-deception, trickery for gain, greed, the minefields of sex and love, power, money, outright wrongdoing, provided a complex network of failed right conduct and a wonderful parade of fools.

This was formulated into a very detailed series of 'Thou shalt nots'. Life in Jacobean England was highly regulated. There were all the formal, official checks upon one's actions – parents, neighbours, employers, the guild, the parish priest, the parish council, the night watch, magistrates and courts. But there were the inner controls, those checks upon wrongful impulses that came from upbringing and conscience – the sense of right and wrong, of honour and virtue, of what God demanded.

In practice, human beings being what they are for the most part – weak, feckless, lazy, selfish – many were indifferent to how they behaved. London bred a huge underclass of 'street people' – prostitutes, beggars, petty criminals, unskilled labourers, the poor in general – lying and cheating their way through existence. Then there were the high status hypocrites and criminals, misbehaving, committing big, profitable scams and with position, rank and money enough to cover their sins and buy off prosecution.

Not only was the individual soul felt to be in terminal decay, but civic life too. Considerable attention was paid in pamphlets, philosophical studies, poems and plays to the question of good government, a particular Renaissance interest. As regards the individual character in drama this relates to conduct towards others and control of oneself, displayed in the perpetual battle to control the passions. As regards community and national politics this relates to theories and real-life examples of good governorship and concepts of civic duty. From Sir Thomas More's *Utopia* (1516) through Elyot's *The Boke Named the Governour* (1531), James's *Basilikon Doron* (1599), to Thomas Hobbes's *Leviathan* (1651), writers were much exercised by the questions, 'What makes a good state?' and 'What makes a good governor?' Shakespeare's history plays and tragedies are much taken up with those complex questions. *Lear* makes a key contribution. Seeing *Lear* as an enactment of bad kingship and its consequences, tends today to be marginalized by greater interest in the personal flaws and *hubris* of the man and father and the unfolding family tragedy, but in an age when civic identity still had priority over personal desires, flawed governorship would be a major theme, seconded by the Gloucester subplot and the questionable household management of Regan and Goneril. *Lear* may be seen as an exploration of the effects of bad leadership. The implications for the real-life social and national political state, the failure of real practice to match idealized theory, are evidenced by the descent into civil war (1642–49) and made more immediately intriguing by the play having been first performed in front of a king and court.

New Philosophy, New Men

A host of new social subtypes was helping destabilize the old orders of society. The new families of the Reformation were, by the time of James's accession and *Lear*, well assimilated into the aristocracy and embedded in the power structure. James's wholesale creation of hundreds of new knights and other titles not only debased the value of such ranks in the eyes of the public, it antagonized the old nobility. Appointing many new men to government and court posts exacerbated tensions further. The fact that many were Scots newcomers arriving with the king made for a fractious atmosphere around Whitehall. *Lear* comments on the loyal service of old courtiers, along with questions of the limits of service, of what it is right to do in the name of your master or mistress when their orders are morally suspect, creating an atmosphere of hidden motives and power plays. Elizabeth raised high men who served her well. William Cecil, Elizabeth's secretary, was made Lord Burghley. Burghley's son, Robert, became secretary of state after Walsingham died in 1590, succeeded his father as Elizabeth's principal minister, smoothed the takeover of James, acted as spymaster for the new king and was rewarded with a peerage as Baron Cecil (1603), then promoted as Viscount Cranborne (1604), and finally Earl of Salisbury (1605). His involvement in security might make him, in Shakespeare's mind, one of the 'scurvy politicians' Lear talks of (IV. vi.). The play world of secrets and lies mirrors the intrigues and deceptions poisoning the corridors of power and the royal apartments. The word 'politician' has a number of related etymological meanings. Often it meant a trickster using 'policy' to cheat. 'Policy' was the word for the intricate lies told to gain what you wanted, the means by which Machiavelli's Prince was advised to achieve his will. It relates to politicians as administrators running aspects of the state and consequently carries the suggestion that politicians are tricksters cheating for their own gain, lying to cover what they are really up to. There was much of that in seventeenth-century government. Lear's court is no utopian administration; as an authoritarian, erratic king, with a venial councillor in Gloucester and a bluff councillor in Kent, Lear possibly runs the country as he runs his family – by personal whim and capricious diktat. The Machiavellian figures of Goneril and Regan seek to marginalize their father with open cruelty and Edmund, by Machiavellian lies and tricks, plots to marginalize his brother. There is the huge *meiny* of Lear's knights, so large that its size alone would be difficult to control. Were they only disruptive when at Goneril's and not before the division of the realm? This is not a court to be proud of. It is a court in tension, ready to split along deep fault lines. Cordelia's 'Nothing, my lord' is all it takes. The vitriolic satire on beadles, usurers, judges and the like broadens the targets. General criticisms of court life are maintained to the end of the drama. About to go to prison, Lear describes himself and Cordelia as spies overlooking the tawdry, silly comedy of changing fortunes at court and imagining themselves laughing

> At gilded butterflies, and hear poor rogues
> Talk of court news; we'll talk with them too,
> Who loses and who wins; who's in, who's out;
> And take upon's the mystery of things,
> As if we were God's spies: and we'll wear out,
> In a wall'd prison, packs and sects of great ones
> That ebb and flow by the moon. (V. iii.)

Great families fell. Royal favour was fickle. Lear's capricious behaviour, violently passionate in its verbal expression, is not unusual. Arbitrary exercise of absolute power was nothing new.[25] Elizabeth could be hysterically angry and dismiss courtiers for misdemeanours, petty or serious, real or imagined. James despatched a stream of men to the Tower for thwarting him.[26] With the irresistible rise of the middle class, successful men were constantly being promoted into the ranks of the privileged and titled. They were not always well received by those who felt their status was being tainted. Promotions for (not always moral) services to the crown, often bought (a means of appeasing ambition and James's constant need for cash), made the hollowness of titles a target for satirical comment. The court crackled with animosities.

The villains present the emerging dangers of individualism that puts self above morality, private profit above decency and humanity. These are the new men (and women) with their new egotistical philosophy. It is part of the context in which Shakespeare and contemporaries viewed those who seek to rise, to gain wealth or consequence through immoral, violent, inhuman means. This applied to the Jacobean tragic writers exposing and punishing the ruthless psychopaths who entertain and horrify as they murder their way to power (in *The Duchess of Malfi*, *The White Devil*, *'Tis Pity She's a Whore*, *The Revenger's Tragedy* and countless others). It also applied to the satirists who decried and mocked underhand, exploitative behaviour by powerful merchant associations, powerful politicians and individuals whose greed became a psychological obsession.[27] Edmund is a more dangerous type of new man, proactively ruthless and devious. The cowardly Oswald (based on the anonymous would-be murderer of the earlier *Leir* play) merely tries taking advantage of a chance situation that comes his way. This reminds how vulnerable masters and mistresses were to ruthless, deceitful servants and how important was the bond of loyalty and honesty between master and servant. Edmund, more chillingly disturbing because he is a blood relative to his victim, uses opportunities as they occur, but also activates 'invention' and fabricates opportunities. Far more amoral than the weak steward, more pushily self-confident and determined, he understands the weaknesses of people and plays upon them. The nature he worships is conscienceless and remorseless. He is unashamed when called Earl of Gloucester before his father is even dead, is supportive (though not present) of the brutal gouging of his father's eyes, unfazed by having to lead an army, unilaterally ordering execution of the captive king and Cordelia, and happily confident in playing off Goneril and Regan against each other. He is a new man in an old Machiavellian way, a villain on his way to power. History is full of such men. His people-management skills would have made him a formidable leader had his personality been virtuous.

A more important group of new men is made new through suffering. They are of most interest in the moral context of the play. Lear, Gloucester, Edgar and Albany suffer, have their old self destroyed and emerge born again, with broader vision, deeper insight, readier sympathy and understanding.

Circumstances and character lead some to rise and others to fall. Industrious habits could (and increasingly did) mean that a hard worker, a thrifty man, a canny opportunist, could rise to a station much higher than that he was born to. These first glimpses of capitalism caused moralists and sermon makers considerable anxiety. Opportunities for making huge fortunes were increasing and with them worries about the insatiable greediness of those who, prioritizing their own private gain above the common good, began to precipitate disgust, envy and disgruntlement among the exploited and those with no chance to improve their own standards of living. The 1590s saw a number of attempts at legislation to regulate merchant enterprises. It was felt that the state had to control unfettered capitalism to ensure it was conducted in orderly and moral ways. In *One and Thirty Epigrams* (1550), Robert Crowley reminds us:

> You are not born to yourself,
> Neither may you take
> That thing for your own
> Whereof God did you make
> But steward and bailiff [...].

Men of ability and drive were encouraged to see their success as the gift of providence more than the reward of their own efforts. As stewards of their own talents they owed God a portion of their profits, paid in doing good works for others. Merchants making huge sums importing spices or cloth from the East had a duty to ensure that the captains and crews of their ships, the dockers unloading cargoes and the market traders or shopkeepers to whom they sold were fairly paid and that the 'superflux' did not all go into their pockets or onto their wives' backs, but into fair wages and charitable works. It was a feature of capitalism that this happened less and less. Acceptable levels of personal gain had to be offset against duty to the community – a medieval idea struggling to survive in a changing and greedy world. Biblical and Christian thinking exhorted believers not to set too great a store by the riches of this world, but to concentrate on enriching the soul. Increasingly, as capitalism began to take hold of European trading, families like the Medici, Bardi, Peruzzi and Strozzi in Florence became powerbrokers loaning to governments. Similar men thrived in England and Germany. Trade growth led to an increase in the entrepreneurial middle class. With more money washing around in London there was an increase in the activities mushrooming to service a thriving city. Foreign visitors were astonished at the amounts of lavish goods in London shops. Duke Frederick of Würtemberg described London as a 'mighty city of business' where 'most of the inhabitants are employed in buying and selling merchandise, and trading in almost every corner of the world [...]. The inhabitants are magnificently apparelled [...]'. He offers an interesting insight on appearance and reality:

> The women have much more liberty than perhaps in any other place; they also know well how to make use of it, for they go dressed out in exceedingly fine clothes, and give all their attention to their ruffs and stuffs, to such a degree indeed, that [...] many a one does not hesitate to wear velvet in the streets, which is common with them, whilst at home perhaps they have not a piece of dried bread.[28]

Merchants' wives dressed like court ladies; snobbery, luxury, extravagance and ostentation flourished. After the improvement in their standard of living the bourgeoisie dreamed of gentrification. That meant selling out of their fortune-making trade, investing the proceeds of the sale, buying a country estate, making more money from the rents of tenants farming their land, and hoping to gain the respect of gentry neighbours. A title increased the chances of that and money could buy a title awarded by a king whose coffers were always empty. This is a society based on the old orders but beginning to change as circumstances altered. It was a difficult transition and made many anxious that there was too much change and basic values were being forgotten or simply discarded. Individualism, a keynote of the Renaissance idea of man, took on dangerous potential when unregulated by law or personal moral self-control.

The audience watching *Lear* brought a memory bank of family-oriented reactions, differing according to age and the nature of the parent–child relationship. Whatever the spectator's story, whatever their assessment of it, they also brought a set of learned values shared by society. Social context varied from family to family depending on the personalities involved and their social position, but would share at points the common values of the culture at large. Social context reflected not only the morality of the past persisting into the present, but the contradictions and conflicts created by current priorities that temporarily interested the time or dominated and coloured their views of the world. Another context is the nature of political experiences and views. Politics is about who has power, how they use it and where they apply it, and who does not have power but wants it and why. Politics in this sense is found as much within families as within nations. *Lear* works on both levels.

Finally there are the historical and literary contexts that help in interpreting a piece of writing. History is something Shakespeare's audience shared – a host of active memories going back into the recently ended Elizabethan era with all its dramas (though their experience and evaluation of it would vary according to religion, rank and age). Similarly, the literary context a spectator brought would vary enormously depending on education, breadth of reading and how often they visited the theatre. Shakespeare's hugely capacious knowledge of history and literature resonates in the allusions, echoes and lessons presented in his dramas. His mind was vibrantly responsive to his surroundings. Sources low and popular, high and cultivated, are absorbed in the play and a huge array of nuanced meanings is cached within the language and situations of a story that references the anxious contemporary scene. For all its being set in a vaguely pagan past, *Lear* is replete with connections to the contemporary court. Though the playwright was vastly better read than almost everyone else in the audience, they all shared a common text. They may have had different degrees of knowledge of it and would certainly have interpreted parts of it in differing ways, but to a large extent, theoretically at least, the Bible was a shared source of values. In practice many, perhaps most, failed to live up to its demands, but they all knew how they were expected to live. It is the deviations from the expected Christian life that provide the play's most dominant context.

Religion was penetrated through and through with politics and politics was mixed up with religion. Thoughts of God, sin, salvation, death, the Devil and damnation were as natural to Jacobeans as breathing. Coming to contemporary political contexts we must remember that the enveloping locus of *Lear* is a court, a world of royal and aristocratic households (a world Shakespeare knew), where 'smiling rogues' bow, scrape, say what is wanted, yet play the villain underneath, and 'Renege, affirm, and turn their halcyon beaks/With every gale and vary of their masters' (II. ii.) while harbouring disrespectful, irreverent, self-interested, vengeful and destructive thoughts, ready to desert to another master who has more power and offers more money. The Fool puts it neatly in his doggerel verse:

> That sir which serves and seeks for gain,
> And follows but for form,
> Will pack when it begins to rain,
> And leave thee in the storm. (II. iv.)

This echoes Machiavelli's analysis of the principle motivation of the court: 'The nobles have more foresight and are more astute, they always act in time to safeguard their interests, and they take sides with the one whom they expect to win.'[29] Machiavelli did not take account of (or perhaps believe in) the loyalty of honest men. Idealism of the sort found in Castiglione and Elyot is countered by Machiavelli's cynical realism:

> One can make this generalisation about men: they are ungrateful, fickle, liars, and deceivers, they shun danger and are greedy for profit; while you treat them well, they are yours. They would shed their blood for you, risk their property, their lives, their children, so long [...] as danger is remote; but when you are in danger they turn against you.[30]

Service was a major form of employment. All households, except the very poorest, had at least a maid or boy. Some had dozens of servants. A royal court had legions of aristocrats, many of whom were less concerned with loyalty than their own status and survival. A good, long-term servant was like a member of the family. A bad one was a disruptive force. Ironically in Lear it is the king who puts family and servant loyalty and love to the test. Theoretically, servants were part of an aristocrat's extended family. In a palace the whole body of people in royal employ was part of the ruler's family. The constantly expanding royal household was problematic, logistically difficult to bed and costly to house and feed.[31] The overcrowding, tensions and rivalries among the court are presented on stage when Lear descends on Goneril's household. Theoretically the sovereign was their father, they his children. He had a duty of care, they a duty of service and loyalty. In practice many servants were simply parasite sycophants and masters slave-driving arrogant snobs. The importance of these bonds of reciprocal care (master/ servant, parent/child), is a recurrent theme in Shakespeare. Both areas of human interface required that personal and professional transactions be based upon truth. Social cohesion depended on both sides doing their duty properly and honestly. Once these bonds were broken, chaos was possible – and in a tragedy, inevitable. Kent and Oswald particularly focus this context. Kent's loyalty to Lear and the orthodox order of things is counterbalanced by his undiplomatic manner, which causes trouble where a sensitive approach might achieve more. Kent's anger is not dissimilar to his master's. Oswald too takes after his mistress; the flattering yes-man, prepared to subvert hierarchy, will do whatever ill-mannered act he is commanded by his feudal mistress, even contemplating committing murder and social subversion, breaking a Commandment and overturning the social order like the servant who killed Cornwall (though his motive was laudably different). Aspects of the courtier's servant life are revealed through Edgar's speeches as Poor Tom. Speaking like a mad seer inspired by the gods, he warns, 'Obey thy parents; keep thy word justly; swear not [i.e., do not take the Lord's name in vain by blasphemy]; commit not with man's sworn spouse; set not thy sweet heart on proud array' (III. iv.). This selection of four Commandments announces Edgar's assuming of the chorus role previously voiced by the Fool. They relate to his father, remind the audience of the common sins of their court, and finish with an admonition against vanity that would be highly relevant to the pampered narcissists watching this disturbing drama. Lear asks, 'What hast thou been?' Ironically it is a question asked of one who has lost his place in society and assumed a false persona by one who is losing his own sense of identity and is in the process of recreating a new one. Edgar answers that he has been:

A servingman, proud in heart and mind; that curl'd my hair, wore gloves in my cap [souvenir love tokens from his mistress], serv'd the lust of my mistress' heart, and did the act of darkness with her; swore as many oaths as I spake words, and broke them in the sweet face of Heaven; one that slept in the contriving of lust, and wak'd to do it. Wine lov'd I deeply, dice dearly, and in woman out-paramour'd the Turk: false of heart, light of ear, bloody of hand; hog in sloth, fox in stealth, wolf in greediness, dog in madness, lion in prey. Let not the creaking of shoes nor the rustling of silks betray thy poor heart to woman: keep thy foot out of brothels, thy hand out of plackets, thy pen from lenders' books, and defy the foul fiend. (III. iv.)

It is a detailed litany of sins typical of young men about town and court: pride, personal vanity, lust, swearing (probably blasphemously), drinking, gambling, insincerity, readiness to believe the worst, violence, sloth, deviousness, greed, irascibility and predatoriness. It ends with warnings against amatory and sexual involvement with women, involvement with moneylenders, and an exhortation to defy the devil. The city dramas of the time are full of young men regularly visiting brothels, entangled in irregular sexual attachments, in debt to moneylenders, and less than God-fearing. *Measure for Measure*, imbued with the same imaginative resonance as *Lear*, presents types from this world. Whether Edgar speaks from personal experience of a young man's raffish life is unknown since his experience is never described, but his depiction of the immorality of seventeenth-century London is accurate. Later the role of shocking the audience by awkward references to the corrupt ways of the world devolves onto Lear. His not-so-mad sayings expose the deeply flawed nature of man and the vile hypocrisy of what is supposed to be a civilized world.

Within two months of James's accession hopes of a new golden age evaporated and uncertainties began accumulating. Crowned in July, by early August a Catholic plot to kidnap him was uncovered and the plague returned to London. Its regular outbreaks always unnerved people. Apart from the natural anxiety about a disease whose origins they did not know, they imagined it was the work of the Devil permitted by God as a punishment for unidentified sins. The context of James I's new court was an unknown quantity. Doubts and fears circulated, but a pattern was emerging. By December 1603 government finances had collapsed in chaos and the king was already bickering with Parliament over money. It would worsen. Puritans and Catholics were disappointed, restless, discontented that no relaxation of restrictions on them had emerged. In fact the opposite looked likely. The court quickly earned a reputation for corruption – physical and moral. Luxury and extravagance, promiscuity, drunkenness and other forms of degeneracy became more and more evident. Large agglomerations of people unavoidably generate rivalries, grievances, hatreds, secrets, changing alliances and relationships. This pot of poison bubbled over when the established order was penetrated by newcomers, foreigners accompanying a new king, and taking posts already occupied.[32] Monarchs have always raised cash by selling titles, honours and posts. The devaluation of distinction did not end there. James created a new rank (1611), the knight baronet, available for £1,905.[33] He also created and sold 19 viscountcies, 30 earldoms, a marquisate and 3 new dukedoms, but remained in debt. Matters worsened when Parliament refused a huge payment request called 'the Great Contract'. The Elizabethan and Jacobeans were keen to have clear differences between the ranks: background, land ownership, income, clothing and spheres of activity were the criteria. Any loss of the sharpness of distinction was a step towards chaos. The tawdry selling of titles provided playwrights with wonderful opportunities for humour, but the money gained did not replenish the public purse and new promotions depleted it further.

Other mental baggage Jacobeans carried was focused in the spate of pamphlets recounting bizarre occurrences. Ghostly appearances, outbreaks of witchcraft, brutal murders, malformed births and unusual weather events were a staple of gossip and fear, for such events were always seen as portents of disaster. The queen's death triggered hoarding of grain and flour. The price of meal rose by four times.[34] Thomas Dekker wrote of 'a hideous tempest' that seemed to herald Elizabeth's death. It 'shook cedars, terrified the tallest pines, and cleft asunder even the hardest hearts of oak'.[35] Lear's wild 'Blow winds' speech might well send tremors of agitated memory through the audience. All natural disasters were seen as God's anger at the nation's sins and a warning to repent and reform. Any unusual event – earth tremor, comet, flood, unseasonable hailstorm – provoked hysterical, moralizing pamphlets and stern homilies from pulpits. This was a belief in transition. A slowly growing movement among scientists, doctors and amateur experimenters sought explanations for natural events in the laws of physics, chemistry or biology rather than in the supernatural, God or magic. In 1609 Robert Gray asserted:

> Amongst us at this day, if any strange accidents do happen, either in the air, or in the earth, or in the waters, [...] we refer them to some material cause or other, being unwilling [...] to acknowledge God to have a hand in this.'[36]

This represents the beginnings of deism,[37] but the belief of the majority, as regards unforeseen, inexplicable and frightening events, was still theocentric as Thomas Beard warned:

> If you be mighty, puissant and fearful, know that the Lord is greater than you, for he is almighty, all-terrible, and all-fearful: in what place soever you are, he is always above you, ready to hurl you down and overturn you, to break, quash, and crush you in pieces as pots of earth.[38]

Though disasters (plagues, diseases, storms, astronomical events) were increasingly thought to have secondary (i.e., scientifically explicable) causes, even Raleigh, prepared to 'boldly look into the second cause', acknowledged of God 'His secret will is the cause of all things'.[39] In 1606 scientific explanations still had the appearance of magic (i.e., diabolism), but the pace of discovery would accelerate steeply during the rest of the century, often co-existing uneasily with the increasing centrality of Christ to many people's lives. The explosion of religious pamphlets in the 1630s and 1640s ran parallel with increasing research into optics, microscopy, astronomy, botany and other branches of science. Yet there were, at the same time, still great swathes of superstitious belief. Witchcraft was an easy explanation for effects that had unseen causes. Witchcraft linked to imagined attempts at social destabilization with religious motives would persist throughout the seventeenth century, despite advances in science and rationalism. It is no coincidence that the career of Matthew Hopkins (self-styled 'witchfinder general') flourished in the midst of the anxieties and suspicions of the Civil War. Samuel Harsnett's *A Declaration of Egregious Popish Impostures* (1603) is an example of prejudice readily reaching for an explanation that demonized the standard scapegoat. Recounting a series of papistical deceptions, it stoked the always-smouldering fires of anguished expectation of Catholic outrages.[40] 1604 was difficult, 1605 worse. In January Barnaby Rich's *Faults, Faults, Faults* deplored the breakdown of love and marriage, clerical squabbles and literary decline, but the general economic depression, agricultural difficulties, scandals and other unsettling alarms were overshadowed in November by the Gunpowder Plot.[41] The evil of the plan to annihilate the social and political leaders created an edgy, suspicious mood, worsened when a great eclipse followed. Such astronomical events were understood by a few but for the majority of the population they were imbued with all sorts of ominous superstitions. 1606 was no better. In January the Gunpowder Plotters were tried and executed horribly. Father Henry Garnett, part of the extended network of Jesuit priests secretly working in England, knew of the plot, but did not reveal it as he was told under the protection of the confessional. He was tried and executed in May. In February 1606 the pamphlet *Strange News from Carlstadt* reported a bloodlike sun, a woman bearing three children – one a blackamoor, one like death, the third with four heads – each speaking bizarre prophecies.[42] Anthony Nixon's *The Black Year* expresses a broader sense of decline with barren fields, oppression of tenants and arts and learning despised. When *Lear* was performed the play's atmosphere of intrigue and treason, secrets and lies, unsettling mad scenes and acts of cruelty and subversion was more than matched by the realities of recent events. The primitive, visceral violence of the play is suited to a pagan world. There are passionate outbursts, curses, two banishments, a beating, three stabbings, a duel, a poisoning, a royal messenger stocked, an appalling sequence involving the king going mad, the blinding of Gloucester, a battle, and the pathos-filled sight of Lear carrying his dead daughter. Enveloping all this is the deeply upsetting atmosphere of vicious rifts, rows, deceptions, lies and cruel words within families. The whole play cuts deeply into the roots of our need for the comforting belief that our family is the source of love and support. All the while the audience knows these are not happenings confined to early society. Lear's world is Shakespeare's, where civilization is as veneer thin as it was in the pre-Christian past. All around were instances of man's inhumanity to man. The recent public executions of the Gunpowder Plotters involved being hanged and while still alive having their hearts cut out. The reality/fiction similarity was obvious. In July most of the audience had been present (like Shakespeare and his company) at Theobalds, the Earl of Salisbury's mansion, where he hosted the visiting King Christian of Denmark. The drunken excesses of the celebrations, the inebriated lady performers in the masque, the copious vomiting of the Danish king, were transgressions of decorum confirming the sense of social disintegration and moral decline recurrent in contemporary literature.

In this play about identity, some want to change their place, others have change forced on them. Lear is changed by anger, morphs again through madness and again through remorse. Gloucester too changes as does Albany. Kent's wonderfully abusive rant (II. ii.) defines the identity of the cringing sycophant Oswald in epithets characterizing a baseborn man with social ambitions. Edgar as Poor Tom answers his own father's question, 'What are you there?' (another uncertainty as to identity) by listing the antics and life of a mad beggar who was once of some status ('three suits to his back, six shirts to his body' [III. iv.]). This is one example of many where words, phrases and images from one part of the play are repeated elsewhere, giving linguistic unity, tying the parts together, suggesting a unified imaginative vision that sees all the parts of this world as of one corrupt whole. The web of interconnecting words, images and ideas runs not only through this play but recurs in other plays of proximal date (*Troilus and Cressida*, *Othello*, *Measure for Measure*, *Timon*), suggesting that the same cynical feelings activated Shakespeare in writing them. Edgar's decline into beggary, common enough, paralleled by the changing fortunes of other characters, reminds us how those rising into power and wealth (Scots favourites, newly dubbed knights, merchant/financiers and monopolists in the city, young men inheriting the family fortune and wasting it in dissipation) never knew how long good fortune would last. Kings too can fall. The 'wheel of fire' (IV. vii.) Lear refers to is an allusion of some impact, for it evokes the powerful medieval image of the Wheel of Fortune that raises up and throws down popes, kings, politicking dukes, merchant bankers, court favourites – a warning echoed in many Bible stories. The fall of a great man is the key pattern of classical tragedy, but in a Christian Renaissance context the downturn of Fortune's wheel was a reminder of the precariousness of life and, importantly, a warning that the fall of evil rulers was a sign of Providence's purpose. Shakespeare's age believed in Armageddon and expected collapse.

Fear was in the air the Jacobeans breathed. Fears about doctrinal differences ripping society apart, fears of excommunication and damnation resulting from cutting England off from Catholicism, must have seethed in the subconscious and conscious mind since Henry VIII's time. The second half of the sixteenth century was awash with anomalous vestiges of the old faith co-existing with the rigours of the new. The outer world might change at the stroke of a pen or at a monarch's behest, but the internal habits of thought and feeling of four to five million people took longer. The ritual details of the Book of Common Prayer controlled Sunday worship in thousands of parish churches, but there was a difference between the conformity of the tongue mouthing responses and the dissent of the heart. No king, bishop or vicar could control the individual conscience. Whatever Henry's motives in destroying the centuries-old religious houses scattered all over the country, ordinary people would have had doubts, reservations and terrified premonitions of God's wrath punishing the land for such impiety. Everyday life was a confusing mixture of new enquiry, the discarding of old doctrines and corrupt superstitions, and little moments of instinctive resort to ingrained superstitious habits. These did not disappear overnight. To live in constant fear of unpredictable disasters, lurches in the Wheel of Fortune, as signs of divine anger might have made men neurotic paranoiacs. Calvin taught that Christians needed to submit to God and trust that nothing happened (good or bad) by the working of chance. All was as God intended. Misfortune might be a deserved punishment for sin, but could also be a chastening good. The story of Job was commonly referenced to enforce the idea that misfortunes could purify and strengthen the sufferer. You had to submit to the will of the Lord. Fear of divine vengeance for misdemeanours receded considerably as the Christian world moved from the medieval into the Renaissance period, but it was still there and became vibrantly active when a sin committed was followed closely enough by some misfortune to make it seem like God's punishment. It was a connection naturally made. In an age of constant religious interaction and constant doctrinal realignment, many people still visited the village wise woman or cunning man. People lived in three worlds. One had ancient pagan, popular roots in the rural community and the natural superstitions that people of all ages cling to. There was also the new world of science that debunked superstition. Then there was the aggressive, new religion, banishing magic and armed with a formidable range of punishments for non-conformity. Lear's calling the gods to curse his daughters would have looked like calling occult powers, but would still be within the belief system to which many in the audience still clung. Lear supposedly lived in pagan times, but Christians still wished ill luck on enemies, seeking the help of a conjuror to bring about misfortune. Such behaviour, ostensibly reprehensible, officially magic, was in reality understandable though growing less and less acceptable. In 1584 it was claimed, 'Three parts at least of the people [remained] wedded to their old superstition still.'[43] There are many scriptural accounts of possession and for the Jacobeans such schizophrenic or multiple personality behaviour had diabolic overtones. Poor Tom's improvised 'ravings' about the fiend that 'vexes' him, the list of devils he recites, highlight how magical and biblical superstition overlap. These scenes inject an extreme tone. The 'raving' of Lear on the heath is the irrational, incoherent venting of anger and disbelief. Incensed at how he has been treated, unable to believe the treatment came from his daughters, his language, references to filial ingratitude being monstrous and of a serpent-like evil, reflect the unnatural behaviour we have seen displayed by him and the sisters. But Tom/Edgar's language ratchets up the tone, moves from the understandable grief of a deeply upset father to a mood on the edge of sanity and then over it. Ironically, everything Tom says, part of Edgar's assumed persona, may be fabricated and not genuinely his own experience. Real or not they were sins committed at court and their lunatic recital is enough to tip Lear into insanity. The scenes in the hovel are like a visit to Bedlam, the London hospital for the insane. Sited near Bishopsgate it was somewhere to visit like the Tower menagerie, the theatres, the bear-baiting arena on Bankside. Visiting the lunatics was just another entertainment. In *Lear* the lunatics come to the audience. It is far from entertaining in the usual sense. Elizabethan and Jacobeans were fascinated by unusual states of mind. Many plays introduce insanity (real or pretended) and other obsessional states. Volpone's infatuation with gold, Hamlet's extreme grief over his father's death and his anger at his uncle, Iago's evil, Othello's jealousy, Richard III's single-minded ruthless pursuit of power, Faustus's obsession with the occult, the various fixations of various malcontents in the Revenge Tragedies, indicate interest in highly charged emotional states. Apart from the obvious excitement such explorations provoked in the audiences, many serious non-fiction writers – moralists, sociologists, medical scientists – described, defined and debated the workings of the human mind, its fragilities and aberrations. Madness mixed with diabolism was a heady, disturbing, frightening combination in any situation. How much more so for a cosseted high-status audience. Describing the degradation of the abject poverty of those 'houseless wretches' at the other end of the social comfort scale was far from the cultivated poetry of court masques. Among references to eating 'the swimming frog, the toad, the todpole, the wall-newt' and Tom's fiend-driven frenzy, eating 'cow-dung for sallets' and swallowing 'the old rat and the ditch-dog', Shakespeare inserts sharp social satire. Targeting not only the wretch 'whipped from tithing to tithing' but through the fictional 'autobiography' of the servingman 'proud in heart and mind', the author attacks the sinfulness of the typical courtier. Vanity, lust, blasphemy and oath breaking, drunkenness, sloth, lying, deviousness, greediness and debt are the transgressions mentioned, but the recurrent sin is lust: 'serv'd the lust of my mistress' heart, and did the act of darkness with her; […] one that slept in the contriving of lust, and wak'd to do it. [...] In woman out-paramour'd the Turk. [...] Keep thy foot out of brothels, thy hand out of plackets [...]' (III. iv.). Shakespeare is blatantly declaring promiscuity as the dominant feature of the court. The hothouse atmosphere of palace life, so many men and women living so close together, naturally led to sexual intrigues, multiple partners and all the attendant emotional drama. Drunkenness and promiscuity were two temptations high on the Non-conformist worst sin list. Along with anger they were the sins that most brought out the animal in man. Yet, as the play's events progress from bad to worse, little acts of kindness, little moments of understanding, hint at an underlying impulse in man that is not so savage, not so selfish. Self-knowledge achieved through adversity, suffering and cleansing lead at the end to a mood of reconciliation, forgiveness, charity, redemption and reconstruction. But at what cost?

Tensions between vestigial Catholicism and the new religion's drive to establish itself led to many inconsistencies. The man who might automatically call on a favourite saint to help him because he had done so since a child might be very vocal in opposing in his parish church any form of religious rite that looked like magic. The desire to banish any supernatural intercession had a long tradition stemming from the underground heresies and Lollardy of the Middle Ages that opposed the increasing doctrinal corruption of a Catholic Church that relied heavily on belief in miracles and saintly intervention. The new church wanted the individual to attend devotedly to his own faith and his own soul. It wanted him to see the priest, speaking in English, praying in English, as his spokesman with God. Edgar's references to the imagined devils Poor Tom 'sees' represented superstitious papistical silliness to most of the audience, perhaps provoking laughter. Yet the Devil and his legions were very real to them, a constant threat. Poor Tom's fiends would have worked on the imagination, evoking haunting fears in the dark recesses of the mind.

Dismantling the Roman Church's infrastructure began in 1534 with Henry VIII's Act of Supremacy, continued in 1536 with the first phase of the Dissolution of the Monasteries, followed by the extensive reforms initiated in Edward VI's brief reign (1547–53). But there were still enemies to fight. Radical Lutheran doctrines worried conservative worshippers, as did the Calvinist idea that some were born predestined to go to Heaven however badly they behaved on Earth and others were damned however virtuous. This raised the question of how much moral behaviour was motivated by fear of punishment (on Earth or in the afterlife). Then there were growing numbers of Puritans gaining power on councils (especially in the City of London), vehemently calling for further church reform to root out Catholic ritual. Mixed with politics and religion were fears of a return to the pre-Tudor baronial Wars of the Roses, focused this time through religious conflict like in France. These related to concerns about who ruled the country and how, especially as the queen crawled toward death. Tensions between Mary Queen of Scots and Elizabeth had threatened civil war. Various plots against Elizabeth created constant uneasiness. These anxieties gave Shakespeare's history plays and tragedies the extra edge of not just being displays of past events, with pomp and ceremony, trumpets and battles, but unnerving suggestions how the past can return to haunt a nation, how unresolved grievances, memories of violence done, injustices committed, hidden like the fissures of an apparently quiescent volcano which, invisibly building pressure, will at some time break into seismic catastrophes in the body politic. Would there be a ferocious papist uprising against James? The general expectation was that there would be civil unrest. Dekker asked,

Who did expect but ruin, blood, and death,
To share our kingdom, and divide our breath?[44]

With concerns growing about the new king's fitness to rule (given his background as son of the plotting Queen of Scots), the spectacle of Lear's behaviour, his daughters' treatment of him and their and Edmund's long-held grievances made tense viewing. Legitimacy seemed besieged.

Much of Shakespeare's work has an underlying motif about fitness to rule. There are examples of good and bad kingship, of how not to rule a city, a household, a family and, most essentially, yourself. There is a persistent concern with the dangers of not controlling your passions. Not knowing yourself (Lear 'hath ever but slenderly known himself'), not knowing your strengths and weaknesses, not focusing the right priorities, not being honest with yourself and others, not making rational judgements, not choosing safe friends and honest servants, not running your household, your family, yourself properly and justly, are persistently discussed during the period. The chronicles offered instructive *exempla* from past history, displaying success and failure among rulers. Elyot's *The Governour* offered a detailed treatise on the education essential for those born to greatness, achieving it or having it thrust upon them. Great place demanded moral principles if duty was to be properly performed. Transient fads and fancies, passing whims, innate personality defects, favouritism and other faults could all affect just conduct.

New centuries always create fearful anticipations of disaster. Contemporary literature reflected these fears in poetic satires and satiric dramas expressing a sense of England having lost its way morally and that the world had become old and run down. Marston's satiric poem *The Scourge of Villainye*, his plays *The Malcontent*, *Antonio and Mellida* and *The Dutch Courtesan*, and Dekker's *The Honest Whore* reflect moral ambiguity and concerns about the state of society, castigate the intrigues, lies, machinations of courts and present a range of psychopathic villains as disturbed and fascinating as Edmund, but far more bloodthirsty. Shakespeare's Great Tragedies and Problem Plays contribute to this gloomy psychic state. *Lear*, Jonson's *Volpone* and John Day's *Isle of Gulls* all appeared about the same time and, though very different in style, present worlds where flattery, greed, hypocrisy and pretension are dominant features of a parasitical humanity where people are likened to the animals their major humour (personality trait) most resembles. Gloucester's picture of his times sums up the sense of the world's decay:

> Love cools, friendship falls off, brothers divide: in cities, mutinies; in countries, discord; in palaces, treason; and the bond crack'd 'twixt son and father. This villain of mine [Edgar] comes under the prediction; there's son against father: the King falls from the bias of nature; there's father against child. We have seen the best of our time: machinations, hollowness, treachery, and all ruinous disorders follow us disquietly to our graves. (I. ii.)

Edmund mocks his father's pessimistic credulity, but uses the same picture of social disintegration to fool his brother into believing in predictions of disaster. As he does so we realize he is describing what has already happened and what will happen: '[…] unnaturalness between the child and the parent; death, dearth, dissolutions of ancient amities; divisions in state; menaces and maledictions against King and nobles; needless diffidences, banishment of friends, dissipation of cohorts, nuptial breeches […]' (I. ii.).

Though there was a natural tendency to sensationalize and emphasize the negative aspects of human sinfulness and God's warnings through violent natural events and grotesque unnatural events (like a calf born with two heads), there was a reverse to all that. Continued survival (the storm that dispersed the Spanish Armada, the numerous unsuccessful plots against Elizabeth and then against James) indicated to some that England was a chosen nation, elected by God for special protection, justifying the Fifth Monarchists' belief that the reign of King Jesus would begin in England. Special nation status resonates through John of Gaunt's 'sceptered isle' speech in *Richard II* (1593–96), where the dying duke calls England 'this blessed plot':

> This other Eden, demi-paradise,
> This fortress built by Nature for herself
> Against infection and the hand of war (II. i. 42–4)

This myth enabled Shakespeare and other playwrights to see English history in terms of good management leading to happiness and God's support, while mismanagement led to the misery of war and withdrawal of God's guardianship.

Chapter 10

THE LITERARY CONTEXT

The Text Alone

The environment of the text itself, speaking for itself, standing independent of other texts and contexts, comprises the relationships the characters have with each other (their obvious exterior relationships and hidden interior feelings), the emotions they evoke in an audience and the question whether it works as a piece of drama. As a story on its own, *King Lear* is about relationship breakdown within two high status families. The main plot concerns the fall of a very old king planning to withdraw from rule and live with his youngest daughter. As part of the ceremonial step down/handover he divides his kingdom based upon his three daughters' declarations of love for him. The two eldest declare insincerely and are given their portion, but the third (who loves him more and truly) refuses to say anything more than that she loves her father as any daughter should according to nature and duty. Exploding with anger the disappointed father disposes of his third daughter's portion to the other two, marries her off to the King of France and foists himself on the others a month at a time. The resulting tensions lead to a complete dissolution of the normal family bonds, the rejection of the father and his subsequent mental breakdown. Omit the status of the characters and you have (up to a point) a story that could apply to any family, because *Lear* is a tale that goes to the roots of human relationships. It lays bare the unsettling fact that sometimes there is little real love within families and much of what passes for it is merely courtesy designed to secure material goods. Such was the profile of many Jacobean high-status families. Once independent, unloving children can discard the restraining politeness of civilized culture and behave as they truly wish to do. Lear's allocation of his land is like any parent moving out of his house and disposing of his goods. The ensuing tensions when he moves into the two eldest daughters' households is little different in essence from the inevitable difficulties of any aged parent moving into a married child's home. The conflicts escalate because this parent brings with him a large and inevitably disruptive entourage and still expects to be treated like a king. Lear's sense of impotence enrages him and when exacerbated by the attitudes and actions of daughters who do not really love him he goes mad. The return of the loving daughter to help rescue, cure and succour her father is an act of positive human kindness counteracting feelings that the family is doomed as a social unit. However, the fact this story is about a royal family makes a difference, for larger issues and many more people's lives and futures are involved than if this was a simple domestic quarrel in an ordinary family. Throughout the narrative sides are taken by characters and by the audience. The isolated, rejected father has loyal supporters who protect and aid him. Armies are mobilized, civil war breaks out, deaths ensue and loyalties are tested. At its most basic level this is a disturbing exposure of naked ambition and plain hatred, demonstrating family life is not always as loving and supportive as complacently assumed. At a more complex level it is a story that questions the parenting of Lear and Gloucester and why they produced the emotionally stunted, distorted personalities of Goneril, Regan and Edmund, yet also produced the unswerving humanity of Cordelia and Edgar. There are hints that favouritism has created such different child psychologies and that Goneril, Regan and Edmund might have developed differently had they felt less neglected. The play works as a harrowing narrative regardless of all external contexts, but the contexts enrich it immeasurably.

King Lear's Place in Shakespeare's Oeuvre

The relationship of *Lear* to Shakespeare's preceding and succeeding work is a matter of identifying recurrent themes and attitudes (like the concern with kingship and governance), considering whether *Lear* 'fits' with the other three Great Tragedies, and identifying ideas and views new to this piece and developments in theatrical handling.

The obvious connection is with the other Great Tragedies (*Hamlet*, *Othello* and *Macbeth*). Appearing 1600–1606, focusing largely on the fall of a central male character, showing the collapse of domestic relationships, they also question the nature of rule and the precariousness of the tenure of power and personal happiness when worked upon by disgruntled plotters. They explore the depths of human evil and the psycho-emotional complexities and frailties of the 'hero'. Date-wise the major comedies are intermixed with the impulse that created the intense and disturbing dramas of the tragedies. Both genres share concern with misjudgement and personal mismanagement pivoted on failure to control emotions, failure to discern the real from the apparent. The moods and outcomes are as different as laughter and tears, but the underlying moral lessons are similar: man is a giddy thing, easily deceived by himself and/or others, and subject to the misleading deceptions of passion and appetite. Similar themes and moral approaches are evident too in the Problem Plays of the same period (*Troilus and Cressida, All's Well That Ends Well, Measure for Measure*). Like *Antony and Cleopatra* (1606–07) and *Timon of Athens* (1605–08), the Problem Plays combine the fall of an individual with a deeply cynical sense of the broad decay of society around them. The theme of appearance and reality is recurrent, expressed in the discrepancies between what people say and what they do. The capacity for clothing to disguise the realities of what people are is another recurrent metaphor in *Lear* as in all Shakespeare's work. Society in crisis (militarily and personally) featured too in the range of English history plays where kingship, a central aspect of *Lear*, was originally displayed and dissected.

The Literature of the Time

Lear relates to contemporary literature, to other tragedies, has affinities with other writers as regards mood, *fin de siècle* views and general philosophy of life, and shares satirical targets with the City Comedies. It was once believed that Shakespeare is not topical or satirical, that Jonson, Marston, Middleton, Dekker, Beaumont and Fletcher are more grounded in specific critiques of their times, while Shakespeare, though including some references to contemporary events, tends to be more concerned with the broad, universal problems of humanity divorced from the particularities of here and now. This view is inaccurate. Between 1600 and 1606, Shakespeare became more engaged with contemporary social decadence, with moral decline and with political questions connected to kingship, rule, power and punishment. This reflects a moralism evident in many playwrights, pamphleteers, polemicists and priests. The view that the time was out of joint is evident in *Troilus* (1601–02), *All's Well* (1602–04), *Measure For Measure* (1604) and *King Lear* (1605–06). The last two particularly deal with similar problems of flawed leadership, the nature of government, authority and the complex ambiguities of both princely and personal morality. Verbal echoes link the two, both have a more than usual number of references to subjects of current concern and set the action within the moral matrix of sin and virtue. The social problems underlying the plots are ones a London audience would recognize. It is as if the plays originate from a common strand of thought and feeling, expressing a black melancholy about the nature of human beings. Yet within this period Shakespeare also wrote *Much Ado, As You Like It* and *Twelfth Night*. No biographical evidence explains the bitterness of the author, but both *Measure For Measure* and *King Lear* share an extreme darkness about humanity. Perhaps the more he saw of life the more cynicism bit.

Shakespeare was immersed in the world of the theatre and the writers who inhabited it. Whatever he read or saw on the stage left traces in his own work; he acquired impressions, images, words and phrases, storing them for later use, as is common to all writers. He was also immersed in the outer world of the Bankside, where theatres were interspersed with brothels, cheap taverns and crowded rickety tenements. Humanity teemed here, from rich to poor and everything in between: a world where cutpurses, conmen, silken courtiers going to the Globe (or a brothel) rubbed up against prentices on an afternoon jolly which might end in the pit of the theatre – after a suitably liquid lunch. There was the world north of the river where he lodged in Silver Street from at least 1603–05. Nearby was Cheapside, the City's commercial and civic artery, heaving with market traders and shopkeepers, the bustle, stink, emotions and dramas of everyday life. Cheapside was a wide thoroughfare used ceremonially for mayors and kings to process from the City to Westminster or the reverse, but chiefly functioning as the money, food and general goods hub of London, with stalls and shops and all the noise and activity associated with buying, selling and haggling. There were tallow chandlers, drapers, tailors, haberdashers, general mercers, timber sellers, butchers and above all goldsmiths. The luxury goods shops had a Continent-wide reputation. Silver Street housed a number of silversmiths' workshops.[1] Nearby Wood Street, Milk Street and Poultry indicate the products they chiefly sold. On Bread Street, running off the south side of Cheapside, was the Mermaid Tavern, where Shakespeare met to eat, drink and talk, talk, talk with Jonson, Middleton, Marston and other writers working for the King's Men. Though writing a play was a solitary activity, there was collaboration and much sharing of ideas and gossip. The Mermaid sessions probably generated many ideas that became interwoven in subsequent plays. In an age before newspapers, tavern chat circulated news and rumour, not always distinguishing between them.

Shakespeare was also intermittently part of another world – the court. A leading member of the King's Men, he was frequently involved in command performances at whatever palace the king happened to be in, for he and the other senior members of the company were made Grooms of the Chamber and, as members of the royal household, wore the royal livery.[2] This locus too had its dramas, its passions and emotional tangles. Literary influence, everyday life and the closed life of the court all intermix in *King Lear*.

The dominant literary genre of the time is the play, though pamphlets, poetry, sermons and other written polemic forms abounded and could be influential.

The *Essayes* of Michel Montaigne (translated by John Florio, published in 1603) make a vital input to questions of sibling relationships, paternal autocracy and general views of the nature of mankind. Samuel Harsnett's extremist anti-Catholic pamphlet *A Declaration of Egregious Popish Impostures* (1603) provided some of the language, diabolic allusions and the atmosphere of deception. Add to these the literary-historical sources of the Lear story and we begin to see how the world of letters contributed to the texture, tone and imaginative core of the play. But the vibrant tensions of the real world are mixed into the text too. These came from Shakespeare's own observations and ever-alert ears, but they have a literary origin too in the topicality of the plays of the 1600s.

The general tone of the theatre and of theatre people naturally had an important effect upon *Lear*. Shakespeare spent much of his working, money-earning time in the Globe or at Blackfriars, as actor, writer, director and co-sharer in the business. Leisure time was spent with writers, discussing ideas, works in progress, what rival theatres were producing, what the company was about to present, what was popular with audiences, what pieces had failed, the mood of London and the state of the world, much as any group of work colleagues might. Fashions in the styles of plays reflected authors' tastes and educational backgrounds but also the demands of theatregoers. They constantly changed. Comedy was always a good bet for pleasing the public. Tragedy or serious topics were less certain, as Jonson discovered when his Senecan-style political tragedy *Sejanus His Fall* (1603) was rejected by the Globe audience. Chronicle histories (popularized by Marlowe's *Tamburlaine*, performed 1587), using the exotic foreign past or recent British history, were always likely to succeed. These introduced political themes not always possible to handle if they were too contemporary, but the King's Men also began to develop interest in stories of the fall of powerful men. This opened a market for tragedy focusing and sublimating current fascination with courtiers and favourites who rose, flourished magnificently, then fell spectacularly. The current political firmament was replete with falling stars not directly portrayed on stage, for the story of their eclipse raised questions about the rule of the monarch. The conduct of historical or fictional figures could represent *hubris* humbled and the audience could be left to make the contemporary identification. Increasingly there were city men whose rise to power and fall into infamy could be used as subject matter for tragedy or tragicomedy. Undercapitalized merchants overspeculating and civic politicians overreaching themselves attempting to move into the landowning nobility made apt subjects for didactic examples on the stage. Court corruption added to the popularity of tragedy that continued into the late Stuart period of Charles II. Marlowe and Shakespeare combined chronicle history and tragedy, but also refined plays that focused on the personal downfall of charismatic fictional individuals, as in *Faustus* (performed 25 times between 1594 and 1597), *The Jew of Malta* (first performed in 1592) and the four Great Tragedies.

By the 1600s two subgenres were in fashion – the Revenge Tragedy and the satirical City Comedy. The first type came to prominence with Thomas Kyd's immensely popular *The Spanish Tragedy* (first performed c. 1582), followed by a flood of court-centred bloodthirsty stories of revenge carefully planned and cruelly executed. After *Hamlet* (1600), among the most well known are Marston's *Antonio's Revenge* (1601) and *The Malcontent* (c. 1603), Tourneur/Middleton's *The Revenger's Tragedy* (1606), Webster's *The White Devil* (1612) and *The Duchess of Malfi* (1612–14) and Middleton/Rowley's *The Changeling* (1622). Varying degrees of revenge form part of many dramas. In *Lear* Edmund is associated with this theme in desiring to oust a sibling and punish his father. Edmund plays a fairly minor role in terms of lines and scenes, though his effect on people's lives is greater than his presence on stage. While fascinating in his evil, he is not a sympathetic figure with a genuine, acceptable reason for wishing to be the instrument of retribution. He is a self-appointed nemesis, a Prodigal Son punishing a Prodigal Father, motivated by self-interest, not by the drive to administer the 'wild justice'[3] of deserved punishment. He may have some psycho-sociological excuse for his discontent, but an audience would judge his cruelty and unnaturalness to be monstrous, beyond reasonable sympathy and unforgivable. Gloucester is guilty of lust, levity and neglectful fatherhood – but does he deserve what happens to him? There is revenge too in the behaviour of Goneril and Regan as they punish Lear for his favouritism to Cordelia. But the matter goes deeper than that. They are retaliating for his long-term patriarchal autocracy, his dictatorial repression of them, holding on to wealth and power for so long. We may understand their viewpoint, may sympathize with their resentment at having been so long dependent on him. Shakespeare, unlike all the sources, has them as women already married, with personal lives, their own establishments and a desire to rule. Their behaviour breaks the Fifth Commandment, is inhuman, unkind and unnecessary, and runs counter to all considerations of decency that require tolerance, understanding and sympathy towards the very elderly, particularly a parent, however irritating and erratic.

City Comedy grew in response to the increasing importance of commerce in London and its emergence as a mercantile, financial, trading and transport centre rivalling Antwerp, Amsterdam and Venice. The expansion of its population and the flood of money running through it precipitated numerous social tensions. London became a decadent showcase for luxury consumerism, therefore attracting shallow wannabes and shady swindlers. At all social levels there were people who affected style and fashion, were ambitious for notoriety, celebrity and power. At all social levels there were parasites and tricksters scrounging and scamming money out of the foolish or unwary, providing playwrights with immense opportunities for comedy and satire. While would-be courtiers, dressed à la mode but without a penny in their purse, were mocked according to longstanding satiric tradition, humorous treatment of ambitious citizens and their snobbish wives and children proliferated too. This reflected the rising profile and power of this relatively new force in urban society. The fabulous wealth of some provoked traditional complaints about luxury, vanity, avarice, envy and pride. These in turn triggered comments and judgements about materialism, loss of spiritual values, and questions of charity, poverty and crime. The old binary opposition of the industrious and the idle apprentice reappears in City Comedies to focus attention on conduct and misconduct. The status, definition and behaviour of gentlemen are endlessly scrutinized. Plays had become the 'brief chronicles of the time', reflecting growing tensions between the ranks as they began to change, blur and separate more widely. Satire is a tricky style, not always understood but often offensive. The 1597 satire *The Isle of Dogs* by Jonson and Thomas Nashe aggravated the authorities and was closed for being a 'lewd plaie' full of 'slanderous matter'. If it satirized the queen that was sedition. In 1559, very soon after her accession, Elizabeth I had issued a proclamation forbidding plays to discuss 'matters of religion or of the governance of the estate of the Commonwealth'. Such concerns were the province of 'grave and discreet persons', 'men of authority, learning and wisdom', not to be aired before or by the general public.[4] From 1581 until his death in 1610, as Master of the Revels Edmund Tilney demanded the Revels Office see all plays before they could be performed. No copy of the text of *The Isle of Dogs* exists, but its content was enough to have Jonson and two actors arrested and imprisoned. Tilney's sensitivity (or concern for the nation's moral health) was matched in 1605 by the king's own irritability when *Eastward Ho!* mocked the Scottish accent and the Scots' greedy depredations in London. The authors were imprisoned briefly. Jonson's persistent echoing of updated Juvenalian satirical targets in *Every Man out of His Humour* (1598), *Volpone* (1606) and *The Alchemist* (1612) created a lively atmosphere of criticism of contemporary mores. In May 1606 an increasingly touchy king and increasingly defensive Commons passed the Act to Restrain Abuses of Players, with fines of £10 for each profane usage of the name of God or Jesus Christ during a performance – a blunt form of censorship that missed the point. It was society that needed cleansing. Shakespeare, as a keen observer of human greed, vanity, cruelty and selfishness, was drawn to offer his own satirical comments. *Lear* has a portion of such social criticism, suggestive of a wider corruption that expressed the split between the hypocrisy and veniality of those in comfortable authority and the masses of poor becoming poorer. The pre-Christian settings of *Timon* and *Lear* avoid the danger of blasphemy. Shakespeare never quite sits square in any of the subgenres. His history plays present more than history, his love romances have cynical undertones, his satirical Problem Plays address more than the normal targets. Equally, this tragedy, while telling the story of the king's fall, is a parade of sin replete with satirical comments on usurers and civic authorities, but mostly courtiers and governance.

The Gorboduc effect

Crucial to the development of the chronicle history-tragedy is Thomas Norton and Thomas Sackville's *Gorboduc*, performed for the queen by the student lawyers of the Inner Temple in 1562, printed 1571 and reprinted 1590. The latter edition is one Shakespeare may have known, for the subject matter parallels that of *Lear*. Claimed as the first play to use blank verse, *Gorboduc* is very evidently a declamatory piece lacking realistic dialogue. Its long Senecan-style speeches are turgid in the extreme, without the metrical variation creating different paces within the lines that makes *Faustus*, *Hamlet* and *The Duchess of Malfi* such effective, attention-holding theatrical vehicles. Norton and Sackville's stately lines are more like public speaking exercises for trainee lawyers. Many early history plays are similarly slowed down by long set speeches (even the very popular *Tamburlaine*), but as the theatre boom progressed the style became more natural, with broken lines, interruptions, metrical variation and differing registers, all creating a more realistic tone and a less formal, ceremonial sound. This is very evident in *Lear*.

    Gorboduc is a political play. Its plot comes from ancient Britain's 'history' several generations after Lear. Transgressing traditional primogeniture, King Gorboduc divides his kingdom between his two sons. The elder, angered at his diminished inheritance, raises an army to wrest the other half of the realm from his younger sibling. The latter, hearing of the military preparations, makes a pre-emptive strike. The elder is killed. His mother (who favoured him) takes revenge by killing her younger son. Horrified, the people rebel and slaughter the old king and queen; the nobles rise against the people, defeat them, and in the ensuing power vacuum are drawn into an extended and destructive civil war. The formal argument of the play, given at the beginning, concludes by commenting that the land was 'for a long time almost desolate and miserably wasted'.[5] Dumbshows precede each act; these are mimes in which the actors allegorically represent the imminent action and dialogue. For the reader the printed text gives a brief summary explaining and interpreting it morally and politically. The first, for example, declares,

'A state knit in unity doth continue strong against all force, but being divided, is easily destroyed.' The plot expresses persistent Elizabethan fears of invasion or bloody Catholic-engineered internal division. History, thus early, became a stalking horse for the presentation of contemporary political ideas. Popular history plays in the 1590s were a means by which to explore, through Britain's past, political ambitions, plotting of bloodthirsty coups and all the destructive by-products of civil conflict haunting the contemporary English psyche. The same fears resurfaced in the early years of James's reign and are echoed in *Lear*.[6] Similarly, the foreground of *Gorboduc* is a family tragedy with underlying political and didactic motifs warning about civil war. Each act (except the last) ends with the Chorus pointing out the political message of the preceding action. The first-act Chorus advises stability in a state, achieved by conformity to tradition, for change is dangerous: 'Each change of course unjoints the whole estate' (I. ii. 444). It closes with a warning, analogous to *Lear*:

And this great king that doth divide his land
And change the course of his descending crown,
And yields the reign into his children's hand,
From blissful state of joy and great renown,
A mirror shall become to princes all,
To learn to shun the cause of such a fall. (I. ii. 458–63)

The second-act Chorus warns against rule by young princes 'not bridled with a guiding stay' (II. ii. 296), against 'growing pride' and 'greedy lust' for power:

[...] woe to wretched land,
That wastes itself with civil sword in hand!
Lo thus it is, poison in gold to take,
And wholesome drink in homely cup forsake. (II. ii. 318–21)

Act III's closing Chorus foresees nationwide disjointure in terms and themes that figure significantly in the instability in *Lear*:

The lust of kingdom knows no sacred faith,
No rule of reason, no regard of right,
No kindly love, no fear of heaven's wrath;
But with contempt of gods, and man's despite,
Through bloody slaughter doth prepare the ways
To fatal sceptre and accursed reign.
The son so loathes the father's lingering days,

Ne dreads his hand in brother's blood to stain.
[...]
Thus do the cruel flames of civil fire
Destroy the parted reign with hateful strife.
And hence doth spring the well from which doth flow
The dead black streams of mourning, plaints, and woe.
Of justice, yet must God in fine restore
This noble crown unto the lawful heir. (III. i. 171–92)

Act IV's Chorus promises retribution for 'greedy lust', 'cruel heart, wrath, treason and disdain'. In a biblical echo later repeated in *Macbeth*, divine vengeance is expected; Jove will send the 'dreadful Furies', for 'Blood asketh blood, and death must death requite' (IV. ii. 348–64). The final act closes with Lord Eubulus, a voice of reason and caution. He has little hope that Parliament, where 'each one for himself, or for his friend', will vote for self-interest, will reach a suitable result in electing a new king. He hopes for divine judgement and intervention:

For right will always live, and rise at length,
But wrong can never take deep root to last. (V. ii. 438–41)

Elizabethans and Jacobeans believed that right will triumph and God will punish the bad. Even in the bleakness of *King Lear*, Edgar the punisher apparently takes up the crown to renew the rule of virtue.

The opening of *Gorboduc* has a dysfunctional family theme like both families central to *Lear*. Queen Videna deprecates her husband's planned splitting of the kingdom because it will 'spoil' her elder son's 'birth-right and heritage' (I. i. 26). It is 'against all law and right' (I. i. 28), but Gorboduc, with Lear-like obstinacy, 'hath firmly fixed his unmoved mind' (I. i. 46). There is a hint of less-than-affectionate upbringing in the queen's comment that Gorboduc is 'in kind a father, not in kindliness' (I. i. 18). The wordplay on 'kind' and 'kindliness' is echoed in the Fool's ironic quibble, 'Shalt see thy other daughter will use thee kindly' (I. v.), not meaning in a kind way but according to her nature – cruelly, like her sister. This pun encapsulates the two sorts of nature portrayed in *Lear*: the cruel survival-of-the-fittest animal nature Edmund and the eldest sisters display (reflected in the text's many animal images), and the tender, kind nature that some humans can show (Edgar, Kent, the Fool and Cordelia). This latter form, particularly associated with Christian culture, is embodied in texts like 'Love one another' (John 13:34–5) and 'Love thy neighbour' (Romans 13:9).[7] (See further discussion in the *Arcadia* section, page 184.)

Gorboduc persistently comments on the folly of dividing the kingdom into two rival realms where one ruler is disgruntled at losing what he regards as his birthright, thus limitedly addressing the ongoing controversy about the inequities of primogeniture. The lords are invited to debate the move. One naively declares that kings rule for 'public wealth, and not for private joy' (I. ii. 171), so personal power seeking should not distract the brothers if they focus on their subjects' welfare. Another, more wary, recommends the king divide the realm but retain rule as father and king to avoid rivalry, and enable the sons to learn to rule their portion of the land:

And oft it hath been seen, where nature's course
Hath been perverted in disordered wise,
When fathers cease to know that they should rule,
The children cease to know they should obey. (I. ii. 274–7)

For him, a father's continued supervision is vital:

[…] Nature hath her order and her course,
Which (being broken) doth corrupt the state
Of minds and things […]. (I. ii. 289–90)

Eubulus, the king's secretary, opposes division altogether:

Within one land, one single rule is best:
Divided reigns do make divided hearts;
But peace preserves the country and the prince. (I. ii. 329–31)

He foresees trouble, given the jealous, ambitious nature of men:

Such is in man the greedy mind to reign,
So great is his desire to climb aloft,
In worldly stage the stateliest parts to bear,
That faith and justice, and all kindly love,
Do yield unto desire of sovereignty. (I. ii. 332–6)

Gorboduc, seeing no cause 'to fear the nature of my loving sons' (I. ii. 409), goes ahead with his plan as naively blind as Lear. Noticeably no such discussion occurs in Lear's court. He has decided on 'the division of the kingdom' and so shall it be. Eubulus is proved right, there is civil unrest, and when that is put down by a coalition of lords, there is still the danger of a coup led by the Duke of Albany.[8] The Duke of Cumberland pleads for unity to defend the land from 'greedy lust and […] usurping power' (V. ii. 303) and for Parliament to elect a king from among themselves. This process is anachronistic (there being no such institution in pagan times), but perhaps reflects the practice of Celtic pre-Roman Britain to make decisions through state councils. The last words are given to Eubulus, who sums up the wreck of 'this noble realm'. He foresees the bloodshed consequent on the need to defeat Albany's grab for power:

> These are the plagues, when murder is the mean
> To make new heirs unto the royal crown. (I. ii. 400–401)

His comment is resonant considering the train of plots to assassinate Queen Elizabeth.[9] Thwarted though they were, their existence created an atmosphere of instability and fear such as pervades *King Lear*. Poison, regicide, deceptions and plots pervade the Great Tragedies, reflecting the contemporary political context.

The Montaigne effect

Michel de Montaigne was a French philosopher whose *Essais* (1580) widely range through topics interpreted through the views of classical pundits but filtered through his own life and experiences. He writes on idleness, liars, friendship, repentance, relationships and the education of children. The amalgam of accepted opinions from the classics with a modern man's own views is something the Renaissance valued highly, valorizing the individual's experience rather than merely conceding to classical or biblical authority. This was to be a key signifier in the development of the rationalist individualism that helped form the eighteenth-century Enlightenment. No independent proof exists of Shakespeare having read Florio's translation of Montaigne, but academic studies identify many words and phrases used in Shakespeare's plays written after the Florio translation that did not appear in his earlier work. Verbal and thematic echoes in Gonzalo's speech on the ideal commonwealth (*The Tempest*) and in the discussion of father–son relationships, inheritance and respect for the elderly in *Lear* suggest very strongly that Shakespeare had read Montaigne's essays 'On the Cannibals', 'On the Affection of Fathers for Their Children' and 'An Apology for Raymond Sebond'. Bate asserts that Florio's translation was 'formative of the philosophical vision of *King Lear*'.[10]

Topics and ideas common to both may stem from a shared humanism basing much human conduct on the broad tenets of religion, but circumstantial evidence links the two men, suggesting Montaigne's attitudes did at least become memory traces that re-emerged when the playwright put quill to paper. Florio, once tutor to the Earl of Southampton, remained in contact with him in later life. Southampton was a patron/friend/acquaintance of Shakespeare, so it seems possible Florio and Shakespeare met and the book was discussed, loaned and read. One thing is clear: the dramatist had read the essays. Over a hundred single common words and 23 passages are echoed in *King Lear*.[11] More important than single word or phrasal similarities are the philosophical parallels. In the light of what the characters experience in *Lear*, Montaigne's comments such as 'Repentance begs for burdens'[12] and his references to the 'evil' of 'ambition'[13] are evidence of a common Western ethical tradition. 'Lying is indeed an accursed vice'[14] is hardly an original view, but it is followed by: 'It is only our words which bind us together and make us human. If we realised the horror and weight of lying we would see that is more worthy of the stake than other crimes.'[15] Thus, the matter takes on heightened significance in the light of how devastating are the effects that stem from the purposeful misuse of language in *Lear*.

In 'That No Man Should Be Called Happy until after His Death', Montaigne considers examples of wealthy and powerful people who ended miserably. He attributes this to the envy of the gods, demonstrating their 'power and dominance' over human fortune (Christians would see it as God teaching humility): 'For just as storms and tempests seem to rage against the haughty arrogant height of our buildings, so it could seem that there are spirits above us, envious of our greatness here below.'[16] He quotes Lucretius in corroboration: 'Some hidden force apparently topples the affairs of men, seeming to trample down the resplendent fasces and the lictor's unyielding axes, holding them in derision.'[17] This recalls Gloucester's cynical dictum 'As flies to wanton boys are we to the gods/They kill us for their sport.' *Lear* is full of references to the gods' power, calls for their justice, the influence of the stars and the uncertainty of human fortune. The unsettling rational cynicism of Montaigne's unblinking gaze upon the vileness of man seems to chime with the bleakness of *Lear*. Gloucester's superstition echoes the view that 'the credit given to miracles, visions, enchantments, and such extraordinary events chiefly derives from the power of the imagination acting mainly on the more impressionable souls of the common people'.[18]

More chilling is the picture of men's preying on another's weaknesses that evokes Edmund and the sisters, Lear's comments on beadles, usurers and cozener, and Edgar's depiction of a courtier:

The merchant can only thrive by tempting youth to extravagance; the husbandman, by the high price of grain; the architect, by the collapse of buildings; legal officials, by lawsuits and quarrels between men; the very honorariums and the fees of the clergy are drawn from our deaths and vices. [...] And what is worse, if each of us were to sound our inner depths he would find out that most of our desires are born and nurtured at other people's expense.[19]

Shakespeare's cynical comment on authority ('a dog's obey'd in office') parallels Montaigne's views on nations 'who receive and admit a Dogge to be their King'.[20] This questions just what authority consists of. Is obedience automatically due to whoever wears the insignia of power? Is obedience due to the king ordering an illegal or unworthy act? Associated with this image of the dog obeyed simply because of the office he holds is Shakespeare's recurrent concern with appearance and reality. The history plays show robes and coronets do not make the wearer noble. *King Lear* shows how dressing up – with misleading words as much as with costume – creates false impressions. Corrupt, hypocritical judges are targeted by both Montaigne and Shakespeare, as are the ideas that man can 'see' without his eyes, that through folly we can find wisdom, and madness can bring clearer vision. The connection to the play is not just through common discussion of the parasitic livelihoods that rely on the weakness or misfortunes of others. It is embodied in the predatory animalistic imagery and the ruthlessness of Edmund and the sisters' ideology when divorced from any ameliorating principle of love: 'the younger rises when the old doth fall'. The ubiquity of sin, the role and nature of women, and the commonness of double standards among authority figures are topics both writers discuss.

It is in 'On Affectionate Relationships' that relevant connections emerge most clearly. This addresses the vexed question of parent–child relationships and just how close they could or should be:

> From children to fathers it is more a matter of respect; friendship, being fostered by mutual confidences, cannot exist between them because of their excessive inequality; it might also interfere with their natural obligations: for all the secret thoughts of fathers cannot be shared with their children for fear of begetting an unbecoming intimacy; neither can those counsels and admonitions which constitute one of the principal obligations of friendship be offered by children to their fathers.[21]

He considers too the problem whether (or if) fathers should hand over some (or all) control of the family and its fortune. Sibling relationships, central to the Lear and Gloucester plots, is another family dynamic Montaigne considers. While bonds can be strong between brothers or sisters, inheritance can cause friction. There should be no automatic expectation siblings will remain friends:

> The name of brother is truly a fair one and full of love [...]. But sharing out property or dividing it up, with the wealth of one becoming the poverty of the other, can wondrously melt and weaken the solder binding brothers together. [...] Moreover, why should there be found

between them that congruity and affinity which engender true and perfect friendship? Father and son can be of totally different complexions [personalities]: so can brothers. [...] And to the extent that they are loving relationships commanded by the law and the bonds of nature , there is less of our own choice, less 'willing freedom'. Our 'willing freedom' produces nothing more properly its own than affection and loving-friendship.[22]

Bearing in mind how crucial the theme of 'the misuse of words' is to *Lear*, the word 'brother' is used equivocally as Edmund convinces the gullible Edgar of Gloucester's displeasure. Edgar uses the term neutrally (possibly with affection), while Edmund says 'brother' as a mask, suggesting active, confiding, friendly, trustworthy, protective concern, thus averting suspicion while planning to supplant his gullible sibling.

In 'On the Cannibals', Montaigne recounts how a party of natives visiting France

noticed that there were among us men fully bloated with all sorts of comforts while their halves were begging at their doors emaciated with poverty and hunger: they found it odd that those destitute halves should put up with such injustice and did not take the others by the throat or set fire to their houses.[23]

This touches upon Lear's consciousness of the abyssal difference between the lives of the nobility and that of the 'poor naked wretches'.

The most relevant essay, 'On the Affection of Fathers for Their Children', raises questions about primogeniture and the difficulties of fathers of advanced age continuing to 'bear bags'. Relevant to rich families, where sons are not expected to work, is the old conundrum of what to do with the idle children of the idle rich once educated and of age. Fundamental is the belief that 'a true and well-regulated affection should be born, and then increase, as children enable us to get to know them'.[24] Children should be cherished 'with a truly fatherly love' but also judged if they are unworthy. Montaigne warns that offspring should not be indulged 'as pet monkeys' when young, but then treated sternly when mature. He recommends consistency: that the generous toy giver should not become 'miserly and close-fisted' once the child is of age.[25] The matters of shared influence and access to family money were much in debate from the 1580s wherever property, inheritance and the maintenance of aristo-gentry males were part of the domestic dynamic. Montaigne states frankly, 'I find it cruel and unjust not to welcome them to a share and fellow-interest in our property – giving them full knowledge of our domestic affairs as co-partners when they are capable of it.'[26]

Edmund laying his plot against Edgar, claims to Gloucester: 'I have heard him oft maintain it to be fit that, sons at perfect age, and fathers declin'd, the father should be as ward to the son, and the son manage his revenue' (I. ii.). This view, parallel to Montaigne, is relevant to Lear's situation. The essay suggests a father economize on his own expenditure in order to provide for his children, for 'it is unjust to see an aged father, broken and only half alive, stuck in his chimney-corner with the absolute possession of enough wealth to help and maintain several children, allowing them all this time to waste their best years without means of advancement in the public service'.[27] Montaigne sees money as the heart of the problem. Young aristo-gentry males, educated but with no function in life and lacking disposable income, caused persistent friction. Bacon, saw this too:

> The illiberality of parents, in allowance towards their children, is an harmful error, makes them base, acquaints them with shifts, makes them sort with mean company, and makes them surfeit more when they come to plenty. And therefore the proof is best when men keep their authority towards their children but not their purse.[28]

As Montaigne recommends, 'The soundest way of sharing out our property when we die is [...] to follow customary law.'[29] This would not disperse Edmund's bitterness. The 'plague of custom' is precisely what irks him, along with the fact that Gloucester has done little to integrate him into the family ('He hath been out nine years, and away he shall again') or arrange for his employment at court. Montaigne's next comment is telling: neglected children 'are driven by despair to find some way, however unjust, of providing for their needs'. The 'unbending meanness' of fathers made thieves and tricksters of sons.[30] City Comedies are full of such low gentlemen. Montaigne, aware that money is a power marker and that old men no longer in high office will hold onto their wealth as a means of keeping respect, points out that filial respect should be founded on our virtues and abilities and their love based on our goodness and sweetness of character not on our title or money. The letter Edmund claims Edgar sent echoes closely these aspects of Montaigne: 'This policy and reverence of age makes the world bitter to the best of our times; keeps our fortunes from us till our oldness cannot relish them. I begin to find an idle and fond bondage in the oppression of aged tyranny, who sways not as it hath power, but as it is suffer'd' (I. ii.).

To Montaigne, 'This defect of not realizing in time what one is, of not being aware of the extreme decline into weakness which old age naturally brings to our bodies and our souls [...] has ruined the reputation of most of the world's great men.' But, 'That is not to say we should make a binding gift of our property and not be able to go back on it.' A sensible father would 'retain [...] general authority over affairs'.[31] Lear does not think through the complex consequences of his decisions and presumes on the decency of Cordelia in his plan to settle with her. If he planned to give her a third of the kingdom, how would that fit with her marrying either Burgundy or France? Did he see her as queen of a double kingdom? This happened under the Normans and Plantagenets, but was neither easy to administer nor successful. Elyot prized circumspection in governors. Lear singularly lacks that crucial political ability to look at the different scenarios, foresee problems and have fall-back strategies to deal with them. Even in his intentions for dividing the kingdom, Lear ignores the plan's inherent weaknesses, naively thinking that equal shares will solve the problem and that each sister will happily rule her portion without coveting what the others have. His improvised Plan B, forced on him by Cordelia's failure to conform to his fantasy, pays no heed to just what his position is to be. He seems to want to dispose of responsibility but keep authority and respect. If there has been a distance preserved between Lear and his elder children it explains the detached coldness of their treatment of him. His hasty rearrangement, after banishing Cordelia, leaves him with no power to cope with the rejections he experiences, leaves him at the mercy of two ruthless, unfilial, ungrateful daughters and with nowhere to go. Montaigne is clear about maintaining 'gentle relations with my children' to 'encourage in them an active love and unfeigned affection for me' and feels 'it is also unjust, and mad, to deprive our grown up children of easy relations with their fathers by striving to maintain an austere and contemptuous frown, hoping by that to keep them in fear and obedience'.[32] He cultivates openness and expresses his views and feelings frankly, wishing for no misunderstandings, either in his favour or against.

In the crucial adaptations Shakespeare made in dramatizing the simple, bland, linear chronicle narrative of *King Leir* and the other sources, Montaigne contributed vital ideas to the complex ambiguities and psychological richness of a tragedy that is painful and unsettling.

Sources

This is a game of 'spot the difference'. Most of Shakespeare's plays are not original ideas, but developments of pre-existing stories. *Lear* is no different. The content of the source stories is less important and much less interesting than what Shakespeare does with the themes and how he changes the story – how he extends the characters he takes on, drops some and introduces new ones. Most of the sources are dull and primitive. Shakespeare broadens the reader/viewer's sense of the complex human issues involved, exhibits a deeply sensitive understanding of human motives, hopes and fears, and displays sophisticated theatrical craft, while his linguistic skills show his superior imaginative creativity.

Some of the audience probably knew the story already. *The True Chronicle History of King Leir* was performed at the Rose Theatre, Bankside in 1594.[33] A printed text of this play (published 1605) gave Shakespeare a chance to reread and reacquaint himself with the handling at the time he was writing his version. He probably knew the story from Holinshed's *Chronicles of England, Scotland, and Ireland* (1577), a book he consulted often for his history cycle. Other versions appear in *The Mirrour for Magistrates* (1574, 1578, 1587, 1610), and Spenser's *The Faerie Queene* (1590; II. x.). The subplot came from Sir Philip Sidney's poem *Arcadia* (II. x.). The historical setting, flimsy and unconvincing as it is, may have been partially triggered by William Harrison's *An Historical Description of the Iland of Britaine* or William Camden's *Remaines Concerning Britaine* (1606). It is also claimed that an Italian fairy tale 'Love Like Salt' is a source because in it a king rejects his youngest daughter (of three) because her declaration of how she loves him ('as meat loves salt') does not meet with his approval. She organizes a banquet served without salt on the meat; the guests complain and she explains the meaning of her declaration. The triple child situation, where one is good but misunderstood, the others appearing good but proving bad, is a common pattern in fairy tales. The connection with *Lear* seems tenuous and the pattern coincidental. The following sources, showing the elements Shakespeare chose to keep and develop and those he discarded, offer insights into the creative process.

Holinshed's version[34]

Some editors have assumed the bulk of the story comes from Holinshed (1577, 1587) and the 1594 play. Holinshed dates Leir's reign from 'the yeare of the world 3105' (between 837 and 800 BC), describing him as 'a prince of right noble demeanor, gouerning his land and subjects in great wealth'. His daughters were 'Gonorilla, Regan, and Cordeilla, which daughters he greatly loued, but specially Cordeilla the youngest farre aboue the two elder'. In 'vnwieldie' old age, he 'thought to vnderstand the affections of his daughters towards him, and preferred hir whom he loued best, to the succession ouer the kingdome'. Gonorilla and Regan declare they love him more than life itself and 'farre aboue all the creatures of the world', respectively. Cordeilla declares, 'Knowing the great loue and fatherlie zeale that you haue always borne towards me [...] I have loued you ever [...] as my naturall father.'

She finishes by saying, 'If you would more vnderstand of the loue that I beare you, assertaine your selfe, that so much as you haue, so much you are worth, and so much I loue you, and no more.' Leir, 'nothing content' with this, possibly misunderstands her to mean she loves him for his material wealth. She may in fact be saying, 'Measure my love for you by how much I show my love for you. You have all my love and you are worth all my love.' Leir marries Gonorilla to Maglanus, the Duke of Albany, and Regan to Henninus, the Duke of Cornwall, and declares they shall inherit half of the kingdom each after his death and 'the one half thereof immediatlie should be assigned to them in hand'. Cordeilla gets nothing, and is sent away to marry Aganippus, 'one of the twelue kings that ruled Gallia' (France), who had requested permission to wed her. Later, the dukes, 'thinking it long yer the gouernment of the land did come to their hands', resort to arms, 'reft from him the gouernance' and assign him a portion of land and maintenance later 'diminished' further. Leir is particularly saddened by the 'vnkindnesse of his daughters, which seemed to thinke that all was too much which their father had […] in so much that going from the one to the other, he was brought to that miserie, that scarslie they would allow him one seruant to wait vpon him'. Eventually, 'such was the vnkindnesse, or (as I maie saie) the vnnaturalnesse which he found in his two daughters', Leir flees to Cordeilla, is well received and held in honour. His son-in-law gathers an army, invades Britain, defeats the sisters and restores Leir to the throne. He dies two years later after a reign of 40 years. Cordeilla reigns for five years then is taken prisoner by her nephews, who, 'disdaining to be vnder the gouernment of a woman', raise a rebellion. In despair she commits suicide. This is a bare narrative outline compared with what Shakespeare does with it, developing into dominant themes Leir's sense of the unkindness and unnaturalness of his daughters' behaviour.

Geoffrey of Monmouth[35]

The ancient folk tale of Lear goes back to Geoffrey of Monmouth's *Historia Regum Brittaniae* (*The History of the Kings of Britain*, 1136). This Latin text, that Holinshed abridged, is a pseudo-history[36] built from legends and folk stories about ancient Britain before, during and after the Romans, much of it fictional, though there are instructive themes related to how society works and how leaders lead. In all the early versions Leir survives and reassumes his throne assisted by Cordelia.

Interesting additions to the story emerge from this much earlier version. Leir intends to give the largest part of the kingdom to whoever loves him most (assuming that will be Cordelia). Goneril, as in Holinshed, swears she loves him more than her life, Regan more than any other living creature. Geoffrey describes Leir as 'her credulous father' and gives a motive to Cordelia. Seeing Leir is deceived by the 'blandishments' of her two older sisters, she decides to test his rational discrimination.

> My father [...] can there really exist a daughter who maintains that the love she bears her own father is more than what is due to him as a father? [...] Unless, indeed, she were trying to conceal the truth by joking about it. [...] I have always loved you as my father [...]. I feel no lessening of my affection [...]. If you are determined to wring more than this out of me, then I will tell you how much I love you and so put an end to your enquiry. You are worth just as much as you possess, and that is the measure of my own love for you.

This seems to focus material worth, though it is still possible to read it as, 'You possess my love and are worth just as much of my love as you have. My love matches your worth.' Because she 'apparently really meant what she had said' Leir is very angry, feels scorned and withdraws her share of the kingdom. 'With the advice of the nobles' he marries Goneril and Regan to Maglaurus and Henwinus 'to share between them one half of the island for as long as he, Leir, should live, and after his death they should inherit the entire kingdom of Britain'. When Leir grows weak with age the dukes rebel and take 'the remainder of his kingdom [...] and with it the royal power'. There is not a complete break, for Maglaurus (Albany) agrees 'to maintain him, together with one hundred and forty knights, so that he should not end his days alone [...] in obscurity'. After two years Goneril complains of his 'attendants' 'wrangling with her own servants' about insufficient rations. She speaks to Maglaurus and then orders her father 'to content himself with the service of thirty soldiers'. Leir goes to Regan, but before a year is over 'a quarrel [arises] between the two households', and Regan orders him to dismiss all except five 'retainers'. Returning to Goneril Leir is refused entry unless he keeps only one 'soldier-attendant'. The comments Geoffrey attributes to Goneril are interesting in terms of the power balance they display: 'She upbraided her father for wanting to go about with such a huge retinue now that he was an old man with no possessions at all. She refused steadfastly to give way [...]. For his part he had to obey her.' Leir, 'loathing [...] the misery' he is reduced to, crosses to France. In a tearful outburst of self-pity he remembers the happiness the Fates have snatched away from him and the military glory he once achieved with 'so many hundred thousand fighting-men', battering down the walls of enemy cities and laying waste the provinces of his foes. 'Oh, spiteful Fortune! Will the moment never come when I can take vengeance upon those who have deserted me in my final poverty?' He also acknowledges the truth of Cordelia's words, finally seeing they were ironic: 'As long [...] as I had something to give, so long did I seem worth while to the other two, for it was my gifts they cared for, not me myself.' The rest of the story is like that told by Holinshed (though more detailed). The question remains whether Shakespeare knew of Geoffrey's work or read it. Latin editions were published (Paris 1508, 1517; Heidelberg 1544) but there is no way of ascertaining whether Shakespeare had access to a copy or could have translated it. His friendship with Jonson in the 1600s would have been a means by which the Leir story could have been made available to him. Jonson, an ex-pupil of Camden, kept contact with the antiquarian. Camden criticized the inaccuracies of Geoffrey, so clearly had seen the text. There are so many elements in Geoffrey's account that are echoed in the play that it seems likely Shakespeare knew this version, perhaps through discussion with Camden. Geoffrey devotes a chapter to the supposed prophecies of Merlin, which the Fool references (III. ii.).

King James knew the Lear story before Shakespeare's play was written or performed. He warns his son to respect the principle of primogeniture or 'ye shall leave the seede of division and discorde among your posteritie: as befell to this Ile, by the division and assignment thereof, to the three sonnes of *Brutus, Locrine, Albanact*, and *Camber*'.[37] A marginal note cites 'Polid. I', referencing Book I of Polydore Vergil's *Anglica Historia* (1532), which chronicles the British kings up to William I. Vergil follows Geoffrey's version, but is doubtful some of the kings ever existed, particularly the Brutus line that led to Lear. The following translation gives Vergil's version of the story much as James knew it:

Leyrus his son came next, who reigned many years, excellently and prudently. He founded the town of Leicester in the interior of the island and only had three daughters. And when he was at a very advanced age he decided to marry them to certain of his lords and divide his property equally, but he bequeathed this only to his two elder daughters because they seemed to love him more. But later, contrary to what he had thought, he found them and their husbands to be ungrateful, cruel and disloyal. But his youngest daughter, Cordilla, endowed with manners and beauty, had been given in marriage to a certain French lordling. She (endowed by nature with a pert wit), asked if she loved her father more, answered that she always carried her father in her eyes, and always would, although it might happen in the future that she would love another more ardently (meaning her husband). Leyrus, indignant at this answer, wise though it was, gave her to the French lordling sans dowry, as he was smitten with the girls beauty. But not long thereafter he was robbed of his kingdom by his sons-in-law, who thought they had been waiting too long for his death, and was compelled to take refuge with Cordilla. And by her he was restored to his throne and, his sons-in-law killed, reigned for three years. During that time Cordilla came back to Britain, having lost her husband, and at the people's bidding gained her father's kingdom. Meanwhile Morgan and Conedag, the sons of her sisters, most grudgingly submitted to a woman's government, and were ashamed to bear such a vile yoke of servitude any longer. And so, having collected an army, they began to lay waste to everything with slaughter, arson and plunder, in order to draw the woman into a battle. Soon thereafter they encountered her, defended by only a small army, captured her, and cast her in prison. Here this excellent lady (who wanted nothing but a man's sex to surpass the glory of the kings who preceded her), grief-stricken over the loss of her kingdom, killed herself five years after she had begun her rule.[38]

Knowing the events in this form would not have aroused the king's doubts as to its suitability for performance in court.

The Mirrour for Magistrates

Wherein may be seen by example of others, with how grievous plagues vices are punished; and how frail and unstable worldly prosperity is found, even of those whom Fortune seemeth most highly to favour.[39]

This collection of instructive verse stories was intended to guide men in positions of leadership, warning them of the mistakes and punishment of illustrious figures from the past. First published in 1559, it set out, as its first editor William Baldwin declared, to show

how [God] hath dealt with some of our countrymen your ancestors, for sundry vices not yet left [...]. For here as in a looking glass, you shall see (if any vice be in you) how the like hath been punished in other heretofore, whereby, admonished, I trust it will be a good occasion to move you to the sooner amendment.

The accounts of the misfortunes and fall of figures from medieval English history were written by various contributors. Each subsequent edition added new instructive *exempla* of the vicissitudes of power, so that by 1587 it had accumulated nearly a hundred tales of power gained then lost. In the 1574 edition John Higgins and Thomas Blennerhasset offered a selection from the semi-fictional 'history' of Lear's time. As Leire ended happily restored to power, he is not central to their account. It is Cordila who narrates her story. In doing so, she cannot but include the course of Leire's misfortunes. Higgins's contribution, in awkwardly scanned seven-line verses rhymed a/b/a/b/b/c/c, is set in a Christian context:

> For sith I see the prest to heare that wilt recorde,
> What I *Cordila* tell to ease my inwarde smart:
> I will resite my story tragicall ech worde,
> To the that giuest an eare to heare and ready art,
> And lest I set the horse behinde the cart,
> I minde to tell each thing in order so,
> As thou maiste see and shewe whence sprang my wo. (lines 29–35)[40]

This presents a number of immediately obvious changes made by Shakespeare in realigning his story. He removes the explicit Christian element, removes Cordila as the central figure (though he keeps her sensitivity to suffering and her victim role) and takes on the image of the cart before the horse, proliferating it into many other images of a world turned upside down, of order subverted. Cordila tells how Leire 'of vs all [...] in age did dote', and 'minding hir that loude [loved] him best to note' decided 'to giue, where fauoure most he fande [found]'. She claims that 'men me iudgde more wise/ [...] /And fayrer farre'. Her sisters 'did despise' her 'grace, and giftes', hinting at deep-seated sibling tensions. Despite their attempts at disparagement, Leire still loved her most:

> But age so simple is, and easye to subdue:
> As childhode weake, that's voide of wit and reason quite:
> They thincke thers nought, you flater fainde, but all is true:
> Once olde and twice a childe, tis said with you,
> Whiche I affirme by proofe, that was defined;
> In age my father had a childish minde. (lines 58–63)

This introduces the childishness of the old king. Though some mention is made in *Lear* of the king's foolishness, little suggestion is made of early stage dementia. Shakespeare emphasizes his being strong-minded, irrational, wilful and irascible, and that the thwarting of these qualities pushes him to madness.

The *Mirrour's* senile king plans to wed his daughters to three peers and 'deuide and parte the lande' (64–5). He calls his older daughters to 'tell me eche how much you do me loue' (70). 'By flaterye fayre they won their fathers hart:/Which after turned, him and me to smartt' (76–7). Leire asks Cordila to prove her love, seeing it as a simple confirmation of what he thought he already knew ('For why he wonted was to loue me wonders well'). Cordila says:

> I loude you ever as my father well,
> No otherwise, if more to know you craue:
> We loue you chiefly for the goodes you haue. (lines 82–4)

She explains this bluntness: 'Thus much I said, the more their flattery to detect [expose]' (85). Her irony misfires. Leire responds 'with Ire', declaring:

> Thou never shalt, to any part aspire
> Of this my realme, among thy sisters twayne,
> But euer shalt vndotid [without dowry] ay remayne. (lines 89–91)

He gives Gonerell to 'the king of *Albany* [Scotland]' and Ragan to the 'Prince of *Camber* [Wales] and Cornwall'. 'These after him should haue his kingdome all', while Cordila is given away in marriage with no dowry to the king of France, Aganippus, who, hearing of her reputation and beauty, sends an embassage requesting her hand. She is sent off to France and 'ioyes enioyd'.

> My father Leire in Britayne waxed aged olde,
> My sisters yet themselues the more aloft t'aduance,
> Thought well they might, be by his leaue, or sans so bolde:
> To take the realme & rule it as they wold.
> They rose as rebels voyde of reason quite,
> And they depriude him of his crowne and right. (lines 121–6)

Once again it is by armed rebellion the daughters augment their power. The king is allowed 'threescore knightes & squires' but in six months Gonerell and her husband 'refte' [snatched away] half his attendants. He is disrespected by 'the meaner vpstarte gentiles' and decides '*Raganes* loue to trye'. After a year 'without a noy' his retinue is reduced to ten and he is shown 'dayly spite'. Returning to Scotland, 'beastly cruell shee' (Gonerell) reduces his servants to one and 'bad him content himself with that or none'. This toing-and-froing is simplified and concentrated in Shakespeare. Now regretting his 'rigour' with Cordila, and admitting 'I finde the wordes thou toldste mee to to true' (161),[41] Leire remorsefully seeks sanctuary with Cordila, who kneeling and weeping begs her husband to assist the restoration of the king, which is achieved 'by martiall feates, and force by suiectes [subjects] sword and might'. Leire reigns three years and is succeeded by Cordila for five before she is dethroned and imprisoned by her nephews. Higgins apostrophizes her changed circumstances:

Was euer lady in such wofull wreckful wo;
Depriude of princely power, berefte of libertie,
Depriud in all these worldly pompes, hir pleasures fro,
And brought from welthe, to need, distresse, and misery? (line 241)

He descants descriptively on her fall from palace to prison, from two kingdoms to a dungeon, from being served by ladies to being accompanied by vermin, from 'holsom ayre to lothsom smell'. The goddess Despair visits her in prison and offers various forms of suicide. Cordila prays her nephews suffer retribution and Despair strikes the fatal stabbing stroke. This account, while repeating the Holinshed and Geoffrey ending, carries with it much of the emotional register Shakespeare was to bring to the play. Shakespeare makes Lear the central tragic figure. Cordelia, though marginalized in terms of her contribution to the action, has her moral importance maintained in the middle of the play by Kent's references to her and by her father's growing realization of her truthfulness and worth. Shakespeare portrays closely Lear's physical and mental fall, concentrating the emotions of the conclusion by having both die after losing the battle to regain the realm and due to the cruelty of man (a man introduced from a new subplot). The changed ending and the more widespread suffering makes Shakespeare's version more bleak. In Lear's 'birds i' th' cage' speech (V. iii.) Shakespeare transmutes the closing image of the pain and dirt of the prison in the *Mirrour* into an imagined place of escape from the world's horrors and hypocrisies. Physical discomfort and disgust turn into a *de contemptu mundi* vision of serenity.[42] That hope is snatched away when Cordelia is hanged, and her executioner slain by Lear in a final act of heroism, before he too dies of a combination of stress (physical and emotional), deep, soul-destroying disappointment and what may be a heart attack. The poem states, '[…] my father well this realm did guide'. The *Mirrour*'s happy ending – father and good daughter reunited, successful regaining of the throne, and a death while ruling well and in peace – is rejected by Shakespeare. The *Mirrour*'s accounts of the downfall of men of high degree prompts contemplation of the mutability of fame and offers a pattern of tragedy just when the drama and that particular form of it became fashionable.

The Faerie Queene[43]

Spenser retells the history of British kings in Book II, Canto X. Six 9-line verses (a/b/a/b/b/c/b/c/c) suffice to cover the tale. Leyr 'in happie peace raind' and though he had no male issue his daughters 'were well vptraind,/In all that seemed fit for kingly seed'. He decreed he would divide his realm equally between the daughters, but in 'feeble age' he 'with speeches sage/Inquyrd, which of them most did loue her parentage'. Gonorill loved him 'more then her owne life' and Regan loved him more 'then all the world'. Cordelia 'lou'd him, as behoou'd [as it was fitting]'. This 'simple answere, wanting colours faire/ [...] him to displesaunce moou'd [moved]' and he divides the kingdom between the other two. After the weddings of the daughters ('the wise *Cordelia*/Was sent to *Aganip* of *Celtica*'), Leyr 'thus eased of his crowne', passes 'a private life led in Albania [Scotland]' and for a long time did not regret 'to bene from rule deposed downe'.

> But true it is, that when the oyle is spent,
> The light goes out, and weeke [wick] is throwne away;
> So when he had resigned his regiment [regime],
> His daughter gan despise his drouping day
> And wearie waxe of his continuall stay.

Leyr decamps to Regan and is initially well treated, but she eventually begins to think he will never go: 'Her bountie she abated, and his cheare empayred'. The king realizing 'loue is not, where most it is profest', goes to Cordelia and is received 'with entire affection'. She gathers an army and 'to his crowne she him restor'd againe'. After Leyr's death, Cordelia rules until her nephews, 'woxen strong,/Through proud ambition', rebel. Weary of her long imprisonment Cordelia hangs herself. This is the first mention of her dying thus.

Arcadia[44]

Book II, Section 10 of Sir Philip Sidney's long prose pastoral romance tells of two princes, Pyrocles and Musidorus, sheltering from a storm in a Galacian cave.[45] They overhear a 'pitifull disputation' between a young man leading 'an aged' one who is also blind. The story of the 'unkinde' king of Paphlagonia,[46] related first by his son and 'then by the blind father' provides the Gloucester subplot.[47] Both are 'poorly arayed' yet have 'a kind of noblenesse' unsuited to their afflicted state. The older man asks the younger if, since he will not 'leade me to that which should end my griefe & thy trouble', he will leave him to his misery and save himself as his son's kindness reproaches his (the father's) 'wickednesse'. The princes reveal themselves, ask what misfortune has brought them to this place and are informed by the son, Leonatus, that the old man, his father, ex-king of Paphlagonia, was ousted from power and blinded by 'the hard-harted vngratefulnes' and 'vnnaturall dealings' of another son. Struck down by misery, the old man beseeched his companion to lead him to a rock where he might commit suicide. Leonatus asks the princes whether they 'feele what duetifull affection is engraffed in a sonnes hart', and will take the old man to a place of safety. The old man interrupts, telling how he was deceived by 'a bastarde sonne [...] of that base woman my concubine, his mother [...] to mislike, then to hate, lastly to destroy' Leonatus, his son by 'lawful marriage'. Fooled by 'poysonous hypocrisie, desperate fraude, smoothe malice, hidden ambition, & smiling enuie', the father ordered his servants to lead Leonatus into a forest and kill him. They released Leonatus, who, fleeing to a neighbouring country enlisted as a soldier. Successful in military service he hears that his 'vnlawfull and vnnaturall' brother has taken control in Paphlagonia. All 'fauors and punishments passed by him, all offices, and places of importance, distributed to his fauourites', the father is left with 'nothing but the name of a King'. Eventually the bastard son throws him out, blinds him and leaves him to poverty-stricken misery. Making himself king, the son sets up a brutal regime enforced by foreign mercenaries garrisoning citadels that become 'the nestes of tyranny'. The people are afraid to offer alms to their ex-king. Leonatus returns and takes care of him. The bastard son arriving at the cave with soldiers to kill his brother, the two princes join in defending him. Plexirtus, the bastard, is deserted by his people and Leonatus is crowned by his tearful, grateful father, who publicly acknowledges his faults, kisses his son and dies. Plexirtus, formed by nature for 'the exercise of craft', surrenders to his brother, hoping 'by humbleness to creepe, where by pride he could not march'. Leonatus's desire for revenge transmutes into forgiveness. One strong effect in this tale is the repetition of the words 'unnatural' and 'unkind'. In *Lear* 'nature', 'unnatural' and 'unnaturalness' are used over forty times. There is a philosophical context to this lexical pattern; it occurs because the essential ethical polarities of good and bad can be seen in two different types (or interpretations) of nature. The cruel and ruthless nature of animals (tigers, foxes, kites, etc.), the nature Edmund calls upon, the nature of marauding warlords, is ruthlessly pragmatic, competitive and without compassion. In his book *Leviathan* (1651) Thomas Hobbes referred to man's life as 'solitary, poor, nasty, brutish, and short' if not protected by a society or political community based on co-operation.[48] Without community (family, village, tribe, etc.) men would prey on each other like animals in a savage, primitive, might-is-right world. Hobbes claimed nature can be counterbalanced by men working together to protect themselves from brute-force robbers. Montaigne says, 'There seems to be nothing for which Nature has better prepared us than for fellowship.'[49] This mutual co-operation is a signifier of civilization and incorporates Christian beliefs that validate the exercise of sympathy, help, decency and respect for the individual. Without this socialization, Hobbes says, there would be no industry and commerce, 'no arts; no letters; no society; and which is worst of all, continual fear, and danger of violent death'. Shakespeare is dramatizing the contemporary discourse about the two different natures, but by killing Edmund, discards the New Testament principle of forgiving those that trespass against us for the more dramatically satisfying retribution and punishment principles of the Old Testament. This offers a duel, a confession of sorts, a deserved death. The reconciliation of legitimate son and erring father is kept for its pathos and its redemptive, healing value. The suicide rock is also kept (though turned into an imaginary cliff perhaps reminiscent of what Shakespeare saw on the company's visit to Dover).[50] The false suicide has moral value as a means of turning Gloucester's despair into stoic acceptance of God's will in keeping with orthodox theology. Strongly linking the two texts is the characterization of evil in the illegitimate son. Unkindness and unnaturalness, emphasized in the original, are retained by Shakespeare and firmly bedded within the domestic triangle of negligent father and two sons. What Shakespeare does is to provide a motive for Edmund's discontent, a broadly drawn personality for the bastard, and a clever and plausible series of ploys by which he is able to supplant his brother. Theatrically, the lies, shifts and inventive opportunism of Edmund arrest attention and create tension.

The True Chronicle Historie of King Leir[51]

Philip Henslowe's diary for 6 and 8 April 1594 records the play's first public performances at the Rose Theatre, acted collaboratively by the Queen's Men and Sussex's Men. It was entered in the Stationers' Register on 15 May as *The Moste Famous Chronicle Historye of Leire King of England and His Three Daughters*. It was printed in 1605 as THE *True Chronicle Historie of King Leir, and His Three Daughters, Gonorill, Ragan, and Cordella*. The title page claimed that 'it hath bene divers and sundry times lately acted', suggesting a recent revival, though similar phrases were often used to suggest a piece's popularity and encourage sales. Just why it should be revived after 10 years is unclear. Perhaps the new king's push for the England/ Scotland union made it seem relevant and topical. The revival of *The True Chronicle* possibly spurred Shakespeare to start (or continue) his own treatment of this old legend/history of flawed kingship. Perhaps he saw the revival to remind him of its text and see if there were any features he could use. Revamping another company's play, giving it new approaches and emphases, was common among dramatists always desperate for new pieces to keep the cash flowing. Clearly this early version had some influence on

Shakespeare when he decided to render the narrative his own way. Some critics see it as the prime source. Yet while the politics are relevant there is little of interest as regards the more complex psychological explorations Shakespeare offers. Leir does not go mad, there is no Fool, no Edgar with his assumed madness, Albany does not emerge as a man of principle. Though there is some sibling rivalry between the daughters, the motives and transgressive ambitions of Gonorill and Regan are largely absent and there is still the happy ending. The value of *The True Chronicle* is that it clearly prompted Shakespeare to think about the Lear story and what in it warranted reworking. It also raises topical political concerns about misgovernance and civil war. Verbal echoes hint strongly that Shakespeare had assimilated the text in his head and cannibalized what he needed. In the seventeenth-century style of cutting and pasting, many dramatists patched and adapted old plays and presented them as new, sometimes simply rewritten in more contemporary language and structured in a less old-fashioned way. That appears the case with *Leir* becoming *Lear*. The original had a longish title and was marketed as a 'chronicle' (a history). Simplifying the title highlights the play as a personal drama. Exploring the central character's psychology became a feature of Renaissance drama, valorizing the growing fascination with individuation. In medieval times the individual was less important than the group. In the Renaissance the views, feelings, experiences and assessment of personal experiences were valued, as possible guidelines or warnings to others.

Leir and his nobles open the play returning from the funeral of 'our (too late) deceased and dearest Queen'. He asks for advice on 'the disposing of our princely daughters', commenting how they 'receyued/A perfit patterne of a virtuous life' from their mother. This establishes a setting in which Christian values inform the play's ethical framework. These are not directly evident in Shakespeare. Maternal influence is acknowledged (whereas in Shakespeare the queen is mentioned only once and fleetingly) and there is a suggestion that the father does not really know or understand his daughters – part of the psycho-emotional subtext of *Lear*. In Shakespeare's characterization Lear seems congenitally incapable of seeking advice.

Leir acknowledges that he feels close to death, is weary of life, and

would fayne resigne these earthly cares,
And thinke vpon the welfare of my soule
Whiche by no better meanes may be effected,
Then by resigning vp the Crowne from me,
In equall dowry to my daughters three.

An untrustworthy councillor, Skalliger, suggests dividing the kingdom with a jointure to each according to their profession of love. Leir says they will all get an equal share, though he still goes through with the silly love test charade. Another noble regrets there is no son and heir and suggests matches with

> [...] some of your neighbour Kings,
> Bordring within the bounds of Albion,
> By whose vnited friendship, this our state
> May be protected gainst all forrayne hate.

Leir reveals that the kings of Cornwall and Cambria (Wales) 'motion loue' to Gonorill and Ragan. Cordella does not want a king 'vnlesse loue allowes'. She alone associates marriage with love. Leir hopes to beguile her and match her 'to some King within this Ile'. Another courtier, Perillus (a milder proto-Kent figure who becomes the outcast king's companion and acts as virtuous counsellor in opposition to Skalliger) warns, 'Do not force loue, where fancy cannot dwell.' Lear devises a 'stratagem'; as Cordella declares her love for him he will ask her to grant him a request – to accept his choice of husband. It is an unworthy trick to get his way, but it is patriarchy in action. Perillus warns again, prophetically:

> Thus fathers think their children to beguile,
> And oftentimes themselues do first repent,
> When heavenly powers do frustrate their intent.

Gonorill reveals her jealousy that Cordella always copies their fashions, that she is 'nice [...] demure [...] sober, courteous, modest, and precise', and that everyone says she exceeds them in beauty and virtue. Ragan longs to find 'some desperate medicine' to 'dimme the glory of her mounting fame'. Gonorill admits she is already half-promised to Cornwall (not Albany, as in Shakespeare). Skalliger betrays Leir's secret intent to the sisters and reveals the plan to marry them to Camber and Cornwall, and Cordella to 'the rich King of Hibernia [Ireland]', then divide the kingdom for their dowries. Skalliger's mentioning the love test offers an opportunity for revenge by so flattering Leir that Cordella cannot compete and will not agree to marry the Irish king. Gonorill foresees the outcome:

> So will our father think, she loueth him not,
> Because she will not graunt to his desire,
> Which we will aggrauate in such bitter termes,
> That he will soone conuert his loue to hate:
> For he, you know, is always in extremes.

This comment is made more explicit at the end of Act I, Scene i of *Lear*, exemplifying how Shakespeare picked up little points for more detailed characterization.

In *Leir* the king is initially made more sympathetic by being given the opportunity to address the audience. His soliloquy indicates the emotional turmoil he is experiencing:

> Oh, what a combat feels my panting heart,
> 'Twixt childrens loue, and care of Common weale!
> How deare my daughtes are unto my soule,
> None knows, Ah, little do they know the deare regard,
> I hold their future state to come:
> When they securely sleepe on beds of downe,
> These aged eyes do watch for their behalf.

There is differentiation in Leir's love: Gonorill is 'deare', Ragan 'kind', but Cordella 'sweet'. Concerned for their 'future state', his 'throbbing heart is pearst with dire annoyes' while they sleep serenely. Ironically he dismisses his doubts 'for the world affords not children more conformable' but acknowledges a presentiment of trouble about dividing the kingdom. He presents the love test as a means to see who 'will soonest yield vnto their fathers hest [demand]'. It is a test of obedience to patriarchal will. Gonorill declares, 'I thinke my life inferior to my loue' and says she would commit suicide to prove it. Ragan declares,

> O, that my simple vtterance could suffice,
> To tell the true intention of my heart.

Cordella's aside responses – 'Did never flatterer tell so false a tale' and 'O, how I doe abhorre this flattery!' – guide the audience's assessment. Her answer to Leir's expectant request ('Speake now, Cordella, make my ioyes at full/And drop downe Nectar from thy hony lips') is initially less blunt in content than in *Lear*:

> I cannot paynt my duty forth in words,
> I hope my deeds shall make report for me:
> But looke what loue the child doth owe the father,
> The same to you I beare, my gracious Lord.

She says little more than this in explanation other than to deny she was ever a flatterer. In Shakespeare she defends and explains her position. Here she is cut off sharply by her father, who calls her a 'bastard Impe, no issue of King *Leir*'. He instantly announces dividing the realm between Gonorill and Ragan:

> I presently will dispossesse my selfe
> And set vp these vpon my princely throne.

Leir's anger is less explosive than in Shakespeare. He calls Cordella peremptory and proud, accuses her of being 'father-sick' and wanting him dead. She begs he should not mistake her and hints at the insincerity of her sisters: 'My toung was neuer vsde to flattery.'[52] She is banished only from court. Unsure where to go, she puts herself in the hands of 'him which doth protect the iust'. The scene is closed by Perillus, saddened to see his king ignoring advice that would have shown him 'the hidden tenure of her humble speech': 'I grieue, to see my Lord thus fond [foolish],/To dote so much vpon vayne flattering words'. He sees the hidden import of Leir's reaction: 'Reason to rage should not haue giuen place'. Folly, unreason, anger and unreadiness to take advice are set up as causes, as they are in Shakespeare. There is none of the extreme emotion in banishing Kent (for Perillus stays with Leir) and Cordella's rejection is fairly low key too, but there are many echoes of ideas taken up and embellished by Shakespeare.

The next action concerns the Kings of Cornwall and Cambria on their way to meet their arranged spouses, each already informed he is to receive 'halfe his Seignories'. As in *Lear*, the resigned king's actual status is not worked out clearly, though it is clear in both plays that the arrangement is unworkable. The sisters reveal how they have blackened Cordella to their father, further incensing him against her. When he receives his new sons-in-law, he is still angrily adamant against advice:

> Cease, good my Lords, and sue not to reuerse
> Our censure, which is now irreuocable [...].
> I am as kind as the Pellican,
> That kills itselfe, to saue her young ones liues:
> And yet as ielous as the princely Eagle,
> That kills her young ones, if they do but dazell
> Vpon the radiant splendour of the Sunne.

His 'censure' is 'irreuocable', a term Lear uses (I. i.). Shakespeare's king is more passionate in his anger. Leir's image of being 'as kind as is the Pellican' is echoed when Lear, slipping into madness at the sight of Poor Tom, assumes Tom's state is caused by his daughters and talks of 'those pelican daughters' (III. vi.), shifting the focus from parental altruism to the greed of the children.[53] Leir gives his daughters in marriage to the kings of Cornwall and

Cambria,[54] asking them to draw lots to see who gets which part of the realm, then dispossesses himself, making 'you two my true adopted heyres'. Just what exactly Leir thinks he is doing in dividing the land and shifting rule, and just what his own position is, is as indeterminate as in Shakespeare. Perillus, talking of the other lords, suspects that 'loue or feare tyes silence to their toungs'. He speaks up for Cordella not to be disinherited. Leir threatens him with death ('Vrge this no more, and if thou loue thy life') as Lear threatens 'Kent, on thy life, no more' (I. i.) and blocks any further discussion:

Who euer speaketh hereof to mee agayne,
I will esteeme him for my mortall foe.

In a biblical echo Perillus introduces the seeing/not seeing imagery so dominant in Shakespeare:

Ah, who so blind, as they that will not see
The neer approach of their owne misery?[55]

He exits promising to do all he can for Cordella.

Lear's hurtful giving away of a dowerless Cordelia to the King of France is differently and less tightly handled in *Leir*. The Gallian king and Lord Mumford (a prototype for the Fool) come to Britain disguised as pilgrims to see if Cordella is as beautiful and virtuous as rumoured. Overhearing her bewailing how 'the fickle Queene of Chaunce' and 'fortune' have dealt with her, but accepting 'it is the pleasure of my God:/And I do willingly imbrace the rod', the Gallian king asks if she would accept a king if one came a-wooing. Wealth and power, she replies, would have no influence upon her as long as she loved him better than anyone else. He reveals himself and they go off to marry. It is not a convincing scene and is not handled as neatly as in *Lear*.

In soliloquy Perillus reveals that now 'she sees hee hath no more to giue', Gonorill is aggravated 'to see her father liue' and has reduced his 'pension' (allowance) by half. He will disguise himself and accompany the king, doing all he can to advise Leir for the best. His departing speech critiques the times:

Oh, whom should man trust in this wicked age,
When children thus against their parents rage?
She calls him foole and doterd to his face,
And sets her Parasites of purpose oft,
In scoffing wise to offer him disgrace.
Oh yron age! O times! O monstrous, vilde,
When parents are contemned of the child!

Shakespeare develops these flaws much more fully.

In a weaker version of the scene in *Lear*, in which Goneril orders Oswald to disrespect the king and his retinue, Gonorill complains to Skalliger of enduring 'such quips and peremptory taunts [...] daily from my doting father', who snaps at everything she says or does, criticizes her 'new fashioned gowne' and complains at her expense on banquets. She is annoyed Ragan has nothing to pay and Skalliger suggests she reduce Leir's allowance. This prompts her to stop all payment so that her father is forced to find other accommodation. The opportunity for the drama of an out-and-out row is lost. Lear's face-to-face argument with Goneril escalates the tension unbearably and drives the king close to apoplexy and breakdown. Skalliger's parting comments reintroduce the theme of the danger of flattery and misused language Montaigne had deplored:

> Go, viperous woman, shame to all thy sexe:
> The heauens, no doubt, will punish thee for this:
> And me a villayne, that to curry fauour,
> Haue given the daughter counsel 'gainst the father.
> But vs the world doth this experience giue,
> That he that cannot flatter, cannot liue.

Another opportunity for drama is lost when Leir annoys Gonorill and she simply flounces out. In a moment more upsetting in *Lear*, the king (feeling he can do no right) breaks into tears. The *True Chronicle*'s Perillus (now in disguise) expresses sympathy but is countered by Leir, who advises that it is bad policy 'to confort with miserable men' and that he should 'get fauour 'mongst the mighty, and so clyme'– comments paralleling the Fool's remarks on letting go your hold 'when a great wheel runs down a hill' (II. iv), though Shakespeare shifts these ideas of loyalty and flattery into the more painful encounter at Gloucester's castle. The family tensions are there, the references to subversion of gender roles and child–parent relationships too, but are often reported rather than represented, diminishing the onstage conflicts and therefore reducing the drama. Flattery is similarly highlighted as dangerous when loosed in a court and elicits the proverbial 'What's got by flattery, doth not long indure' from Perillus. His advice that Leir try the hospitality of his other daughters prompts the king to acknowledge how he was 'causelesse' in dispossessing Cordella and is now punished for his blindness. He decides to visit Ragan. These exchanges contain hints of what Shakespeare would take up and develop, but lack the tension, the nasty, edgy comments and the Fool's stinging commentary on the unfolding follies and transgressions of nature. Missing too are the troublesome interchanges between an angry Kent and a servile Oswald.

The next scene has the subversive Ragan congratulating herself that everyone obeys her:

I rule the King of Cambria as I please:
The States are all obedient to my will.

She knows that while Gonorill lives in royal state,

My father with her is quarter-master still,
And many times restraynes her of her will.

She declares she would not submit to that and would send him packing. These transgressions are augmented back in Gonorill's palace when her husband sends a message to see Leir has arrived safely and Gonorill intercepts it. Voicing the horrible hope that Leir falls sick and dies she plans to write to Ragan

[…] such thunderclaps
Of slaunders, scandal, an inuented tales,
That all the blame shall be remoued from me.

This childish letter dishonestly claims Leir has criticized Ragan, abused Gonorill, caused friction between Cornwall and her 'and made mutinyes amongst the commons'. She promises the messenger 'a hye way of preferment' for endorsing her fabrications. The letter suggests Ragan have Leir killed and Gonorill asks the messenger if he will do it. Adding to the horror he blasphemously declares, 'By this booke I will' and kisses the letter as if it had the authority of the Bible.

Leir and Perillus arrive at Ragan's palace, the king talking of himself as 'but the shadow of my selfe', an image Shakespeare reuses. Ragan says aside, 'I must dissemble kindnesse', runs to her father and kneels weeping to see him come so unworthily (i.e., without a train and poorly dressed). When all have entered the palace Ragan confides to the audience that she will make him 'truely say, he came from bad to worse'. She reads her sister's letter while the messenger anticipates more secret work 'and more crownes [money]'. Ragan is concerned her father has heard 'that I do rule my husband as I list' and has come to force her to acknowledge 'my Lord to be my head'. Asked if he is prepared to murder Leir the messenger replies, 'I weigh no more the murdering of a man,/Then I respect the cracking of a Flea' and offers to kill her husband as well. Female subversion of hierarchy is evident and murder casually accepted. Meanwhile Cordella's husband, seeing she is depressed by the loss of her father's love, offers to send an ambassador to Cornwall to make peace and invite Leir to visit them.

Leir and Perillus are lured to a thicket outside the palace, thinking to meet Ragan to secretly discuss family matters. Leir wakes from a troubled dream that Gonorill and Ragan stabbed him a hundred times but that Cordella came and poured healing balsam in his wounds (linking her to Christ). The messenger admits the purpose of his errand. Leir expresses readiness to die, but adds that Hell stands gaping to receive a killer. At that moment thunder and lightning frighten the messenger and he shows them Gonorill's letter suggesting that Leir should be murdered. Perillus declares:

Oh iust Iehoua [Jehovah], whose almighty power
Doth gouerne all things in this spacious world,
How canst thou suffer such outrageous acts
To be committed without iust revenge?
O viperous generation and accurst,
To seeke his blood, whose blood did make them first!

While Leir says it is God's will he should be killed, Perillus warns the messenger that the king is 'the high anoynted of the Lords' and that he should 'keepe thy hands still vndefilde from blood' or be haunted afterwards by those who suborned him seeking his life for fear he will talk. Furthermore, in death he will suffer 'for euer tyed in chaynes [...] in the hottest hole of grisly hell'. Thunder cracks again, the messenger quakes, drops his daggers and flees. Leir still wishes to die, but Perillus persuades him to seek refuge with Cordella. In *Lear* this despair and the attempt to cure it is shifted to the Gloucester story. At this stage, the effects of Leir's deteriorating physical and emotional conditions are somewhat dissipated by short intervening scenes monitoring the lack of progress made by the Gallian ambassador in finding out about Leir's situation and Cordella and her husband's anxiety about the lack of information. Cordella believes Gonorill will dissuade Leir from accepting the invitation to France, 'For she to me hath always bin vnkind.'

Ragan tells Cambria she believes 'the detested Witch' Cordella has enchanted Leir away as he has disappeared. She claims she loathes her life now she is deprived of her father and longs for death. With unintended irony Cambria replies,

The heauens are iust, and hate impiety,
And will (no doubt) reueale such haynous crimes.

Disguised, Cordella and her husband, about to embark for Britain, meet an exhausted Perillus and Leir. They maintain their disguise until they learn what has happened. Leir gives vent to his despair:

Ah, Gonorill, was halfe my Kingdomes gift
The cause that thou didst seeke to haue my life:
Ah, cruell Ragan, did I giue thee all,
And all could not suffice without my bloud.

He regrets his treatment of Cordella. She leads him to a table to eat. She calls him 'good old father' and he calls her 'good young daughter' because she is like a daughter he had. Admitting he was 'too much vnnaturall [...] so haue I lost the title of a father', Leir recounts what the sisters have done and at this point Cordella, unable to hold back, reveals herself, kneels and asks his pardon for all faults she committed from birth. The Gallian king suggests invasion 'to redresse this wrong'.

Back in Britain Ragan, eager to push matters to the test, stridently criticizes the male leaders around her and the patriarchal system that excludes her from leading her forces.

O God, that I had bin but made a man;
Or that my strength were equall with my will!
These foolish men are nothing but mere pity,
And melt as butter doth against the Sun.
Why should they have pre-eminence ouer vs,
Since we are creatures of more brave resolve?
In braggart anger she sneers at men who are afraid
To give a stab, or slit a paltry Wind-pipe,
Which are so easy matters to be done.

The French army lands and find British forces defecting to them. A noble spokesman declares Leir as long wished-for, assuring him,

But all the Country will yeeld presently,
Which since your absence haue bin greatly tax'd,
For to maintayne their overswelling pride.

In a parley the French king accuses Ragan and Gonorill of seeking Leir's life. Their denial causes an outburst from Leir:

Out on thee, viper, scum, filthy parricide,
More odious to my sight then is a Toade.

Shown the letters between the sisters, Ragan rips them and both deny the murder plot. Battle lines are formed, and when Cornwall announces the day is lost and everyone is deserting to Leir, a stage direction indicates, 'Alarums and excursions, then sound victory'. The winning side gathers, Leir delivers a final speech in rhyming couplets, thanks 'the heauens' and the French king, whom he calls 'my sonne'. Leir's offer to resign in favour of the French king is rejected. Leir finally admits to Cordella, 'Thou louedest me dearely, and as ought a child.' 'Sound Drummes and Trumpets. Exeunt. FINIS.'

This triumphant ending, omitting the next stage with Cordella's death in prison, merely assuages an unsophisticated liking for happy endings and the victory of virtue. Shakespeare's adjustments of focus and development of new features (narrative and psychological) make his version more febrile, tense and ultimately horrific.

A real-life Lear?

One possible source is not fiction but fact. A recent law case provided some uncanny parallels to the Lear story. Shortly before the probable period of *Lear's* composition, Sir Brian Annesley, a wealthy gentleman of Elizabeth I's court (thus possibly known to Shakespeare), became senile. In 1603 the elder two of three daughters tried to have him certified insane and incompetent to manage his finances or estate.[56] It seems possible that Lady Grace (the eldest daughter) saw the will, disliked the terms, and sought power of attorney in order to declare incompetence due to insanity. That would have put her father's property in her hands. Cordell, the unmarried youngest daughter contested this and wrote for support to an old acquaintance of her father, Sir Robert Cecil, the King's Secretary. When Annesley died (July 1604), his will was successfully defended by Cordell, who inherited most of the family property. An executor of the upheld testament was Sir William Harvey, married to the Countess of Southampton, mother of Shakespeare's one-time patron, the Earl of Southampton.[57] The chain of connections suggests strongly the possibility that this story of family conflict over the division of property (Annesley had an estate in *Kent*), the accusation of *insanity* and the name *Cordell* coalesced in Shakespeare's mind with the ancient Leir story, the play and book versions of it, prompting him to rework a narrative offering so many resonant opportunities. Apart from the 'coincidence' of the name Cordell, there is the idea of madness. In all written source versions, despite extreme anger with his youngest daughter and anguish at his treatment by the older two, even in his most despairing moments the king does not go mad. It is an innovation that contributes unsettling intensity and tension and allows Shakespeare to give Lear lines that are enlightened, satirical and bitter.

Analysing sources shows how a writer's acquisitive memory accumulates bits and pieces from life and reading, stores them, then uses them later, transforming them to do the job he requires. It also shows the skill of Shakespeare in taking narrative and turning it into sharply focused, emotion-filled dialogue. How much more value Shakespeare added in turning raw, simple accounts into moving drama, filling out the simple love declarations in the sources with rhetoric that has the verbal semblance of truth but is just too 'glib and oily' to be genuine. He develops the king's simple displeasure in Holinshed and Higgins into an overemotional reaction that speaks of hysteria and senility, an indulged mind unused to opposition and incapable of coping with disappointment. He adds God-defying *hubris* and shifts Albany's character from simple evil ambition into an essentially good man overshadowed by a transgressive wife, but who finds a voice to express his principles and the courage to do what is right. He introduces a subplot paralleling the savage subversions of the main plot and dramatically intersecting with the main characters. This enables the crucial impact on the outcome caused by Edmund's death warrant for Lear and Cordelia. He gives us the Fool, Kent and Poor Tom and, in changing the ending, has created one of the most harrowing and pitiable dénouements in world drama.

A *final source*

How many of the audience knew any of these earlier forms of the story is less important than how resonant viewers would have found the socio-political framework of Shakespeare's version. Living memory would make the story vibrantly topical. Rival dukes, war with France, civil war, plots, torture, poisoning, a study of kingship, loyalty and disloyalty and the division of a kingdom were topical themes – in real life and in drama. Knowing any earlier versions of the king who divided his realm was unnecessary, for each individual came to the theatre pre-prepared. Upbringing made them well acquainted with the teachings and values of the Bible and the requirements of the Christian life, and made such values an instinctive part of their thinking. Commandments broken, sins committed and virtues displayed or not displayed on stage would automatically shape their evaluation of the action in front of them. The Lear situation was addressed by Plutarch in his *Moralia* (*Moral Essays*). 'Whether an Aged Man Ought to Manage Publike Affaires' indicates Shakespeare was not the only writer concerned with the effects of age on the ability to run a state. Philemon Holland published his translation in 1603, coinciding with the final stages of the succession crisis, with the aged queen hanging on desperately to life and power. The old may have experience and wisdom valuable to the state, but in Plutarch's view physical decline brings a preference for pleasures rather than the rigours of administration. For Campbell, 'Lear […] is divesting himself of cares which he no longer wishes to carry. And it is equally apparent that he is doing it not in the interest of the recipients of his benefits but because he seeks release from duties that are burdensome.'[58]

The most important literary context of *Lear* is the biblical contribution. There are few verbal echoes, but the contrast between proper conduct and sinful behaviour is there by implication throughout. By the end of the play Lear's world has been ripped apart. We witness two families disintegrate. What makes this worse is that they do it to themselves. A father banishes his daughter, two daughters reject their father, a son plots against his father and brother, an earl has his eyes gouged out, a servant kills a duke, a princess kills a servant, a son contemplates parricide, an earl's son kills a steward, a brother commits fratricide, a queen is hung, two sisters kill each other, and a king goes mad and dies of grief. These sensational events cross multiple boundaries of acceptable behaviour, invoking the deeply embedded taboos of the Ten Commandments, the Seven Deadly Sins, and by implication the Seven Virtues, provoking expectations of a chain of cause and effect leading either from sin to punishment to repentance to forgiveness or from sin to punishment to non-repentance to death and damnation. What causes these events is a sequence of character collisions exposing the differences between moral and socio-political expectations and the realities of how the social and political worlds work, the discrepancies between how civilized people are supposed to act and how the impulses of 'savage and unnatural' passions can make them act. These collisions take place within the familial structure of several 'courts' – first Lear's palace, then Gloucester's castle, Albany's palace, the 'court of the gods' or the 'court of nature', the court of arbitration (Edgar/Edmund's duel) and the court of audience judgement. The discrepancies are brought starkly to light by a quartet of ruthless power seekers who bring down the social order of the older generation. Transgressive acts, triggered by the failure of the ruling older elite to govern suitably, expose the vulnerability and gullibility of those administering an old system. Lear and Gloucester are punished for their failings as rulers, parents and individuals. Both less than effective fathers, the sins of king and earl have distorted the emotions of some of their children and all, deserving and undeserving, are brought down in the consequent collapse. The sins of the fathers are visited upon the children and are returned upon the fathers and society in general by those children. The Commandment/virtue matrix enables the audience to judge the actions it sees involving honouring parents and not committing adultery, coveting, killing or lying. It fits with a second matrix of mortal sins – pride, wrath, lust and avarice – the unspoken biblical/ethical contexts.

Standard expectation of the fifth act of a tragedy demanded bloodshed – a cleansing of 'disease' whether in the public, national, political, familial or personal spheres. *Lear* comprises all three, inevitably creating a sense of widespread disaster. The body count, coming within a few scenes, includes Oswald, Gloucester, Goneril, Regan, Cordelia, Cordelia's executioner, Edmund and finally Lear himself. It is hinted too that Kent may soon die of a psycho-physiological collapse, a loss of the will to live. The deaths are concentrated: Oswald in Act IV, Scene vi and the other fatalities seen or reported within forty lines in Act V, Scene iii, three relatively short scenes later. The number of troops killed in the battle is unknown, but subliminally they add to the sense of widespread destruction. This is a landscape suitable for tragedy and the spectators saw the constituents of tragedy displayed: a figure of power (protagonist) falling (*peripeteia*), villainous behaviour (antagonists), recognition of failings and ignorance becoming aware (*anagnorisis*), tragic flaws (*hamartia*) exposed, and *hubris* (pride) punished (nemesis). The retributive destruction is personal but has national dimensions. The extent of physical and emotional devastation is imaginatively expressed by Kent's reaction to the distraught king bearing his dead daughter's body. He asks 'Is this the promis'd end?' Edgar and Albany reply:

> EDG.: Or image of that horror?
> ALB.: Fall and cease. (V. iii.)

They are referencing another context: the long-held Christian belief that a 'Last Day' would come, the end of the world, when all current states and current rulers would cease to have power, Christ would come to Earth – the 'Second Coming' – and all would be judged, the quick (living) and the dead. The judgement was envisaged as a weighing – men assessed by their virtue or sinfulness, and their destination (Heaven or Hell) determined. This motif in a play about the end of the world (or the end of *a* world) had vibrant resonances for Shakespeare's age. A well-known Old Testament story tells of the arrogant Babylonian king Belshazzar who was 'weighed in the balances' and 'found wanting'. His father, Nebuchadnezzar, had been warned that his overexertion of power would be punished. He was driven out of his court. Then at a huge, lavish feast, his son Belshazzar saw a vision of a hand writing on the wall in a strange language. The prophet Daniel translates the message to mean 'God hath numbered thy kingdom and finished it. Thou art weighed in the balances and art found wanting. Thy kingdom is divided and given to the Medes and Persians' (Daniel 5:26–8). That night the king is slain and his kingdom taken over by the Persians. It is a story of *hubris* punished, of excessive behaviour leading to loss of power, of a king's persistent pleasure seeking distracting him from properly administering his kingdom. The 1606 audience would know the story and would have long ago absorbed the idea of divine intervention in the affairs of mismanaged states and individual misconducted lives. All disasters were seen as warnings from God. People linked this with a belief that society was in a state of moral decay leading to a point of such deterioration that God would end the world and send his Son to reign. This would be preceded by sensational events: the Jews converting to Christianity, the Ottoman Empire defeated and Rome falling. Christ and his saints would rule the Earth for 1,000 years (Revelation 20:4) or all eternity (Daniel 13:18). Meanwhile, God regularly sent warnings to sinful man. Europe experienced intermittent waves of millenarian expectation, but discussion of it increased with the Reformation, which made Bible access easier. The prophecies of Daniel and of the Revelations of St John the Divine were favourite reading for those who longed for the fall of the Antichrist. Just who the Antichrist was differed from sect to sect depending on their prejudices. On 9 October 1603 Christopher Hooke, preaching about the visitation of the plague and God's wrathful indignation, declared:

> God complaineth with grievous accusations both against Court and Country, against Church and Commonwealth, for the sins of blasphemy, of drunkenness, of pride and covetousness, of horrible witchcraft and sorcery, of immeasurable bribery; of buying and selling offices in the Commonwealth and dignities of the Church, of insatiable avarice, and ambition in both, and in neither a care or conscience to perform their duty to the common good but to their own gain and commodities.[59]

Throughout this period people anticipated the end of this corrupt world and the commencement of the rule of King Jesus. Ironically, Lear himself called on the gods to:

> Smite flat the thick rotundity o' the world!
> Crack nature's moulds, all germens spill at once,
> That make ingrateful man! (III. ii. 7–9)

A lesson in being careful what you wish for.

Chapter 11

THE CONTEXT OF TRAGEDY

And this great king that doth divide his land
And change the course of his descending crown,
And yields the reign into his children's hand,
From blissful state of joy and great renown,
A mirror shall become to princes all,
To learn to shun the cause of such a fall. (*Gorboduc*, I. ii. 458–63)

Tragedy is as old as human sorrow. The medieval concept was of a great man's fall due to the instability of all human affairs. This focused on the caprices of Fortune as the cause of personal disaster. Renaissance tragedy, also concerned with 'the Fall of Princes' and acknowledging the erratic, unjust turning of Fortune's wheel, additionally explores the central character's *hamartia* (the fatal individual psychological flaw or weakness) and the degree to which humans create their own disasters. Elyot's *The Boke Named the Governour* (1531) provided an educational programme to encourage proper conduct in any man that governs people. The verse stories in *The Mirrour for Magistrates* (1559) illustrate, from history and legend, the different disasters that have befallen prominent figures. Both *King Lear* and *Mirrour* indicate interest in the means by which power may be lost; they are both mirrors in which rulers of whatever status (from father to king) can see how they may resemble the figure under discussion. Shakespeare's tragedies all focus similarly on the personal psychology that puts a powerful figure in a vulnerable position. There are other external factors like other men's power plays or the plotting of malevolent antagonists that accelerate or exacerbate the fall of an otherwise good and strong ruler, but essentially it is the central figure's own weaknesses that precipitate his fall. People in the 1600s were particularly interested in stories portraying the decline of men of power and place. They saw it regularly in their own socio-political milieu and looked to famous people of the past as instructive *exempla*. The vacillating fortunes of the Earls of Leicester and Essex were recent memories and the recurrent rises and falls of Sir Walter Raleigh were an ongoing saga. The decline of such figures still had a huge impact on the mass of people and their failings are thus of importance as warnings and instruction. In *King Lear* two figureheads fall and their families with them.

There is perhaps something not entirely upsetting in seeing an overconfident, arrogant fool brought low. Being too grand, too successful, too full of yourself and too indifferent to moderation and the claims of humility was to court retribution. Such is the overconfidence and autocratic behaviour of Lear at the beginning. An audience may feel pity at his suffering and death but consider them deserved. Blind to his own faults initially, addicted to demanding and getting his way, we watch his clouded judgement begin to clear, and we begin to pity his inevitable destruction as a regal persona and his physical/mental decline.

The theoretical basis for tragedy came from classical sources, the chief being Aristotle's *Poetics*. This collection of lectures defines and analyses the key features of Greek tragedy. It was known in the Renaissance through a Latin translation from Arabic and was increasingly becoming part of European thinking about tragedy. A tragedy is a representation (*mimesis*) in action and words of the fall of a great man from prosperity to misery, not necessarily ending with his death. It presents a story (*mythos*), complete in itself, with a beginning, middle and end, employing dignified language suitable to its serious theme and including a degree of spectacle. The tragic process is defined as follows: a man of power (the *protagonist*), at the height of his prosperity, of otherwise good qualities, thinking his world is safe and he is happy, makes a mistake of judgement and action (knowingly or unknowingly). His miscalculation comes about because of a weakness or flaw (*hamartia*) in his personality and is caused by an excessive pride (*hubris*) in his ability to judge and act without due attention to morality and the gods (or God). His pride in himself will falter, due to his flaw: a tendency to jealousy, ambition, irascibility, impulsiveness, lust – any emotion experienced to an irrational extreme. In any event it will transgress the moral boundaries of his time and offend the gods. Unaware of the mistake initially, the character continues his life. Gradually a problem emerges as a result of his mistake. It may be military, political or personal. Matters deteriorate, his fortunes begin to reverse (*peripeteia*), complications become inextricable, the hero becomes aware of his mistake and recognizes his fault (*anagnorisis*) before disaster (*catastrophe*) strikes (perhaps his own death at the hands of the opponents [*antagonists*] he has aroused, but death is not a necessary outcome). The progress towards the outcome (*dénouement*) involves escalating suffering (physical, emotional, mental or any combination) and creates in the audience a sense of sorrow for the protagonist and fear that if such things can happen to men of special abilities, with power, privilege and wealth, they can wreck our lives too. This pity and fear creates such strong feelings in the audience that they are purged of emotion, washed out and exhausted, but also filled with a sense of how little their own problems are by comparison. This process is called *catharsis*. One other feature of tragedy is the sense the protagonist (and the audience) has of being hopelessly entangled, trapped in a process he cannot stop. He is fated to disaster whatever he does.

The Greek and Roman worlds, so influential in Jacobean thinking, both believed that reasonableness and harmony were achieved by maintaining balance, what the Greeks called *sophrosyne*. Lear lacks what Epicurus called 'flexibility' and Montaigne called 'pliableness'. He is too extreme, too autocratic. The Epicurean requirement of adjustment to the different needs of life at different times was seen as key to surviving and living life well (i.e., morally, wisely and rationally). It was a view Christians endorsed.

Critical focus on *Lear* prioritizes the king, his flaws and the sadness of Cordelia's death. Understandably, his fall and whether it fits Aristotelian or medieval-Renaissance concepts of tragedy has exercised critics from Samuel Johnson to Jan Kott.[1] It is after all an eponymous tragedy and there is the inevitable question whether the punishment for his sins is disproportionate. Is he 'more sinned against than sinning'? But alongside the fall of a great man (or a man with great power) are the interconnected subsidiary traumas experienced by Cordelia, Edgar, Gloucester and Kent, and the plots and punishments of Goneril, Regan and Edmund – plenty enough to horrify and occupy critics. While tracing Lear's painful pilgrimage to its conclusion,

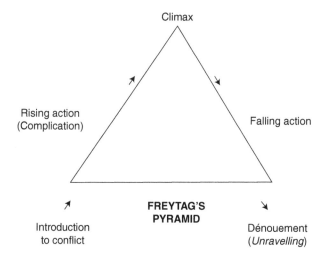

Shakespeare interlards the dialogue with critical comments to unsettle and embarrass his audience. These might be missed as the human tragedy builds in the growing excitement of a live performance. In the quiet process of private reading we can detect and dissect these satirical attacks.

Dramatic progress follows the sequence indicated in Freytag's Pyramid. The rising action introduces the initial problem (Lear banishing Cordelia and planning to stay with his other daughters) and complicates this with the Lear and Gloucester entanglements, caused by the scheming of the villains.

Once set going the action builds through a series of minor climaxes or disasters – the lead-up to Lear's going into the wilderness, Edgar's flight, Lear's madness, Gloucester's blinding – before the main climax of the battle and a series of deaths. The emotional graph is a steep and steadily climbing anguish, the scenes becoming incrementally more horrifying. The shape of the action is perhaps less an isosceles triangle than an irregular one with a steep fall from climax to outcome. In Shakespearean tragedy the climax comes in the final scene. This climax comes in stages – the battle, the deaths of Goneril and Regan, the Edgar/Edmund duel and the entry of Lear bearing the dead Cordelia. These coincide with the revealing (or unknotting) of the secrets and plots that bring the characters to the final scene.

Chaucer's prologue to *The Monkes Tale* (*The Canterbury Tales*) gives a standard definition of the subject matter of tragedy:

> Tragedie is to seyn a certeyn storie,
> [...]
> Of him that stood in great prosperitee
> And is y-fallen out of heigh degree
> Into miserie, and endeth wretchedly.

The Monk lists a sequence of famous men who fell: Lucifer, Adam, Samson, Hercules, Nebuchadnezzar, Belshazzar, Zenobia, Nero, Holofernes, Antiochus, Alexander, Julius Caesar, Croesus, etc.). This standard recital of mythical, classical and biblical figures is augmented by more recent instances of misfortune: King Pedro of Spain, King Peter of Cyprus and Count Ugolino of Pisa (who figures in Dante's *Inferno*). The Monk is interrupted by the Knight, uneasy at hearing this 'hevinesse', preferring tales of poor men who 'clymbeth up, and wexeth fortunat'. This gives a sense of the depressing effect of tragedy, purging us of all taste for gloom and making us all the more ready to be thankful for our good fortunes. The fall of a prince was an apocalyptic event, since the collapse of central one-person rule (liberal or despotic) affected the whole polity. Given too the quasi-divine status accorded kings and the awed reverence shown to them, for them to fall was shocking. If God's elect could be toppled – by treason, murder or self-inflicted failing – what hope was there for the security of lesser men? A prince's fall was a warning, a reminder of the precariousness of human life. Such a subject demonstrated those personal or political faults to avoid, applied by extension to anyone with power to lose – noble, MP, judge, magistrate, general, ship's captain, head of commercial enterprise, lord of the manor or father of a family. Recent history alone provided copious examples of the intrigues, betrayals, bloodthirsty ambitions, attempted coups and outrageous bids for power that led to the toppling of rulers and traitors alike. The Wars of the Roses and earlier English historical events apart, the sensational violence of political struggles in the Italian city-states and elsewhere proved an exotic, endlessly fascinating source of settings and stories to explore. Catholic Europe was connected in English minds with devious plots and ingeniously cruel methods of killing. Thomas Kyd's *The Spanish Tragedy* (1581), *the* play that captured the popular imagination, regularly recalled for performance (unusual in those days), set the mould for violent tragedy and the fashion for dramas that centred on revenge. The element of revenge in *Lear* is inherent in the grievances Goneril and Regan bear against their father and in Cordelia's invasion, but is most clearly developed in Edmund's attempts to displace first his legitimate brother and then his father. The inventive machinations of the deprived child Edmund are as fascinating to the audience as the clever opportunism of Iago and Richard III. Elizabethan-Jacobean tragedy's great contribution is in the subtle interrelated psychological dynamics of hero and villain. In *Lear*, while acknowledging that the king-father is autocratic, dogmatic and too-readily angered, and the two elder sisters justifiably embittered, the audience may well experience a slowly building sympathy for the old man.

The model for early Elizabethan tragedy was the work of Seneca. Francis Meres links the Roman writer with the rising star of English theatre: 'As Plautus and Seneca are accounted the best for Comedy and Tragedy among the Latins, so Shakespeare among the English is the most excellent in both kinds for the stage.'[2] The stories that were the bases for the great Greek tragedies (Aeschylus's *Oresteia* and Sophocles's *Oedipus* trilogy) were often known through other sources than the originals – Chaucer's poetry and Ovid's *Metamorphoses* for example – but in the early 1500s the Greek texts of Sophocles and Euripides were becoming available. By the 1550s Seneca too was gaining ground as a model for classroom translation and study, initially through his prose works, valued for their liberal *sententiae* contemplating matters relevant to men in public office. His meditations on personal loss and exile appealed too. *De Ira* (*On Anger*) is particularly relevant to *Lear* – a powerful plea for the control of the lower, baser emotions. This ethical line and stoic approach coincided with contemporary religious thought and the

Christian tradition of quietist endurance of suffering. Gradually, Seneca's tragedies too gained attention. Scholarly tragedies, in Latin, written in European universities, owed much to the influence of Seneca's flamboyant rhetoric. Rhetoric was still a major part of the undergraduate degree course. Public speaking competitions and dramatic performance were seen as suitable training, for many students would become public leaders or priests. The earliest evidence of Seneca performed in English was *Troades* at Trinity College, Cambridge (1551), followed by *Oedipus* and others. But another impetus came from the developing public theatres, where dramatists (many from Oxbridge) exploited his sensational and bloody storylines. The later dominance of Revenge Tragedy is traceable to this Senecan influence, its persistence evidenced by recurrent quotation and parody of his work far into the period. He provided three examples of the ghost device, whereby a returning spectre informs the hero/revenger of the cause of his or some other person's death. This incites the action. The ghost of Hamlet's father is well known, but many other plays rely on this Senecan device. Other appealing features were the passages of lyrical description and the flourishes of oratorical language used for dramatic moments. This explains the presence in so many early Elizabethan tragedies of long, action-stopping speeches. Audiences used to long sermons were attuned to listening to and untangling the meaning of sometimes turgid descriptions. By the time of the Great Tragedies, however, Shakespeare's experience had taught him how to break up long speeches with dramatic interjections.

The Tenne Tragedies, edited by Thomas Newton (1581), collected the translations of Seneca's dramas.[3] In this edition, writers discovered plots focused on revenge carried out in highly bloodthirsty ways. Seneca's implicit critique of high-handed autocratic rule by absolutist monarchs/emperors was much to the taste of English dramatists, as was the condemnation of courts corrupted by favourites and parasites, scheming ladder climbers and hangers-on. This, and the examples from contemporary and recent political history available in Holinshed, created a taste for violent stories involving redress of personal wrong. Court settings offered satirical opportunities aimed at the sycophantic toadyism found in myth and history, inevitably evoking identification with contemporary life. In the claustrophobic domestic setting of *Othello* and in the closed, court/family setting of *Hamlet*, revenge and tragedy are given their cleverest and most psychologically complex treatments, but since Christianity demanded retribution for all wrongdoing, a way of reinforcing God's omniscience and omnipotence, literature was required to demonstrate that sin would be punished, and so in *Macbeth* and *Lear* too we see the bad punished on the field of battle. Believing that God knew of all sins committed, audiences expected villains to be punished sooner or later. The Latin saying 'Cave, cave, deus videt' (Beware, beware, God is watching) and innumerable biblical texts reminded Christians they lived in a culture where sin was expected to be discovered and followed by retribution. People tended to want to take revenge themselves, in the ancient tradition of the revenge vendetta – the *lex talionis* (law/right of retaliation). Vengeful people very reluctantly handed over this traditional 'duty' to the courts. Christianity tried to control the 'eye for an eye', 'take the law in your own hands' instinct. Theology stressed vengeance as the prerogative of God: 'Vengeance is mine; I will repay, saith the Lord' (Romans 12:19). But the desire to retaliate personally against those dishonouring or murdering a member of the family persisted, especially among the aristo-gentry, with their warrior-culture background and their oversensitive 'code' of 'honour'. While nodding deferentially in the direction of law, order and Christian values, the Revenge Tragedies, from *Horestes* (1567) to the derivative bloodbaths of Caroline drama, took advantage of the public's love of gory payback stories acted out onstage. Revenge Tragedies involve disguise, intrigue and plotting, as the murderer and the avenger scheme to outwit each other. Real or pretended insanity is common and numerous secondary deaths obligatory.

Lear, prompted by the Fool and his own dawning understanding, senses quite early that he was wrong in his assessments of his daughters and acknowledges of Cordelia, 'I did her wrong' (I. v.). Further recognitions are to come. The audience is always ahead of Lear's awareness of his folly, but part of the tragic mode is that audiences are helpless observers. The story follows his decline, evoking feelings of pity and fear in the spectators. For Aristotle tragedy concentrates these effects by having one plot, one setting and a timescale of 24 hours (the unities). The language should be dignified, in keeping with the lofty subject, and the cause of the 'fall' should similarly be serious, not trivial. Because Greek drama in general (and tragedy in particular) was a public religious celebration, there is an ethical underpinning honouring and supporting the gods by showing non-normative behaviour being punished as a reaffirmation of community-held values. Noticeably, Shakespeare deviates from these rules. The timeline is indeterminate (but clearly more than a day), the locations various, and there is a subplot mirroring the main plot thematically and narratively. This deepens the sense of family breakdown with the royal family's divisions and betrayals repeated in another high-status family. The lexis has multiple registers: the high rhetoric of formal ceremony delivered in blank verse; improvised, stream-of-consciousness prose, mixing classical images with demotic phrases in a pastiche meant to represent a sane man pretending to be mad; broken blank verse, indicating extreme emotion that extends from anger to mental breakdown; and prose exchanges full of abusive epithets, snatches of song and rhyme and an example of peasant dialect. Mixing diverse language forms – structurally and lexically – reflects social and personal norms disintegrating. Once the 'storm' – symbolizing normality collapsing – has blown itself out, there is a return to more controlled, formal language as the survivors attempt to reconstruct their world. This skilled use of language reflecting action and mood is an identifiable feature of the mature craftsmanship Shakespeare displays at this phase in his career. It contrasts graphically with the more straight-laced, dull, unvarying formality of many plays from the early Tudor period.

Another common feature of tragedy is Nemesis, the ancient Greek goddess of retribution, representing the belief that whatever wrong you do will be done back to you, through the gods or a human agent of punishment. Nemesis (Greek for paying what is due) was a remorseless goddess pursuing perpetrators, for years if necessary, until vengeance was taken. The wrong done initially might be against the hero or another person (as in Clytemnestra's murder of her husband, Agamemnon, in the *Oresteia*). The gods then sent someone to avenge the wrong (like Orestes, son of Clytemnestra, and Agamemnon, deciding his duty to his father was greater than to his mother). The initial wrong might also be committed by the protagonist somehow dishonouring the gods. This pride, arrogance and overweening confidence (*hubris*) was the pride that goes before a fall. Overconfidence in yourself (like Lear's dogmatism) is a weakness, a flaw. Other personality defects could be flaws. A particular failing might not inhibit performance as a leader at all until circumstances put you in a position where the flaw becomes active. It could be one you might be completely unaware of until it is activated and begins to destroy your peace of mind, your world or your life. The tragic flaws that destroy the heroes of Shakespeare's Great Tragedies are variously defined. Lear's might be described as irascibility, ill-judgement in old age, believing flattery is truth, being too naive or being too strong. The love test, a piece of silly old man's sentimentality, is the *hubris* of a man too confident he knows how things will work out and then incapable of responding rationally and calmly when his expectations are disappointed. The Romans saw retribution as linked to *invidia* (envy). A king brazenly, arrogantly believing every decision he makes is divinely inspired would arouse the gods' envy, incurring punishment for thinking he was untouchable, invincible and irreproachably right. *Invidia* can be seen as a sense of injustice that needs righting, a restoration of humble moderation. A king who is too autocratic needs to be humiliated. *Lear* has much to do with punishment and humbling.

Tragic dénouements (conclusions; literally 'unknotting') are catastrophic. In *Lear* it is the unexpected deaths of Cordelia and the king. After Lear's terrible suffering, reconciliation with Cordelia looks hopeful, but the temporary lull in horror is inevitably shattered. Unnecessary victims are part of the hopelessness of tragedy. Once tragedy becomes possible innocent victims are unavoidable. Albany wins the battle and would obviously free the royal pair, but mischance allows Edmund to dispose of them before Albany can do anything. In tragedy, anything that can go wrong will. The opening scene shows that Lear's character weaknesses make suffering and conflict inevitable. The tragedy lies in the unavoidability of suffering but is heightened by the sense that Lear and Gloucester could act differently, do not, and suffer more than is proportionate to their failings. Both are redeemed by reunion with their rejected children, acknowledging their guilt and becoming more enlightened (about themselves, the world and who is untrustworthy), but death is inevitable. It is not tragic if the hero is destroyed by an unexpected disaster. The destruction is tragic when set in motion by a self-initiated action stemming from the protagonist's inner weakness. Once reconciliation is impossible between Lear and Goneril, then Lear and Regan, tragedy becomes impossible to halt. The exposure of a king's vulnerability reminds us of the insecurity of all our lives. For the audience – helpless to help, witnessing the falling apart of another being's life – the experience is harrowing. To watch a man go mad is almost unbearable. It is painful to watch the protagonist being responsible for his own tragedy, provoking it by his decisions and actions. It is not tragic if, like a puppet, he is manipulated by outside forces. Having initiated his own downfall the hero is increasingly subject to situations he cannot control and which overwhelm him. The machine is unstoppable. But, through suffering, the hero, punished and purified, emerges sadder and wiser.

Gloucester sums up man's vulnerability:

As flies to wanton boys are we to the gods;
They kill us for their sport. (IV. i.)

He is wrong. It may appear that Fate, Fortune and the gods punish us arbitrarily, but Gloucester brought his suffering on himself. Lear punishes Cordelia for embarrassing him in public, Goneril and Regan punish Lear for his treatment of them over a long period, Edmund punishes his father for neglect and society for ignoring his qualities. Edgar punishes Edmund. Theologically everything that happens is God's will. Edgar sums up the working of Fate:

The gods are just, and of our pleasant vices
Make instruments to plague us:
The dark and vicious place where thee he got
Cost him his eyes. (V. iii.)

ROTA  FORTUNÆ

With domineering hand she moves the turning wheel,
Like currents in a treacherous bay swept to and fro:
Her ruthless will has just deposed once fearful kings
While trustless still, from low she lifts a conquered head;
No cries of misery she hears, no tears she heeds,
But steely hearted laughs at groans her deeds have wrung.
Such is the game she plays, and so she tests her strength;
Of mighty power she makes parade when one short hour
Sees happiness from utter desolation grow.
(Boethius, *The Consolation of Philosophy*, II. I.)

Edmund agrees, seeing his own fatal defeat in single combat as the working of Fortune (i.e., Divine Providence): 'The wheel is come full circle; I am here' (V. iii.). Beginning as nothing, rising rapidly to brief eminence, thrown down and ending as nothing again. The Wheel of Fortune (*Rota Fortunae*) was a popular image reflecting the unreliable and capricious nature of one's fortunes. It was how the classical world explained the workings of Fate, providing an apt image of great men falling from power to misery and/or death – central to the idea of tragedy. Fortuna, goddess of Fate (a woman, i.e., a symbol of arbitrary changeability), was frequently depicted as blindfolded to express the arbitrariness and impartiality of good or bad luck. In the Middle Ages, though the wheel image was often invoked, it was increasingly connected not with an unpredictable goddess but with the will of God. God – omnipotent, omniscient – planned everything. A fortunate rise in luck or an unforeseen disaster were not the work of untrustworthy Fate, but of Providence. John Knox rejected the idea of Fortune as heathen. Elizabethan bishop Thomas Cooper summed up the Anglican view: 'That which we call Fortune is nothing but the hand of God, working by causes and for causes that we know not'; nature was 'nothing but the finger of God working in his creatures'.[4] He saw plagues not as natural, preventable medical problems: 'Whensoever misery or plague happeneth to man, it cometh not by chance or fortune, but by the assured providence of God.'[5]

Albany sees Goneril's suicide and Regan's poisoning by Goneril as 'judgement of the heavens' (V. iii.). Lear impotently threatens punishments and invokes punitive curses, calling the gods to witness and act. The Fool's joke about Lear putting down his breeches to be punished by his daughters is suggestive of a new development in thinking, associating punishment with human agents acting on God's behalf or on their own behalf. Tragedies in general remind men how fragile their hold on life and happiness is and how devastation is a judgement on their conduct. The moment when the hero finally realizes the mistake(s) he has made, how events are leading towards collapse, can be heart-rending. The ending itself is meant to bring about feelings of pity and fear that effect a purging or *catharsis*. The idea is that in witnessing such horrific events happening to people who, while making foolish judgements, are not essentially bad, the play appeals to our sympathy and so works upon our emotions that we are completely cleansed of emotion and feel helplessly battered into dumbness. Despite Lear's foolishness, his disproportionate bad temper, we do slowly begin to sympathize with this old man's plight. This process is echoed in the phases of Gloucester's punishment. The hope felt when Lear is reunited with Cordelia is snatched away when they are defeated. Sadness turns to outrage at the wickedness of Edmund's decision to have them executed. The close of the play is curiously muted. Edgar's final speech seems absurdly inadequate and impotent:

The weight of this sad time we must obey;
Speak what we feel, not what we ought to say.
The oldest hath borne most: we that are young
Shall never see so much, nor live so long.

This echoes Ephesians 4:14–15:

> [...] we henceforth be no more children, tossed to and fro, carried about with every wind of doctrine, by the sleight of men, and cunning craftiness, whereby they lie in wait to deceive; But speaking the truth in love [...].

Relevant to a play involving civil war is Richmond's more expansive plea for healing and reconciliation at the end of *Richard III*:

> England hath long been mad, and scarred herself;
> The brother blindly shed the brother's blood,
> The father rashly slaughtered his own son,
> The son, compelled, been butcher to the sire.
> [...]
> Abate the edge of traitors, gracious Lord,
> That would reduce these bloody days again,
> And make poor England, weep in streams of blood!
> Let them not live to taste this land's increase
> That would with treason wound this fair land's peace!
> Now civil wounds are stopped, Peace lives again:
> That she may long live here, God say Amen!

Perhaps the scenes just witnessed are so disturbing that the participants (and audience) are left speechless, unable to express inexpressible emotions.

Chapter 12

THE FAMILY CONTEXT

The Sins of the Father: Familial Transgression in *King Lear*

I the Lord thy God am a jealous God, visiting the iniquity of the fathers upon the children unto the third and fourth generation of them that hate me. (Exodus 20:5)

Lear is a family-centred play about two dysfunctional families. Because so much about the families' pasts is omitted we cannot complete their psychological profile, cannot accurately answer the inevitable questions that arise. How long has Lear's family been a one-parent unit? To what extent was Lear's queen able to educate and form the sisters? How did Lear behave as a lone father? What was the relationship like between the sisters? What was the emotional atmosphere surrounding the marriages of Goneril and Regan? What contact has Gloucester had with Edmund prior to his return? What contact was there between the brothers? Some of these backstory features are present in the sources, but Shakespeare ignores them and we have only hints suggesting tentative answers. Lear as a king can only be assessed by his present behaviour. A few comments from Goneril, Regan, Kent and Cordelia show how he is judged by those around him. There is the loyalty too of the Fool and those of the entourage who stay with him.

The play has been largely seen in personal terms, a tragedy of family breakdown, focusing Lear's personality and the bonds that should tie families together, but which, when broken, assist their collapse. Because the two disintegrating families are high status, their fall has wider social, political and national consequences and, within the text, social, political and national resonances abound. The bonds broken and the most important transgressions are familial ones. The war is textually marginal, yet significant to the audience because of its outcome. The broad context was the ever-present fear of foreign invasion, heightened by the transitional period of a new king (only three years into his reign) attempting to establish his rule. The recent past and current anxieties were part of the mental context brought to the performance, but the national dimension is minor. The major thrust of the story and main interest would have been Lear. The disturbing breaking up of his personality destroys his reign, disassembles his family, disperses his household and leads him to madness and death.

The basic unit of human life is the individual. The basic unit of social life is the couple. That social unit extends through children. The parent–child relationship is absolutely fundamental to the social framework. The family is the brickwork of society. It is through the interaction of parents and children that the younger generation is taught how to live, how to survive and how to act and react in relation to other units in the surrounding community. Loving, feeding, clothing, caring for and educating their children is the duty of fathers and mothers. Love felt for a parent is created by their being loving. The capacity for loving is learned by a child being shown love. It is not expressed only by words, but by deeds; if a child is not loved, not shown love, does not see and feel the expression of parental love, it grows up limited in ability to love others and with an overdeveloped tendency to self-love. The family is ideally thought of then as the means by which love is taught and handed on. It is, theoretically (and often in practice) a unit of affectionate support. But, the family can also be the source of immense negative forces. To Freud it was the centre and origin of repression and the distorting effects of repression. It can be a repository of murderous grievance and it is that disturbing aspect that we see represented in *Lear*. Tolstoy said, 'Each unhappy family is unhappy in its own way.'[1] These are very unhappy families.

Social harmony depends in part on the harmonious, loving, supportive nature of the families within its communities. If the constituents of unified family life break down, the security of society at large is endangered. Something has clearly gone wrong in the Lear and Gloucester families; Goneril, Regan and Edmund's behaviour displays that. Ostensibly it is material greed that precipitates the conflicts – not just a question of who gets what inheritance, but of how to negotiate a workable *modus vivendi* for elite family children old enough to want independence but without means to be so. The contemporary debate about whether male heirs should be given partial independence is presented by Edmund as the supposed view of Edgar: 'I have heard him oft maintain it to be fit that, sons at perfect age, and fathers declin'd, the father should be as ward to the son, and the son manage his revenue' (I. ii.). To Gloucester this is 'unnatural' and 'worse than brutish'. Middleton's City Comedies display highly predatory money-focused behaviour within families. In *A Mad World My Masters* Follywit, a demobbed soldier in disguise, robs his grandfather to get the money he desperately needs. The grandfather, Sir Bounteous Plenty, is not curmudgeonly or miserly, making the grandson's behaviour all the more shocking. Follywit puts the problem clearly:

Let sires and grandsires keep us low, we must
Live when they're flesh as well as when they're dust. (II. ii. 44–5)

This raises a legitimate question: how can sons maintain themselves if brought up to be idle, have no professional training and therefore no source of income? The source of their disaffection, their ruthlessness, is in the parenting models they have had *and* in their own moral choices. The sins of the fathers have made some of the children what they are. Gloucester's legitimate heir is decent, forgiving, has fortitude and looks set to be the next king. Lear's loved, favourite, youngest child risks and loses her life to redeem her father. Why are they different from their siblings? Were they born innately good or have they been shown more love? Is it pure chance? In *The Tempest* (1611) Miranda states, 'Good wombs have borne bad sons' (I. ii. 16). Many would see the differences between the offspring as a sign of some plan by God to use the bad children as agents of punishment and the good as imitations of Christ, illustrating man's better qualities – forgiveness, care and reconciliation. Both fathers succeeded in parenting Edgar and Cordelia more effectively than their other offspring. In considering *Lear* we are initially horrified by the appalling public spectacle of a ferocious family row. It is exceptionally unsettling to see an old man pathetically demanding his children parade their love for him, then losing his temper when one refuses to play his silly game. The King of France says of Cordelia,

This is most strange,
That she that even but now was your best object,
The argument of your praise, balm of your age,
The best, the dearest, should in this trice of time
Commit a thing so monstrous, to dismantle
So many folds of favour. (I. i. 213–18)

Lear had earlier admitted:

I lov'd her most, and thought to set my rest
On her kind nursery. (I. i. 123–4)

It is upsetting to see Lear's hysterical reaction, his curses, his violent comments on Cordelia, his despicable disposal of her in marriage to the prince who asks least. At this time fathers had the absolute right to arrange a daughter's (or a son's) marriage without either their knowledge or consent. Only the most dictatorial father would do that, but many unions were so arranged. What is worse for the audience is being privy at the end of Act I, Scene i to the assessments of Lear by his other daughters. Clearly his crazy, impromptu decision to live with them alternate months does not suit them and he will not have an easy time with this highly suspect arrangement.

The events of the play are unusual and sensational, crossing the boundaries of acceptable behaviour. Outrageous as they are they invoke for the audience those taboos and values, the unspoken biblical contexts, already discussed. The reversals of nature, the transgressions of the family bond – explicitly, a father banishing his daughter, another proscribing his son an outlaw, two daughters 'banishing' their father and a son betraying his father – build throughout the play in a constant process of horror. The consequences mount and reverberate until Lear enters in the last scene bearing his dead daughter in his arms, an extreme reversal of nature, not part of normal process. Originating largely in the speeches of the Fool, Edgar and Lear, within this enveloping framework of reversals the text is filled with images reinforcing the central transgressions: Albany's 'milky gentleness'; his wife's 'steely' nature; Lear bearing his 'ass on thy back o'er the dirt', making his daughters 'thy mother' and giving 'them the rod' and putting 'down thine own breeches'; the hedge sparrow that feeds a baby cuckoo and then has 'it head bit off by it young'; 'the cart draws the horse'; 'an obedient father'; 'a man's brains [...] in's heels'; the sight of a man in tears; Kent dishonouring Oswald by beating him with his sword instead of fighting like a gentleman; and a tailor making a man. The language parallels the action in turning nature upside-down. Putting Kent, a royal messenger, in the stocks is an action inappropriate to his status, showing 'small respect [...]/Against the grace and person of my master' (II. ii.). Royal servants had a sort of diplomatic immunity, but Kent is being treated like the 'basest and contemned'st wretches/For pilferings and most common trespasses' (II. ii.). Regan justifies the action with another reversal of decorum, putting her sister's will before respect to her father, with no attempt to conciliate:

> My sister may receive it much more worse,
> To have her gentleman abused, assaulted,
> For following her affairs. (II. i.)

Edgar, outlawed, on the run, assumes a disguise inappropriate to his status, 'to take the basest and most poorest shape' (II. iii.); Kent will be 'set [...] to school to an ant'; the 'unsightly' Lear – a king, a father – kneels and begs his daughter to feed him, give him a bed and clothe him (II. iv.); in all cases nature is subverted. Goneril, unashamedly announcing a change of gender roles when the drums of war begin to beat, tells Edmund:

I must change arms at home and give the distaff
Into my husband's hands. (IV. ii. 17–18)

She goes to extremes when her letter to Edmund is revealed by Albany and she declares,

The laws are mine, not thine:
Who can arraign me for't?' (V. iii.)

Not only is she defying patriarchy but setting herself above the law. Her imperturbable arrogance expresses itself in her simply walking away and refusing to answer any further questions. It is the Devil's implacable evil. Indeed, Albany has already seen her as a 'devil' and a 'fiend' (IV. ii.) and she has already shown a refusal to acknowledge guilt or express repentance. Running alongside these subversive, thought-provoking comments and distortions of normative expectation are thoroughly unsettling exposures of the unjust or corrupted normalities of society. There are the Bedlam beggars Edgar has seen that give him the idea for his disguise. Many were tricksters shamming fake disabilities to scam charity, but there were genuine unfortunates, some mentally unstable, some homeless paupers, some who had dropped into unemployed poverty through the economic unevenness of the time. To the authorities, 'Vagrants were a menace to the social order because they broke with the accepted norms of family life. If the ideal was the patriarchal household, they had no part in it, and for that reason they were considered pariahs.'[2]

Edgar has been forced out of his less than happy patriarchal household, as has Lear. Both will achieve a re-establishment of that bond – briefly – but the play as a whole seems to reflect contemporary anxieties about threats to family life that might herald the dissolution of society and the 'promis'd end'. A worse threat than the transients roaming the highways of England were those of higher rank who appear respectable but hide their sins. Lear calls the gods to expose the 'wretch'

That hast within thee undivulgéd crimes,
Unwhipped of justice; […] thou bloody hand;
Thou perjured, and thou simular of virtue
[…]. Caitiff, to pieces shake,
That under covert and convenient seeming
Hast practised on mans life. (III. ii. 50–56)

The Fool joins the exposure of wrongs, foreseeing 'confusion' if it should come to pass that a 'priest' was 'more in word than matter' (more concerned with the fine turn of phrases than with the lesson they are preaching). He foresees 'confusion', when 'brewers mar their malt with water' or 'nobles' teach their tailors how to make their fashionable clothes. This is ironic, for such things were already common happenings. He ironically foresees a time when every law suit is correctly judged, no squire is in debt, there are no poor knights, people stop slandering each other and no pickpockets move among crowds – things never likely to come to pass.

Albany, beginning to oppose his wife, warns:

That nature which contemns its origin
Cannot be bordered certain in itself. (IV. ii. 32–3)

The image is of a tree branch (evoking the idea of a family tree) splitting off from the main trunk, unable to sustain itself and dying:

She that herself will sliver and disbranch
From her material sap, perforce must wither
And come to deadly use. (IV. ii. 34–6)

'Material sap' is the essential, original life force, referring not just literally to the sap of the tree but to the parent (i.e., Lear). In warning that this route is dangerous Albany uses an image of further unnatural, transgressive behaviour:

Humanity must perforce prey on itself,
Like monsters of the deep. (IV. ii. 48–9)

The overwhelming build-up of animal imagery reflects the growing savagery of the play and reflects the same-species destructive savagery of a civil war. Man is the only creature that goes to war purposely to kill his own kind in bulk. Albany suggests unnatural human violence has reached monstrous proportions. To the Elizabethans and Jacobeans monsters were unnatural, mutant, quasi-diabolic, cross-species combinations of animals, subverting God's natural order. Albany's prediction is vindicated in the expected fifth-act bloodbath. This landscape is suitable for tragedy and the accumulated reversals demonstrate the consequences of family dissolution.

Setting the play in a pagan past enables Shakespeare to represent savage passions without appearing to attribute them to his own times. It is evident that the 'Nature' Edmund addresses (I. ii.) is a ruthless goddess of the self, and the terms of Lear's imprecations against his daughters are of a cruel pagan type akin to 'the barbarous Scythian' (I. i.). Lear invokes this 'Nature' in his a curse on Goneril:

Hear, Nature, hear! Dear Goddess, hear!
Suspend thy purpose, if thou didst intend
To make this creature fruitful!
Into her womb convey sterility!
Dry up in her the organs of increase,
And from her derogate body never spring
A babe to honour her! (I. iv.)

This is a horrible, sinful thing for a father to wish upon a daughter. The images and language throughout the play reflect the primitive emotions and actions of the plot. Significantly, Lear's language becomes more conciliatory, more gentle, more broadly sympathetic to others (though not hypocrites or wrongdoers) once he has suffered and gained a wider understanding of his failings and a clearer vision of how the world is arranged.

The transparent non-Christian disguise allows rethinking of political and personal moralities related to contemporary issues provoked by the play. The audience could see that and judge the action before them within a set of well-established values. That value system would deplore Lear's over-autocratic patriarchy in the opening scenes, condemning it as peremptory and arbitrary. It would deplore the levity, immorality and gullibility of Gloucester and condemn the parent–child power axis displayed throughout. It would perhaps be ambivalent about the master–servant relationships displayed, condemning the self-serving obsequiousness of Oswald, but unsure how to judge Kent and the Fool. This was a society in which, in even the lowliest households, the loyalty and honesty of servants was the bond next in importance to those of the family. An unsettling part of the horror of the play is seeing how a break-up within the key family in the realm spreads into the surrounding social structure, generating other abnormalities. In addition to the train of broken familial taboos already mentioned, a wife usurps her husband's role as household head, an earl's outlawed son becomes a houseless beggar, a king sleeps in a hovel and a statusless bastard leads an army and orders the death of a queen. Amid this chaos, cruelty, destruction and madness, a fool is the wisest character on stage. This host of transgressive situations made *Lear* a highly disturbing play for an audience that believed social hierarchies guaranteed order and feared any breakdown of this system heralded 'the promis'd end'. But this was an age that believed God's wrath might end the world suddenly and violently. Apocalypse was always possible. The first rumblings of seismic change are audible in the opening lines of the play. Beginning *in medias res* (i.e., jumping into the middle of events), Gloucester and Kent discuss the imminent division of the kingdom. Favouritism by Lear towards Albany hints at possible family tensions. Expectations about the division seem so evenly balanced ('equalities are so weigh'd that curiosity in neither can make choice of either's moiety') that no one can tell who will get what. We later see the dukes are vastly different sorts of men – one ruthless and ambitious, the other quietly reflective and virtuous. The planned division is disturbing, highly precarious and foolish. Dividing anything causes contention over how it is divided and whether the division is fair; grievance is almost certain. Someone will feel injustice however equitable a division is made. This is not sharing sweeties, it is political madness and will put the audience on alert.

The two courtiers turn to discuss the third person on stage: Gloucester's bastard son. Another dangerous family inequity emerges. Primogeniture, the established custom, means Edmund would legally inherit nothing.[3] However undeserving Edgar might be, however profligate, weak-minded and unfitted, he would get everything. The 'whoreson must be acknowledged', and is – after a fashion. Gloucester admits Edmund is his lovechild and has been brought up – elsewhere. Edmund has been 'out' for the last nine years and the Earl intends 'away he shall again' – hardly sympathetic parenting.

Rich men commonly spawned illegitimate children. The arrangements made for the education and upbringing varied enormously depending on the decency and conscience of the errant parent. Some kept them in the family, bringing them up with the legitimate offspring. Others kept them in a separate household, looked after and educated. Some would cast adrift mother and child with perhaps a lump sum and a warning to keep away. Gloucester has re-established contact, but not maintained careful watch. So we have a disgruntled, neglected bastard and a legal son who has all the benefits. It is a recipe for sibling conflict.

Bacon warned against encouraging rivalry: 'Men have a foolish manner (both parents and schoolmasters and servants) in creating and breeding an emulation [rivalry] between brothers during childhood, which many times sorteth to discord when they are men, and disturbeth families.'[4] Rivalry here has been caused by different treatments in upbringing. Ironically, lack of distinct primogenitive inheritance in the Lear family will lead to destruction, but sibling jealousy is again operative. In the absence of a male heir Goneril should inherit. Envy of Cordelia is caused by her being father's favourite. Envy between the elder two is caused by sexual jealousy over the favours of Edmund. Exacerbating Gloucester's neglect of 'the whoreson' is the jokingly off-hand, vulgar way he speaks of Edmund's mother and his begetting, as if Edmund is not there or it does not matter what is said of him. But this cipher will count. The amused, neatly worded insults – 'She had, indeed, Sir, a son for her cradle ere she had a husband for her bed [...]. Yet was his mother fair; there was good sport at his making' – reflect a venial, easy-going attitude to creating an unwanted child. It was transgressive, for all its commonness among those of rank and title; it broke the bonds of matrimony, betraying the wife who a year before bore Gloucester an heir. Lust was a mortal sin and the Seventh Commandment warned, 'Thou shalt not commit adultery'. Gloucester will be cruelly punished for his sins. As Edgar says to his dying brother, 'The dark and vicious place where thee he got/Cost him his eyes' (V. iii.). The situation has a fairy-tale feel to it: once upon a time there was a man who had two sons; one was as evil and devious as the Devil, the other as good, unsuspecting and suffering as Christ. Edmund is a classic case of disaffected youth – excluded from the normal family situation, excluded from paternal love, envious of his older brother (who presumably experienced contact of some sort with both parents), resentful of 'the plague of custom' that excludes him from inheritance and all the other social interactions an earl's son would normally expect. Neglected and deprived, he angrily dedicates himself to a goddess who stands for a ruthlessness that ignores the Christian moral tradition.[5] 'The younger rise as the old doth fall' is natural, but Edmund is prepared to speed the process by foul means. Civilized values applaud the process by which with love the older generation cares for the younger when it cannot fend for itself, acts as mentor as it approaches maturity. It also supports the process by which the declining generation is cared for by the younger. Both processes are cemented by love. That necessary ingredient seems missing in *Lear* initially. Bacon, considering the problem of ensuring all the children in a family are cared for, deprecates cases where 'one or two of the eldest [are] respected, and the younger made wantons [i.e., spoiled], but in the midst some that are as it were forgotten'.[6] Bacon, like Montaigne, suggests it is important to ensure lack of money does not force younger offspring into misdemeanours: 'The proof [outcome] is best when men keep their authority towards their children, but not their purse.'[7]

Throwing money at the Edmund problem will not placate his grievances. They are too deep-seated. Gloucester's readiness to 'work the means' to help Edmund inherit does not deflect his 'loyal and natural boy' (II. i.) from plotting to undermine brother and father and 'get' the entitlement he thinks his due. He achieves this through 'invention' and 'practices' that will let him, 'if not by birth, have lands by wit' (I. ii.). He can do great damage now he is 'inside the castle', transgressing first by lying: the fake letter, his glosses on it, and the fabricated anger he tells Edgar his father has against him. Lies soon turn to deceptive actions, leading to complicity with the savage maiming of his father. Blood leads to blood (from his arm, his father's eyes and his own death). Though not there when Gloucester's eyes are gouged, Edmund knows of his father's perilous plight in the hands of Cornwall and Regan – and does nothing to stop it. As the French army approaches, Regan remarks,

> [...] Edmund, I think, is gone,
> In pity of his misery, to dispatch
> His nighted life. (IV. v.)

Though he does not find Gloucester, just thinking of parricide was gravely sinful. Edmund has that embittered defect that characterizes villains and detaches them from humanity. His lack of a loving upbringing and his monumental resentment against his father have left him without the ability to empathize, unable to imagine what his actions do to others or what others feel. Or perhaps he can imagine and does not care. Excluded from society he uses society's naive, unsuspecting gullibility to subvert it and get what he wants. Standing outside all norms of decent behaviour, he smiles and flatters Cornwall and Regan, attracts the interest of Goneril and quickly takes Cornwall's place as military leader. A Protean shape changer, he has the opportunist's skill in appearing to be whatever his companions want: loyal son, loyal brother, loyal co-commander or putative lover. He uses the court's ways and means to further his aims. The sisters lied to get their inheritance, he lies to get his.

Lear's family has a similar parable-type feel: once upon a time there was a man with three daughters.... Given the didactic nature of art during the Renaissance, an instructive pseudo-morality play is one way to interpret *Lear*. An educated, Bible-conscious spectator would see the play developing the idea of the sins of the fathers visited upon the children, but with the twist that the children turn those sins against their fathers.

The belief that children will be made to suffer for parental wrongs/ failings also appears in Numbers 14:18 and in *The Book of Common Prayer*. It is an idea that an audience would recognize. As Lear exposes his parental shortcomings, the presupposition formed regarding Gloucester begins to take definite shape also. The play *will* demonstrate how the transgressions of the younger generation punish the sins of the two fathers. In an age that believed all men were sinners, that sins would be paid for one time or other, and that 'the wages of sin is death', we can, even this early in the drama, see the retributive context of the opening lines.

This 'morality play' mood and the dramatic tension increase when the imperious, overbearing Lear announces,

> [...] Know that we have divided
> In three our kingdom; and 'tis our fast intent
> To shake all cares and business from our age,
> Conferring them on younger strengths. (I. i)

The plan is filled with dangerous possibilities. It is folly to divide the infrastructure of a unified state into what will have to become three separately run political set-ups, let alone hope to make a fair partition that will appease all parties and expect that post-devolution there will be peaceful co-existence between the three new states.[8] When we see that the recipients of Lear's division are three such sisters, future troubles seem inevitable.

It is a commonplace that family rows go deep, that grievances can go way back. What are we to say of a political act that is to be decided by a competition of declarations of love? Lear's phrase 'Know that we have divided in three our kingdom' implies he has already made the allocations, so why the competition?

> Which of you shall we say doth love us most?
> That we our largest bounty may extend
> Where nature doth with merit challenge. (I. i.)

This seems to offer a bigger portion of land to whoever makes the most meritorious claim of love. It is a piece of humiliating fakery – fake on Lear's part if he has already apportioned the kingdom, certainly fake on the part of Goneril and Regan's extravagant claims of love, and humiliating to all the sisters. Lear is asking them to make very personal statements in a public situation. It is foolish and insensitive, but when Lear seems to determine the division immediately after Goneril's fake rhetorical declaration and then turns to Regan for her attempt to win a bigger share, the king has stepped into the world of madness. It is a crazy game, a show, a piece of nonsense to please a clearly unstable old man. Lear asks Cordelia what she can say 'to draw/A third more opulent than your sisters?' Is he really dividing the country impromptu, determining who gets what by the largeness of their claims of love? If so he should judge only after all claims are made. Mad enough to think of dividing the kingdom, he is mad enough to divide it according to the declaration each makes. His behaviour is transgressive on the personal and national level. It appears he has already mentally divided the kingdom on the assumption that Cordelia, with whom he has already decided to live, will make the most appealing declaration. The sisters all know Cordelia is father's favourite ('he always lov'd our sister most' [I. i.]), his 'joy'. Perhaps the elder two hope a fortuitously worded declaration will gain a little extra, presumably agreeing to play the game because 1. they do not want to lose out on anything going, and 2. they know Lear is not a man to cross. Is he fit to run either kingdom or family? Is it all just an elaborate plan to cajole his daughters into pleasing him in public? That would be more fakery, making it appear they win their portion according to their declaration when in fact the matter is already decided, and he really wants the pleasure of hearing how much they love him. Cordelia's refusal to play this game puts her father and her sisters to other sorts of test – how truly Lear loves Cordelia and how true the sisters' claims are. The banishment and the hastily 'forced' marriage, disproportionate and cruel, are examples to Goneril and Regan in transgressing the bounds of civilized behaviour. Given the chance to behave decently in housing and caring for their wayward, unstable father, they use the opportunity to get rid of him. This treatment of a man in his eighties would be cruel in any context. Shakespeare's audience would judge it in the light of the Fifth Commandment and the respect owed a king. Goneril displays further transgression by encouraging a subordinate to be rude to an ex-king because he now has no power. 'A dog's obey'd in office', but once out of office a fallen placeman is treated like a dog.

Lear shows further unfitness to rule in responding to Cordelia's refusal by foisting himself on the other daughters for alternate months, showing impetuosity when calm circumspection is needed. His proposal to be housed with 'an hundred knights' – declaring he will resign his power and revenue but still be called king and treated with all the usual ceremonies – is unworkable and mad. He correctly describes himself later as 'a very foolish fond old man'. Dividing the realm is politically naive, a piece of unworthy showmanship divorced from the realities of how people express their feelings and how they feel about having to express them. 'Which of you shall we say doth love us most?' This pathetic question has no place in normal adult family relations, let alone in the public sphere, surrounded by courtiers and with national political consequences. The situation is unrealistic, a fantasy scenario from fairy story and parable, but highlights some real-life features and heralds further transgressions that pinpoint rather uncomfortable questions about the real nature of family and hierarchical bonds. Money, inheritance and property divide families and cause the most vicious arguments and fallings out. Whatever Lear's failings as king and father, Cordelia loves him, putting the matter in simple, stark, realistic terms:

> [...] I love your Majesty
> According to my bond; no more nor less.
> [...]
> You have begot me, bred me, lov'd me: I
> Return those duties back as are right fit,
> Obey you, love you, and most honour you. (I. i.)

She loves him because he is her father, loves him according to the established expectations of society. Any deeper personal feelings she is not prepared (or able) to voice. Her love is not expressed by words, but by deeds ('I am sure my love's/More ponderous than my tongue' [I. i.]). It is not what the authoritarian king wants to hear, but he does not understand the difference between the public sphere and the private. Bringing the private into the public in demanding these declarations transgresses the role of king and father by blurring the distinctness of the two. Unintentionally, Cordelia's blunt honesty forces Lear to make another bad, mad, impromptu decision that sets the course towards inevitable catastrophe.

Lear questions uncontrolled patriarchy. Underlying the two parent–children groupings in the play is the question of just how much real love existed between parents and offspring in a time when marriages were often arranged, and many mothers and fathers (the latter particularly) among the political elite were often not only physically and emotionally distant from each other but detached from the nursery, took little interest in their growing children and were emotionally cold when they were together. Patriarchal strictness, if not ameliorated by love and softer, shared moments, did not encourage close, loving bonds. Duty, the Commandment to honour thy father and thy mother, did not necessarily encourage love. Authoritarian males could be distant and family interactions often coldly formal. Parents (particularly fathers) were often figures of awe. Angry fathers could be like the wrath of God if disobeyed or thwarted. Montaigne deprecates this:

> I am against the custom of forbidding children to say 'Father', and requiring them to use some other, more respectful title, as though Nature had not sufficiently provided for our authority. We address God Almighty as Father and scorn to have our own children call us by that name.[9]

Noticeably, in making their love declarations in the formal situation of the gathered court, Goneril calls her father 'Sir' and Cordelia 'my lord' and 'Good my Lord'. Similar formality is shown by Regan when she meets the angry king at Gloucester's castle ('your Highness', 'Sir', 'my Lord'). This distance may perhaps be because there are servants and nobles present, may be intentional because they are arguing or may be suggestive of difficulty in expressing affection. The formality is broken once when, cruelly, Regan says, 'I pray you, father, being weak, seem so' (II. iv.). In Act II, Scene i, when Edmund pretends he is wounded by Edgar, he calls Gloucester 'Father, father!' It is a plea for sympathy. Usually he calls him 'sir' or 'your lordship'. The Bible provides numerous examples of brutality by father against child and vice versa. Early modern European history records ruthless, brutal behaviour by titled parents towards sons and daughters and similarly ruthless acts by children. The lure of power, wealth and position exposed just how little love could exist within families. Closer to home, the Revenge Tragedies portray the violence generated within families when such goals are at stake. Kent attempts to intervene in the name of honesty, in the long-held belief that the faithful councillor is more trustworthy and valuable than the flattering courtier. Kent knows he is transgressing the deference expected from a courtier to a king ('be Kent unmannerly,/When Lear is mad' [I. i.]). Speaking truth to power is dangerous in an age of absolutism, but Kent maintains his love and loyalty, returns from his banishment to serve, care and be guardian in the king's madness and homeless isolation, creating a new family for Lear.

Gloucester's transgression began many years back. Edmund was 'away' nine years, formative years in which awareness of isolation from a father would have grown, been felt strongly, and increasingly aggressively resented. Unsurprisingly, he is vengeful. Lear's family may also have suffered long-term dysfunctionality. Lear's queen has possibly been long dead, so the sisters have grown up with a quick-tempered autocratic father and without a female role model (no nurturing older gentlewomen are presented).

The court leaves with the standard 'Flourish. Exeunt [...]', but in emotional disarray. Goneril and Regan provide an interesting psychological profile of the king, biased but giving insight into this grotesque family, and indicating clearly some of the transgressions that have become the norm with Lear. He is inconsistent ('how full of changes his age is'), has been for some time ('the observation we have made of it hath not been little'), and this latest reversal of former affection ('he always lov'd our sister most') is irrational, extreme and ill-judged ('and with what poor judgement he hath now cast her off appears too grossly'). His outburst and dogmatic rejection of Cordelia is due to 'the infirmity of his age' and 'yet he hath ever but slenderly known himself'. This tendency to violent emotional responses is a 'long-engraff'd condition' and he has never, even at the height of his intellectual and emotional powers, been calm and rational in judgement ('The best and soundest of his time hath been but rash'). Not trusting Lear to retire gracefully and relinquish his authority, the sisters fear this deep-seated erratic irascibility will only increase with 'the unruly waywardness that infirm and choleric years bring with them'. When next we see him he is in a confrontation with Goneril of the sort they anticipated. His self-imposed position, having supposedly given up power but still behaving like a king, makes a serious rift inevitable.

This opening scene incorporates latently all the potential for tragedy, introduces the themes, and sets the tragic machine ticking over. When next we see Lear his blindness and lack of control will set it in unstoppable motion. In the words of Anouilh's Chorus in his tragedy *Antigone*:

The spring is wound up tight. It will uncoil of itself. […] The least turn of the wrist will do the job. Anything will set it going […] and the tragedy is on.

The rest is automatic. […] The machine is in working order; it has been oiled ever since time began, and it runs without friction. Death, treason and sorrow are on the march; and they move in the wake of storm, of tears, of stillness.[10]

Lear is a tragedy ready to happen. The sins of the fathers, already psychologically visited upon the children, will now be physically returned by those children. The tragic machine waits throbbing. How horrific and destructive its path will be the audience cannot imagine.

Part II

THE WORLD TURNED UPSIDE DOWN

Chapter 13

SINS, TRANSGRESSIONS, SUBVERSIONS AND REVERSALS

In this scene-by-scene identification of the boundaries crossed as the drama progresses, Commandments broken, Deadly Sins committed, and other lesser failings and socially subversive comments or actions are marked in **bold** print. The items identified relate to the moral matrices discussed in Part I. Read this section in conjunction with the play.

The play presents an unbroken parade of transgressive and subversive actions that reverse, ignore or simply brush aside normative expectations. Many have a religious dimension – unsurprising considering the primacy of religious practice and the audience's familiarity with the Bible's requirements of conduct. Other actions offend common sense, civilized behaviour and ordinary human decency. Court life and regal rituals were increasingly scrutinized, questioned and mocked in this period. The whole subgenre of revenge tragedy, with its court-centred plots, critiques the conduct of courtiers. James I's court, his household and his failure to live up to the principles of *Basilikon Doron* are the subtext of the play, clearly evident despite the pretended pagan setting. Modern readers knowing the period cannot but sense how critical the play is of Jacobean England and the court in particular. How much more pointed it must have seemed to those gathered in Whitehall in 1606.

Act I, Scene i

The drama begins with discussion of an intention that goes against common sense. **Dividing a kingdom** would alert even those least knowledgeable about political science. Gloucester's jokes about his bastard child display **levity**, making light of serious matters. Earldom was a highly respected ancient rank, going back to the much-revered Saxon period, a time accorded 'golden age' status, before the 'Norman yoke' was imposed upon the land, yet here is an earl venially boasting of a sexual exploit. This is **bad taste, fornication, adultery, lechery** and **poor parenting**.

Lear's **ostentatious** trumpet fanfare entry heralds floods of actions and reactions breaking many rules. The fanfare was a normal method of announcing a monarch's arrival, but it is accompanied by the **peremptory** command, 'Attend the Lords of France and Burgundy, Gloucester.' Though an accepted part of formal ceremony, the manner indicates Lear's usual **autocratic, high-handedness** (as king and father). A more sensitive father would not force his daughters to display private emotions in public. It seems to be a device for **displaying his power**, to know how loved he is and to please his self-esteem (**vanity**). Goneril and Regan are both guilty of **simulation** (pretending to feel an emotion) and **dissimulation** (the hiding of one's true feelings). This is **lying, flattery** and **hypocrisy**. Much was written at this time concerning the dangers of flattery in court. Bacon calls these tricks 'hiding and veiling of a man's self [...] when a man industriously [purposely] and expressly feigns and pretends to be that he is not'.[1] This is later evident in Edmund's deceitful behaviour. There are, Bacon concedes, times when secrecy can be wise and thoughtful. This **lying** is for personal gain and is wrong because it misleads Lear. Cordelia is guilty of **political short-sightedness** and personal **naiveté** in refusing to play along. More mature judgement would lead her to say enough to please her father and allow him to follow his plan of living with her. Her embarrassment at being asked to publicly avow her feelings overwhelms her and her reply is shockingly curt. Lear, **impetuously** concluding she does not love him, **rashly** decides to banish her and live by turns with the other daughters. Naiveté is less serious (though it has unforeseen consequences) than breaking the Commandments about not **bearing false witness** (as the elder two have) and **failing to honour your parents** (as all three do). Lear's extreme reaction to Cordelia's 'Nothing, my lord', is **excessive**, shows **lack of self-control**, and the sin of **wrath**, worsened by his **responding suddenly and violently**. **Hot temper**, not a positive kingly quality, may be regarded as a tragic flaw (or one of them). Rational judgement and considered action were especially demanded of rulers. Lear shows neither, so transgresses as monarch and father. Kent's determination to speak out is **disrespectful** but he feels 'duty' should not 'dread to speak' when a loyal servant and counsellor sees 'power to flattery bows'. He rates loyal, sensible adult advice more highly than respectful politeness and intricate court etiquette. Exemplifying the true friend and counsellor who speaks the unpalatable truth, Kent offers an **image of reversal** in describing Lear's behaviour as like killing the doctor and rewarding the 'foul disease'. James I had promised to be 'a good physician' when he came to the throne. He was not, any more than Lear. The power of Kent's image here is in the idea that if the doctor is the source of a disease the patient has no more chance than a country whose monarch is 'diseased'. Disease imagery recurs when Regan talks of 'the infirmity of his age' and Goneril agrees, 'The best and soundest of his time hath been but rash.' 'Sound' means healthy, so even at his best Lear was **imbalanced** and **impetuous**, compounding his irrational **spite** in banishing Cordelia by also banishing Kent for speaking out of love, loyalty and common sense. He sees as a virtue never reversing a decision once made, berating Kent for trying to make 'us break our vows,/Which we durst never yet'. James I was notoriously difficult to shift in his views. So too was Elizabeth I. Her motto, *Semper eadem* (Always the same), is positive and negative. Immovability is a mark of consistency and resolution if a decision is sound, but is here **obstinate** and **precludes taking advice**. Wise kings have counsellors and consider other courses of action. Foolish ones make snap decisions and stick with them ('I have sworn; I am firm'). When Lear angrily orders Kent 'out of my sight', the earl takes up the image and advises him to 'see better' and let Kent be 'the true blank of thine eye' – that is, the white bull's eye in the target's centre (i.e., the wise counsellor, whose advice helps make valid decisions). Sight metaphors run throughout. Clear vision and blindness or defective sight are integral to the ideological development of the drama; Lear mad understands matters more truly and Gloucester blind sees which son is true and which is not. Ironically, Lear swears 'by Apollo', a god whose religion was based on the maxim 'Nothing in excess'. How different from Lear.

Campbell sees Lear's volcanic anger as stemming from injured self-esteem.[2] His public demand for declarations of love has been refused and his public image is embarrassed. His foolish demand is suitably treated by **flattery** that fools him and honesty that angers him.

The two older sisters planning to curb their father indicate some of the causes of this rift in the past behaviour patterns of the 'rash' king. Their immoral **secrecy, plotting, deception** and **dishonourable behaviour** towards their father is made subversive by being devices of women and daughters: **ambition** had negative aspects, but would be thought more disturbing in women and daughters. Normative **gender roles are subverted** and fundamental **social principles threatened**.

Act I, Scene ii

The foundations of family soundness are under even more grave and direct threat as Edmund announces himself and his intentions. He **betrays** father and brother, **transgressing the Commandment to honour your parents** and with hints of a Cain/Abel or Esau/Jacob **fraternal rivalry** founded in **envy**. Dante put traitors to kindred in the lowest sector of Hell. Bacon nominates a bastard among those 'apt to envy others' because 'he that cannot possibly mend his own case will do what he can to impair another's'.[3] The soliloquy marks Edmund as irredeemably **heathen**, devoted to a pagan goddess, but he speaks like a Renaissance man who has read Machiavelli and will use people's credulity to undermine his brother and promote himself. He is a **malcontent** (a recurrent figure in Revenge Tragedies). His concept of the nature he claims to worship is of the ruthless beast, the selfish snatch-what-you-want ideology of survival of the fittest. **Predatory will** is only controlled by civilized moral expectations to stop each person acting upon individual desires. These are the 'customs' that 'plague' Edmund, the fussy 'curiosity of nations' that established primogeniture as the means by which inheritance rights are organized. Montaigne wrote, 'Nothing is really in our power but our will; it is on the will that all the rules and duties of Man are based and established.'[4]

This suggests duty is an abstract theory only activated if a person's will accords with the requirement of duty. According to his philosophy, Edmund's prime duty is to satisfy his own will to power. Custom and law deny him any right to patrimonial land. It is never made clear how, if at all, Edmund will benefit from his father's death. He bases his plan on the principle that throughout history has driven men grasping for power: if you really want something, grab it. Such men succeed until they go too far and are eventually toppled. Edmund seems not to consider being an obedient son, living with and being known and valued by his father. His immediate remedy for being undervalued is undermining his brother and pushing him out of the nest, like the Fool's cuckoo. He knows gullibility is the weakness of the good – and he will exploit it, will **subvert good conduct, lie, forge, slander** and **libel**. His remarks on the host of foppish spawn of legitimate marriages, conceived without love and probably within arranged unions, are embarrassing for such fathers and sons in the audience. How many would there be who only had position and power because of their birth? How many heirs to title and fortune were hopeless fools, libertines and knaves, with younger brothers much more suitable and capable but without any prospects? His intention to 'top th' legitimate' is **subversive** and **malignant**, threatening to overturn primogeniture. It promises a Machiavellian plot and therefore has dramatic effect in generating interested anticipation, though we may suspect that his supreme confidence in himself is **hubristic** and carries the seeds of his downfall. There is **no modesty, moderation or humility** in Edmund. Almost immediately he begins deploying a series of tantalizing **innuendos and lies**, like the Devil – 'the Father of Lies'. This is a vital, creative mind and we watch it at work, responding to the opportunities offered by Gloucester's ready gullibility, admiring even while we know it is **evil**. A wise man reserves judgement, but Gloucester's lack of knowledge of Edgar, his readiness to believe him capable of thinking and saying what Edmund alleges, indicates another father ignorant of his child's character, too **prone to jump to conclusions**. Gloucester, shocked at Lear's sudden departure from the palace, limiting his own power, confining himself to an allowance, is about to react similarly. As Lear mistakes Cordelia in her verbal expression ('Nothing, my lord'), so Gloucester, ironically, is drawn into suspecting Edmund's letter contains compromising matter by his intentionally suspicious answer, 'Nothing, my Lord'. Gloucester does not know his son's handwriting and believes Edmund's punning confirmation that it is Edgar's 'character', with no thought of **forgery**. Gloucester believes Edgar has made transgressive statements and clearly does not know his own son or does not trust him. Lear too mistakes Cordelia's 'Nothing' as meaning she does not love him as he thought she did. Experience and instinct should tell both fathers this is not so. To give him credit, Gloucester does voice surprise ('Had he a hand to write this? A heart and brain to breed it in?') but is hurried into conviction by Edmund's cogent explanations of how deviously the letter came to hand and an apparent verbatim statement of Edgar's belief that 'sons at perfect age, and fathers declin'd, the father should be as ward to the son, and the son manage his revenue'. Given no time to consider, convinced by Edmund's apparent concern to provide definitive evidence, Gloucester betrays a **lack of faith in Providence** with his belief that astrological forces are at work undermining different aspects of society. This hits at the **foolish superstitious tendencies** of an age when, despite nominal Christian faith, people still went to men like Simon Forman, William Lilly and John Dee for zodiac-based predictions and believed in old sayings about good and bad luck ensuing from the tiniest chance events in everyday life. Gloucester, apparently much influenced by his beliefs in the way the stars affect human life, is marked as a man of the old world and its ways. Edmund too knows the relevant jargon, though he is not a believer. The talk of 'these late eclipses' and the rest would be understood by the audience, for visiting astrologers and cunning men was a primitivism common among all classes. Gloucester, a man of rank, a leader of men, presumably one of Lear's oldest council members (if Lear can be believed to ever take counsel), should by age and experience be more circumspect, but is, as Edmund says, '**credulous**'. The terms Gloucester uses to describe Edgar – '**unnatural**', '**brutish**', 'worse than brutish', 'a **monster**' – are more applicable to himself (and Edmund). Edmund **pretends** to be unwilling to believe Edgar is so ruthless, but offers verbal 'evidence' to counter each objection his father makes. Edgar is no better. His '**foolish honesty**' (gullible naiveté) marks him as another easy

victim, along with Cordelia, Lear, Gloucester and Albany. He too is hurried
along without time to consider whether Edmund's account is genuine. None
of these characters has the wit to bide their time or even consider that the
way things appear may not necessarily be the way they truly are. Edmund's
deviousness is clear in his readiness to justify all means that fit his personal
purpose. He emerges fully developed as the standard **malcontent** villain of
Revenge Tragedy and naturally raises interest in what he will do and how.
Rejecting astrology (for he will make his own fortune), he is sceptical, one
of the '**new men**' rejecting old beliefs in 'planetary influence'. Believing he
would have been what he was whatever the combination of stars at his birth,
he suggests that his character ('rough and lecherous') is due to his parents.
He is perhaps suggesting that his father compounding with his mother out
of wedlock and his subsequent marginalization have made him what he is,
'moulded more by the example of parents than by the stars at their nativities'.[5]
Nature and nurture combine in Edmund to create an **envious** outsider able
to access sources of power. Edmund has a low, cynical view of his own kind.
Rejecting the influence of the planets on people's personalities, he dismisses
the 'whoremaster man' and his 'goatish disposition', listing only negative
types – villains, fools, knaves, thieves, treachers (traitors), drunkards, liars
and adulterers. The rest of humanity are presumably honest simpletons like
his father and brother. Gloucester's litany of reversals and bonds broken
('Love cools, friendship falls off, brothers divide [...]'), are resourcefully
repeated by Edmund ('**unnaturalness between the child and the parent [...]**,
dissolutions of ancient amities; divisions in state [...]') to convince Edgar
it is all true. The echo of Gloucester's complaints is Edmund's take on the
events he witnessed at court, re-emphasizing the unnatural reversals we have
witnessed, and establishing the dominant mood of the subsequent play.

Act I, Scene iii

The shift to Goneril's palace instantly introduces more **transgressive
behaviour subverting the family.** After only a fortnight's stay there is friction
between Goneril's household and Lear's train of knights. The atmosphere
is volatile because Lear struck a gentleman of Goneril's retinue for 'chiding
of his Fool'. This petty incident brings tensions to a head. Goneril claims,
'By day and night, he wrongs me [...]. He flashes into one gross crime or
other [and] sets us all at odds.' The verb 'flashes' suggests the **thoughtless
impetuousness** of Lear acting **without consideration** for others. The phrase
'all at odds' foreshadows the greater confrontations to come. Great events
have small beginnings. The Fool has said something, perhaps in his blunt
personal manner, a gentleman of Goneril's household has reprimanded him

and the king has hit the man for daring to upbraid a royal servant. It is a tiny indication of the uncertainty of the ex-king's position, still behaving as if he were top of the pyramid. The blow is a physical expression of **wrath**. A king might do such a thing and was allowed to do so by virtue of his power, but it would be regarded as **ungentlemanly** and **unfitting**. His **disruptive** behaviour is similarly unsuitable for a guest, even a royal one. Patience and forbearance were kingly qualities. Sir Thomas Elyot required those who lead men to consider consequences of actions, display 'honourable [...] demeanour', dignity and prudence. Kings faced many irritating situations, but were expected to repress the desire for instant angry retaliation and calmly put the matter into perspective. Lear seems angered by the tiniest cross, perhaps encouraging his knights to grow 'riotous'. Goneril's answer is again **contrary to the Fifth Commandment, unladylike** and **childish**. Tit-for-tat is not a rational, civilized action. Encouraging servants to show disrespect is **socially subversive** and **bad manners**. Goneril probably exaggerates the misconduct of Lear and his train, looking to confront him. Clearly she has grounds for complaint, but it is also evident both have high opinions of their status and the respect due to them. Collision is inevitable. That things are going seriously wrong is encapsulated in the comment 'Old fools are babes again', a reversal of normative respect shown to elders, but also a blunt statement of Lear's condition: he is **infantile, egotistic, demanding** and **spoiled**. Her intention to use 'checks as flatteries' (thwarting a child's wilful behaviour with rebukes rather than soothing) is subversive and inappropriate in a child. Clearly Goneril intends to **create a confrontation**. This **turning upside down of nature** – an old man being like a baby, a daughter behaving like a mother – is disturbing. More so is the cruel **contempt** Goneril shows:

> Idle old man
> That still would manage those authorities
> That he hath given away! (I. iii.)

She does not consider discussion with her father any more than he considered discussion with Cordelia. If he does not like her view, he can go; she will not be 'over-rul'd'. She has her father's **autocratic, dogmatic** will. Her readiness to **set her servants against the king** and his train cuts at the roots of a key bond within society; it is extremely subversive to use your power as employer and promoter to encourage dependent wage-earners to behave contrary to the exemplary conduct of Castiglione. Next to family, the bond between master/mistress and servant was crucial to social stability. The Captain's readiness to carry out Edmund's execution order on Lear and Cordelia shows how catastrophic subverting hierarchy can be. He is promised it will 'make thy way/To noble fortunes' (V. iii.). Goneril is releasing the natural savagery and cruelty of 'might is right' when she sets up her servants to seek confrontation, a **barbarism** reflected in the linguistic references to wolves, kites and foxes.

Act I, Scene iv

Kent returns disguised as a servant prepared to undergo hardship ('serve where thou dost stand condemn'd') out of love and loyalty. Kent's return is **counter to the king's verbal edict** and carries a death sentence. The **disobedience** is transgressive but marks intense loyalty. An earl dressing down and pretending to be a gentleman-servant **crosses the boundaries of hierarchy**. Visually it involves a costume downgrade. In a play where people hide their real selves and fail to behave according to the expectation of their rank, disguise by means of clothes is a visual emphasis of the need to cloak yourself when danger or necessity demand but is also used by those with evil intentions. It symbolizes the **blurring or masking of identity**, adding to the **confusion of appearance with reality**. In Kent's case it is in order to do good. In Edgar's case disguise is necessary to avoid capture, trial and punishment (though trial might give him the opportunity to deny Edmund's claims). Disguising their true natures enables Goneril and Regan, dressed as princesses, elite figures, to hide their true feelings and intentions. Noble ladies with **ignoble hearts**, their behaviour runs counter to their appearance. This is a world where the old certainties, like clothing indicating your calling or rank, are confused. This scene carries many more paired examples of **norm reversals**, for though it is only two weeks since Lear and his retinue infested Goneril's household, flashpoints have already emerged. The entry of Oswald, the archetypal **obsequious self-serving** servant, brings immediate conflict with Lear and Kent through the 'weary negligence' he shows. The rules of courtesy require him to respect a guest. Since that guest is his mistress's father, the requirement is greater still. The fact this guest is also an ex-king (though still bearing the title) makes the demands of courtesy even stronger. Oswald shows how thin a veneer of civility overlays our essential selfishness. His rationale is: 'This man no longer has any power so I don't have to respect him. My mistress pays my wages and is the means of any future personal advancement, so I will follow her orders rather than do what is proper.' Kent and Lear both exhibit **disorderly, ungentlemanly conduct**; Lear strikes Oswald, Kent trips him and manhandles him. Ironically, while behaving in this manner, he warns, 'I'll teach you differences'. Kent himself ignores these 'differences' when he calls him a 'lubber'. To abuse a princess's household steward crosses the bounds of courtesy even if his behaviour deserves it. Many established 'differences' (social demarcations) are contravened during the play, but more important bonds will be broken which turn social critique into tragedy.

The Fool's entry accelerates the audience's awareness of what turnarounds are happening, for this character, with the freedom allowed to his role, points out very sharply how things are being turned topsy-turvy. He says what others dare not and what he says is cruel. It is his profession to be a transgressor – to reprimand or mock the great, to tell cruel truths in order to make Lear realize his **folly**. He begins by turning loyalty on its head and calls Kent a fool for allying himself to one out of favour, warning 'and thou canst not smile as the wind sits, thou'lt catch cold shortly' (I. iv.). There would be many in the audience who switched allegiance as one royal favourite fell and a new one rose. Early in James's reign it became obvious how he liked to surround himself with young men to whom he showed special affection. His favourites received great largesse – presents of jewels, clothes, valuable monopolies, estates and peerages. Most courtiers were **parasites** hoping to gain something from the king – and James was known to be extravagant, wasteful and unwise, once giving a knighthood to a goldsmith for drilling a hole in a diamond for him. Lear's threat of 'the whip' prompts the Fool's quip about how truth is not a favourite, it is a dog to be whipped out of the house (as Lear will be driven out) to the kennel (gutter) while the bitch called Lady (Goneril) is allowed indoors by the fire. Dogs as images of flattery and conditional loyalty recur many times throughout the play. Here one dog stands for truthfulness, the other for the fawner seeking comfort and gain.[6] The importance of honesty in human transactions was established in the Commandment 'Thou shalt not bear false witness'. It is a bedrock concept for all interactions, social or personal. This play rests on a shifting quicksand of lies, deceptions, smiles hiding hatred and false assertions that seem true because we tend to believe what people say. Once we realize people lie to cover real motives and feelings, all sense of security is gone. This essential texture of the play, the difference between appearance and reality, recurs throughout Shakespeare's works. The Fool's awkward truths continue to punctuate the scene as he plays a little charade in which he asks Lear to represent the lord 'that counsell'd thee/To give away thy land' – himself. They stand side by side – the sweet fool (i.e. the Fool with his jests and his relatively trouble-free life) and the bitter one (Lear, with his self-inflicted miseries and more to develop later). He continues with a pointed topical attack on the court sitting in front of him, saying that if he had a monopoly of folly (which he does not as it is widespread) 'lords and great men [...] would have part'. When he came to the throne James declared he would deal with the monopoly problem. Elizabeth's Declaratory Act prohibited the spread of monopoly grants, but despite setting up a commission to limit monopolies, James soon began granting them to importunate courtiers. This created a conflict area between the Crown and the House of Commons. Monopolies could make cash for James (by outright sale to a courtier or a regular share of the profits) but reduced the national income, for monopoly taxes went to the monopoly owner. The Fool specializes in pointing out sharp reversals: 'thou bor'st thine ass on thy back o'er the dirt'; 'thou mad'st thy daughters thy mothers'; 'thou gav'st them the rod and putt'st down thine own breeches'; the daughters will whip him for telling the truth and Lear will whip him for lying. In saying this the Fool references self-interested inconsistencies of action that lead to a loss of moral certainty. A savage metaphor, **reversing parent–child** power, is the cuckoo biting off the head of the parent sparrow that fed it. Lear's painful path to acknowledging how foolish he was in trusting the **counterfeit affection** expressed by two of his daughters is what earns him the audience's pity and gives the play its drive. Moral correction is painful. A character in Middleton's *Michaelmas Term* (1605) remarks, 'Man is ne'er healthy till his follies bleed' (V. i. 15).

Goneril's description of the misconduct of Lear's 'insolent retinue', even if exaggerated to suit her case, raises questions relating to the ideal behaviour of men of 'name' and to the 'rank [...] riots' of James's male courtiers. The Renaissance debated tirelessly what made a gentleman and certainly decorous public comportment was key since all gentlemen were presumed to have a public role. Realizing at last his **folly** and **loss of judgement**, feeling his honour impeached by her remarks, his responses are instantly **extreme** ('degenerate bastard', 'marble-hearted fiend', 'detested kite'). It is as if his long-repressed dislike of her suddenly erupts in passionate rejection. There is, unsettlingly, no law that says a child must love its parent (or vice versa). To honour your father and mother (as the Commandment demands) is not the same as loving them. *Showing* honour to someone is not the same as honouring them. Sincerity is essential. Lear's curse that Goneril be barren or that her child (if she has one) should 'be a thwart disnatur'd torment to her', is an alarming, **unfatherly** and **unnatural** reversal of norms. The usual joy at grandfatherhood is turned horrifically on its head with a curse that in the event turns on him, as his two children become torments to him. Another deeply upsetting reversal is his bursting into **tears of anger**, frustration and impotence at finding Goneril has already dismissed 'fifty of my followers at a clap [...]!' (I. iv.). The tears indicate that whatever words of defiance he spits, Goneril has unmanned him. Lear himself feels 'asham'd/That thou has power to shake my manhood thus'. He swears he will pluck out his own eyes if he weeps again, perhaps subliminally planting the idea of blinding in his daughter's mind, to resurface in Act III, Scene vii. Storming out, the king makes the hollow hubristic rhetorical boast he will 'resume the shape which thou dost think/I have cast off forever'. He will take on several other personae, but never again the 'shape' seen at the beginning of the play. Falling from power is a feature of tragedy, but the process of falling is enlightening and the Lear of the final act is wiser though sadder. This man, so used to having his way without question, loses all self-control when thwarted (a child-like trait). His rage is human, impotent. There is nothing godly or regal here. It is as if a king should 'play bo-peep' (i.e., play the part of a shepherdess) – a double role reversal, from king to lowly shepherd, from man to woman. Albany's entrance at the end of the confrontation presents another reversal of gender roles. Goneril dismisses his reproach with 'Pray you, content', criticizing his 'milky gentleness'. He weakly, meekly accedes to her with the timid 'Well, well; th'event' (i.e., let us see how it turns out). Some viewers would be horrified at this, others would see it as common enough female behaviour. The first phase of Lear's emasculation as king and father ends with him temporarily homeless, preparing to seek refuge with Regan. That will come to nothing and he will truly be without shelter. This situation evokes Matthew 8:20: 'The foxes have holes, and the birds of the air have nests; but the Son of Man hath not where to lay his head.' In his unavoidable psycho-drama, Lear, like Christ, will go into the wilderness and suffer.

Act I, Scene v

The Fool's quip that if a man's brains were in his heels he might get chilblains reverses normal body positions. The punchline suggests Lear is safe from chilblains because he has no wits if he thinks Regan will be any more hospitable than Goneril. Lear is moving in a mad world, where normal expectations of family kindness and sympathy no longer exist; he is mad to reject his most loving daughter and trust the rhetoric of his two 'pelican daughters', mad to banish Kent, mad to think a hundred knights could co-exist harmoniously in a strange household if they did not behave with delicate awareness, mad to give away all hold on material power. Common sense, which he lacks, would warn him to keep some money and power in his own hands and somewhere to lay his head. A king of his age should have experience that would make him capable of foresight, seeing what the consequences of his impetuous actions might be, and circumspectly plan ahead in case matters should go wrong. Lear has his first premonition of the incipient danger of losing his grip on reality:

O! let me not be mad, not mad, sweet heaven;
Keep me in temper; I would not be mad! (I. v.)

Madness is the **opposite of man's natural state** as a rational, logical, carefully considering creature. Sanity is normal, though constantly besieged by deranging appetites and passions. The Fool, in an arresting moment of dramatic impact, makes a parting comment that might well be aimed at those light-hearted, flippant young women in the audience who giggle at Lear's plight:

> She that's a maid now, and laughs at my departure,
> Shall not be a maid long, unless things be cut shorter. (I. v.)

One can imagine him pointing at the rows in front of him, finger moving along to include all the viewers, saying any virgin finding this funny lacks the sense to keep her virginity long. It is a hit at the moral thoughtlessness of the waiting gentlewomen at court, seeing everything as a laugh and nothing as serious. The female part of the court was no more decorous or mature than the males: 'The ladies about the Queen spend their time these days in children's games [...]. This exercise is sometimes used from 10 of the clock at night till 2 or 3 in the morning.'[7] In other respects they were similar to the men: 'There is much **plotting** and **malice** among the ladies of the court striving for the offices of honour about the Queen.'[8] Change 'ladies' to 'gentlemen', 'Queen' to 'King' and, handy-dandy, what is the difference?

Act II, Scene i

Full of ironies to come unexpectedly true later, this scene extends and deepens the sense of family break-up and wider collapse by developing the Gloucester subplot further. Edmund, pursuing his plan to gain his father's trust and replace his brother, hints of rumours of a **rift between the dukes**. Curan (a courtier) asks Edmund, 'Have you heard of no likely wars toward [...]?' The division of the realm has quickly generated a **rivalry** that threatens civil war. Moral polarity between the Dukes will develop further, but political division comes to nothing with Cornwall's death and the sides uniting to face invasion. The scene displays Edmund's superb **stage-managing** (manipulation) of his '**credulous**' father and 'noble' brother, even opportunistically using Cornwall's imminent arrival at Gloucester's palace to scare Edgar into flight, hinting Cornwall comes to question Edgar about speaking against him. Edgar's certainty of innocence is insufficient for him not be anxious to escape when Edmund hears his father coming. While shouting out as if trying to stop his brother, Edmund reassures him of his support, encouraging him: 'fly, brother'. To him, the terms 'brother' and 'father' are just words, they carry no affection, no identification with them through shared memories. Once again language carries the meanings of the play as it did with the brutal animal imagery of Act I. Edmund is what Gloucester made him – a young man **without feelings** for family, **without bonds**. His creative improvisation is masterly, fabricating a scene in which he supposedly tried to stop Edgar persuading him to murder their father. He goes so far in his **lies** as to wound himself and accuse Edgar of attacking him. His comment to the audience 'I have seen drunkards/Do more than this in sport' is another topical criticism of the crazy behaviour of inebriated Roaring Boys terrorizing London streets. Claiming Edgar mumbled 'wicked charms, **conjuring** the moon', Edmund taints his brother with **sorcery**. With cruel irony he even pretends he spoke up for the very child–father bond he lacks, claims he assured Edgar that 'the revenging gods/'Gainst parricides did all the thunder bend'. This dramatic irony will redound against Edmund. He later seeks his father's life and the 'strong bond' that binds child to father will show forcefully in Edgar's tender care of the blinded earl. The gods will be revenged – but against Edmund's unnaturalness. With Lear-like **readiness to rush to extremes**, Gloucester promises death to Edgar and anyone concealing him, yet this will be the child who, like Cordelia, sets aside grievances to care for a parent. In an unconscious irony that will cost him dear, Gloucester calls Cornwall his 'worthy arch and patron' – words again **disconnected from truth**. The unworthy heir theme is further developed when, in response to Edmund's claim that Edgar called him 'thou unpossessing bastard!' (an unsubtle prompt to Gloucester which works), Gloucester, with unwitting irony, calls Edmund a 'loyal and natural boy' and declares he will make him his heir, thus **transgressing the law** prohibiting bastards from inheriting. The medieval church keenly supported this legislation to disincentivize lechery.

Cornwall and Regan assume **false sympathy** as they test Gloucester's response to two anti-Lear remarks: that Edgar was the king's godson and that he was one of the 'riotous knights'. The earl does not take the bait, but Edmund confirms his brother was of the depleted entourage and Regan declares the king's companions must have encouraged Edgar to kill his father in order to have his revenue to waste, evoking the prodigal behaviour of many young men at court.[9] Edgar, as Poor Tom, develops this in more detail (III. iv.), speaking either from experience or observation. In further ironies, Cornwall recognizes Edmund as a son of 'virtue and obedience' (praise the audience knows is undeserved) and Gloucester (shortly to be blinded by the duke) is called 'our good old friend'. This scene works by indirection and opposites, and features several **false claims** and epithets. Some are known to be false by the speaker, others are known to be wrong by the audience only. This complicity adds tension as we wonder whether the truth will ever out. The scene closes with Gloucester declaring, 'Your Graces are right welcome.' This resonates with ironies. Regan and Cornwall fled their castle to avoid sheltering Lear. The audience senses if they meet Lear again, they will be no more hospitable than Goneril.

Act II, Scene ii

This scene deals with **unwise righteous anger**. Kent's contempt for Oswald leads him into **ungentlemanly** and **undiplomatic** behaviour. Abusing a servant is unbecoming an earl (and **not sensible** given Lear's already precarious situation with his daughters) and **unsuitable** for a king's messenger. Like heralds or ambassadors, royal messengers had special protected status, but Kent's inability to guard his tongue leads to **indecorous conduct** and then to downright **discourtesy** to the duke and his wife. Like Lear, Kent is **irascible**. He is **abusive** and **snobbish** about Oswald wearing a sword, and yet **dishonourably** draws his own sword to do **violence**. Kent's responsibility for **stirring up trouble** will have consequences when Lear is provoked by the disrespect shown his messenger. The angry earl's abuse is a useful mouthpiece for some vitriolic comments on the servile yes-men of the court, though it is disguised as general remarks upon obsequious servants anywhere:

> A knave, a rascal, an eater of broken meats; a base, proud, shallow, beggarly, three-suited, hundred-pound, filthy worsted-stocking knave; a lily-livered, action-taking, whoreson, glass-gazing, super-serviceable, finical rogue; one-trunk inheriting slave; one that wouldst be a bawd in way of good service. (II. ii.)

This outburst, full of rank-conscious terms, indicates how low Oswald is in the hierarchy and how shameful he is as a man. He is a 'knave' (low class and **dishonest**), a 'rascal' (**untrustworthy**), an 'eater of broken meats (a low servant licking up leftovers, not eating with or like gentlemen). He is 'base' (of low origins), yet 'proud' (sinfully **thinking better of himself than he should**, given his origins). Being 'shallow' suggests he is **materialistic** and has **no genuine moral principles**, while 'beggarly' suggests that in being paid he is no better than a beggar asking for money. He is not gentleman enough to clothe himself, but reliant on his employer's customary annual clothing donation of three suits. He has only one trunk (servants were allowed a box of personal possessions) and does not wear silk stockings like a gentleman but dirty worsted ones. This is a reminder of the often-broken sumptuary laws prohibiting one rank from wearing dress suitable to another. The ragged Lear bedecked with flowers, the near-naked Poor Tom and Kent himself dressed as a servant are examples of the **transgression of dress codes** and signifiers of the breaking up of normative behaviour. This applies metaphorically to those who **dress finely but behave basely**. Furthermore, Oswald is a litigious **coward** going to law rather than fighting like a gentleman; he is called a bastard ('whoreson'), **vain and foppish** ('glass-gazing') and fussily ready to do anything over and above normal duties in order to curry favour. Kent even suggests he would be a 'pander' (a pimp/procurer) because of his readiness to do whatever his employer asks, good or bad.

Kent's anger is **excessive**, compensating for his inability to rectify his beloved master's situation by venting anger against someone of the opposing faction. He insults Goneril, calling her '**Vanity** the puppet' and **loses control** to the extent of threatening to fight Edmund when he enters, disturbed by the noise. He knows him to be Gloucester's son but demeaningly calls him 'goodman boy' and 'young master' and threatens to 'flesh' (cut) him. The audience may agree with Kent's comments and understand his anger, but would see the inadvisability of it. His **unbecoming language** for a man of his age and rank indicates what uncontrolled anger leads to.

Among his comments are some pointedly relevant critiques. Kent contributes to the imagery and theme of unnaturalness, saying of Oswald, 'Nature disclaims in thee: a tailor made thee.' The steward is an **artificial** construct, identified by his clothes. Proverbially the clothes made the man; in other words, a tailor could create the impression or appearance of a lady or gentleman merely with fine clothes. The person wearing them might be physically decayed underneath but appear elegant, or the gentleman's outfit might be a misleading sham (as Kent believes of Oswald). Cornwall is both **disrespectful** and correct when he calls this messenger 'beastly knave', for Kent is behaving indecorously. He is also right to ask, 'Know you no reverence?' Kent is **not showing due respect** because he has not quite fully realized his role, reacting as an angry earl when supposedly he is a royal messenger. Claiming 'anger hath a privilege' is wrong. He has no voice save to present his master's message. The rest of what he says causes trouble that leads to a further transgression, but it enables Shakespeare once more to point the finger at the court. Kent explains he is angry with Goneril's steward inappropriately wearing a sword, which by law is only permitted to gentlemen. A gentleman was defined as having education (particularly at university level), a coat of arms, family history of gentry status, skill in arms and independent means without having to earn money by work. Kent goes further, delivering a diatribe against 'smiling rogues' (servile smiling rascals) who cause disagreements between husband and wife. ('Like rats' they 'oft bite the holy cords a-twain'.) In the broader context Shakespeare is targeting servants who make themselves available as a sexual alternative to a spouse. Fornication was not an improbable accusation among the various levels of the royal household. In the more immediate context this comment applies to

Oswald furthering Goneril's plans, about which Albany is already unhappy. Kent attacks those servants **flatteringly encouraging bad passions** in their masters, playing up to whatever their master's mood might be and changing their view to fit the prevailing attitude.

A man 'whose disposition [...]/Will not be rubb'd or stopp'd', Cornwall too transgresses by his own **anger**. Like Lear he is used to getting his own way and **reacts forcibly** if thwarted. Putting the messenger in the stocks is grossly **disrespectful** to his father-in-law. Gloucester declares the stocks are for the 'basest', a 'low correction' for 'pilf'rings and most common trespasses'. Cornwall knows this but **wilfully** goes ahead. Even punishments were stratified according to the rank of the culprit, so Cornwall is **subverting custom** as well as displaying his **unsuitability for power**. Careful consideration and balanced judgement were key in administering justice. **Hasty, arbitrary punishment** was not kingly. The public had been shocked when on his way to take up the throne James, at Newark in Nottinghamshire, had a pickpocket caught working the crowds executed on the spot (without trial). Having insulted the duke and duchess by saying he has seen better-looking faces than theirs, Kent belatedly tries to flatter them and remind them of the respect they owe the king. It is too late. He is stocked and Regan spitefully insists he stay there overnight. This is another **abuse of power** through **hasty, impassioned judgement**. Regan acts according to the new morality of self, more concerned what her sister will think if her servant's abuser is unpunished than she is to honour her father by treating his messenger honourably.

Alone in the stocks, unaware of the degree to which he has contributed to further conflict within the royal family, Kent reminds us of the growing **unnaturalness** of the play as he refers to a letter from Cordelia and his hope that she will come to remedy 'this enormous state' (i.e. abnormal). He calls on Fortune to turn her wheel more favourably. More circumspect conduct by him would have been more useful than blind hope in the benevolence of Fortune.

Act II, Scene iii

Edgar's enforced disguise **breaks the dress code** of the time. In such a status-conscious society the markers of rank were highly visible. The power of clothing as marker of rank has been discussed elsewhere. Presented here **reversed in extreme visual form** it will have a powerful dramatic effect when Edgar meets Lear. The description of the Bedlam beggars thronging the roads, visiting 'low farms [...], poor pelting villages, sheep-cotes and mills' to 'enforce their charity', exposes the state of society. The mad and homeless are soliciting aid from those only a step or two above them. Where are the government, the parish Poor Law officers, the local rich families enacting the Corporal Works of Mercy? We are told that such wretches are 'whipp'd from tithing to tithing'. So much for the scriptural exhortation to 'love one another' (John 13:34–5). Edgar, later to be instrumental in opening Lear's eyes to the sufferings of his people, is learning to 'feel what wretches feel'. His season in purgatory will strip away the ragged follies of his previous time as a comfortably-off heir to an earldom and possible member of the king's entourage. Stripped of identity ('Edgar, I nothing am') and clothing and his appearance changed to those of the disadvantaged and homeless, he undergoes a period of suffering, acts as guide and carer for his father, reasserts his bond with him, saves him from **despair**, defeats his brother in single combat and emerges as a wiser, sadder man and the next sovereign. A remarkable pilgrimage.

Act II, Scene iv

This scene vibrates with tension as the inevitable definitive rift between Lear and his eldest daughters occurs. It is suffused with angry, bitter arguments, set immediately alight at the sight of Kent in the stocks. The Fool jokes at the **subversion** of God's finest creation (man) being hobbled like horses, dogs, bears and monkeys. Kent's account of how his welcome at Regan's was superseded by Oswald's is another **turning upside-down of protocol**. The Fool points out that fathers who retain financial control will encourage kind behaviour in their children, unsettlingly suggesting that money might be the sole nexus between some parents and children. Lear's **anger** causes the first physical symptoms of extreme stress – heart palpitations and sensations of suffocation through shortness of breath. He expresses it in another **image** of rebellious **usurpation** where the **natural state is altered** by the sensation of the lower body swelling up **out of its place** towards the heart. Kent **lies** when asked if he did nothing else to cause trouble and seriously underplays his **provocative, unbecoming, disrespectful language and conduct**.

When Kent asks why the king's train is so reduced the Fool comments on the general self-interest of courtiers, advising, 'Let go thy hold when a great wheel runs down hill' and latch on to the next 'great one that goes upward'. Knaves would follow this advice, but loyal followers (like himself and Kent) will remain with a master revered and loved. These ideas are put more pithily (and prophetically) in another of his admonitory rhymes aimed at the audience:

That sir which serves and seeks for gain,
And follows but for form,
Will pack when it begins to rain,
And leave thee in the storm. (II. iv.)

In an age when loyalty – to country, monarch, overlord, family – was much valued (Dante put traitors in Nether Hell), **disloyalty** in hard times was thought exceptionally **dishonourable**. Lear **loses his temper again** when Cornwall and Regan deny him audience ('images of revolt and flying off') – the **double dishonour** of refusing a king's and a father's command. He experiences another physical attack as his stress levels rise further at seeing Kent still stocked. Seemingly on the edge of a heart attack, he calms a little when the Duke and Duchess appear. This does not last as Regan questions whether he has treated Goneril with sufficient respect, suggesting she probably had good grounds for restraining 'the riots of your followers'. A series of **reversals** are evident here as Regan talks to her father like parent to child, suggesting he should be advised by a responsible adult who understands his situation 'better than you yourself'. Lear contributes to the **subversion of decorum** by kneeling and facetiously begging for 'raiment, bed, and food'. This '**unsightly**' trick is followed by a violent curse against Goneril, repeating the **unnatural sentiments** of Act I, Scene iii. With heart-breaking irony Lear claims Regan knows better than her sister

> The offices of nature, bond of childhood,
> Effects of courtesy, dues of gratitude. (II. iv.)

At this moment, with dramatic effect, the scene is interrupted by a blaring trumpet announcing Goneril's arrival. Henceforward the daughters' **cruelty** escalates. Its intensity focuses in Regan's remark, 'I pray you, father, being weak, seems so'. They coldly argue his train down from fifty to none, with no conception of how we all like to have things or people about us that remind us of our former life. Lear reminds Regan, 'I gave you all.' Her reply is chilling: 'And in good time you gave it.' This is **brutal, callous** and **selfish**. There is no love here, simply **self-interest** and **materialism**, as if we only pretend love for a parent until we have got all they can give. One reason this play is so painful to watch – apart from the physical horrors presented – is its stripping away of all the comforting beliefs in familial closeness, displaying a family that is as cruel as beasts. Bacon applauded Machiavelli's works because they 'openly and unfeignedly [...] describe what men do, and not what they ought to do'.[10] It takes stern fortitude to look unflinchingly at this scene. Not all families are like this, but it is how many political elite families in English history behaved. The Tudors, the family many of the audience would have known and served, had experienced internecine parent–parent, parent–child and sibling–sibling struggles. The history plays recently performed reflected badly too on elite families in their murderous **struggles for power**. Here was the same ambition, hatred and heartlessness, set even further back in history and representing family members as little more than wild beasts. Consistent animal imagery throughout the play reinforces the idea of how, without vigilance, virtue, love and human existence are derogated to that lower, appetite-driven, primitive level of creation. Without those more divine qualities of love, protectiveness, reason, moderation, charity and tolerance, 'man's life is cheap as beast's'. As an omen of disruption to come the storm is heard outside as Lear leaves behind this cruel abnormality for another cruel state – insanity's isolation. In his madness he will be guarded by those who retain love and respect for him, but he is outcast in his own mad world. Regan, cruel to the end, shows no compassion, saying it is too dangerous to shelter such a 'desperate train' as attends the king and he has to learn from the mistakes he has made:

> [...] to wilful men,
> The injuries that they themselves procure
> Must be their schoolmasters.

Cornwall counsels Gloucester to 'come out o'th'storm'. None can shelter from the storm they have released through their transgressive behaviour. It will envelop them all.

Act III, Scene i

The Gentleman and Kent verbally create the ferocity of the storm, describing Lear 'contending with the fretful elements'.[11] This Gentleman, here and elsewhere acting as a means for Kent to convey information, shows the loyalty Lear has generated, staying with the king as his Wheel of Fortune 'runs down a hill'. The Fool too is with Lear, desperately trying to laugh him out of his angry sense of injury. Kent's trust in the anonymous Gentleman encourages revelation of further decay in the state. There is an unacknowledged 'division' growing between the two dukes. Their rivalry, not yet openly admitted, is 'cover'd/With mutual cunning'. This secrecy hints at a Machiavellian game of deception – public smiles but private plotting. Both dukes have servants in their households feeding intelligence to France. These 'spies and speculations' add to the atmosphere of mistrust and machinations. The revelation that a French military force has entered 'this scatter'd kingdom' with covert parties landing at some of the ports provides anticipation for the audience of some attempt by the representatives of good to prevent further dissolution of the state. Roughly halfway through the drama we sense the balance beginning to swing towards Lear.

Act III, Scene ii

Lear is not mad yet, but he is in a state of high emotional turmoil defying the elements, calling them to destroy him and the world. It is a normal reaction, when experiencing severe disappointment and upset due to a deeply held belief in someone, to think we want the wreck of everything. Lear's language expressing his fury and despair involves **images of disorder**: floods so extreme churches will be under water and the world flattened by 'all-shaking thunder'. The drowned churches symbolize the **overthrow of religion** and the striking flat of 'the thick rotundity o'th'world' and the breaking of 'Nature's moulds' represent a call for the **overthrow of the gods' creation**. This **defiant blasphemy** does not accord with the quiet stoical acceptance required of Christians. The audience would see Lear as defying God's plan, but as a pagan he would know no better. Everything that happened was thought to be God's will and with His foreknowledge. Shakespeare here mixes supposedly pagan beliefs with Christian ones. The king's paranoid obsession with ingratitude focuses on his daughters. He accuses the thunder, lightning and rain of being 'servile ministers' in league with them.

The Fool tries to make a joke out of the idea of a man whose sexual desires lead him into marriage before he has a house to live in. It is a distant reference to Lear's impracticality in dispossessing himself and relying on the kindness of unkind daughters. The king, unaware of the Fool, talking to himself, realizes, even in his extremity, that he needs to calm down or he will induce some sort of brain episode. 'I will be the pattern of all patience' is ironically what he should have been before. With this mood change Lear becomes more philosophical and critical in his comments. He sees the storm as a means of the gods exposing their enemies and lists some culprits: the criminal who has not confessed his **crime** and remains **unpunished**, the **murderer** ('bloody hand'), the **perjurer**, the **hypocrite** pretending to be virtuous after committing incest, the wretch who covertly **plotted someone's death**. He calls all **those who have hidden crimes** to confess ('Rive your concealing continents') and beg 'these dreadful summoners grace'. The terms 'summoners' and 'grace' have particular effect. A summoner was an official of the ecclesiastical courts who delivered the official court summons for having committed some sort of sin. The word 'grace', a Christian concept, was the favour of God. If you had grace by nature it meant you were a naturally good person, that God was in you. 'Grace' could also mean the sense of relief you would feel after confessing a sin and begging forgiveness (which Lear is calling upon these imaginary sinners to do). Throughout this speech it is not inconceivable that the actor might look round the audience. It is unsettling when an actor fixes his eyes upon you. It is certain that among the gathered courtiers there would be many who had used 'covert and convenient seeming' to get out of trouble, or get what they wanted. The tone of this speech is not pagan, its terms are Christian and immediately understandable by an audience brought up with Christian values. The degree to which they had strayed from them would be the measure of their guilt at hearing these comments.

Kent asks his master to rest in a hovel near the castle walls, while he tries again to 'force/Their **scanted courtesy**' and regain shelter in Gloucester's castle. He has already been denied. Giving shelter, particular in bad weather, was regarded as a traditional duty owed by all ranks to benighted travellers. Refusing it was a sign of **discourtesy, inhospitableness** and **selfish callousness**.

As if grace had entered him, Lear, feeling his 'wits begin to turn', shows consideration to the shivering, soaked Fool. In his turmoil, on the edge of madness, he becomes more alert to others. While the king and Kent enter the hovel, the Fool delivers what he calls a 'prophecy' that satirically analyses seventeenth-century England. He claims to envisage a time when 'the realm of Albion' will collapse in chaos ('confusion') and people will walk because all will be humble and not wish to display their wealth through finely caparisoned horses or extravagant coaches. Unlikely. This state will come about when priests are full of fine words and empty of important lessons (which they already often were), when brewers water their beer (a common fraud), when **nobles** are so trivially minded they are **more concerned with the latest fashion** than their duties, teaching tailors how they want their clothes to look (already the case in the **vain**, fashion-mad court), when no heretics are burned but young men (because they have had sex and caught syphilis, a widespread STD, the symptom of which was a burning sensation in the penis). This references young men visiting prostitutes, catching syphilis, then presenting themselves as would-be husbands to rich heiresses,[12] encapsulating the **sexual looseness** of the age, an example of **hypocrites** pretending to purity and virtue. The reference to every case in law being right is a hit at the dogmatic judge or **arrogant** lawyer, who claim their legal conclusions are always correct and just. **Bribery, twisting the truth**, peremptory and **biased judgements** were common abuses within a legal system skewed in favour of the powerful and rich. Squires were often in **debt** and dramas of the 1600s are full of cash-strapped knights, all flash and show, but expecting to be respected. People love **spreading slanderous rumours** and hearing bad of others. **Reputation-destroying tales** filled the court. Cut-purses (**thieves**) were always found in crowds. **Usurers** keep secret their accumulated gold, never counting it in the open any more than pimps and prostitutes donated money for building churches. This list of actual abuses and impossible reforms is an indictment of the age. The Fool steps out of the remote setting and into contemporary England.

Act III, Scene iii

Gloucester tells Edmund the castle has been commandeered by Cornwall and Regan. This **'unnatural dealing'** and the **enforced confiscation** of his property is **counter to all law and normal proceeding**. It is a monstrous piece of **subversion of the basic property right** which all Englishmen were entitled to expect. The situation is worsened by its being retaliation for the pity Gloucester showed in requesting Lear be allowed to shelter in the castle. This **dictatorial**, unnatural behaviour is exacerbated by Cornwall and Regan threatening Gloucester with their displeasure if he talks about Lear, speaks in support of him or tries to help him. It is as if the old king has been outlawed like Edgar. Edmund's Machiavellian tendency to deception is neatly expressed by insincerely 'agreeing' the duke has been **'savage and unnatural'**. Gloucester has a letter informing him of foreign forces having landed and reveals his intention of joining the king's side in the inevitable war. He foolishly tells Edmund to talk to Cornwall while he secretly does what he can to relieve the king. His loyalty, courage and preparedness to risk death to help his 'old master' sharply contrast with Edmund's readiness to **betray** him. Edmund immediately informs the duke, an action he thinks worth reward. **Ruthless dishonesty** and **unscrupulous ambition** combine as Edmund manoeuvres for advancement, **dishonouring his father** and **showing himself without honour**. His **inability to forgive** past treatment contrasts with the news of Cordelia's attempts to aid her father. One action speaks of **hate**, the other of **love**. Strong here is the contemporary fear that the **impulses to self-aggrandisement and self-advancement** and the **preferencing of the individual will** were changing society for the worse. The closing couplet, a common device for emphasizing a point at the end of a scene, is chilling. It expresses Edmund's **completely evil heartlessness**. No Christian feelings are operative here:

> This seems a fair deserving, and must draw me
> That which my father loses; no less than all:
> The younger rises when the old doth fall.

Act III, Scene iv

Contrasting **unnatural behaviour by a son** to his father is kindness shown not to a relative but to someone for whom great love, loyalty and respect are felt. Kent and the Fool try to shepherd the old king out of the storm and into shelter. It is humanity's humanity at work. Lear points out he hardly feels the cold and wet, for strong emotion blocks out other pains as he struggles to come to terms with the '**filial ingratitude**' that 'beats' like a 'tempest' in his mind. Filial ingratitude is as **unnatural** as a mouth biting the hand that feeds it.

The more sensitive, chastened Lear ushers the Fool into the hovel and then prays. The concerns expressed show the degree to which sudden and unusual suffering has opened the king's eyes to the plight of others. Wondering how the ragged poor can endure the storm, homeless and unfed as they are, he admits not thinking of them sufficiently in the past. They were his responsibility, but in the **pride of pomp and power** he took 'too little care of this'. He raises the point that Dives knowingly ignored; the rich and powerful need to 'take physic', to 'medicate' their souls, purge (a common meaning for 'take physic') their pride in their own importance and experience for themselves 'what wretches feel' as a reminder of their duty to 'shake the superflux to them'. To give the poor what you had in abundance and did not need was a duty. Moralists addressed this persistently, but human moral 'blindness' (an appropriate image in *Lear*) is such that the message needs constant reiteration. Human sympathy soon evaporates and mankind sinks back into **greedy sloth, selfishness** and **spiritual complacency**. Social transgressions associated with the detachment of the court and the upper sort from the mass of people are largely implied here rather than directly stated, but the actor-king is like a preacher and the audience like a congregation gathered to hear wisdom and advice. A large gathering of 'pomp' (those who are magnificent, well-dressed, proud, etc.) was there in front of Lear.

Poor Tom's eruption on stage triggers numerous new satirical attacks. Masquerading first as a mad beggar, Edgar comments on the **lack of human charity** shown to such figures ('Who gives anything to poor Tom?') then, fabricating a life as a 'servingman', he unleashes criticisms of a host of court immoralities. Interspersed are broader warnings:

Take heed o'th'foul fiend. Obey thy parents [a Commandment]; keep thy word's justice [a Commandment]; swear not [a Commandment]; commit not with man's sworn spouse [a Commandment]; set not thy sweet heart on proud array [the sin of vanity and showy clothes].

Poor Tom's 'servingman' may well be Edgar drawing upon his knowledge (personal or observed) of the court. It does not sound like the life of an ordinary domestic. **Concern with appearance**, recurrent **lustful** references, claims of **swearing and breaking oaths, drinking too much, gambling, insincerity, violence, sloth, deviousness, greed, ready belief in malicious rumours, predatoriness** and **debt** make this a recognizable litany of the sins of many young hangers-on at court. The list might make any gathering blush with guilt – how much more so a court audience already notorious for decadence. Tom's state provokes Lear's new philosophical bent and nascent charity as he sees him reduced to his basic vulnerability, and tries to lend him his own clothes (another stage in Lear's disassembling regality). Tom's account of being 'whipp'd from tithing to tithing, and stock-punish'd, and imprison'd' is no more than the truth of how an **institutionally punitive and uncharitable society** dealt with homeless vagrants. His fall from being a man with 'three suits to his back, six shirts to his body', a horse and weapons is a warning to those watching of how anyone may fall. Everyone there would know of those who rode high on Fortune's wheel and ended on the scaffold, in prison, in rags or in Bedlam. Jacobeans were fascinated by tales of falls from fortune (they saw plenty of them) and descents into madness. *The Duchess of Malfi* presents a scene in a madhouse and a duke who becomes mad through intense incestuous sexual jealousy. Othello's reason is on the very edge in his incoherent jealousy, Hamlet fakes insanity, *Eastward Ho!* has Harebrain and Security as two unstable jealous husbands, and Volpone is a money-mad monomaniac. The most impactful madman was Kyd's Hieronymo, the unhinged father seeking bloody revenge in *The Spanish Tragedy*. Edgar's compelling act representing a madman is chilling and exciting in its stream-of-consciousness speeches laced with references to **diabolic possession and persecution**. Gloucester, watching Tom, makes the unwittingly ironic remark, 'Our flesh and blood [...] is grown so vile,/That **it doth hate what gets it**.' Hatred of a parent seems unnatural and vile, yet it is central to the play's disturbing exposure of human cruelty. He is unaware this is his son (though his comment makes it clear he is thinking of him) or that his bastard hates him and is plotting against him. Amid the nerve-jangling pretend insanity of Edgar and the real madness of Lear now his wits have turned, the storm continues in the background as a derailing descant that makes the scene almost physically and emotionally unbearable. Yet there are little touches of care and concern.

Act III, Scene v

Edmund **blackens his father** in order to rise to a great place himself. Replacing his brother is insufficient; he now **greedily** wants Gloucester's title and property, pretending to deplore it ('I must repent to be just!') but readily giving up the secret letter betraying Gloucester's knowledge of the French invasion, then **faking** regret that Gloucester was committing treason and that he detected it. This deprecation is unconvincing to the audience but his shallow deceit is not picked up by Cornwall, who all-too-readily names Edmund as earl and sends him to find his father and arrest him. Cornwall seems to sense Edmund's **readiness to do anything, however morally reprehensible, in return for advancement**. Cornwall's promise that Edmund will 'find a dearer father in my love' is a **grotesque reversal of a deep-seated human bond** – one monster siring another.

Act III, Scene vi

Lear's **anger**, fierce disappointment and **longing for revenge** (an irrational fixation) have now completely turned his wits, triggered by Tom's pretended insanity. He thinks constantly of violent retribution. Tragedy always has an undercurrent that expresses the viewer's desire to see justice done to the villains and those mistreated. Lear's longing for justice against Goneril and Regan is played out in the mock trial he imagines. It is not yet clear how or whether the audience's longing for justice will be achieved. Lear's pathetic charge that his imaginary Goneril 'kick'd the poor King her father', is a laughable accusation – if one felt like laughing. His imaginary Regan has 'warp'd looks' that tell clearly what her heart is like. The mad Lear sees more clearly than when he was nominally sane. His claim '**Corruption in the place!**' resonates in several ways – the corrupt behaviour of the dukes and their wives, the corruption of Jacobean law courts, and the corruption of the court where the play is being performed. As Edgar begins to find it difficult to continue counterfeiting, Lear enters deeper into his real madness. There is a moment's glimmer of possible sanity as the king says to Tom, 'You, sir, I entertain for one of my hundred' (unless meaning his followers are sinful 'fools and madmen').

Gloucester's news of a plot to murder Lear horrifically combines potent taboos: **parricide and regicide**. Lear is escorted to Dover and supposed safety, indicating that goodness does survive and loyalty will risk its life to do right.

Act III, Scene vii

If the previous scene was hard to bear with its unsettling verbal comments, the sight of a madman and the demoralizing situation of Lear, this scene upsets in a physically visceral way. Before he even enters we know Gloucester is in deep trouble. Cornwall calls him 'traitor', begging the question whether the duke's will is law. Ordering the earl not to 'sustain' Lear carries no legal weight. It would if Cornwall were a legally appointed justice and this a legal trial. This is **naked *realpolitik*, Machiavellian ruthlessness**. It says, 'Gloucester is my prisoner, I will punish him, because I can.' James would recognize the absolutism here in instant 'justice', having exercised it himself. Regan and Goneril display **autocratic cruelty**; the first wants him hanged and the other demands, 'Pluck out his eyes.' This would elicit a gasp of horror in the audience. It is laughably absurd delicacy on Cornwall's part to send Edmund away so he may not have to watch 'the revenges' taken. The terms used, the punishments called for, seem excessive in view of what Gloucester has actually done. It looks like spitefulness because he disrespected them and ignored their demands. The official excuse would be his knowledge of foreign invaders. We learn that the party of good is regathering itself and that some thirty-five dismissed followers have rejoined the king and, along with some of Gloucester's dependants, are escorting Lear to Dover. This irks Cornwall and he calls for 'the traitor Gloucester' to be bound like a thief. Once again, as with Kent's stocking, **respect for rank is ignored**. Cornwall acknowledges he cannot sentence the earl to death without a proper trial ('the form of justice'), but because he has the power to do so he will yield to his **wrath**. In the spirit of *realpolitik* he says men can blame him, but they cannot stop him. Ironically, this **hubristic brag**, this intended naked **abuse of power** is misplaced confidence, for he will be fatally wounded. The earl's entry evokes spitefulness in his tormentors. He is verbally insulted ('ingrateful fox', 'filthy traitor', 'villain') and physically assaulted (Regan plucks his beard). These are **grossly disrespectful** to anyone, even more so to someone who is an aristocrat like themselves. It **transgresses courtly decorum** and is **vile behaviour** from one human being to another. As Gloucester says "tis most **ignobly** done' (i.e. low, not like a noble). In an unfortunately inopportune moment he defiantly declares he will *see* 'winged vengeance overtake such children'. This alludes to the Furies of classical myth (sometimes described with bird or bat wings) and combines with Christian ideas of divine retribution. The word 'see' prompts Cornwall's memory of Goneril's demand they should pluck out Gloucester's eyes and leads to a moment of **physical cruelty** common in Elizabethan-Jacobean dramas. Bloody and gruesome acts were popular with audiences, for the wild justice they sometimes represented, for the excitement some people derive from witnessing acts of extreme violence and for curiosity as to how the actors would achieve the illusion. This gratuitous, impromptu maiming was possibly achieved by tipping Gloucester's chair back onto the floor with servants crowding round and kneeling to hold the chair, obscuring the earl from sight ('Fellows, hold the chair'), while Cornwall simulates gouging the eyes with the heel or spur of his boot ('Upon these eyes of thine I'll set my foot').[13] The horror is worsened by Regan's joke: 'One side will mock another; th'other too.' As the servant steps forward to remonstrate with Cornwall one of those kneeling could apply a concealed phial of blood to the face. The vengeance Gloucester called for is immediate. The servant who fatally wounds the duke is committing an act of **social subversion**, but is simultaneously the instrument of justice. Regan's running him through the back with a sword

counters the expectation of her sex being tender and nurturing, but neither she nor Goneril have ever acted according to assumed behavioural norms. When Cornwall has finished his appalling job ('Out, vile jelly!/Where is thy lustre now?') the traumatized Gloucester calls for Edmund only to be told of his **duplicity**. Ironically, disillusion brings instant awareness of his '**follies**' in trusting the wrong son; at the moment of blinding he 'sees' his mistakes. Our sense of justice is appeased by Cornwall's death. Punishment for Regan's mocking remark that Gloucester should 'smell/His way to Dover' will come later. The underlying **contempt** of some of the nobility **for those below them** is evident in Cornwall's order that the dead 'slave' should be thrown 'upon the dunghill'. This inhuman attitude recalls Bacon's approval of Machiavelli for writing about the reality of human action, not the fantasies of idealists. Again we are reminded how good is found in unlikely places as two servants discuss assisting Gloucester and dressing his wounds.

Both sinning fathers have been punished. The bulk of the transgressions have been committed. More are to come, fewer in number, but more serious.

Act IV, Scene i

Edgar assesses his situation with laudable stoicism; it is better to know you are condemned than be **flattered** to your face and despised behind your back. This judgement also echoes the misleading of Lear. The idea of the two-faced **hypocrite** who flatters a person but then denigrates them to others is pertinent for a court audience. Flattery involves lying about your true feelings; a form of **false witness**. Edgar's equanimity is shattered when Gloucester is led in. His despairing cry of 'World, world, O world!' is followed by acceptance that death is not to be shunned, fought or feared, for it is the merciful end to the 'strange mutations' we suffer in life. The trinity on stage is a powerful pietà.[14] The blinded earl, forehead bloodily bandaged, marks **man's savagery to man**. The old man guiding him signifies the tenderness of human charity. The ragged beggar symbolizes a suffering Christ, reviled by those who should have loved him, and man reduced to his basic level yet retaining decency and kindness. Like Lear, Gloucester in adversity finds a wisdom he lacked before: 'I stumbled when I saw.' This odd reversal of normality echoes how Lear's madness activated an inner eye seeing into the heart of things. He declares 'our mere defects' can 'prove our commodities' ('our faults can help us prove what are our best possessions', i.e., his blindness over Edmund now shows Edgar was the true son.) He understands that while 'prosperity doth best discover vice, […] adversity doth best discover virtue'.[15] Failings as a parent, gullibility and sin – lust, adultery and faulty parenting – led to punishment, but also led through pain to clearer knowledge of what was valuable in his life.

He expresses a longing to be with Edgar. That son, devastated by what he sees, is about, however, to be given a chance to rehabilitate himself through caring for and saving the life of his father. He rehabilitates Gloucester by leading him away from the **despair** of

> As flies to wanton boys are we to th' Gods;
> They kill us for their sport

to the acceptance of whatever life brings. He learns Job's lesson not to repine at what God sends you in life. Despair was sinful because it ignored the belief that whatever happened was part of God's plan.

Gloucester's comment on being escorted by Poor Tom ("Tis the times plague, when madmen lead the blind') hints at a broad critique of Shakespeare's own difficult times, when leaders did not seem to be able solve England's religious, economic or political problems or did not care to. Reassuming his beggar role, Edgar lists the fiends that possess him and associates each with transgressions: 'Obidicut, of **lust**; Hoberdidance, prince of **dumbness** [keeping silent when you should speak up for what is right]; Mahu, of **stealing**; Modo, of **murder**; Flibbertigibbet, of **mopping and mowing** [grimacing moaners]'.

Before starting for Dover, Gloucester indicates how suffering has opened his 'moral' eyes by giving Edgar his purse – an act of 'shaking the superflux' to a needy man – then contextualizing the act as necessary redistribution of unwanted wealth:

> Let the superfluous and lust-dieted man,
> That slaves your ordinance, that will not see
> Because he does not feel, feel your power quickly;
> So distribution should undo excess
> And each man have enough. (IV. i.)

The mutilated, blood-marked father led by the ragged son touchingly exemplifies human co-operation and intra-familial kindness.

Act IV Scene ii

From the physically outcast son to the morally outcast: Edmund and Goneril already seem to have an understanding, making him a would-be **fornicator**, her a would-be **adulteress**. Goneril **sneers disrespectfully about her 'mild husband'**. Oswald announces a **reversal of a reversal**. Albany, previously subordinate to his proud wife, is reverting to the orthodox gender role. Pleased to hear of the invasion, he deprecates Goneril's return (after hearing how she has behaved), and accuses the servant of having '**turn'd the wrong side out**' in calling Gloucester a traitor and Edmund loyal. After the previous scene this reinforces the sense that the powers of good are finally roused. Goneril disrespects Albany further by criticizing his 'cowish terror' and **reluctance 'to undertake'** (take up his leadership role). She does this in front of a servant and a would-be lover, declaring her own transgression in **subverting normality**:

> I must **change arms at home**, and **give the distaff**
> **Into my husband's hands.**

A distaff (a stick on which women fixed the flax from which the spindle hung in spinning flax into thread) symbolized the female side of a household and its domestic duties. She shows further **inability to judge in a morally correct way** by calling Oswald 'trusty servant'. He will shortly show **readiness to betray Goneril** and serve Regan, believing it will advance him socially. Giving a favour and a kiss to Edmund **betrays her marriage vows**. Once more she shows her inability to see things rightly, complaining of Albany, 'My Fool usurps my body.' She preferences the ruthless, ambitious bastard who responds to her **lust** above the decent man who sees her faults and advises her of them.

Albany's entrance leads straight into disagreement. Ultra-patriarchalists would disapprove of an **overproud woman**, **shrewishly arguing** with her master. Albany rightly assesses the moral and psychological dangers in her treatment of her father.

> That nature [disposition], which contemns its origin,
> Cannot be border'd certain in itself;
> She that herself will sliver and disbranch
> From her material sap, perforce must wither
> And come to deadly use.

Goneril's **unprincipled inhumanity** shows in her dismissive response: 'No more; the text is foolish', provoking Albany to more definitive condemnation of the '**barbarous**' and '**degenerate**' acts of women who are 'tigers, not daughters'. He sees an unthinkable outcome for society:

> Humanity must perforce prey on itself,
> Like monsters of the deep.

The **predation of humans by other humans is monstrous**, an **unnatural subversion of life** with social significances. Cannibalistic preying on humans evokes thoughts of war, commerce, how neglecting your duty as a wealthy man of rank helps destroy those you are meant to protect. Everyone in the audience lived off the hardships of others. The image of courtiers as parasites or carrion-feeders was common in contemporary literature. Representations of courts and courtiers in Revenge Tragedies use similar images. Goneril's answer simply diverts the argument into accusations of **cowardice and tardiness** in not reacting to the threat of invasion, but Albany persists:

> See thyself devil!
> Proper deformity shows not in the fiend
> So horrid as in a woman.

The idea of a **woman behaving like the devil**, becoming **deformed**, evokes traditional beliefs about female tenderness; that view subverted was all the more horrible. He tells her she is changed, has covered up her female self, become a monster and devil, and that if she were not a woman he would tear her apart. Legally he is entitled to beat his wife if she misbehaves. Perhaps he is afraid to or is restrained by her status as a king's daughter. Perhaps he respects her right to be protected by her husband from physical assault even when it is he who wishes to punish her. She mocks his views with a sneer: 'Marry, your manhood – mew!' This has been variously interpreted as his manhood is mewed up (locked away) or simply a derisive 'miaow' as a way of saying, 'Your manhood is like a pussycat' (i.e., soft).

The gender confrontation – the man principled but restrained from physical retaliation, the woman **indifferent to his moral views** – is interrupted by a messenger. The 'moral divorce' of Goneril and Albany is temporarily suspended, but becomes part of the future action and part of the dénouement. Learning of Gloucester's blinding, Albany is appalled but suitably feels Cornwall's death proves the gods avenge quickly. His sense of justice probably coincides with our own. Goneril, untouched by the earl's treatment, is more concerned newly widowed Regan might poach Edmund. Albany pledges to thank Gloucester for supporting the king and revenge his blinding. This encourages hope that good is beginning to gather itself.

Act IV, Scene iii

Hope persists as we hear how Cordelia received news of what has been happening to her father. An audience, almost certainly anti-French, would find it psychologically subversive to see a French king invading British soil.

This danger is diverted by his withdrawal, which foregrounds Cordelia. Her expected **rage** at her sisters' conduct is suitably **controlled**:

[...] She was a queen
Over her passion; who, most rebel-like,
Sought to be king o'er her.

A potential **double transgression is averted** as rage (a sin) and passion (emotion) are quietly kept within bounds by tears that do not become excessive sobs and vengeful threats. She expresses disgust at the **shamefulness** of the **unladylike** nature of her sisters. Men might behave savagely, but ladies (educated, well brought up, high born, sensitive, moral) remained decorously calm even in times of great emotional stress. It is reported that Lear too (in moments of clear thinking) feels shame at his unkindness to Cordelia and refusal to give his benediction to her. Here, regret and shame for anger, control of passion and sympathy for suffering mark acceptable Christian qualities in both father and daughter.

Act IV, Scene iv

Further evidence that good survives shows in the exchange between Cordelia and the Doctor, but we are reminded there are problems still to be solved when we hear of Lear madly singing and dressed with flowers. Contrasted with the formality of the 'drum and colours [flags]' accompanying Cordelia's entry is the **picture of reversal** we see with Lear in his royal clothes, but **crowned with flowers**. It is as if he has returned to nature before his resurrection. It is a disorienting, destabilizing image, like Edgar's ragged beggar appearance before he is cleansed. Cordelia gives reassurances she has come with 'no blown ambition' but out of 'love, dear love' and concern for what is 'our ag'd father's right'. This intended return to normality focuses Lear's right as a king, what is right in terms of an old man's human dignity and the human decency he has a right to expect.

Act IV, Scene v

At Gloucester's now **usurped** castle, Oswald's report that Goneril 'is **the better soldier**' emphasizes the **gender reversal**. Regan **callously** regrets letting Gloucester live since he 'moves/All hearts against us'. The supposedly brute commoners show natural sympathy, **shaming heartless** nobles who obey the established power. But 'a dog's obeyed in office'. Regan's **covetous jealousy** of her sister and Edmund betrays her **vulgar passions** and her **overemphasis** of **fleshly desires**. Like Goneril she exhibits none of the qualities cultivated women were expected to possess. Her **petty, devious** readiness to **subvert a servant** is evident in her wheedling Oswald into supporting her claim to Edmund. Her machinations hit upon the way to persuade him:

> If you do chance to hear of that blind traitor,
> Preferment falls on him that cuts him off.

He is happy to commit a **gratuitous murder** in order to show 'what party I do follow'. Prepared to deceive both sisters, playing one off against the other, the only party he follows is his own. Traditional Christianity valorized putting others before oneself. The new Renaissance **individualism** put self before everyone.

Act IV, Scene vi

Edgar supposedly leads his father to the top of a cliff. Gloucester senses his companion has changed. He is told he is deceived (as indeed he had been by both sons, in different ways) and that 'in nothing am I chang'd/But in my garments'. This is another reversal reversed. As Poor Tom, Edgar claims he only has better clothes. As himself he implies he is the same Edgar who loved and loves his father, but he is changed in his clothing (from nobleman to ragged beggar to peasant). Gloucester asked the Old Man who escorted him to find Tom better garments, so in the process of rehabilitation, returning to the earl's son, Edgar slowly morphs from near-naked beggar to peasant, and his style of talking alters and improves too – becoming less disjointedly lunatic, more coherent and more cultivated in register.

The fake suicide is another pretence in a play in which things are rarely what they seem, words not meaning what they say and clothes hiding who the wearers really are. Turning Gloucester from sinful despair to Job-like acceptance is assisted (along with another voice change into a local dialect) by the suggestion that Poor Tom was a fiend. The escape from the Tempter encourages the earl to 'bear affliction'. This partial salvation is interrupted by the mad Lear. Now in his own imaginary world, he remembers inspecting his troops, watching archery practice, marshalling halberdiers and hawking, but soon returns, like any monomaniac, to his obsession with his daughters and how they '**flattered** me like a dog'. In a moment of **absurd reversal**, dressed in his royal costume but 'fantastically crowned with flowers', he claims he is 'every inch a king' and imagines his subjects shaking nervously at his look. Sad memories of the awe he once inspired lead him to imagine a crowd of criminals whom he pardons, like Christ with the woman taken in adultery. Perhaps the sight of Gloucester triggers thoughts of the earl's adultery, for he launches into a lecture about the age-old problem of sexuality. The church was always worried about how to control or discourage sexual activity. It was a problem too for the civil authorities in prostitute-filled London trying intermittently to close the brothels. It was a problem in the court. Thousands of young men gathered in London seeking their fortune. Young women too flocked to the court looking for places as waiting gentlewomen or for a golden, titled marriage. Then there were all the **aspiring** daughters of wealthy citizens hoping to marry rank. City and court were seething with **sexual longing**. As the usually coy Ophelia sings in her unrepressed madness:

> By Gis and by Saint Charity,
> Alack and fie for shame,
> Young men will do't if they come to't –
> By Cock they are to blame. (*Hamlet*, IV. v. 58–61)

In a similar vein the tapster/pimp Pompey Bum (*Measure for Measure*) discusses the question of dealing with sexuality with the wise, moderate magistrate and co-ruler of Vienna, Escalus:

POMPEY: Does your worship mean to geld and splay all the youth of the city?

ESCALUS: No, Pompey.

POMPEY: Truly sir, in my poor opinion, they will to't then. If your worship will take orders for the drabs [cheap whores] and the knaves [rascals], you need not fear the bawds [pimps, panders, madams].

ESCALUS: There is pretty order beginning, I can tell you. It is but heading and hanging.

POMPEY: If you head and hang all offend that way for ten year together, you'll be glad to give out commission for more heads. (II. i. 227–37)

Pompey, like Lear, sees extreme crackdowns on the sex trade (i.e., executing **fornicators**), as leading to a need to raise the birth rate. Lear's solution is: 'Let copulation thrive [...] for I lack soldiers.' Both acknowledge the irrepressibility of the sex drive and the impossible tension between its control and the need for a rising population. Though the population of London had risen steadily since 1500, the national birth rate had dipped.

The king's wild mind swings from applauding copulation to imagining a woman, a 'simular of virtue', pretending she is better than she is while seething with a 'riotous appetite'. The theme of **hypocrisy**, running throughout the play, now focuses on criticizing the double nature of women: domain of the gods head to waist and of the lustful centaurs below. This virgin/whore double view of women is traditional. Female sexuality is associated here (as in much clerical writing) with the Devil and the punishing fires of Hell ('the sulphurous pit'). This outburst of long-internalized feelings prompts Gloucester to call Lear's breakdown a **'ruin'd piece of Nature!'** His erratic mental forays create a tension that heralds the **approaching apocalypse.** Lear speaks like the Fool as he descants on how 'a man may see how this world goes with no eyes', how you can 'look with thine ears'. He slips from these **reversals of nature** to further examples of **hypocritical social corruption:** the judge who berates a thief but is corrupt himself (taking bribes or turning a blind eye to crimes committed by elite men), the beadle (parish officer) whipping a prostitute while lusting after her himself, the magistrate lending money at exorbitant rates while sentencing a petty cheat ('cozener'). His argument is 'handy-dandy' – turn them around and you cannot tell the difference. This view is expressed in *Measure for Measure* when Escalus, hearing charges against a pimp arrested by a constable, sees how clever the pimp is and how stupid is the representative of the law, and asks, 'Which is the wiser here, Justice or Iniquity?' (II. i. 169). It is deeply cynical but realistically suggests authority is a cheat; if a justice, a beadle or a magistrate was a dog dressed up he would still be obeyed. Too often **corruption in the king's court** filtered down to authority figures. Examples at the top gave leave to those lower down the system. This is Shakespeare in the satirical mood so disturbingly evident in *Measure For Measure* and *Timon of Athens*. He accuses all **authority figures** of being **hypocrites** no better than the people they condemn. Curiously, one of the most potent images of reversal is drawn from the simple, everyday idea of a beggar approaching a farm, asking for alms and being chased off by the farmer's dog: 'the creature run from the cur'. A dog given authority over a human being is a powerful image of **the world turned upside down.** Lear concludes with a fatal stab at the **double standard of justice:**

> Thorough tatter'd clothes small vices do appear;
> **Robes and furr'd gowns hide all.** Plate sin with gold,
> And the strong lance of justice hurtles breaks;
> Arm it in rags, a pigmy's straw doth pierce it.

In claiming he has 'the power/To seal th'accusers lips' he speaks as a king whose will can achieve anything, especially **perversion of the law.** He finishes with a blow at the 'scurvy politician' who claims he knows what will happen rather than admit he has no idea how to solve current problems or avert future ones. This is only the rambling of a madman, so neither James nor his ministers would think themselves accused.

A gentleman sums up this madness as an extreme **subversion of rank and nature**:

A sight most pitiful in the meanest wretch,
Past speaking of in a King!
But offers hope in the one daughter
Who redeems nature from the general curse
Which twain have brought her to.

The ambiguity here cleverly suggests that the sinfulness of Goneril and Regan **inviting the curse of war** is associated with Adam and Eve's Original Sin. Likening the current situation to the cataclysm of the Fall would impact powerfully on an audience reared in a biblical culture.

The scene closes with a dramatic shift from theoretical sins listed by Lear to the purposed sin of Oswald intending to kill the blind earl. He hubristically declares,

That eyeless head of thine was first fram'd flesh
To raise my fortunes.

The intention (**murder, social transgression** – a steward killing a noble) and the reason are both revolting. Edgar is right to call him 'a serviceable villain' (punning on 'villain', a rogue, and 'villein', an old word for a serf, a lowly farm worker, the property of his master). The discovery of Goneril's letter to Edmund keeps the audience mindful of further deception. Her **adulterous intentions** are clear and Edgar rightly declares,

O **indistinguish'd space of woman's will**!
A plot upon her virtuous husband's life.

Women are not spared in the analysis of the dissolution of this society. 'Will' means not just what she wishes to achieve (murder), but means lust as well (thus including her intentions towards Edmund); 'indistinguish'd space of woman's will' means 'how limitless is woman's sexual desire'.

Act IV, Scene vii

This reconciliation and healing scene is the last hopeful and heart-warming scene in the play. Kent, reborn, discards his disguise as the king's servant. Cordelia too is reborn in the sense that the tongue-tied young woman of Act I is now an articulate and philosophical queen. Lear, reborn, wakes thinking he has died and Cordelia is a spirit. Lear, on his 'wheel of fire' weeps tears 'like molten lead', acknowledges he is 'old and foolish', admits he wronged Cordelia, and asks that she 'forget and forgive'.

Act V, Scene i

Public and private collide again as the prosecution of the impending war becomes entangled in an **adulterous love triangle**. Edmund, decisive in manner, organized in planning, seems cut out for military command, while Albany is 'full of alteration/And self-reproving'. The upcoming battle appeals to Edmund's determination to thrive and gatecrash the governing hierarchy. Albany is hesitant because he does not see the justification of opposing Lear. Military matters are diverted by Regan's interrogation into Edmund's relationship with her sister. **Jealousy and sibling rivalry** focus on the false new Earl of Gloucester and will run parallel with the fortunes of war. Goneril says she would rather lose the battle than lose Edmund to her sister. This **transgresses a governor's duty**, which is always primarily to the state and its people. Albany comments that already the rule of each half of the kingdom has been heavy-handed ('the rigours of our state') and some with 'most just and heavy causes' have sided with the invaders. Goneril interrupts, firmly declaring these 'domestic and particular broils' are not the priority. Her manner is **contrary to expected female conduct**. Yet it is not an entirely **sincere** comment for she immediately shows she is still aware of the Regan–Edmund problem.

Edgar gives the duke the 'love letter' from Goneril to Edmund and asks Albany, if he is victorious, to allow a champion to fight in prosecution of the letter. Asking that the customary form of a challenge be adhered to, with a herald calling upon the champion to present himself, implies a return to normative behaviour. Edgar says this will not be necessary if 'you miscarry' [lose] for then 'machinations' will be at an end, assuming Edmund will either be dead or taken prisoner to face trial for his plotting. This too would be a return to normality for the old regime and legality would have been restored and justice done. The scene closes with Edmund's amused reflections on the two rival sisters. This soliloquy is **sincerely insincere** as he plays with the idea of having both, one or neither. As an opportunist Machiavellian, he will await the outcome of the battle, using Albany's nominal leadership, then see which sister wants him enough to kill Albany. He does not consider what his next step would be once the duke was dead, but determines to **thwart** Albany's **intended mercy** to the king and Cordelia. He declares his situation demands action, not wasting time dithering about what to do. Indeed he responds to the victory by immediately ordering Lear and Cordelia be executed.

Act V, Scene ii

The outcome is swiftly determined. The battle is heard offstage then reported by Edgar hurrying his father to safety. The stage direction 'Alarum; afterwards a retreat' is more detailed in the Folio and Quarto, with the French powers marching across stage with flags flying and drums beating. This creates more of a sense of the imminent action. There will presumably be sounds offstage simulating fighting, and then a retreat back across the stage. The timescale here is not a realistic representation of how long it might take to form battle lines, manoeuvre, engage, fight and retreat. It is symbolic and stylized. Its brevity emphasizes the injustice of Lear's loss, reinforced in the next scene when he and Cordelia enter as prisoners. Edgar, perhaps angrily, perhaps sharply, upbraids his father for being 'in ill thoughts again' and wanting to stay where he is and 'rot'. 'Men must endure' life, its process and its departure. This Christian approach, diminishing the value of life or death because the afterlife is more important, is encapsulated in his dictum 'Ripeness is all'. Edgar voices orthodoxy. Being prepared for death by living a good life meant, for a contemporary Christian, that whenever death came it could be embraced in the assurance of Heaven.

Act V, Scene iii

Lear's defeat is a major difference from all the sources. From here on Shakespeare develops his own ending. Edmund's triumph as he leads in his captives would seem wrong, unjust in the extreme, but it enables Shakespeare to work upon the audience's emotions, making them suffer even further. This is the process of *catharsis* ratcheting up the pity and fear of the audience to such a degree they can hardly bear any more, leaving them washed out or purged. The audience's angry sadness builds as Lear talks of them both in prison like captive but singing birds. He imagines her kneeling to ask his blessing, as was normal. What is a **reversal of custom** is that, in response to her kneeling for benediction, he will kneel and beg forgiveness. There is a humility in him now absent at the start of the play. With that calmer mood of praying, singing and telling stories, the satirical king returns, imagining viewing the 'gilded butterflies' (gaudily dressed courtiers) and laughing to hear sad fools retelling petty, unimportant court news. These are the last few mocking remarks aimed at the audience. He imagines talking about the successes and failures at court, seeing 'packs and sects of great ones' rising in favour and falling out of it like the 'ebb and flow' of the moon. It is a final dig at those who **think so highly of themselves**, but who are just the playthings of Fortune, time and machinations.

The peaceful reconciliatory mood is broken by Edmund briskly arranging their murder. Contrary to the articles of war, he has them taken untried to prison for execution. He gives a death warrant to the captain, whom he has already promoted and to whom he promises 'noble fortunes' for obeying these orders. Once again **unscrupulous ambition** uses the unscrupulous ambition in another to accomplish evil. By a nice piece of justice, this captain will be killed by Lear, but sadly not before Cordelia is hung. This comment on the nature of some people would resonate round an audience where similar lackeys carried out immoral orders simply because they are given by a figure of power.

Lear is taken away and the victors gather to discuss their next moves. Edmund, **economical with the truth**, announces that he has thought fit to send the captives to prison. Albany, pointing out that Edmund is 'but a subject of this war', prompts responses from the sisters, sparking off the open emergence of their **sexual rivalry**. Underlying the arguments are questions of precedence. Edmund has **arrogantly assumed** more power than Albany is prepared to acknowledge. The sisters argue about who has prior claim to Edmund. In a world where **'degree' has been 'shaked'**, tearing up the rules creates collisions between those who think they have a claim to power or position. Anarchy destroys itself by its own principles. Underlying tensions erupt as Regan calls Edmund 'General' and offers her 'soldiers, prisoners, patrimony' and herself. She is **subverting procedure** by delegating her military rights to an inferior, though at the same time **upholding normal hierarchy** by submitting herself to male control. It is **a very forward act**, triggering Albany into arresting Edmund for **'capital treason'** (planning to kill a head of state – himself – though he does not know a worse plan is afoot). He also arrests Goneril, 'this gilded serpent' who has 'subcontracted' herself to another man while legally 'contracted' to her husband. This is **subversion of marriage** and a **transgression towards God** in so far as marriage is a holy sacrament. Albany challenges Edmund (by the traditional duelling code: throwing down his glove) and Edmund accepts; Regan gasps that she is sick and Goneril makes it clear she is responsible. The poisoned, dying Regan is led away as the herald formally announces the combat. After the traditional three trumpet calls, Edgar appears in yet another disguised shape: as **armed vengeance**, the instrument of justice. These reassertions of orthodox values, customs and hierarchies are presented against the suspense of what might be happening to Lear and Cordelia. While an audience may want to see the villains get their just deserts, there is anxiety, pity and fear for the innocents. Edgar indicts Edmund as a **would-be assassin** ('conspirator 'gainst this high illustrious prince') and a **traitor** ('false to thy gods, thy brother, and thy father'). Edmund, ever the rule breaker, transgressively waives his right 'by rule of knighthood' to know his opponent's identity. As he falls defeated Albany cries out, 'Save him! Save him!' This is ambiguous. Does he want him saved to face trial? Or is it a sign that he wishes even this 'toad-spotted' evil man to be redeemed at the last moment. Though Edmund has been 'cozen'd and beguil'd' in fighting an anonymous opponent, there is **justice in a deceiver deceived**. Refusing to submit, as Albany presents her with her own damning letter, Goneril declares no one has authority to arrest her for 'the laws are mine, not thine'. This **double subversion puts herself above her husband**, and **above the law**. Courageously Edmund admits his crimes and forgives his killer. Edgar at last can step out of his disguise. Removing his helmet, reborn, able to reassume his name, he announces himself dramatically: 'My name is Edgar, and thy father's son.' He gains heightened dignity in summarizing the moral import of what has happened:

> The Gods are just, and of our pleasant vices
> Make instruments to plague us;
> The dark and vicious place where thee he got
> Cost him his eyes. (V. iii. 170–73)

Some gentlemen in the audience might have felt a little hot under the ruff to reflect on the awkwardnesses attached to their own illegitimate offspring. Edmund agrees Edgar's comments are true and that he started as nothing with nothing and is back where he started: 'The wheel is come full circle; I am here.' In explaining what has happened to him, Edgar emphasizes the religious nature of his 'pilgrimage'. He became a guide, a leader, a provider for his father (a **reversal of the parental role**) and a spiritual mentor too in averting his despair. At the end he reassumed the child's role and 'ask'd his blessing' before the weakened and broken earl died. He announces too another role player revealed in Kent's reappearance as himself. He hints at Kent's approaching death when, deeply moved by retelling Lear's sufferings, 'the strings of life/Began to crack'. Jolted back to the present, when the murder of Regan (by Goneril's poison) and Goneril's suicide are reported, Albany sees this as a 'judgement of the heavens'. This is another example of **normal attitudes being restored**; the gods have delivered punishment, but the victims deserve no sympathy. Edmund's death is ignored as 'a trifle'. Albany's comment that divine judgement 'makes us tremble' but 'touches us not with pity' recalls the pity and fear Aristotle deemed necessary for the cathartic end of a tragedy.

Kent enters asking to see the king. The audience's suspense over his fate is now to be satisfied. Edmund, on the edge of death, finally admits authorizing the death warrant he and Goneril sent against Cordelia. Thus she is literally responsible for **killing one sister** and technically guilty (commissioning by proxy) of **killing the other**. Guilt for this encourages her **suicide**.

The final, greatest transgression of the play is the **subversion of life by death** as Lear carries in his dead child. It provokes a sense of the end of the world in Kent, Albany and Edgar. Pity dominates as Lear desperately seeks to see if Cordelia still lives. His wandering comments, jumping erratically from one topic to another but always coming back to his lost daughter, are difficult to bear. Albany resigns his power in favour of 'this old Majesty' and promises their rights restored to Edgar and Kent. He announces further reaffirmation of justice and normality's return:

> All friends shall taste
> The wages of their virtue, and all foes
> The cup of their deservings.

But Albany breaks off seeing Lear's final moments have come. The king reiterates the usurpation of life by death and the **injustice** of Cordelia being dead while dogs, horses and rats still breathe. Albany once more, as senior in rank, invites Kent and Edgar to rule and 'the gor'd state sustain'. Kent declines, as he knows he is close to death himself, and so the newly resurrected Christ figure, Edgar, is left to assume the crown. Cleansed, humbled by his sufferings, he has grown in moral stature as the play progressed towards its catastrophe. His closing speech is very downbeat, almost platitudinous.

> The weight of this sad time we must obey;
> Speak what we feel, not what we ought to say.
> The oldest hath borne most: we that are young
> Shall never see so much, nor live so long.

Characters speaking openly and frankly what they felt was not much evident in the inciting and rising actions of the play. Saying what was expected was too evident. The **devastation of war**, the **devastation of families** and the **brutality and misery** released were such as are not often seen, though some in the audience would live to see the horrors of 1642–49 and the execution of the young prince among them.[16] The stage direction 'Exeunt, with a dead march' provides a traditional formality that suggests the return of peace and a **return to normality**. The futures of those who clapped the bowing players were to be neither peaceful nor very normal.

NOTES

Introduction

1 Examples of family dysfunctionality were increasing (see Beier, *Masterless Men*, 56), as were alcoholism, crime, bastardy and syphilis. Poverty triggered outbreaks of familial violence even in settled communities, let alone among houseless vagabonds. Among the wealthy, the emotional coldness of distanced parenting led to an increase in the sorts of tensions displayed in the Lear and Gloucester households.

2 Tillyard, *The English Renaissance: Fact or Fiction?*, 27, 28.

3 *The Prince*, XV, 90–91.

Prologue. Grim Expectations

1 Henry was made Duke of Cornwall at James's accession in March 1603. Charles was given the hereditary title for the second son of Scots kings, Duke of Albany, in 1604.

2 Title page of the 1608 printed text. Some of the court may have known the story from the earlier play or from chronicle histories. There were no theatre programmes then, though public theatres advertised forthcoming performances on posters; 'Goe read each post, view what is plaid to day' (Marston, *The Scourge of Villanie*, 5).

3 Chambers, *The Elizabethan Stage*, IV, 366.

4 John Earle (*Microcosmographie*, 1628, H3r), quoted in Gurr, 218. Earle claims the 'waiting-women Spectators' flocked to public theatres to see their favourites.

5 William Harrison, quoted in Gurr, *The Shakespearean Stage*, 212.

6 See Peck, *Northampton: Patronage and Policy at the Court of James I* and *Court Patronage and Corruption in Early Stuart England*.

Chapter 1. The Historical Context: An Overview

1 Weldon, *The Court and Character of King James I* (1650).

2 See Nichols, *The Progresses, Processions, and Magnificent Festivities of James the First*.

3 Troynovant was the ancient name for London, supposedly founded by Brutus leading a band of Trojan exiles. This pseudo history in Geoffrey of Monmouth filtered through Holinshed into a play, *Locrine*, performed c. 1595.

4 James's inaugural speech to Parliament declared, 'I am the husband, and the whole island is my lawful wife; I am the head and it is my body' (McIlwain, *The Political Works of James I*, 272). Revisionist historians have tried to rehabilitate James, but the overwhelming evidence of the time is highly critical of him.

5 Davies, *The Early Stuarts*, 7.

6 After John Calvin, the radical French Protestant reformer.

7 Machiavelli had referred to 'the great changes and variations, beyond human imagining, which we have experienced and experience every day' (*The Prince*, 130; written 1513, published 1532). In 1606 the European world was still morphing from its medieval past.

8 Historical Manuscripts Commission, *Calendar of the Manuscripts of the Most Honourable the Marquess of Salisbury*, vol. 12, 272.

9 Peck's work uncovers how privy councillors gathered advisors from court, scholarly and merchant communities. Much counsel was focused on self-interested profit making by the networks involved and the king ignored what would not increase his revenue or simply went his own way, exercising absolute, personal power.

10 After Giovanni Boccaccio's collection of stories of the tragic falls of illustrious men, *De Casibus Virorum Illustrium*.

Chapter 2. The Elizabethan World Order: From Divinity to Dust

1 The Catholic Church had imagined another level: Purgatory, an escape route for avoiding Hell. Venial sinners, after death, could purge their souls of sin and make themselves suitable for Heaven. Masses paid for by money left in wills were believed to assist in cleansing the soul of the departed. Protestantism saw Purgatory as a doctrinally suspect, corrupt moneymaking scheme and dropped it from Anglican teachings.

2 Uranus was not discovered until 1781.

3 In *The Boke Named the Governour* (1531).

4 See Revelation 21.

5 A *Defence of Iudiciall Astrologie* (quoted in Thomas, *Religion and the Decline of Magic*, 414).

6 A court comprising privy councillors and judges, initially instituted to try cases of suspected treason by powerful lords the ordinary courts were unable to bring to book. Under the Stuarts it became a means of curbing the Crown's political opponents, most of whom belonged to one or other of the dissenting religions.

7 A tribe with eyes in their shoulders and a mouth in their chest was reported by Raleigh after his 1595 trip to Guiana and recorded in Hakluyt's *Voyages* (viii).

8 *Psychomachia* is the struggle between good and evil for the mind/soul of man. Portrayed in early drama as a good and a bad angel – advising or tempting the protagonist (as in *Faustus*) – by the 1600s they lost their allegorical state, becoming metamorphosed into secular characters, like a good friend and false friend or a wise, disinterested adviser and a flattering self-seeker.

9 For revisionist analyses of the times, see Bouwsma, *The Waning of the Renaissance*.

10 Literacy was accelerating and cheap books and pamphlets increasingly numerous. By 1600, 25 per cent of males and 10 per cent of women could read (Mortimer, *The Time Traveller's Guide to Elizabethan England*, 102). In London male literacy was 80 per cent.

11 Its reliance upon mind, reason and will marks the Renaissance's divergence from medievalism.

12 The church tried to keep track of unlicensed presses producing heretical or treasonable matter, but smuggled imports from Holland and the mobility of printers made it very difficult to police thought.

13 *City of God*, 548.

14 Revelation has Hell underground. In *Paradise Lost* (1667) Milton has Hell specially created by God from the materials of Chaos to receive the falling angels after their defeat and expulsion from Heaven.

15 Beier, *Masterless Men*, 125.

16 Formalized by St Thomas Aquinas, one of the formative medieval Christian thinkers. Hell's hierarchy is variously organized by different writers.

17 Incubi were male demons thought to have sex with sleeping women. Succubi were female demons coupling with men.

18 *Nichomachean Ethics*, X. 9. 199.

19 Increasingly, successful merchants like Cranfield, Ingram and Swinnerton were drawn into government advisory groups. Some inevitably took advantage of the opportunities for jobbery. See Peck, *Northampton*, ch. 7.

20 A royal proclamation announced a recall of monopolies, ordered lawyers to cease excessive charges, instructed royal household officials not to abuse their positions when procuring goods for the court, and (a sop to the Puritans) banned bear baiting, music, plays and 'disordered exercises' on Sundays. These intended reforms were forgotten once James secured power.

21 Nichols, *Progresses, Processions, and Magnificent Festivities*, 128–32. A benefice was a parish post for a priest. 'Placemen' held court or government posts, often through family influence.

22 *Basilikon Doron* (*King's Gift*), a conduct book for kings justifying the principles of Divine Right.

23 Shuger, *Habits of Thought*, 1.

24 Many gained military experience fighting the Spanish in the Netherlands.

25 Increasingly the better sort invested in speculative ventures (industrial, commercial and colonial).

26 'Roaring Boys' were gangs of upper-class young men who went out to get drunk and fight. Some groups planned attacks and muggings.

27 Both Elizabeth and James often struck servants and courtiers.

28 Gentry and noble families put younger sons to professions and trades so they should have an income, since land and fortune were bequeathed to the eldest male.

29 Chapman et al., *Eastward Ho!*, I. i. 114–16, 138.

30 Cited in Stone, *The Crisis of the Aristocracy*, 27.

31 Ashley, *England in the Seventeenth Century*, 18.

32 Ashley, *England in the Seventeenth Century*, 18.

33 Thomas Wilson, *State of England* (quoted in *Camden Miscellany*, vol. 16, 43).

34 Kishlansky (*A Monarchy Transformed*, 44) describing the huge network of family members given posts under the influence of the Duke of Buckingham, James's favourite.

35 Edmund Bolton, the antiquarian, refers to 'the vent of Virginia' as used by the government to resettle the idle multitude (Peck, *Northampton*, 119).

36 See Beier, *Masterless Men*, 14, 16.

37 Recently discovered legal documents show Shakespeare being fined for hoarding food, presumably to sell at inflated prices (*Sunday Times*, 31 March 2013). His role as a moneylender puts a hypocritical slant on his comments about usurers and tarnishes his stance as someone concerned for the poor.

38 Burton's *The Anatomy of Melancholy* (1621) explores this multiplicity of psycho-emotional types.

39 Campbell (*Shakespeare's Tragic Heroes*) interprets heroic flaws from physiological diagnoses.

40 'Those who have deliberately preferred a life of irresponsible lawlessness and violence become wolves and hawks and kites' (Plato, *Phaedo*, 134). See also Leviticus 11:14, where kites are listed with many other birds that are 'an abomination'.

41 See Cressy, *Agnes Bowker's Cat*, ch. 2.

42 Cf. 'All the law is fulfilled in one word, [...] Thou shalt love thy neighbour as thyself. But if ye bite and devour one another, take heed that ye be not consumed one of another' (Galatians 5:14–15).

43 Socrates calls bees, wasps and ants 'social and disciplined creatures' (Plato, *Phaedo*, 134).

44 In Webster's *The White Devil*, the corrupt Duke Brachiano is described as a yew tree. This tree was traditionally associated with graveyards. Brachiano causes deaths and dies horribly as punishment for his failure to give virtuous shelter.

45 *The White Devil* (1612), III. iii. 49–50.

46 Hugh Thomas, *Rivers of Gold*, xvii.

47 After his visit he built Guiana into a fabulous treasure resource to encourage James to support his colonization of the place. His *Discovery of Guiana* (1591) refers to 'the great and golden city of MANOA, which the Spaniards call EL DORADO' and laid out his plans to colonize 'for return or profit' but also as a 'let or impeachment' to the Spanish (cited in Hill, *Intellectual Origins of the English Revolution*, 159). He fell foul of James's pro-Spanish policy.

48 'The Order for the Burial of the Dead' (*The Book of Common Prayer*, 86).

49 Gawdy, *Letters*, 132. A sewer seated you at table and served you.

50 Quoted in De Lisle, *After Elizabeth*, 205. Scaramelli revealed to the signory that English politicians, aristocrats and courtiers blamed the government for 'having sold England to the Scots'.

51 Gawdy, *Letters*, 131.

52 Quoted in De Lisle, *After Elizabeth*, 210, from *The Calendar of State Papers Relating to English Affairs, Existing in the Archives and Collections of Venice* (London, 1900), vol. 10, 1603–07.

53 'Demystifying the Mystery of State: *King Lear* and the World Upside Down', *Shakespeare Survey* 44 (1992): 78.

54 'On Anger', 810.

55 Bacon, 'Of Anger', 226. Bacon's translation.

56 By 1604 eight hundred and thirty-eight new £30 knights had been created.

57 Aristotle, *The Politics*, 67. See Castiglione, *The Book of the Courtier*, 298.

58 *Basilikon Doron*, 4. All quotes from the EEBO Editions reprint of the 1682 edition.

59 Migration into London prompted the growth of extramural suburbs where crime and poverty were rife. See Beier, *Masterless Men*, 43.

60 Nichols, *The Progresses, Processions, and Magnificent Festivities of James the First*, 327 (emphasis added).

61 Daunton, *Progress and Poverty*, 137.

62 Historical Manuscripts Commission, *Calendar of the Manuscripts of the Most Honourable the Marquess Salisbury*, vol. 12, 272.

63 Clapham, *Elizabeth of England*, 98.

64 Peck, *Northampton*, 156.

65 Strype, *Memorials of Thomas Cranmer* (1690), rec. 114.
66 Wootten, *Divine Right and Democracy*, 94–98.
67 For confrontations between congregants and clergy see Cressy, *Agnes Bowker's Cat*, ch. 9.
68 See Bunker, *Making Haste from Babylon*, 103. Some Mayflower separatists came from Nottinghamshire, West Riding and Lincolnshire. John Cotton, Puritan minister of St Botolph's, Boston, also gathered followers round him.
69 *Basilikon Doron*, 18, 19, 18.
70 Brathwait, *The English Gentleman*, 115.
71 Brathwait, *The English Gentleman*, 115.
72 Webster, *The White Devil*, III. ii. 161–63.
73 Percy, *Advice to His Son*.
74 See Adelman, *Suffocating Mothers*.

Chapter 3. Sin, Death and the Prince of Darkness

1 Wycliffe, Prologue to the Apocalypse, 493.
2 After fornication (prohibited sex), nonattendance was the second most common offence.
3 Chute, *Shakespeare of London*, 241.
4 *A Declaration of Egregious Popish Impostures* (1603). For borrowings see Muir, *Review of English Studies*, 1951.
5 Lucifer was Prince of Light before he fell. The Testaments call the Devil a prince. As darkness denotes sin joining the two terms is natural. Edgar's comment, 'The Prince of Darkness is a gentleman; Modo he's called, and Mahu' (III. iv.) takes these names from an anti-papist pamphlet by Samuel Harsnett and links evil with the sham politeness of gentlemen that masks devious intent.
6 *Basilikon*, 12–13. See *Two Elizabethan Puritan Diaries*, ed. M. M. Knappen.
7 Dabhoiwala, *The Origins of Sex*, 41. Family dysfunctionality of different sorts was also worryingly increasing (see Beier, *Masterless Men*, 56), not only among the homeless, but in settled communities and in the governing classes.
8 Nearly half of all babies never reached their first birthday. High mortality among teenagers affected not just the poor but ended many direct dynastic lines. James's eldest son, the promising and popular Prince Henry, would die aged 16 (probably of typhus). Shakespeare lost his only son aged 11. Jonson lost his first son aged 7.
9 The anonymous *Memorial* (addressed to James on his accession) demanded the reintroduction of the Edwardian reforms, more practising preaching ministers, strict observance of the Sabbath and the banishment of the ring exchange in marriage and other 'superstitious' remnants of popery. Cited in De Lisle, *After Elizabeth*, 192.
10 'To Philosophize Is to Learn How to Die', *The Complete Essays*, 96.
11 *Basilikon Doron*, 13.
12 Such a network of astrologers, mathematicians, atheists and navigators is discussed in Christopher Hill, *Intellectual Origins of the English Revolution*, ch. IV. There was an uncertain mix of genuine scientific discovery and superstition and magic among these groups. The 'Wizard Earl' of Northumberland, one of the Raleigh group, experimented in alchemy.
13 Dollimore, *Radical Tragedy*, 189.
14 Raleigh, *History of the World* (1603–13), II, 214 (1820 edition). Cooper, *Certaine Sermons* (1580), cited in Thomas, *Religion and the Decline of Magic*, 91.

15 Bacon, *The Advancement of Learning*, 157.
16 See Botticelli's painting *The Abyss of Hell* (1480).
17 'Servingman' does not mean a lowly menial, but a person of probably gentry status serving someone of greater rank.
18 *A Direction for the Government of the Tongue*, 1593. Cited in Cressy, *Agnes Bowker's Cat*, 141.
19 See Campbell, *Shakespeare's Tragic Heroes*, ch. 14.
20 *Confessions*, VIII, 7.
21 Dabhoiwala, *The Origins of Sex*, 42.
22 'Of women's unnatural, insatiable lust, what Country, what Village doth not complain?' (*The Anatomy of Melancholy*, 656–57).
23 'If they cannot contain, let them marry: for it is better to marry than to burn' (I Corinthians 7:9).
24 A placket is an opening in a skirt or petticoat by which a man could gain access.
25 Luxury means lust (from Latin, *luxuria*).
26 Polecats, stoats and weasels were thought to be highly sexed. A fitchew was slang for a prostitute.
27 *On the Good of Marriage*, ch. 21.

Chapter 4. The Seven Cardinal Virtues

1 *The Book of the Courtier* (1528), 87–88.

Chapter 5. Kingship

1 One-fifth of all plays from 1588–1608 were histories (Harbage, *Shakespeare and the Rival Traditions*, 85, 260).
2 Hill, *Intellectual Origins*, 175.
3 Hill, *Intellectual Origins*, 177.
4 City-state (Greek). In theology, morality and political theory a person was seen as a state, governed well or ill.
5 Plato's *Republic* is the starting point (much referenced in James's *Basilikon Doron*), but others took up the theme – Xenophon (*Cyropaedia*), Isocrates (*Oration to Nicocles*), Cicero (*De Officiis*), Seneca (*De Clementia*), John of Salisbury (*Policraticus*, 1159), St Thomas Aquinas (*De Regimine Principum*, c. 1265), Erasmus (*Education of a Christian Prince*, 1516), Machiavelli (*Il Principe*, 1532).
6 All quotes from the unpaginated Scolar Press facsimile reprint.
7 Cf. Castiglione, *The Book of the Courtier*, bks I–III.
8 It was not, at this time, usual for sons of the nobility to go to university. This had begun to change by the end of the sixteenth century, but for reasons of social prestige rather than concern for education (see Secor, *Richard Hooker*, 76).
9 Elyot applauds the Saxon king Edgar for unifying the disparate, weak, petty kingdoms of England.
10 Stone, *Crisis of the Aristocracy*, 617.
11 Republicanism or anti-monarchism were not yet discernible movements, but Buchanan's *Law of Kings* (1579) and Raleigh's *Prerogative of Parliaments* (1603) were beginning to question absolutism and suggest ways of controlling it.
12 Speech to Parliament (1610). See Wootten, *Divine Right and Democracy*, 107.

13 Chute, *Ben Jonson*, 130.

14 Marginal note, *Basilikon*, 62.

15 *The Duchess of Malfi*, I. i. 11–15. The same speech mentions the French king clearing his court of 'flatt'ring sycophants, of dissolute,/And infamous persons […]'.

16 'Of all the responsibilities that fall to a prince, the most important is justice. And to maintain this, there should be appointed to hold office men of wisdom and probity, who must be good as well as judicious' (Castiglione, *The Book of the Courtier*, 307).

17 Polydore Vergil recounts it and a marginal note in *Basilikon* (62) references Vergil, so James knew the story. The printed text of the early play, *King Leir*, appeared 1605.

18 'On the Vanity of Words', 343.

19 The authors of *Eastward Ho!* were briefly jailed for mocking the Scots.

20 This note must have been added for the 1603 edition as the plot postdates the 1598 first edition.

21 According to Winwood's *Memorials* it was 'twice represented by the King's Players, with exceeding concourse of all sorts of people; but whether the matter or manner be not well handled, or that it be thought unfit that Princes should be played on the stage in their life-time, I hear that some great Councellors are much displeased with it, and so 'tis thought shall be forbidden' (Winwood, 470; cited in Harrison, *A Jacobean Journal*, 172).

22 Camden's very popular *Britannia* (1586) only goes back to the Roman invasion. Earlier monkish histories relied on legend and fabrication to fill out the pre-Roman past.

23 Buchanan also taught Montaigne at the Collège de Guyenne in Bordeaux.

24 Nichols, *The Progresses, Processions, and Magnificent Festivities of James the First*, 327. Ben Jonson wrote part of the address. Later critical of the political state in *Sejanus* (1603), then became involved with court masque production as a covert means of instruction.

Chapter 6. Patriarchy, Family Authority and Gender Relationships

1 Ephesians 5:22–23. See also I Corinthians 11:3.

2 Genesis 3:16.

3 *Hallelujah* (1641).

4 *Basilikon Doron*, 54.

5 *Basilikon*, Doron 58.

6 *Basilikon Doron*, 60–61.

7 Education in the classics brought many males into contact with negative examples of female behaviour, particularly among Roman empresses.

8 *De Cultu Feminarum*. Cited in Ellerbe, *The Dark Side of Christian History*, 115.

9 Homily XV to the People of Antioch.

10 Cited in Starr, *The 'Natural Inferiority' of Women*, 45. Clement also advocated equality of the sexes and women being admitted to leading roles in the church.

11 *Malleus*, sect. 1.

12 The comment is from the incestuously obsessed Duke Ferdinand in *The Duchess of Malfi*, II. v. 6.

13 Similar orthodoxy is voiced by unmarried, inexperienced Luciana in *The Comedy of Errors* (1588–93) II. i. 15–25.

14 A gull was a fool, someone gullible.
15 Cited in Stone, *The Crisis of the Aristocracy*, 615.
16 Stone, *The Crisis of the Aristocracy*, 614.
17 See Dusinberre, *Shakespeare and the Nature of Women*, 2–4.
18 Cordelia defines Burgundy's love as based on 'respect [public status] and fortunes' (I. i.).
19 *Seuen Deadly Sinnes of London*, 44.
20 Further detail in Berry and Foyster, *The Family in Early Modern England*; also see Stone, *The Family, Sex and Marriage in England, 1500–1800*.
21 See Schleiner for discussion of the small coteries of women authors.
22 *Norton Anthology of English Literature*, vol. 1, 1553–55.
23 The letters between the gentry couple Sir John and Margaret Winthrop in the second decade of the seventeenth century testify to both a loving marriage and a highly articulate woman. Similarly, Lovell recounts the affection Bess of Hardwick achieved with her several husbands.
24 *Basilikon Doron*, 61–62. A marginal note indicates James knew these pseudo-historical characters from Polydore Vergil's *Anglica Historia* (1532).
25 Dusinberre, *Shakespeare and the Nature of Women*, 216.
26 Dusinberre, *Shakespeare and the Nature of Women*, 63.
27 Dusinberre, *Shakespeare and the Nature of Women*, 300.
28 Dusinberre, *Shakespeare and the Nature of Women*, 278.
29 See, for example, Elizabeth Hoby (Laoutaris, *Shakespeare and the Countess*) and Elizabeth Talbot (Lovell, *Bess of Hardwick*) – both formidable and not always pleasant women.
30 'Almost half of all babies died within twelve months of birth' (Lovell, *Empire Builder*, 1) and the teenage deaths of longed-for heirs litter the records. Elizabethan and Jacobean family monuments in churches display sad little sculpted groups of dead children.
31 Stone, *The Family, Sex and Marriage*, 37.
32 See Dusinberre, *Shakespeare and the Nature of Woman*.
33 Mothers often bequeathed money or property to a younger son to ensure he was not left destitute when his father died and left all to the eldest.
34 See Schleiner, *Tudor and Stuart Women Writers*.
35 The early 1600s saw increasingly punitive action by various authorities against fornication, adultery, incest, homosexuality and prostitution. See Dabhoiwala, *The Origins of Sex*, ch. 1.
36 Berry and Foyster, *The Family in Early Modern England*, 3.
37 Berry and Foyster, *The Family in Early Modern England*, 3.
38 Berry and Foyster, *The Family in Early Modern England*, 3.
39 William Gouge, *Of Domesticall Duties* (1622).
40 *The First Blast of the Trumpet against the Monstrous Regiment of Women* (1558).
41 'On the Affection of Fathers for Their Children', 448.
42 Stone, *The Family, Sex and Marriage*, 136.
43 Behn's first play was *The Forced Marriage* (1670). Before this, masques and dramas for private reading were female authored.
44 Mulcaster citations in the *Norton Anthology*.
45 *Norton Anthology*.
46 Stone, *The Family, Sex and Marriage*, 143.
47 'The Epystle of the Translatour', from Hoby's translation (1561).

48 See Campion in *Norton Anthology*.
49 *Norton Anthology*, 1036–39. For the texts of Speght, Swetnam and others see Butler, *Female Replies to Swetnam the Woman-Hater*.
50 Castiglione, *The Book of the Courtier*, 47, 108.
51 Sermon 1, September 1522.
52 'The word and works of God is quite clear, that women were made either to be wives or prostitutes' (*Works* 12, 94). 'God created Adam master and lord of living creatures, but Eve spoilt all, when she persuaded him to set himself above God's will. 'Tis you women, with your tricks and artifices, that lead men into error' (*Table Talk*).
53 See Rubin, *Mother of God*, pt VI.
54 There was a subgenre of books on famous and virtuous women. Christine of Pizan's *The Book of the City of Ladies* and Boccaccio's *De Mulieribus* were most influential.
55 Castiglione, *The Book of the Courtier*, 198.
56 *Anatomy*, pt 3, sect. 2, memb. 1, subs. 2, 650–51.
57 Resentful, beaten servants could not legally run away and leave the parish. That was to become a masterless man/woman and carried a prison sentence. This implication that the servant was the property of the master was yet another of the ancient practices that restricted the liberties of the English.
58 Stone, *The Family, Sex and Marriage*, 137.
59 Stone, *The Family, Sex and Marriage*, 136.
60 Stone, *The Family, Sex and Marriage*, 136.

Chapter 7. Man in His Place

1 Robert Crowley, *Voice of the Last Trumpet* (1550).
2 For attitudes to commercial enterprise Weber (*The Protestant Ethic and the Spirit of Capitalism*, 1904–05) and Tawney (*Religion and the Rise of Capitalism*, 1926) are still relevant. So too is L. C. Knights, *Drama and Society in the Age of Jonson* (1937), chs 1–4.
3 *Peripeteia* is Aristotle's term for the tragic process of reversal of a successful man's fortunes. *Nemesis* is the Greek Goddess of retribution. *Hubris* is the Aristotelian term for the overconfidence that is punished by a fall.
4 See Peck, *Northampton*, ch. 7.
5 Quoted in De Lisle, *After Elizabeth*, 195.
6 *Anatomie of Abuses*, sig. C.11v.
7 Castiglione, *The Book of the Courtier*, 55.
8 Bishop Burnet, 'King Edward's Remains: A Discourse about the Reformation of Many Abuses', *History of the Reformation*.

Chapter 8. Images of Disorder: The Religious Context

1 Cressy, *Agnes Bowker's Cat*, 139.
2 Thomas, *Religion and the Decline of Magic*, 179.
3 Cressy, *Agnes Bowker's Cat*, ch. 9.
4 1606–07 was the period when separatists exiled themselves to Leiden before sailing to America, fleeing increasing persecution. See Bunker, *Making Haste from Babylon*, pt 2.
5 Cressy, *Agnes Bowker's Cat*, ch. 10.

6 Falling asleep during the sermon and disrespecting the vicar were fineable offences.
7 Bacon, 'Of Seditions and Troubles', 104.
8 Peck, *Northampton*, 146.
9 Gawdy, *Letters*, 148.
10 Bate, *Soul of the Age*, 179. An even clearer parallel is Angelo's behaviour in *Measure for Measure*.

Chapter 9. The Contemporary Political Context

1 Davies, *The Early Stuarts*, 1.
2 Gawdy, cited in De Lisle, *After Elizabeth*, 157. Among the newly hatched knights were the sons of pedlars and of a run-down lawyer. They paid less than £8 for the honour.
3 Sir Toby Belch describes the cowardly Sir Andrew Aguecheek as 'a knight, dubbed with unhatched rapier, […] on carpet consideration […]' (*Twelfth Night*, III. iv. 245–46).
4 Davies, *The Early Stuarts*, 9.
5 Davies, *The Early Stuarts*, 8.
6 Quoted in Scott, *James I*, 263. This comment by Roger Aston, a messenger in James's service, provoked laughter at the Privy Council. It soon proved hollow.
7 Sir John Harington, *Nugae Antiquae*, vol. 1, 352. Quoted in De Lisle, *After Elizabeth*, 311. Drummond of Hawthornden notes (a letter, 3 August 1606), 'There is nothing to be heard at court, but sounding of trumpets, hautboys, musick, revellings and comedies' (see Furness edition of *Macbeth*, 1873).
8 The stage direction 'Horns within' was added by Rowe in his 1709 edition of the works. Goneril instructs Oswald to be disrespectful 'when he [Lear] returns from hunting' (I. iii.).
9 In 1604 he bought Royston Abbey, Hertfordshire, furbishing it as a hunting lodge.
10 Quoted in Gibbons, *Jacobean City Comedy*, 40.
11 In 1614 he dissolved Parliament for seven years.
12 Harrison, *A Jacobean Journal*, 305.
13 James arrived in London on 7 May 1603. On 19 May, 'The players that were my Lord Chamberlain's servants are now by letters patent made the King's servants, of whom the chief are Lawrence Fletcher, William Shakespeare, Richard Burbage, Augustine Phillips, John Hemmings, Henry Condell, William Sly, Robert Armin, and Richard Cowley' (Harrison, *A Jacobean Journal*, 30, quoting *Malone Society's Collection*, I. 264).
14 Davies, *The Early Stuarts*, 263. Masques were allegorical performances (often with classical deities and personifications of abstract qualities – Courage, Justice, etc.). They were written for court audiences and had music, song and dance.
15 Chambers, *The Elizabethan Stage*, I, 7, note.
16 Harrison, *A Jacobean Journal*, 90–91.
17 England was never united to Scotland in pre-Roman times. They were two separate regions, divided into large tribal areas ruled by separate kings. The cast list calls Lear 'King of Britain', but this does not include Scotland, Wales or Ireland. A large kingdom straddled the border up to the Firths of Clyde and Forth. North of this line was a Pictish realm.
18 In a decree of 1603 the king required all landowners worth £40 a year to become knights or pay a fine.
19 Servants were traditionally given three suits a year.
20 Davies, *The Early Stuarts*, 263.
21 Harrison, *A Jacobean Journal*, 107, quoting Edmund Lodge (ed.), *Illustrations of British History* (1838), III, 86, 88.

22 'In the Parliament of 1597 a profitable law was made for the repressing of rogues and vagabonds by which much good ensued, but now of late by the remissness of some justices of the peace they swarm everywhere more frequently than in times past' (Harrison, *A Jacobean Journal*, 65).

23 From the 1603 Florio translation, 280. Screech renders it 'We could be excused for having borrowed […] decking ourselves in their beauty, hiding ourselves in their coats: wool, feathers, hide or silk' (539).

24 Harrison, *A Jacobean Journal*, 181, quoting Winwood's *Memorials*, II, 43.

25 Progressing south James indicated readiness to use his sudden access to absolute power, having a pickpocket summarily executed at Newark without trial. He pardoned many prisoners yet left Catholic recusants incarcerated with murderers.

26 James sacrificed Raleigh to keep Spain sweet. Some judges received Spanish pensions shortly after his execution (Hill, *Intellectual Origins*, 154).

27 As in Massinger's *A New Way to Pay Old Debts* (written 1625, performed 1626). Sir Giles Mompesson, MP, a corrupt office holder (aptly named Sir Giles Overreach in the play) used his position to obtain licenses for businesses, charged for doing so and kept the money. His name became synonymous with speculative, accumulative, corrupt aristocratic government. He was found guilty, a fine levied, but he fled to France.

28 Wilson, *Life in Shakespeare's England*, 116.

29 *The Prince*, IX, 68. Cf.: 'Men willingly change their ruler, expecting to fare better' (Machiavelli, III. 34).

30 *The Prince*, IX, 96.

31 The royal palaces had permanent staff. Then there was the travelling court accompanying the king to whichever venue he was gracing.

32 Davies, *The Early Stuarts*, 9.

33 This device raised £90,855 in three years (Peck, *Northampton*, 115; Kishlansky, *A Monarchy Transformed*, 87).

34 Recent research has discovered legal documents pertaining to Shakespeare being fined for hoarding food, presumably to sell at inflated prices (*Sunday Times*, 31 March 2013). His role as a moneylender puts a hypocritical slant on his comments about usurers and tarnishes his stance as someone concerned for the poor.

35 Dekker, *The Wonderful Year of 1603*, 24.

36 *An Alarum to England*. Quoted in Hill, *Intellectual Origins*, 182.

37 Deists believed in God, but believed He did not interfere in human affairs.

38 *Theatre of Gods Judgement* (1597), 412 (1648 edition).

39 *History of the World*, II. 214 (1820 edition).

40 The archetypal event establishing anti-Catholic fears was the 1572 St Bartholomew's Day massacre.

41 Perhaps reminding James of the explosion that killed his father.

42 Harrison, 280.

43 Thomas, *Religion and the Decline of Magic*, 84.

44 Dekker, *The Wonderful Year of 1603*, 26.

Chapter 10. The Literary Context

1 Individual locations are discussed in Stow's *The Survey of London* (1598).

2 Orgel, *The Illusion of Power*, 45.

3 'Revenge is a kind of wild justice, which the more man's nature runs to, the more ought law to weed it out' (Bacon, 'Of Revenge', 72).

4 Quoted in Wickham, Berry and Ingram, eds, *English Professional Theatre, 1530–1660*, 51.

5 All quotes from *Minor Elizabethan Drama: Pre-Shakespearean Tragedy*.

6 Other contemporary plays, notably Jonson's *Sejanus* and *Catiline*, reflect similar concerns.

7 See Danby, *Shakespeare's Doctrine of Nature*.

8 Albania, an old name for Scotland, hinting perhaps at the aims of Mary Queen of Scots.

9 There was an attempt to shoot the queen on her barge on the Thames. The Ridolfi (1570), Throgmorton (1583) and Babington (1586) plots planned to replace her with Mary Queen of Scots. There were also the Don John (1577), Somerville (1583), Parry (1584) and Lopez plots (1594).

10 Bate, *Soul of the Age*, 149.

11 Appendix 6, Muir edition.

12 Montaigne, 'That Our Actions Should Be Judged by Our Intentions', 29.

13 'On Liars', 33.

14 'On Liars', 35.

15 'On Liars', 35.

16 'On Liars', 85.

17 'On Liars', 86.

18 'On the Power of the Imagination', 112.

19 'One Man's Profit Is Another's Loss', 121.

20 Florio's translation, III, 210.

21 'On Affectionate Relationships', in *The Complete Essays*, 207.

22 'On Affectionate Relationships', 208.

23 'Affection of Fathers', 240–41.

24 'Affection of Fathers', 435.

25 'Affection of Fathers', 435.

26 'Affection of Fathers', 435.

27 'Affection of Fathers', 435.

28 Bacon, 'Of Parents and Children', 79.

29 'Affection of Fathers', 446.

30 'Affection of Fathers', 435–36.

31 'Affection of Fathers', 439–40.

32 'Affection of Fathers', 441.

33 Shakespeare was in the Queen's Men in 1594. They performed the play with Sussex's Men. A. L. Rowse suggests Shakespeare may have played Perillus, for his speeches have many close echoes in *Lear* (372).

34 *Holinshed's Chronicle*, 225–27.

35 *The History of the Kings of Britain*, 81–87.

36 Wright comments, 'The *Historia* does not bear scrutiny as an authentic history and no scholar today would regard it as such' (*The Historia Regum Britannie of Geoffrey of Monmouth*, xxviii).

37 *Basilikon Doron*, 62. Vergil's book, giving accounts of British kings from their early legendary beginnings, became another source for dramatists seeking material for history plays.

38 Sir Henry Ellis, *Polydore Vergil's English History, from an Early Translation*, vol. I, Camden 1st series, no. 36 (London: Camden Society).

39 Prologue to the first edition.
40 Campbell, *Parts Added to the Mirrour for Magistrates*.
41 In modern English 'to to true' would read 'too too true'.
42 Literally 'concerning contempt for the world'. It sums up the classical and Christian stance that rejected the hollow vanities of this world in favour of pursuing wisdom and spiritual calm.
43 Quotes from *Poetical Works of Edmund Spenser*, Oxford Standard Authors.
44 From Appendix 5 (Muir edition).
45 Border region between Poland and Ukraine.
46 Administrative region on the Anatolian coast (north Turkey) during the Byzantine Empire.
47 A thirteenth-century poem, *Robert of Gloucester*, provided the original story mediated in Sydney.
48 *Leviathan*, pt I, ch. XIII, 'Of the Natural Condition of Mankind as Concerning Their Felicity, and Misery', 186.
49 'On Affectionate Relationships', 207. 'Fellowship' means company, society.
50 The King's Men were there on 4 October 1605, perhaps to perform at the request of the Earl of Northampton, who was made warden of the Cinque Ports in January 1604.
51 Quotes from Malone Society reprint, ed. R. Warwick Bond. This edition is unpaginated and without act/scene designations.
52 More vivid is Shakespeare's 'I cannot heave/My heart into my mouth'.
53 In folklore the parent pelican pierces its breast to feed its children with its blood.
54 Albany (associated with the kingdom north of the Humber and into Scotland) has been edited out of the story and turned into the King of Wales.
55 Isaiah 6:9–10, Jeremiah 5:21 and Matthew 13:13.
56 Lady Grace Wildgoose (wife of Sir John Wildgoose), Christian Sandys (wife of William, third Baron Sandys).
57 Bullough, vol. 7, 269–71, 276–84, 287–92. After the Duchess's death (1607) Harvey married Cordell Annesley.
58 Campbell, *Shakespeare's Tragic Heroes*, 183.
59 Harrison, *A Jacobean Journal*, 71.

Chapter 11. The Context of Tragedy

1 'Even Dr Johnson, in an age we think of as rationalistic, felt that *King Lear* was more than he could endure, and craved a happy ending' (Orgel, *The Illusion of Power*, 35).
2 *Palladis Tamia* (1598).
3 *Troas* (1559), *Thyestes* and *Hercules Furens* by Jasper Heywood, *Oedipus* (1563) by Alexander Nevyle, *Agamemnon, Medea, Hercules Oetaeus* and *Hippolytus* (c. 1567) by John Studley, *Octavia* by Thomas Nuce, and Newton's adaptation of *Thebais*.
4 Thomas, *Religion and the Decline of Magic*, 91, 92.
5 Thomas, *Religion and the Decline of Magic*, 91.

Chapter 12. The Family Context

1 *Anna Karenina* (1875), 1.
2 Beier, *Masterless Men*, 51.

3 The church actively supported the law preventing children born out of wedlock from inheriting.
4 'Of Parents and Children', 80.
5 Deuteronomy 23:1 bars illegitimate children from joining the congregation.
6 'Of Parents and Children', 79.
7 'Of Parents and Children', 79.
8 In *Henry IV*, pt 1 (1597) the rebels, Hotspur and Glendower, quarrel over a perceived unequal division of the kingdom. The partitioning of Rome's territories creates tensions in *Antony and Cleopatra* (1606–07).
9 'On the Affections of Fathers to Their Children', 441.
10 *Antigone*, 34.

Chapter 13. Sins, Transgressions, Subversions and Reversals

1 'Of Simulation and Dissimulation', 77.
2 Campbell, *Shakespeare's Tragic Heroes*, 174, 195.
3 'Of Envy', 83, 84.
4 'That our deeds are judged by the intentions', 28.
5 George Herbert, cited in Thomas, *Religion and the Decline of Magic*, 384.
6 Cf. 'No animal fawns so much as a dog, and none is so faithful' (Erasmus, *Praise of Folly*, 134).
7 Harrison, *A Jacobean Journal*, 86, quoting E. T. Bradley, *Life of the Lady Arabella Stuart* (1889), II, 190.
8 Harrison, *A Jacobean Journal*, 107, quoting Lodge, *Illustrations of British History* (1838), III, 86.
9 There are historical examples of this. The impoverished gentleman is a recurrent figure in drama.
10 Bacon, *The Advancement of Learning*, 157.
11 Thunder effects were simulated by rolling cannonballs in a wooden trough (or by drum rolls). Lightning flashes could be created by lighting squibs offstage.
12 It was a common complaint that wives were infected by promiscuous, diseased husbands.
13 Peter Brook's 1962 production did it thus.
14 A pietà is a study of the sorrow of the Virgin Mary holding the dead body of Christ. Here it is a supportive trio in which each is both Christ and a sorrowing companion.
15 Bacon, 'Of Adversity', 75.
16 Henry, Prince of Wales, died 1612. Charles, succeeding James in 1625, was executed in 1649.

BIBLIOGRAPHY

Adelman, Janet. *Suffocating Mothers: Fantasies of Maternal Origin in Shakespeare's Plays, 'Hamlet' to 'The Tempest'*. London: Routledge, 1992.

Anouilh, Jean. *Antigone*. London: Methuen, 1964.

Aristotle. *The Nichomachean Ethics*, trans. David Ross. Oxford: Oxford World's Classics, 2009.

_____. *The Politics*, trans T. A. Sinclair. London: Penguin Classics, 1981.

Ashley, Maurice. *England in the Seventeenth Century*. Harmondsworth: Pelican History of England, 1960.

Augustine, St. *City of God*, trans. Henry Bettenson. London: Penguin Classics, 2003.

_____. *Confessions*, trans. R. S. Pine-Coffin. London: Penguin Classics, 1964.

_____. *On the Good of Marriage (De Bono Coniugiali)*, ed. P. G. Walsh. Oxford: Clarendon Press, 2001.

Bacon, Francis. *The Advancement of Learning*, ed. A. Johnston. Oxford: Clarendon Press, 1980.

_____. *The Essays*, ed. John Pitcher. London: Penguin Classics, 1985.

Bate, Jonathan. *Soul of the Age*. London: Penguin Books, 2009.

Beier, A. L. *Masterless Men: The Vagrancy Problem in England, 1560–1640*. London: Methuen, 1985.

Berry, Helen, and Elizabeth Foyster. *The Family in Early Modern England*. Cambridge: Cambridge University Press, 2007.

Boethius, *The Consolation of Philosophy*, trans. V. E. Watts. London: Penguin Classics, 1969.

Book of Common Prayer, 1549, 1569, 1662, ed. Brian Cummings. Oxford: Oxford World's Classics, 2011.

Bouwsma, William J. *The Waning of the Renaissance*. New Haven: Yale University Press, 2000.

Brathwait, Richard. *The English Gentleman* [1631].

Buchanan, George. *Law of Kingship*, ed. R. Mason and M. Smith. Edinburgh: The Saltire Society, 2006.

Bullough, Geoffrey (ed.). *Narrative and Dramatic Sources of Shakespeare*. New York: Columbia University Press, 1957–75.

Bunker, Nick. *Making Haste from Babylon*. London: Pimlico, 2011.

Burnet, Bishop. *History of the Reformation* [1681]. Oxford, 1865.

Burton, Robert. *The Anatomy of Melancholy* [1621], ed. F. Dell and P. Jordan-Smith. New York: Tudor, 1927.

Butler, Charles. *Female Replies to Swetnam the Woman-Hater*. Bristol: Thoemmes Press, 1995.

Camden Miscellany, vol. 16. London, 1936.

Campbell, Lily B. *Shakespeare's Tragic Heroes*. London: Methuen, 1930.

_____, ed. *Parts Added to the Mirrour for Magistrates by John Higgins and Thomas Blennerhasset*. Cambridge University Press, 1946.

Castiglione, Baldassare. *The Book of the Courtier*, trans. George Bull. Harmondsworth: Penguin Classics, 1981.

Chambers, E. K. *The Elizabethan Stage*. Oxford University Press, 2009.

Chapman, George, Ben Jonson and John Marston. *Eastward Ho!*, New Mermaid edition, ed. C. G. Petter. London: Ernest Benn, 1994.

Chrysostom, St John. *Homilies to the People of Antioch*. Online: http://www.ccel.org/ccel/schaff/npl109 (accessed 15 October 2014).

Chute, Marchette. *Ben Jonson of Westminster*. London: Souvenir Press, 1978.

_____. *Shakespeare of London*. London: Secker and Warburg, 1951.

Clapham, John. *Elizabeth of England*, eds. E. Plummer Read and C. Read. Pennsylvania: University of Pennsylvania Press, 1951.

Cressy, David. *Agnes Bowker's Cat: Travesties and Transgressions in Tudor and Stuart England*. Oxford University Press, 2000.

Crowley, Robert. *One and Thirty Epigrams*. London, 1550.

_____. *Voice of the Last Trumpet*. London, 1550.

Dabhoiwala, Faramerz. *The Origins of Sex*. London: Penguin, 2013.

Danby, John. *Shakespeare's Doctrine of Nature: A Study of King Lear*. London: Faber, 1961.

Daunton, M. J. *Progress and Poverty*. Oxford: Oxford University Press, 1995.

Davies, Godfrey. *The Early Stuarts*. Oxford: Clarendon Press, 1976.

Dekker, Thomas. *The Wonderful Year of 1603*, ed. A. L. Rowse. London: Folio Press, 1989.

De Lisle, Leanda. *After Elizabeth*. London: Harper Collins, 2005.

Dollimore, Jonathan. *Radical Tragedy*. Hemel Hempstead: Harvester Wheatsheaf, 1984.

Dusinberre, Juliet. *Shakespeare and the Nature of Women*. London: Macmillan, 1996.

Ellerbe, Helen. *The Dark Side of Christian History*. Orlando, FL: Morningstar & Lark, 2001.

Elyot, Sir Thomas. *The Boke Named the Governour*. Menston: Scolar Press, 1970.

Erasmus, Desiderius. *Praise of Folly*, trans. Betty Radice. London: Penguin Classics, 1971.

Ford, John. *'Tis Pity She's a Whore*, New Mermaid edition, ed. M. Wiggins. London: A. & C. Black, 2007.

Gawdy, Sir Philip. *The Letters of Sir Philip Gawdy*, ed. Isaac H. Geaves. London: J. Nichols, 1906.

Geoffrey of Monmouth. *History of the Kings of Britain*, trans. Lewis Thorpe. London: Penguin Classics, 1966.

Gibbons, Brian. *Jacobean City Comedy*. London: Methuen, 1980.

Gouge, William. *Of Domesticall Duties*. 1622. Norwood, NJ: W. J. Johnston, 1976.

Gurr, Andrew. *The Shakespearean Stage 1574–1642*. Cambridge: Cambridge University Press, 1992.

Harbage, Alfred. *Shakespeare and the Rival Traditions*. New York: Barnes & Noble, 1952.

Harrington, John. *Nugae Antiquae*, ed. Rev. Henry Harrington. London: Dodsley and Shrimpton, 1779.

Harrison, G. B. *A Jacobean Journal*. London: Routledge, 1946.

Harsnett, Samuel. *A Declaration of Egregious Popish Impostures*. London, 1603.

Heinemann, Margot. 'Demystifying the Mystery of State: *King Lear* and the World Upside Down'. *Shakespeare Survey* 44 (1992).

Hill, Christopher. *Intellectual Origins of the English Revolution*. Oxford: Oxford University Press, 1965.

Historical Manuscripts Commission. *Calendar of the Manuscripts of the Most Honourable the Marquess of Salisbury*. Kept at Hatfield House, Hertfordshire.

Hobbes, Thomas. *Leviathan*, ed. C. B. Macpherson. London: Pelican Classics, 1968.

Hoby, Lady Margaret. *The Private Life of an Elizabethan Lady: The Diary of Lady Margaret Hoby*, ed. Joanna Moody. Stroud: Sutton, 1998.

Holinshed, Raphael. *Holinshed's Chronicle*, ed. A. & J. Nicoll. London: Dent Everyman Library, 1965.

James I, King. *Basilikon Doron*. EEBO Editions' reprint of the 1682 edition, 2012.

Kishlansky, Mark. *A Monarchy Transformed: Britain 1603–1714*. London: Penguin, 1996.

Knappen, M. M., ed. *Two Elizabethan Puritan Diaries*. London: SPCK, 1933.

Knights, L. C. *Drama and Society in the Age of Jonson*. London: Peregrine, 1937.

Knox, John. *The First Blast of the Trumpet against the Monstrous Regiment of Women*. 1558. Edinburgh: Akros, 1995.

Machiavelli, Niccolo. *The Prince* [1532], trans. George Bull. Harmondsworth: Penguin Classics, 1961.

Malleus Maleficarum (The Hammer of Witches), trans. Christopher S. Mackay. Cambridge: Cambridge University Press, 2009.

Marston, John. *The Scourge of Villanie* [1599], ed. G. B. Harrison. Elizabethan and Jacobean Quartos. Edinburgh: Edinburgh University Press, 1966.

McIlwain, C. H., ed. *The Political Works of James I*. Cambridge, MA: Harvard University Press, 1918.

Meres, Francis. *Palladis Tamia* [1598].

Minor Elizabethan Drama: Pre-Shakespearean Tragedy. London: Dent Everyman, 1924.

Mirrour for Magistrates. (See Campbell, Lily B.).

Monmouth, Geoffrey of. *The History of the Kings of Britain*, trans. Lewis Thorpe. London: Penguin Classics, 1966.

Montaigne, Michel. *The Complete Essays*, ed. M. A. Screech. London: Penguin Classics, 2003.

Mortimer, Ian. *The Time Traveller's Guide to Elizabethan England*. London: Vintage Books, 2013.

Mulcaster, Richard. *Positions* [1581].

Nichols, John. *The Progresses, Processions, and Magnificent Festivities of James the First*. London, 1828.

Norton Anthology of English Literature, vol. 1. London: W. W. Norton, 1962.

Orgel, Stephen. *The Illusion of Power*. Berkeley: University of California Press, 1975.

Peck, Linda Levy. *Court Patronage and Corruption in Early Stuart England*. London: Routledge, 1993.

_____. *Northampton: Patronage and Policy at the Court of James I*. London: Allen & Unwin, 1982.

Percy, Henry. *Advice to His Son*, ed. G.B. Harrison. London: Ernest Benn, 1930.

Perkins, William. *A Direction for the Gouernment of the Tongue* [1593].

Plato. *Phaedo* (in *The Last Days of Socrates*), trans. H. Tredennick. London: Penguin Classics, 1969.

Rich, Barnabe. *Faults, Faults, Faults* [1605].

Rowse, A. L. *William Shakespeare: A Biography.* London: Macmillan, 1963.

Rubin, Miri. *Mother of God.* London: Allen Lane, 2009.

Schleiner, Louise. *Tudor and Stuart Women Writers.* Bloomington: Indiana University Press, 1994.

Scott, O. J. *James I.* New York: Mason Charter, 1976.

Second Tome of Homilies [1571].

Secor, Philip B. *Richard Hooker: Prophet of Anglicanism.* Tunbridge Wells: Burns & Oates, 1999.

Seneca. 'On Mercy' in *Dialogues and Essays,* trans. John Davie. Oxford: Oxford World's Classics, 2008.

Shuger, Debora. *Habits of Thought.* Berkeley: University of California Press, 1990.

Starr, Tama. *The 'Natural Inferiority' of Women.* New York: Poseidon Press, 1991.

Stone, Lawrence. *The Crisis of the Aristocracy.* Oxford: Clarendon Press, 1966.

_____. *The Family, Sex and Marriage in England, 1500–1800.* London: Penguin, 1979.

Stow, John. *The Survey of London.* 1598. London: Dent, 1970.

Strange News from Croatia [1606].

Strype, John. *Memorials of Thomas Cranmer* [1690].

Stubbes, Philip. *Anatomie of Abuses* [1583].

Tawney, R. H. *Religion and the Rise of Capitalism* (1926). London: Penguin Books, 1990.

Thomas, Hugh. *Rivers of Gold.* London: Penguin, 2003.

Thomas, Keith. *Religion and the Decline of Magic.* London: Penguin, 1991.

Tillyard, E. M. W. *The English Renaissance, Fact or Fiction?* Baltimore: Johns Hopkins Press, 1952.

The True Chronicle History of King Leir, and His Three Daughters, Gonorill, Ragan, and Cordell, ed. R. Warwick Bond. Malone Society reprints. Oxford: Oxford University Press, 1907.

Vergil, Polydore. *Polydore Vergil's English History, from an Early Translation,* vol. 1, ed. Sir Henry Ellis. Camden 1st series, no. 36. London: Camden Society, 1846.

Vives, Juan. *Instruction of a Christian Woman* [1524].

Weber, Max. *The Protestant Ethic and the Spirit of Capitalism* (1904–5). London: Unwin University Books, 1968.

Webster, John. *The White Devil,* New Mermaid edition, ed. C. Luckyj. London: A. & C. Black, 2001.

Weldon, Sir Anthony. *The Court and Character of King James I* [1650].

Wickham, Glynn, Herbert Berry and William Ingram, eds. *English Professional Theatre, 1530–1660.* Cambridge: Cambridge University Press, 2000.

Wilson, John Dover. *Life in Shakespeare's England.* London: Pelican, 1959.

Wilson, Thomas. *State of England* [1600], ed. F. J. Fisher. 1936.

Winthrop, Sir John, and Lady Margaret. *Some Old Puritan Love-Letters,* ed. J. H. Twichell. London, 1893.

Wither, George. *Hallelujah* [1641]. London: J. R. Smith, 1857.

Wootten, David. *Divine Right and Democracy: An Anthology of Political Writings in Stuart England.* Harmondsworth: Penguin, 1986.

Wright, Neil. *The Historia Regum Britannie of Geoffrey of Monmouth.* Woodbridge, England: Boydell and Brewer, 1984.

INDEX